THE

ANGLICAN USE GRADUAL

(Second Edition)

Chant settings for the Minor Propers of the Mass

ADAPTED BY

C. DAVID BURT

PARTRIDGE HILL PRESS

FALMOUTH, MASSACHUSETTS

2022

The Anglican Use Gradual

First Edition 2004
Corrected Version 2007
Second Edition 2019
Corrected Versions 2021, 2022

Published by
Partridge Hill Press
Falmouth, MA

ISBN: 978-0-9793800-7-5

Preface

The great work of G. H. Palmer and Francis Burgess, early in the last century, to provide plainchant settings for the music of the liturgy, endowed the English-speaking world with a rich corpus of chant. It is to be lamented that the Catholic Church did not draw on this heritage when the Mass began to be celebrated in the vernacular. The insistence on "modernized" English made this problematic. At the same time, the Anglican Communion was engaged in its own liturgical upheaval, and in America the traditional *Book of Common Prayer* was replaced by a liturgy using modern English. The Coverdale Psalter of the Prayerbook was replaced with a modern English revision.

This has all led to the desuetude of *The Plainchant Gradual* of Palmer and Burgess and *The English Gradual* of Francis Burgess. Nevertheless, the Ordinariates for Anglicans in the Catholic Church as well the many traditionalist churches that use the Anglican Missal have re-awakened the need for a revision of the Gradual in English.

This is a major revision of *The Anglican Use Gradual,* 2007 which follows the structure of the *Graduale Romanum* and draws upon the musicological work of Dr. Palmer (G.H.P.), Francis Burgess (F.B.), and Winfred Douglas (W.D.). Since *The Plainchant Gradual* of Palmer and Burgess is again available in a reprint, I have eliminated most of the occasional melismatic chants and have included simple psalm tone chants based on Burgess' *The English Gradual* in order to provide a practical book that can be used in most churches. This expanded volume follows the structure and text of *Divine Worship:The Missal,* 2015, and covers all of the minor propers called for in that Missal. An index is included to adapt this book to the Ordinary Time lectionary sequence.

"Anglican Use" refers to Anglican, Catholic, Western Rite Orthodox, or any other congregatons using a liturgy based primarily on Anglican sources.

My sincere gratitude is offered to The Rev'd. Carl Reid, Mr. Stephen Cavanaugh, Dr. Helen Harrison and many others for their help in preparing this volume.

C.D.B.

How this book may be used

The rich musical patrimony of the English Catholic and Reformation tradition contains many elements: psalm tones, plainsong antiphons and mass settings, Anglican chant, hymns, anthems, litanies, and organ music. Catholic worship before the Reformation in England was influenced by the monastic tradition, and elaborate Latin chants were sung by choirs. As the Reformation developed, there was more emphasis on congregational singing and the use of the vernacular, exactly the same thing that we have seen in the Catholic Church in our time. The Anglo-Catholics combined in their service books many pre-reformation elements that had been left out of *The Book of Common Prayer*, and *Divine Worship: The Missal* continues that tradition. Hence we have the option of combining or selecting from many different elements.

The major propers of the Mass are the *Kyrie, Gloria, Credo, Sanctus, Benedictus, and Agnus Dei*. These may be said or sung and many settings are found in hymnals and published choir pieces. The minor propers, where the text is differerent for each Mass, are the *Introit, Gradual, Alleluia, Tract, Offertory, and Communion*. This is principally what is contained in this book, and conforms to the restored text of the minor propers in *Divine Worship: The Missal*. However they are not obligatory. For a said service, the texts may simply be read by the priest at the altar.

This book may be used by a single cantor, a schola, or a full choir. The use of taditional Gregorian notation saves space and should not be an obstacale. In fact this is a good place to start learning this notation which is unavoidable for more advanced plainsong.

For a sung service it has become usual to begin with an entrance hymn. The *Introit* may be sung after the hymn or omitted.

The rubrics in the Missal say that the "Responsorial Psalm" from the Lectionary may be used in place of the *Gradual*. The Reformation introduced congregational reading or singing of verses from the Psalter for Morning and Evening Prayer. More recently psalmody has been introduced in the Mass both in the Anglican Church and in the Catholic Church. Congregations can sing a psalm to accompanied Anglican Chant or plainsong, if given the music. It is common in many Anglican Use congregations to sing a psalm after the Old Testament Lesson, and then have the *Gradual* and *Alleluia* or *Tract* after the Epistle.

The *Offertory* may be sung and followed by a hymn or an anthem.

The psalm verses suggested at the *Communion* may be sung by the choir alternating with the communion antiphon. It is effective to also alternate between the plainsong of the antiphon and the psalm verses in Anglican Chant. This too may be replaced by or followed by a hymn.

CONTENTS

SEASON OF ADVENT
THE ADVENT PROSE

The Advent Prose may be sung in procession before the Introit, or elsewhere in the Mass, on any of the Sundays of Advent. On the Fourth Sunday of Advent, it may replace the Introit.

PROSE *Roráte, cǽli*   *Is 45:8*

Cantors

i.

DROP down, ye hea-vens, from a-bove, *

Choir

and let the skies pour down right - eous - ness.

Cantors

1. Be not wroth ve - ry sore, O LORD, neither remember

in - i - qui - ty for ev - er: thy ho - ly cities are a wilder-

ness, Si - on is a wil - der - ness, Je - ru - sa - lem a

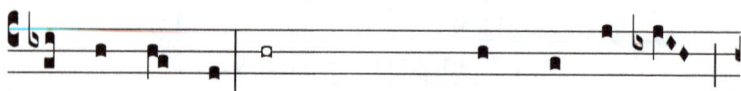

de - so - la - tion: our holy and our beau - ti - ful house,

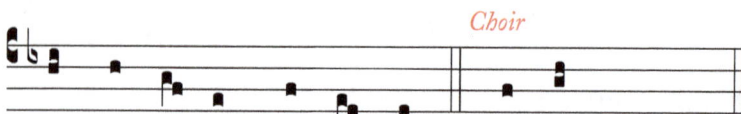

Choir

where our fa- thers prais-ed thee.   Drop down.... *(etc.)*

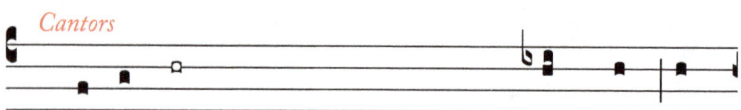

Cantors

2. We have sin - ned, and are as an un - clean thing, and

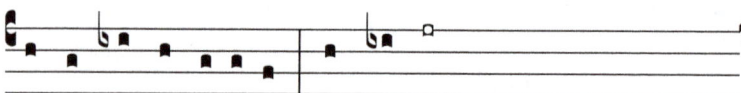

we all do fade as a leaf: and our iniquities, like the wind,

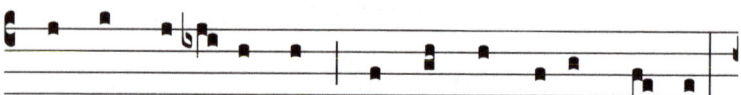

have ta - ken us a - way; thou hast hid thy face from us;

and hast consumed us, be-cause of our in-i-qui-ties.

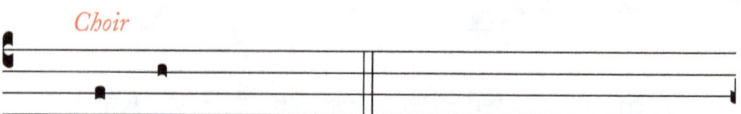

Choir

Drop down.... *(etc.)*

Cantors

3. Ye are my witnesses, saith the Lord, and my servant

whom I have cho - sen; that ye may know me and be-

lieve me: I, e - ven I, am the Lord, and be - side me

there is no Sa - viour: and there is none that can de - li -

Choir

ver out of my hand.   Drop down.... *(etc.)*

Cantors

4. Com - fort ye, com - fort ye my peo - ple, my sal - va -

tion shall not tar - ry: I have blot - ted out as a thick

9

cloud thy trans - gres - sions: Fear not, for I will save

thee: for I am the Lord thy God, the Ho - ly One of

Choir

Is - ra - el, thy Re - deem - er.   Drop down..... *(etc.)*

FAUX-BOURDON *for optional use*
In free speech-rhythm (as plainsong), unaccompanied.

Drop down, ye hea-vens from a - bove,   and let the skies pour down right-eous-ness.

C.F.

10

FIRST WEEK OF ADVENT

INTROIT *Ad te levávi*   *Ps. 25: 1-3*

Cantors

vij.

UN- TO thee, O LORD, lift I up my soul;   O my

God, in thee have I trusted, let me not be con- foun- ded:

Choir

nei- ther let mine enemies triumph over me; for all they

FINE   *Cantors*

that look for thee shall not be a- sham- ed. *Ps.* Show me

Choir   *Cantors*

thy ways, O LORD: and teach me thy paths.   Glo- ry be

to the Father, and to the Son, and to the Ho- ly Ghost:

Choir

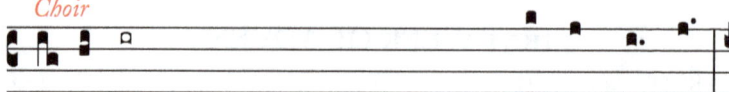

As it was in the beginning, is now, and ev- er shall be:

Full

world with- out end. A- men.   Un- to thee,..., *(etc.)*

Friday: IN. *Dóminus illuminátio mea, (Trinity IV, p. 394)*

GRADUAL   *Universi qui te exspéctant*   *Ps. 25:3,4*

Cantors   *Choir*

OR all they that look for thee: shall not be a- sham-

Cantors

ed, O LORD.   ℣. Make known to me thy ways, O LORD:

Choir

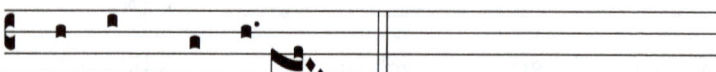

and teach me thy paths.

Friday: GR. *Bonum est confídere, (Trinity XIV, p. 431)*

ALLELUIA *Osténde nobis* *Ps. 85:8*

Cantors   *All*

℣. AL - LE- LE- LU- IA. Al - le- lu- ia.

Cantors   *Choir*

℣. Show us thy mercy, O LORD: and grant us thy

All

sal- va- tion.   Al - le- lu- ia.

OFFERTORY *Ad te, Dómine, levávi* *Ps. 25:1-3*

Cantors

ij. UN - TO thee O LORD, lift I up my soul; O my God,

in thee have I trusted,   let me not be con- foun- ded:

Choir

Nei- ther let mine enemies triumph over me;   for all

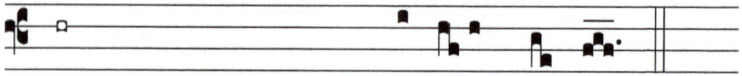

they that hope in thee shall not be a- sham- ed.

COMMUNION *Dóminus dabit benignitátem*   *Ps. 85:13*

Cantors   *Choir*

i.

THE LORD shall show lov- ing - kind- ness: and our

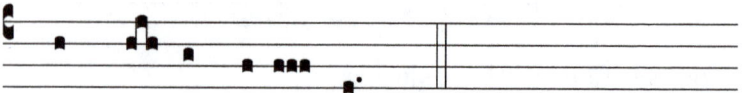

land shall give her in- crease.

Verses from **Psalm 85:1-4,7,8-13** *may be sung.*

Thursday CO. *Manducavérunt, (Epiphany VI, p. 109)*

14

The Advent Ember Days

Being the Wednesday, Friday, and Saturday after
the First Sunday in Advent

Ember Wednesday in Advent

Use the Introit, Gradual, Offertory and Communion for the 4th Sunday in Advent, p. 35ff

Ember Friday in Advent

INTROIT *Prope es tu*   *Ps. 119:151,152,1*

Cantors

vij.

B E thou nigh at hand, O LORD, for all thy com-

Choir

mand- ments are true: as con-cerning thy testimonies,

I have known long since, that thou hast ground-ed them

FINE   *Cantors*

for ev - er.   *Ps.* Bles-sed are those that are un-de-fi-led

Choir

in the way: and walk in the law of the Lord.

15

Cantors   *Choir*   *Full*

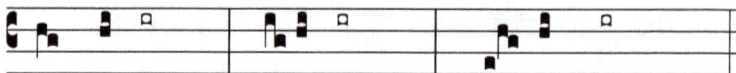

Glo- ry be... *(etc.)* As it was... *(etc.)* Be thou nigh... *(etc.)*

GRADUAL *Osténde nobis*   *Ps. 85:7,1*

Cantors   *Choir*

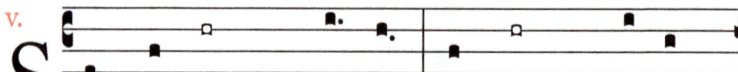

℣.

SHOW us thy mercy, O LORD: and grant us thy sal-

Cantors

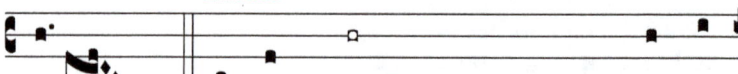

va-tion. ℣. O Lord, thou art become gracious un-to

Choir

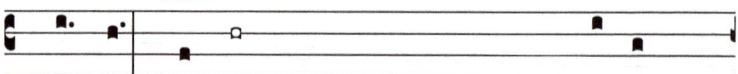

thy land: thou hast turned away the cap-ti-vi-ty of

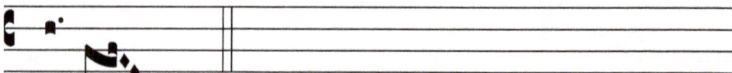

Ja - cob.

OFFERTORY *Deus tu convértens* *(Advent II, Page 23)*

COMMUNION *Ecce Dóminus veniet*   *Cf. Zech 14:5,7*

Cantors

i.

BE- HOLD, the Lord shall come, and all his Saints

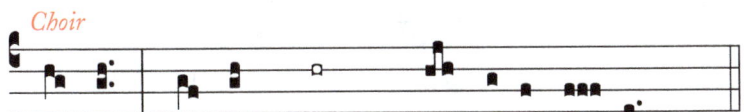

Choir

with him: and there shall be in that day a great light.

Verses from **Psalm 50:1-6** *may be sung.*

Ember Saturday in Advent

INTROIT *Veni et osténde*   *Ps. 80:3,2,1*

Cantors

vij.

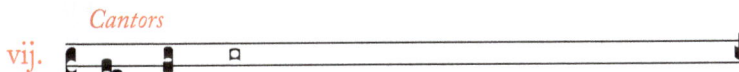

COME and show us the light of thy countenance, O

Choir

Lord, thou that sittest up-on the Che-ru-bim: and we

FINE   *Cantors*

shall be sav - ed. *Ps.* Hear, O thou Shep-herd of Is-ra-el:

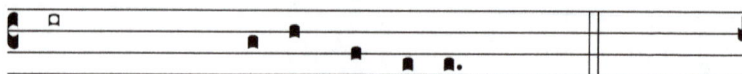

thou that leadest Jo-seph like a sheep.

Cantors *Choir* *Full*

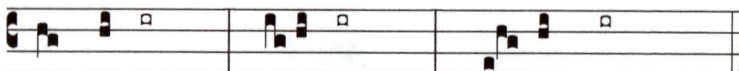

Glo- ry be... *(etc.)* As it was... *(etc.)* Come and show... *(etc.)*

GRADUAL *A summo cælo egressio* *Ps. 19:6,1*

v. *Cantors* *Choir*

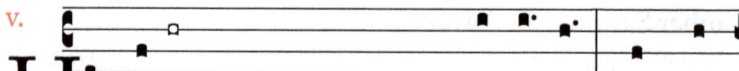

HIS go-ing forth is from the end of hea-ven: and his

Cantors

circuit even to the end there-of. ℣. The hea-vens

Choir

declare the glo-ry of God: and the firmament show-eth

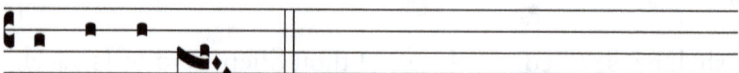

his han-dy-work.

TRACT *Qui regis Israel*   *Ps. 80:1,2*

Cantors

viij.

HEAR, O thou Shepherd of Is-ra-el: thou that

Choir

leadest Joseph like a sheep. ℣ Show thyself also, thou that

sittest upon the Che-ru-bim: before Ephraim, Benjamin,

Cantors   *Full*

and Man-as-seh. ℣ Stir up thy strength, O Lord: and

come and save us.

OFFERTORY *Exsulta satis*   *Zech. 9:9*

Cantors

ij.

RE-JOICE great-ly, O daughter of Sion; shout, O

Choir

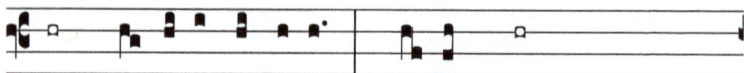

daugh-ter of Je-ru-sa-lem:　be-hold, thy King cometh

unto thee: ho- ly and a Sav-iour.

COMMUNION *Exsultavit*　　　　　　　　　*Ps. 19:5b,6*

Cantors　　　　　　　　　　　　　　　*Choir*

i.

HE re-joiceth as a giant to run his course:　his go-ing

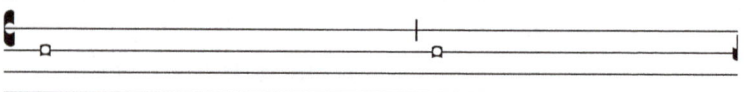

forth is from the end of heaven,　and his circuit even

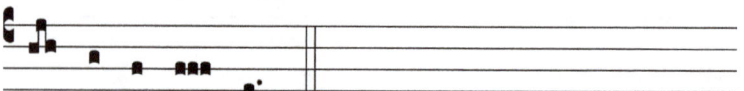

to　the end there-of.

Verses from Psalm 19:1-6 *may be sung.*

Second SUNDAY in ADVENT

INTROIT *Populus Sion*   *Isa. 30:19, 30; Ps. 80*

Cantors

vij.

O PEO-PLE of Sion, behold the LORD is nigh at

Choir

hand to re- deem the na- tions: and in the gladness of

your heart the LORD shall cause his glo- ri- ous voice to

FINE   *Cantors*

be heard. *Ps.* Hear, O thou Shep- herd of Is- ra-el:

Choir   *Cantors*

thou that leadest Jo- seph like a sheep.   Glo- ry be

to the Father, and to the Son, and to the Ho- ly Ghost:

21

Choir

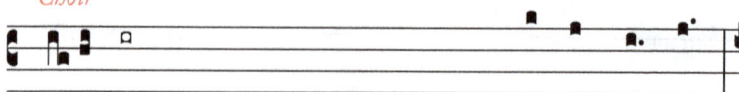

As it was in the beginning, is now, and ev- er shall be:

Full

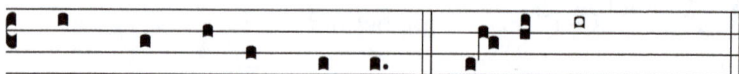

world with- out end. A- men.   O peo- ple..., *(etc.)*

GRADUAL *Ex Sion*   *Ps. 50:2,3,5*

Cantors   *Choir*

v.

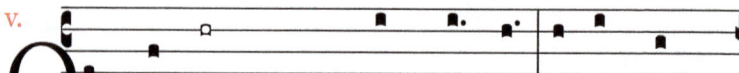

OUT   of Sion hath God ap- pear-ed: in per- fect

Cantors

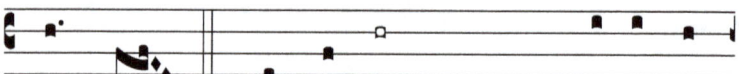

beau- ty.   ℣. Ga- ther my saints to-ge- ther un- to

Choir

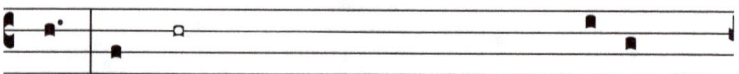

me: those that have made a covenant with me with

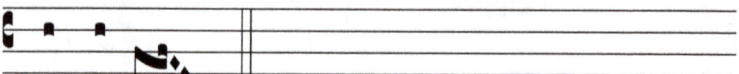

sac- ri- fice.

ALLELUIA *Lætátus sum*   *Ps. 122:1*

Cantors   *All*

AL- LE- LU- IA.   Al - le- lu- ia.

Cantors   *Choir*

℣. I was glad when they said un- to me: we will go into

All

the house of the LORD.   Al - le- lu- ia.

Wednesday AL. *Veníte ad me. (All Saints, p. 620)*
Saturday AL. *Qui séquitur me. (Justin, Martyr, p. 556)*

OFFERTORY *Deus tu convértens*   *Ps. 85:7,8*

Cantors

WILT not thou turn again, O God, and quicken us;

Choir

that thy peo- ple may re- joice in thee?   Show us thy

23

mercy, O Lᴏʀᴅ; and grant us thy sal- va- tion.

Wednesday Oꜰ. *Confortámini. (Sapientiatide. p. 39)*

Cᴏᴍᴍᴜɴɪᴏɴ *Ierúsalem, surge*   *Bar. 5:5; 4:36*

Cantors

E- RU- SA- LEM, haste thee, and stand on high:

Choir

and be- hold the joy and gladness that cometh unto thee

from God thy Sa- viour.

Verses from Psalm 147:12-20 *may be sung.*

Third SUNDAY in ADVENT

INTROIT *Gaudéte in Dómino* *Phil. 4:4-5; Ps. 85*

Cantors

vij.

RE- JOICE in the LORD alway: and again I say, Rejoice.

Let your moderation be known unto all men. The LORD

Choir

is at hand. Be care- ful for nothing; but in every thing

by prayer and supplication, with thanksgiving,   let

FINE

your requests be made known un- to God.

Cantors   *Choir*

Ps. LORD, thou art become gracious un- to thy land: thou

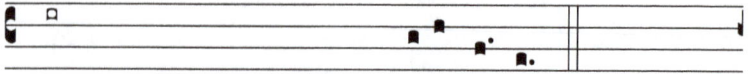

hast turned away the captivi - ty of Ja- cob.

Cantors   *Choir*   *Full*

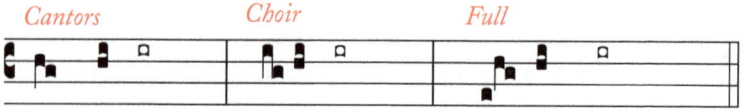

Glo- ry be... *(etc.)* As it was... *(etc.)* Re- joice in ... *(etc.)*

Wednesday: IN. *Rorate.* *(Advent IV, p. 35, unless it is Dec. 17 or 18))*

GRADUAL *Qui sedes, Dómine*   Ps. 80:2-3

Cantors

V.

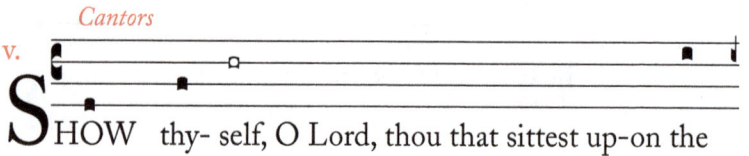

SHOW thy- self, O Lord, thou that sittest up-on the

Choir

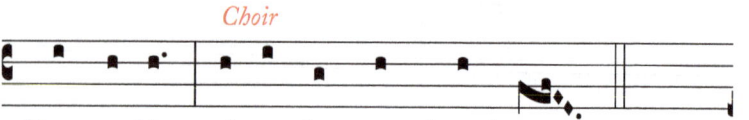

Che- ru- bim; stir up thy strength and come.

Cantors   *Choir*

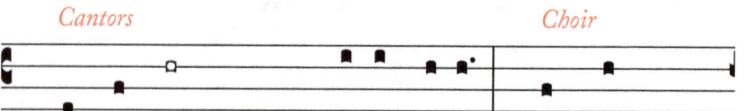

℣. Hear, O thou Shepherd of Is- ra- el: thou that

lead- est Jo- seph like a sheep.

26

Sunday, year B: GR. *Fuit homo. (Vigil of John the Baptist, p. 565)*

ALLELUIA *Excita, Dómine*

Cantors　　　　　　　　　*All*

vj.

AL- LE- LU- IA.　　Al - le- lu- ia.

Cantors　　　　　　　　　*Choir*

℣. Stir up thy strength, O Lord: and come and help us.

All

Al - le- lu- ia.

OFFERTORY *Benedixísti, Dómine*　　　　　　　　　Ps. 85:2

Cantors

ij.

O LORD thou art become gracious unto thy land;

Choir

thou hast turned away the cap- ti- vi- ty of Ja- cob:

27

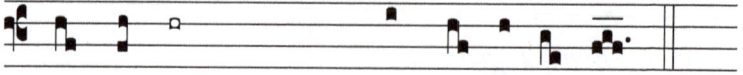

Thou hast forgiven the of- fence of thy peo- ple.

COMMUNION *Dícite: Pusillánimes*   *Isa. 35:4*

Cantors   *Choir*

i.

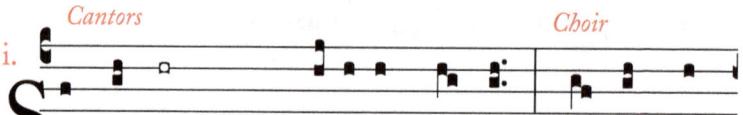

SAY to them that are of a fear- ful heart: Be strong, fear

not;   behold your God will come and save you.

The Second Song of Isaiah, Canticle *Quærite Dominum may be sung.*

Saturday: CO. *Domus mea.*
(Common for the Dedication of a Church, p. 646, unless it is Dec. 17 or 18)

SAPIENTIATIDE
The Great O Antiphons

On the appointed days, these Anthems following are sung or said before and after the *Magnificat* at Evening Prayer. They are also sung or said at Mass as appointed.

O Sapientia   *Dec. 17*

Cantors   *Choir*

O WIS - DOM,* which cam-est out of the mouth of the Most High, and reach-est from one end to an-oth-er, migh-ti-ly and sweet-ly or-der-ing all things: come and teach us the way of pru-dence. o i ou e a e

If the Antiphon is said as a commemoration for Advent, it is followed by the Versicle:

℣. Drop down, ye heavens, from above,
℟. And let the skies pour down righteousness.

29

O Adonai

Cantors   *Choir*

ij.

O A-DO-NA - I, * and Lea-der of the house of Is-

ra-el, who ap-pea-redst in the bush to Mo-ses in

a flame of fire, and ga-vest him the law in Si-nai

come and de-li-ver us with an out-stretch-ed arm.

o i ou e a e

O Radix Jesse

Cantors   *Choir*

ij.

O ROOT of Jes-se, * which stan-dest for an en-sign

of the peo-ples,   at whom kings shall shut their mouths

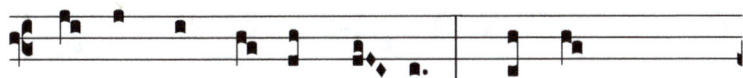

to whom the Gen-tiles shall seek: come and

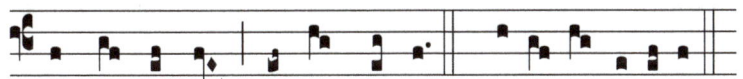

de - liv - er us,   and tar - ry not.   o   i   ou   e   a   e

O Clavis David

Cantors   Choir

ij.

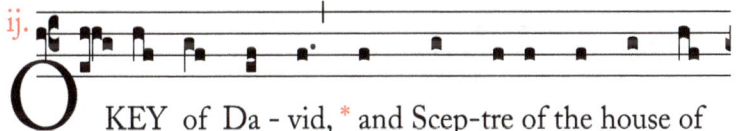

O KEY of Da - vid, * and Scep-tre of the house of

Is-ra-el,   that o-pen-est and no man shut-teth,   and

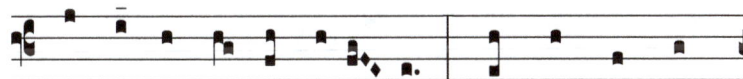

shut-test and no man o-pen-eth;   come, and bring the

31

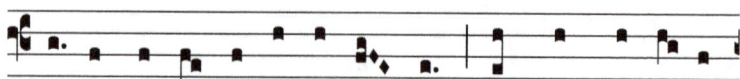

pri-son-er out of the pri-son-house, and him that sit-teth

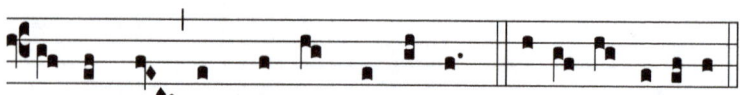

in dark-ness and the sha-dow of death. o i ou e a e

O Oriens *Dec. 21*

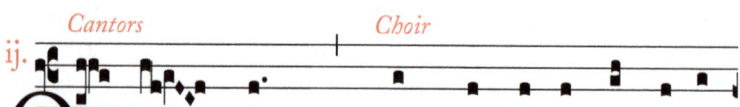

Cantors *Choir*

ij.

O DAY - SPRING, * Bright-ness of the Light e-ver-

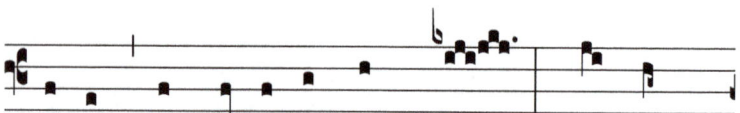

last-ing and Sun of righ-teous-ness: come and

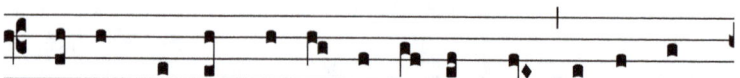

en-light-en him that sit-teth in dark-ness and in the

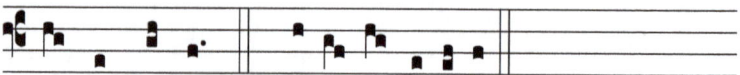

sha-dow of death. o i ou e a e

O Rex gentium   *Dec. 22*

Cantors   *Choir*

ij.

O KING of the Na-tions, * and their De - sire; the

Cor-ner-stone, who ma-kest both one: come and save

man-kind, whom thou form-edst of clay.

o i ou e a e

O Emmanuel   *Dec. 23*

Cantors   *Choir*

ij.

O EM-MAN-U-EL * our King and Law-giv-er

the De-sire of all na - tions and their Sal- va- tion:

33

come and save us, O Lord our God. o i ou e a e

O Virgo vírginum

Cantors   Choir

O VIR-GIN of vir-gins, * how shall this be?

for nei-ther be-fore thee was a-ny like thee, nor

shall there be af-ter. Daugh-ters of Je-ru-sa-lem, Why

mar-vel ye at me? The thing which ye be-hold is a

di-vine mys-te-ry. o i ou e a e

34

Fourth SUNDAY in ADVENT

The propers for Sapientiatide may be used on this Sunday. p. 39 ff

INTROIT *Roráte, cæli*   *Isa. 45:8; Ps. 19*

Cantors

vij.

DROP down, ye heavens, from above, and let the skies

Choir

pour down righ - teous - ness: let the earth open,

FINE   *Cantors*

and bring forth a Sa - viour.   *Ps.* The hea- vens declare

Choir

the glo - ry of God: and the firmament show - eth

Cantors

his han - dy - work.   Glo- ry be to the Father, and to the

Choir

Son, and to the Ho- ly Ghost: As it was in the

35

Choir

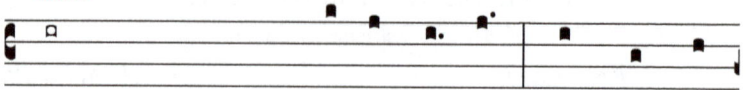

beginning, is now, and ev- er shall be: world with- out

Full

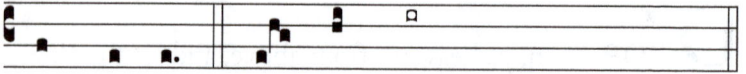

end. A- men. Drop down, ye heavens, ...*(etc.)*

GRADUAL *Prope est Dóminus* *Ps. 145:18, ℣. 21*

Cantors

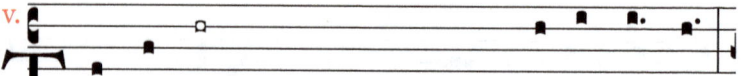

THE LORD is nigh unto all them that call up - on him:

Choir

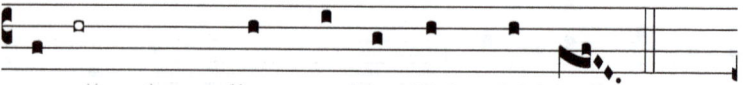

yea, all such as call up - on him faith - ful - ly.

Cantors

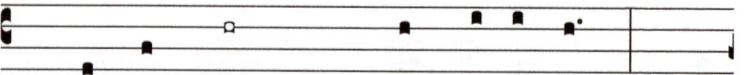

℣. My mouth shall speak the praise of the LORD:

Choir

and let all flesh give thanks un - to his ho - ly Name.

ALLELUIA *Veni, Dómine*

Cantors *All*

vj.

AL- LE- LU- IA. Al - le- lu- ia.

Cantors *Choir*

℣. Come, O LORD, and tar - ry not: forgive the misdeeds

All

of thy peo - ple.   Al - le- lu- ia.

OFFERTORY *Ave, María*   *Lk. 1:28*

Cantors

ij.

HAIL Ma - ry, full of grace; the Lord is with thee:

Choir

bless - ed art thou among women, and blessed is the fruit

of thy womb.

COMMUNION *Ecce virgo* *Isa. 7:14*

i.

Cantors

BE - HOLD, a Virgin shall con - ceive, and bear a Son:

Choir

and his name shall be call - ed   Em- ma - nu - el.

Verses from Psalm 19:1-6 *may be sung.*

From 17 to 24 December

17 December

INTROIT *Prope es tu* *(page 15)*
GRADUAL *Tóllite portas* *(Masses of St. Mary, p. 751)*
ALLELUIA *O Sapientia*

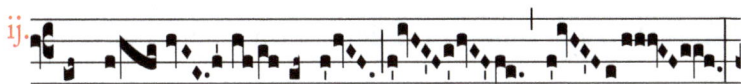

AL-LE-　　　lu-ia.　* *ij.*

or the Alleluia may be sung more simply, thus:

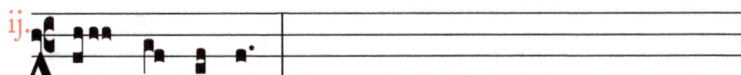

AL -LE- lu- ia.　* *ij.*

*Then follows the appointed O Antiphon (p. 29 ff) and the Alleluia is re-
peated.*

OFFERTORY *Confortámini*　　　　　　　　　　*Isa. 35:4*

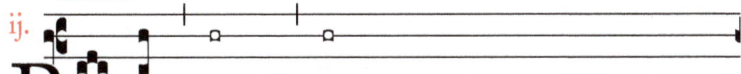

Cantors

BE strong, fear not; for behold, our God will come with

Choir

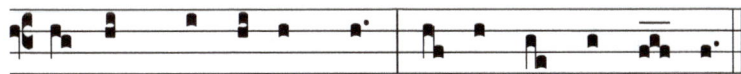

ven-geance and re-com-pense: he will come and save you.

COMMUNION *Ecce Dóminus veniet (page 17)*

18 December

INTROIT *Vení, et osténde*   *Cf. Ps. 80:3,2,1*

Cantors

vij.

COME and show us the light of thy countenance,

O LORD, thou that sittest up-on the Che-ru-bim:

Choir   *FINE*   *Cantors*

and we shall be sav - ed. *Ps.* Hear, O thou Shep- herd

Choir

of Is- ra-el: thou that leadest Jo- seph like a sheep.

Cantors   *Choir*   *Full*

Glo- ry be... *(etc.)* As it was... *(etc.)* Come and show ... *(etc.)*

GRADUAL *A summo caelo egressio (Page 18)*
ALLELUIA *O Adonai (Page 39)*
OFFERTORY *Exsulta satis (Page 19)*
COMMUNION *Exsultavit (Page 20)*

19 December

INTROIT *Ne tímeas*   *Luke 1:13,15,14; Ps 21:1*

Cantors

FEAR not, Zechariah, for thy prayer is heard; and thy

wife Elizabeth shall bear thee a son, and thou shalt call

Choir

his name John: and he shall be great in the sight of the

Lord, and shall be filled with the Holy Ghost, even from

FINE

his mother's womb; and many shall re-joice at his birth.

Cantors

Ps. The King shall re-joice in thy strength, O Lord:

Choir

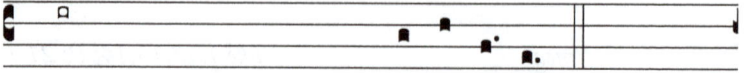

exceeding glad shall he be of thy sal-va-tion.

Cantors   *Choir*   *Full*

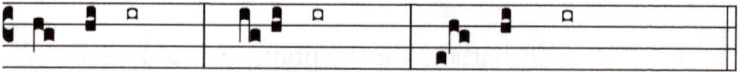

Glo- ry be... *(etc.)* As it was... *(etc.)* Fear not, Zachariah ... *(etc.)*

GRADUAL *In sole posuit*   *cf. Ps. 19:5,6*

Cantors   *Choir*

v.

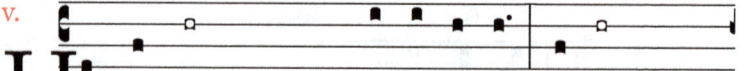

HE hath set his taberna-cle in the sun: and as a bride-

Cantors

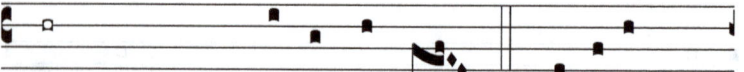

groom, coming out of his cham-ber. ℣ His go-ing

Choir

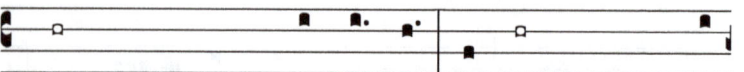

forth is from the end of hea-ven: and his circuit even to

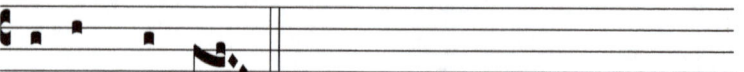

the end there-of.

ALLELUIA *O Radix Jesse (Page 39)*

OFFERTORY *Audi Israel*

HEAR, O Is-rael: be-hold, I, the Lord, will come,

and I will forgive the sins of thy peo - ple.

COMMUNION *Veni Dómine*   *Cf. Hab. 3:3*

COME, O LORD, and tar-ry not: for-give the sins

of thy peo - ple.

Psalm 85:1-7,9-13 *may be sung.*

20 December

21 December

INTROIT *Vení et osténde* *(page 40)*

GRADUAL *Dómine Deus virtútum* *Ps. 80:19,2*

Cantors *Choir*

TURN us again, O LORD God of hosts: show the light

of thy countenance, and we shall be made whole.

Cantors *Choir*

℣. Stir up thy strength, O Lord: and come and help us.

ALLELUIA *O Oriens* *(Page 39)*
OFFERTORY *Exsulta satis* *(Page 19)*
COMMUNION *Exsultavit* *(Page 20)*

22 December

INTROIT *Meménto nostri* *Ps 106:4,5,1*

Cantors

RE-MEM-BER me, O Lord, according to the favour

Choir

that thou bearest un-to thy peo-ple: O vis-it me with

FINE   *Cantors*

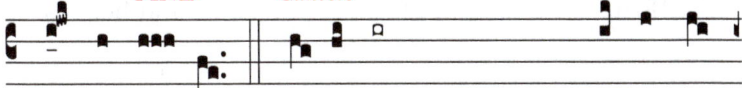

thy sal-va-tion;   that I may see the fe-li-ci-ty of thy

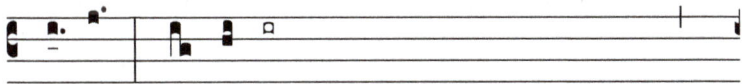

cho-sen,   and re-joice in the gladness of thy people,

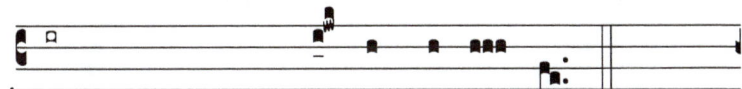

and give thanks with thine in- he- ri-   tance.

Cantors

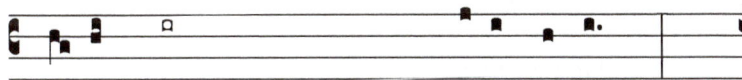

Ps. O give thanks unto the Lord for he is gra-cious:

Choir

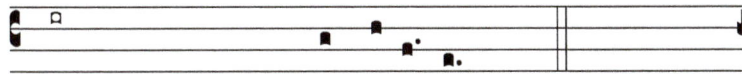

and his mercy en-dur-eth for e- ver.

Cantors   *Choir*   *Full*

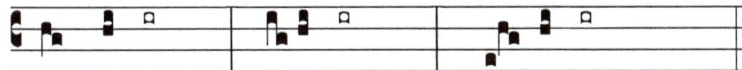

Glo- ry be... *(etc.)* As it was... *(etc.)* Remember me... *(etc.)*

GRADUAL *Excita Dómine.*   *Ps 80:2b,1*

Cantors   *Choir*

STIR up thy strength, O LORD: and come and help us.

Cantors

℣. Hear, O thou Shepherd of Israel, thou that leadest

Choir

Joseph like a sheep: show thyself also, thou that

sittest up-on the Che-ru-bim.

ALLELUIA *O Rex gentium (Page 39)*
OFFERTORY *Audi Israel (Page 43)*

COMMUNION *Magnificat*   *Luke 1:46, 49*

Cantors ... *Choir*

i.

Y soul doth mag-ni-fy the Lord: for he that is

mighty hath mag- ni- fi- ed   me.

Verses from The Magnificat *may be sung.*

23 December

INTROIT *Prope es tu* *(page 15)*

GRADUAL *Tollite portas* *(Masses of St. Mary, p. 751)*

ALLELUIA *O Emmanuel* *(Page 39)*

OFFERTORY *Confortámini* *(Page 39)*

COMMUNION *Ecce Dóminus veniet* *(Page 17)*

24 December

The Morning Mass

INTROIT *Roráte Caeli* *(page 35)*

GRADUAL *Prope est Dóminus* *(page 36)*

ALLELUIA *O Virgo Virginum* *(Page 39)*

OFFERTORY *Ave María* *(Page 37)*

COMMUNION *Ecce virgo* *(Page 38)*

SEASON OF CHRISTMAS

CHRISTMAS EVE

Vigil Mass *or* Christmas Eve falling on a Sunday

INTROIT *Hodie sciétis*   *Cf. Ex. 16:6,7; Is. 35:4; Ps. 24:1*

Cantors

vij.

TO-DAY shall ye know that the LORD will come to de-

Choir   *FINE*

li-ver us: and at sunrise shall ye be-hold his glo - ry.

Cantors

Ps. The earth is the LORD'S, and all that there-in is:

Choir

the com-pass of the world, and they that dwell there-in.

Cantors   *Choir*   *Full*

Glo- ry be..., *(etc.)* As it was..., *(etc.)* To-day..., *(etc.)*

48

GRADUAL *Hodie sciétis*   Cf. *Ex. 16:6,7; Is. 35:4;* ℣. *Ps. 80:1,2*

Cantors

TO-DAY shall ye know that the Lord will come to de-

Choir

li - ver us: and at sunrise shall ye be-hold his glo - ry.

Cantors

℣. Hear, O thou Shepherd of Israel; thou that leadest Jo-

Choir

seph like a sheep: show thyself also, thou that sittest upon

the Cherubim; before Ephraim, Benjamin, and Ma-nas-seh.

ALLELUIA *Crástina die*

AL- LE- LU- IA.   Al - le- lu- ia.

V. On the morrow the iniquity of the earth shall be

blot-ted out: and the Saviour of the world shall reign

o-ver us.   Al - le- lu- ia.

OFFERTORY *Tollite portas*   *Ps.24:7*

LIFT up your heads, O ye gates; and be ye lift up, ye ev-

er - last - ing doors: and the King of glo-ry shall come in.

COMMUNION *Revelábitur*   *Cf. Isa. 40:5*

Cantors   *Choir*

i.

T HE glo-ry of the Lord shall be re-veal-ed: and all

flesh shall see the sal-va - tion of our God.

Verses from Psalm 24:1-8 *may be sung.*

Christmas in the Night

INTROIT *Dóminus díxit*   *Ps. 2:7b, 1*

Cantors ... *Choir*

vij.

THE LORD hath said un- to me: Thou art my Son;

Cantors

this day have I be- got- ten thee. *Ps.* Why do the

Choir

heathen so furiously rage to- ge- ther: and why do the

Cantors

people i- ma- gine a vain thing? Glo- ry be

to the Father, and to the Son, and to the Ho- ly Ghost:

Choir

As it was in the beginning, is now, and ev- er shall be:

Full

world with- out end. A- men. The LORD hath..., *(etc.)*

GRADUAL *Tecum princípium* Ps. 110:3, ℣. 1

Cantors

IN the day of thy power shall the people offer thee

Choir

free-will offerings with an ho-ly wor- ship: the dew of

Cantors

thy birth is of the womb of the morn- ing. ℣. The LORD

Choir

said un- to my Lord: Sit thou on my right hand; until I

make thine e- ne- mies thy foot- stool.

ALLELUIA *Dóminus dixit ad me* Ps. 2:7

Cantors *All*

AL- LE- LU- IA. Al - le- lu- ia.

Cantors *Choir*

℣. The LORD said un- to me: Thou art my Son; this day

All

have I be- got - ten thee. Al - le - lu- ia.

OFFERTORY *Læténtur cæli* *Ps. 96:11*

Cantors

ij. LET the hea- vens re- joice, and let the earth be glad:

Choir

before the Lord, for he is come.

COMMUNION *In splendóribus* *Ps. 110:3*

Cantors *Choir*

i. THE dew of thy birth: is of the womb of the morn- ing.

Verses from Psalm 110 *may be sung.*

INTROIT *Lux fulgébit* *Cf. Isa. 9:2. 6; Lk. 1:33; Ps. 93:1*

Cantors

vij.

LIGHT shall shine today upon us; for unto us the Lord

Choir

is born: and his Name shall be called Wonderful,

Mighty God, the Prince of peace, Father of the world to

FINE

come; of whose kingdom there shall be   no   end.

Cantors

Ps. The Lord is King and hath put on glo-rious ap - pa - rel:

Choir

the Lord hath put on his apparel, and gir-ded him-self

55

Cantors   *Choir*

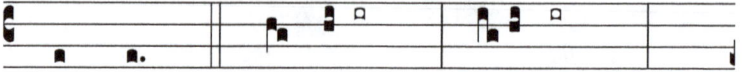

with strength.   Glo- ry be... *(etc.)* As it was... *(etc.)*

Full

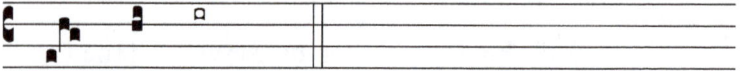

Light shall shine ... *(etc.)*

GRADUAL *Benedictus qui venit*   *Ps. 118:26, 27 ℣. 23*

Cantors

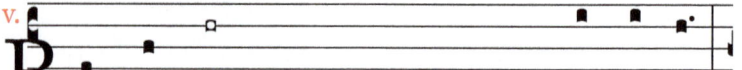

℣. BLES-SED is he that cometh in the Name of the LORD:

Choir   *Cantors*

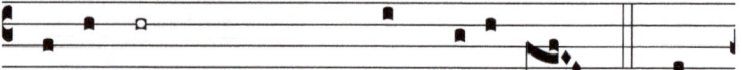

God is the LORD who hath show - ed us light. ℣. This

Choir

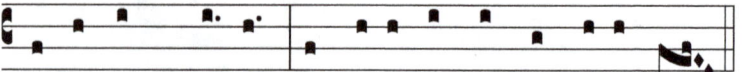

is the LORD's do - ing: and it is mar-vel-lous in our eyes.

ALLELUIA *Dóminus regnávit, decórem*   *Ps. 93:1,2*

Cantors   *All*

vj.

AL- LE- LU- IA.   Al - le- lu- ia.

Cantors

℣. The LORD is King, and hath put on glorious ap-par-el:

Choir

the Lord hath put on his apparel, and gird-ed him-self

All

with strength.   Al - le- lu- ia.

OFFERTORY *Deus enim firmávit*   *Ps. 93:2,3*

Cantors

ij.

GOD hath made the round world so sure, that it can

Choir

not be mov-ed: ev - er since the world began, hath thy

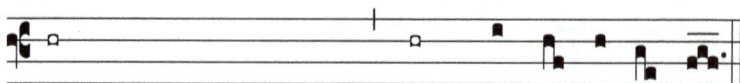

seat, O God, been prepared, thou art from ev-er-last-ing.

COMMUNION *Exsúlta, fília Sion*   *Zach. 9:9*

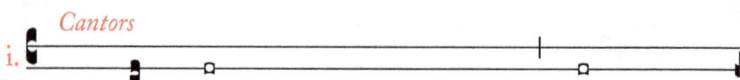

Cantors

i. RE-JOICE greatly, O daughter of Sion, shout, O

Choir

daughter of Je-ru-sa-lem: be-hold, thy King cometh,

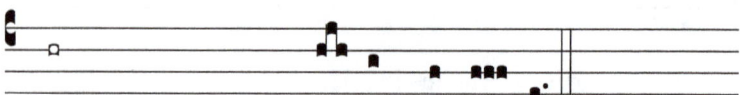

the Holy One and the Sa-viour of the world.

Verses from Psalm 34 *may be sung.*

CHRISTMAS
Day

Introit *Puer natus est nobis*   Isa. 9:6; Ps 98:1

Cantors

vij.

U̲N-TO us a Child is born; un-to us a Son is giv-en:

Choir

and the government shall be upon his shoulder; and his

FINE

Name shall be called, Angel of Migh-ty Coun-sel.

Cantors   *Choir*

Ps. O sing unto the LORD a new song: for he hath done

Cantors   *Choir*

mar-vel-lous things. Glo- ry be... *(etc.)* As it was... *(etc.)*

Full

Un - to us ... *(etc.)*

GRADUAL *Vidérunt omnes*   *Ps. 98:4,5, ℣. 3*

Cantors

℣.

ALL the ends of the earth have seen the salvation of

Choir   *Cantors*

our God: O be joyful in God, all ye lands. ℣. The LORD

Choir

hath declared his sal-va-tion: In the sight of the heathen

hath he openly show-ed his right-eous-ness.

ALLELUIA *Dies sanctificátus*

Cantors   *All*

vj.

AL- LE- LU- IA.   Al - le- lu- ia.

Cantors

℣. A hal-lowed day hath dawned upon the earth;   come,

Choir

ye nations, and wor-ship the LORD: for on this day a great

Light hath des-cend-ed up-on the earth.

All

Al - le- lu- ia.

OFFERTORY *Tui sunt cæli*   *Ps.89:12 & 15a*

Cantors

ij.

THE hea- vens are thine, the earth also is thine; thou hast

laid the foundations of the round world, and all that

Choir

there-in is: righ-teou-ness and equity are the

61

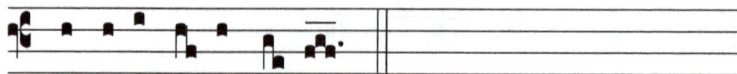

ha-bi-ta-tion of thy seat.

COMMUNION *Vidérunt omnes*   *Ps. 98:4*

Cantors   *Choir*

i.

ALL the ends of the world: have seen the sal-va-tion of

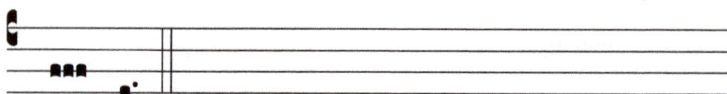

our God.

Verses from Psalm 98 *may be sung.*

THE HOLY FAMILY
Sunday within the octave of Christmas
or, if there is no Sunday, 30 December

INTROIT *Deus in loco sancto*   *Ps. 68: 5,6,35,2*

Cantors

vij.

GOD in his holy habitation; it is he that maketh

Choir

brethren to be of one mind in an house: He will give the

FINE

dominion and preeminence   un- to his peo- ple.
(*in Eastertide:*   unto his peo- ple. Al- le- lu- ia.)

Cantors

Ps. Let God arise, and let his e- ne- mies be scat- ter- ed:

Choir

let them also that hate him flee be- fore him.

Cantors   *Choir*   *Full*

Glo- ry be... *(etc.)*   As it was... *(etc.)* God in... *(etc.)*

63

GRADUAL *Unam pétii a Dómino*   Ps. 27:4

Cantors

℣.

ONE thing have I desired of the LORD, which I

Choir

will re- quire: e- ven that I may dwell in the house of

Cantors

the LORD. ℣. To be- hold the fair beau-ty of the LORD:

Choir

and to vi- sit his tem- ple.

ALLELUIA *Gaudéte, iusti*   Ps. 32:1

Cantors   *All*

vj.

AL- LE- LU- IA.   Al - le- lu- ia.

Cantors   *Choir*

℣. Re- joice in the Lord, O ye righ- teous: for it

becometh well the just to be thank- ful.

All

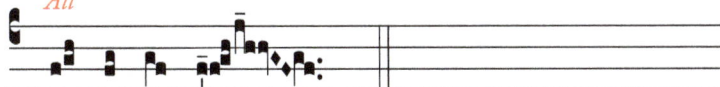

Al - le- lu- ia.

OFFERTORY *In te sperávi*   *Ps. 31:16, 17*

Cantors   *Choir*

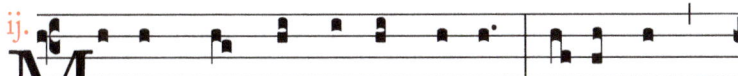

ij.

MY hope hath been in thee, O LORD: I have said,

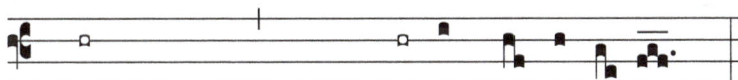

Thou art my God,   my times are in thy hand.
(*Eastertide:* my times are in thy hand. Al- le- lu- ia)

COMMUNION *Fili, quid fecísti*   *Luke 2:48–49*

Cantors

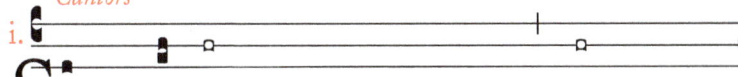

i.

SON, why hast thou thus dealt with us? Behold, thy

Choir

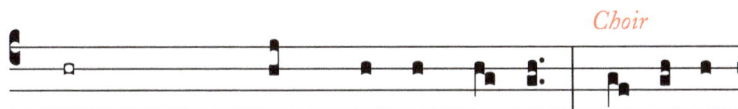

father and I have sought thee sor- row- ing. And he said

unto them, How is it that ye sought me? Know ye not that

I must be a- bout my Fa- ther's bus- iness?

Verses from Psalm 27 *may be sung.*

Sunday Year A: *Tolle púerum* *Matt. 2:20*

Cantors

i.

AKE the young Child and his mother, and go into the

Choir

land of Is - ra - el: for they are dead which sought the

young Child's life.

Verses from Psalm 93 *or* 128 *may be sung.*

Weekdays within the octave of Christmas
*All as on Christmas Day, **Lux fulgébit** or **Puer natus***

ALLELUIA *Multifárie*   *Heb. 1:1,2*

Cantors   *All*

vj.

AL- LE- LU- IA.   Al - le- lu- ia.

Cantors

℣. God, who at sundry times and in divers manners spake

Choir

unto the fathers by the Pro-phets, hath in these last days

All

spoken un-to us by his Son.   Al - le- lu- ia.

JANUARY 1

INTROIT *Salve, sancta Parens* Sedulius; Ps. 45:2,11,12

Cantors

vij.

HAIL, O Mo- ther most ho- ly, who in childbirth

Choir

didst bring forth the Mon-arch: him who o'er heaven and

FINE *Cantors*

earth reigneth for ev-er and ev- er. *Ps.* My heart is

Choir

inditing of a good mat- ter: I speak of the things which I

Cantors

have made un- to the King. Glo- ry be...*(etc.)*

Choir *Full*

As it was..., *(etc.)* Hail, O Mother ..., *(etc.)*

or IN. *Lux fulgébit* *(p.55)*

68

GRADUAL *Diffúsa est grátia* Ps. 45:2, ℣. 4

Cantors *Choir*

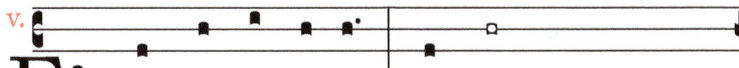

FULL of grace are thy lips: Be - cause God hath

Cantors

blessed thee for ev - er. ℣. Be- cause of the

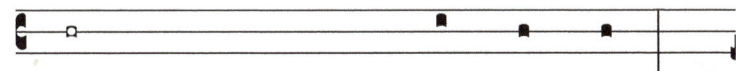

word of truth, of meekness, and righ- teous- ness:

Choir

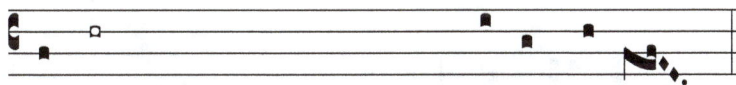

and thy right hand shall teach thee ter- ri- ble things.

ALLELUIA *Post partum*

Cantors *All*

AL- LE- LU- IA. Al - le- lu- ia.

Cantors

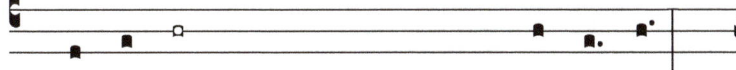

℣. Af- ter childbirth thou remainedst a pure vir- gin:

Choir

Mother of God, in- ter- cede for us.

All

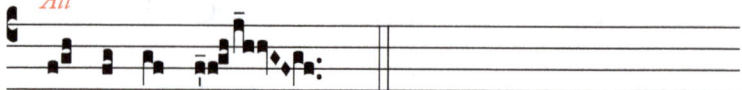

Al - le- lu- ia.

OFFERTORY *Felix namque es*

Cantors

ij.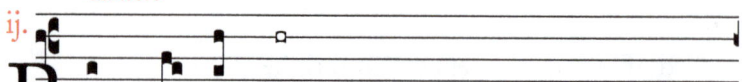

BLES- SED art thou, O Holy Virgin Mary, and most

Choir

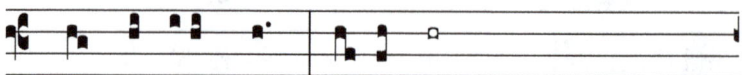

wor- thy of all praise: for out of thee arose the Sun of

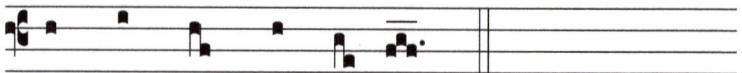

righ-teous- ness, Christ our God.

COMMUNION *Exsúlta, fília Sion*   *Zach. 9:9*

Cantors

i.

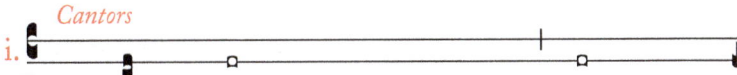

R E-JOICE greatly, O daughter of Sion, shout, O

Choir

daughter of Je- ru- sa- lem: be- hold, thy King cometh,

the Holy One and the Sa-viour of the World.

Verses from Psalm 45:2, 8-13 *or the* Magnificat *may be sung.*

Second SUNDAY after CHRISTMAS

These Propers shall serve for the Second Sunday of Christmas, if there is one, and from 2 January up to and including the Vigil of the Epiphany.

INTROIT *Dum médium* Wisd. 18:14-15; Ps. 93

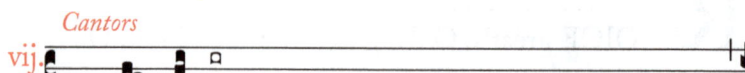

Cantors

WHEN as all the world was in profoundest quietness,

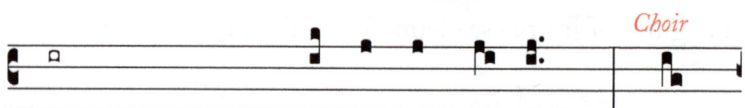

Choir

and night was in the midst of her swift course: thine

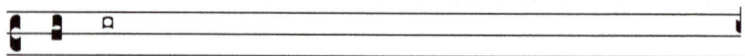

al- mighty Word, O LORD, leaped down from heaven

FINE *Cantors*

out of thy roy- al throne. *Ps.* The LORD is King, and hath

Choir

put on glo- rious ap- pa- rel: The LORD hath put on his

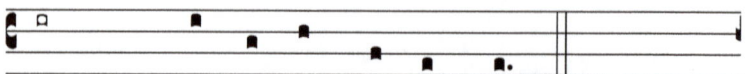

apparel, and gir- ded him- self with strength.

72

SECOND WEEK after CHRISTMAS

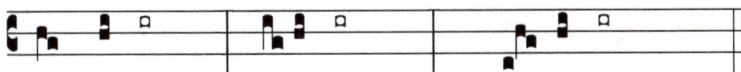

Glo- ry be...*(etc.)* As it was..., *(etc.)* When as all ..., *(etc.)*

GRADUAL *Speciósus forma*   *Ps. 45 :2 ℣. 1*

Cantors   *Choir*

v.

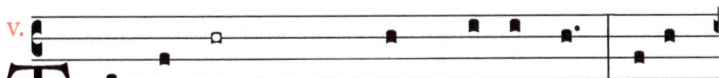

THOU art fairer than the chil- dren of men: full of

Cantors

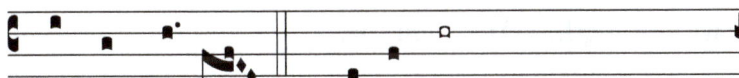

grace are thy lips. ℣. My heart is inditing of a good

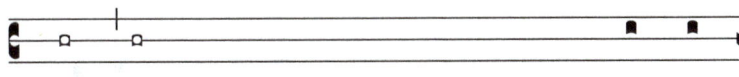

matter; I speak of the things which I have made un- to

Choir

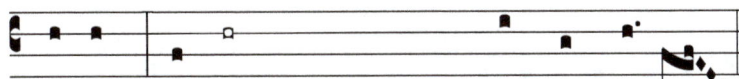

the King: my tongue is the pen of a rea- dy wri- ter.

ALLELUIA *Dóminus regnávit, decórem*   *Ps.93:1,2*

Cantors   *All*

vj.

AL - LE- LU- IA. Al - le- lu- ia.

73

Cantors

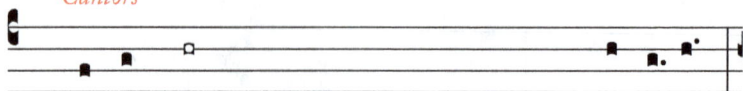

℣. The LORD is King, and hath put on glorious ap-pa-rel:

Choir

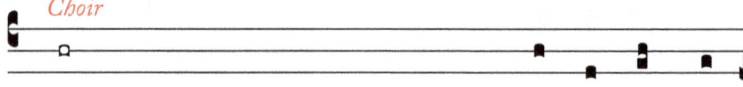

The LORD hath put on his apparel, and gird-ed him- self

All

with strength. Al - le- lu- ia.

OFFERTORY *Bénedic, ánima mea*   *Ps. 103:2,5*

Cantors

ij.

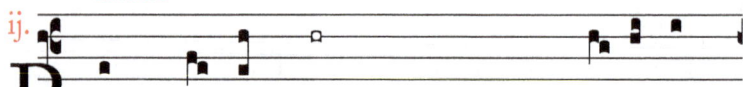

P RAISE the LORD, O my soul, and forget not all his

Choir

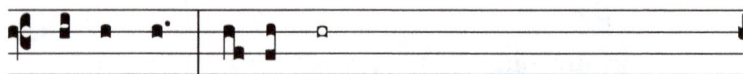

be- ne- fits: who sa- tisfieth thy mouth with good

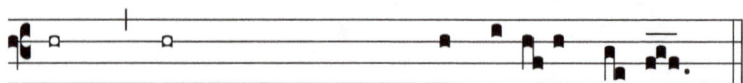

things: making thee young and lus- ty as an ea- gle.

74

COMMUNION *Dómine, Dóminus noster*   *Ps. 8*

Cantors   *Choir*

i.

O LORD our Go- ver- nor,   how ex- cellent is thy

Name in all   the world.

Verses from **Psalm 8** *may be sung.*

JANUARY 6
or THE SUNDAY BETWEEN JANUARY 2 AND JANUARY 8

These Propers, or those for the Second Sunday of Christmas, serve for week-days between the Epiphany and the following Sunday.

INTROIT *Ecce advénit cf. Mal. 3:1; I Chron. 19:12; Ps. 72:1, 10, 11*

Cantors ... *Choir*

vij.

BE-HOLD, he appeareth, the LORD and Ru - ler: and

FINE

in his hand the kingdom, and pow'r, and do - min - ion.

Cantors ... *Choir*

Ps. Give the King thy judge - ments, O God: and thy

Cantors

righteousness un - to the King's Son.   Glo - ry be to the

Choir

Father, and to the Son, and to the Ho - ly Ghost. As it

was in the beginning, is now, and ev- er shall be:

Full

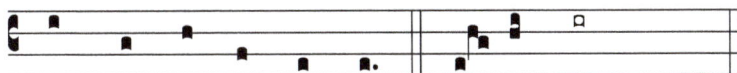

world with- out end. A - men.   Be - hold, he..., *(etc.)*

GRADUAL *Omnes de Saba vénient*   *Isa. 60:6, ℣. 1*

Cantors

℣.

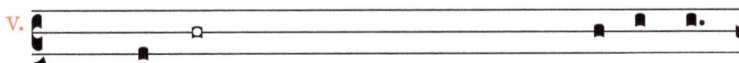

ALL they from Saba shall come, bringing gold and in -

Choir

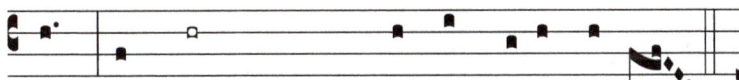

cense: and shall show forth the prais - es of the LORD.

Cantors   *Choir*

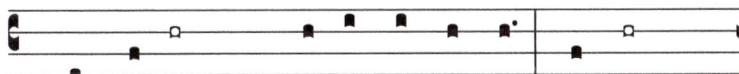

℣. A - rise and shine, O Je - ru - sa - lem: for the glory

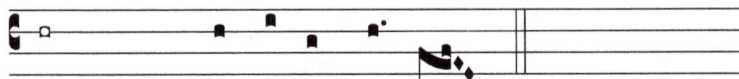

of the Lord is ri - sen up- on thee.

ALLELUIA *Vídimus stellam*   *Matt. 2:2*

Cantors   *All*

vj.

AL- LE- LU- IA.   Al - le- lu- ia.

Cantors   *Choir*

℣. We have seen his star in the East: and are come with

offerings to wor - ship the LORD.

All

Al - le- lu- ia.

OFFERTORY *Reges Tharsis*   *Ps. 72:10, 11*

Cantors

ij.

THE Kings of Tharsis and of the isles shall give presents;

the Kings of Arabia and Sa - ba shall bring gifts:

Choir

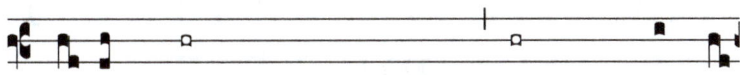

all Kings shall fall down before him; all nations shall do

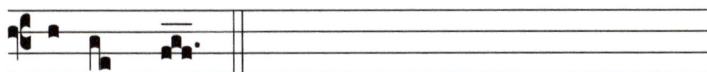

him ser - vice.

COMMUNION *Vídimus stellam*   *Matt. 2:2*

Cantors   *Choir*

i.

WE have seen his star in the East: and are come with

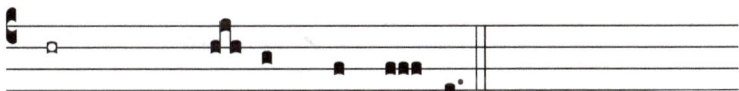

our offerings   to wor - ship the Lord.

Verses from Psalm 72:1-2, 6-7, 9-11, 16-17 *may be sung.*

TIME AFTER EPIPHANY
AND PRE-LENT
SUNDAY after JANUARY 6

Where the Solemnity of the Epiphany is transferred to Sunday, if this Sunday occurs on 7 or 8 January, the Feast of the Baptism of the Lord is celebrated on the following Monday. These Propers, or those for the Epiphany, serve for the weekdays between the Baptism of the Lord and the following Sunday.

INTROIT *Dilexísti*   *Ps. 45: 7,1*

Cantors

vij.

T HOU hast loved righteousness, and ha-ted i- ni- qui-ty;

Choir

where- fore God, even thy God, hath anointed thee with

FINE   *Cantors*

the oil of gladness a- bove thy fel- lows. *Ps.* My heart

Choir

is inditing of a good mat- ter: I speak of the things

which I have made un-to the King.

80

THE BAPTISM of THE LORD

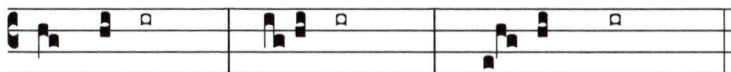

Glo- ry be...*(etc.)*   As it was..., *(etc.)*   Thou hast ..., *(etc.)*

GRADUAL   *Benedíctus Dominus Deus*   *Ps. 72:18*

Cantors

V.

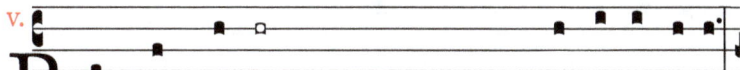

B LES-SED be the LORD God, even the God of Is- ra- el:

Choir   *Cantors*

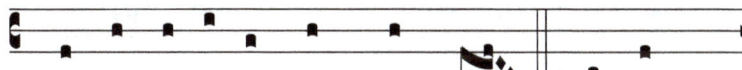

which on- ly do- eth won- drous things. ℣. The moun-

Choir

tains also shall bring peace: and the little hills

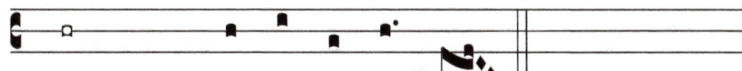

righteousness un- to the peo - ple.

81

ALLELUIA *Invéni David servum meum*   *Ps. 89:21*

vj. *Cantors* *All*

AL- LE- LU- IA. Al - le- lu- ia.

Cantors   *Choir*

℣. I have found David my ser- vant: with my holy oil

Cantors   *All*

have I a-noin- ted him.   Al - le- lu- ia.

or Benedíctus qui venit   *Ps. 118:26–27*

Cantors

℣. Bles - sed is he that cometh in the Name of the LORD:

Choir

God is the LORD who hath showed us light.

All

Al - le- lu- ia.

THE BAPTISM of THE LORD

OFFERTORY *Benedíctus qui venit*   *Ps. 118:26–27*

Cantors

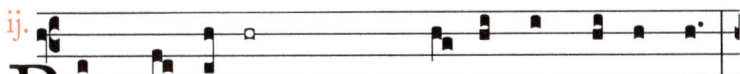

BLES- SED is he that cometh in the Name of the LORD:

Choir

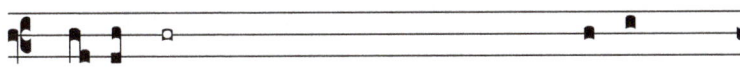

we have wished you good luck, we that are of the

Cantors

house of the LORD. God is the LORD who hath

Choir

show- ed us light. Al- le- lu- ia. Al- le- lu- ia.

COMMUNION *Omnes qui in Christo baptizáti estis*   *Gal. 3:27*

Cantors

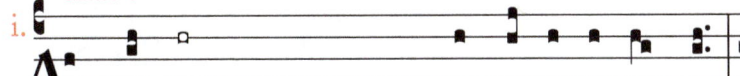

AS ma- ny of you as have been bap- ti- sed in- to Christ

Choir

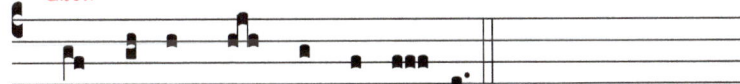

have put on Christ, Al- le- lu- ia.

Verses from Psalm 29 *may be sung.*
83

Epiphany II

INTROIT *Omnis terra* *Ps.66:4,1*

Cantors

vij.

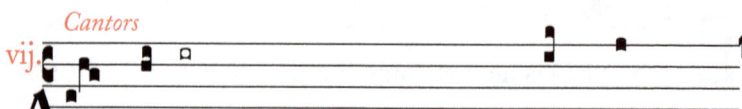

ALL the earth shall worship thee, O God, and

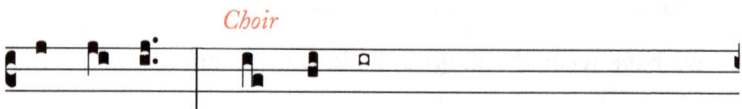

Choir

sing of thee: they shall sing praise to thy Name,

FINE   *Cantors*

O most High- est.   *Ps.* O be joyful in God, all ye

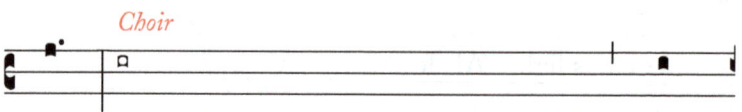

Choir

lands: sing praises unto the honour of his Name; make

Cantors

his praise to be glo- ri- ous.   Glo- ry be ..., *(etc.)*

Choir   *Full*

As it was ..., *(etc.)* All the earth ..., *(etc.)*

GRADUAL *Misit Dóminus*   *Ps. 107:20, 21*

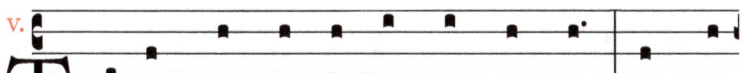

THE LORD sent his word and heal- ed them: and they

Cantors   *Choir*

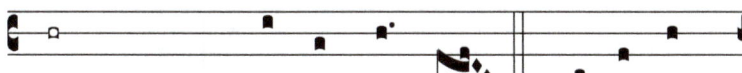

were saved from their des- truc- tion. ℣. O that men

Cantors

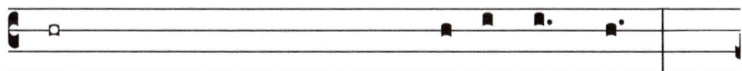

would therefore praise the LORD for his good- ness:

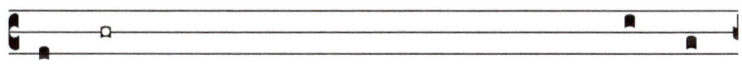

and declare the wonders that he doeth for the chil- dren

Choir

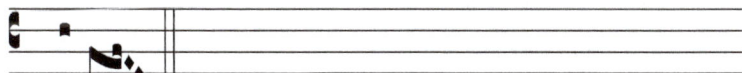

of men.

Year I, Tues. & Thurs. GR. *Iurávit Dóminus (Sep. 3, St. Gregory, p. 598)*

---Friday GR. *Osténde nobis (Ember Friday in Advent, p. 16)*

Year II Weds. GR. *Invéni David (Common of Martyrs, p. 653)*

---Friday GR. *Miserére mei, Deus (Ash Wednesday. p. 126)*

ALLELUIA *Laudáte Deum, omnes ángeli* Ps. 149:2

Cantors *All*

vj. AL- LE- LU- IA. Al - le- lu- ia.

Choir

℣. Praise the LORD, all ye An- gels of his: Praise him

All

all his host. Al - le- lu- ia.

Year I, Tues. & Thurs. AL. *Iurávit Dóminus (Common of Confessors, p. 682)*

---Weds. AL. *Tu es sacerdos in æternum (Common of Martyrs, p. 653)*

----Fri. AL. *Osténde nobis (First Sunday of Advent, p. 13)*

or AL. *Ego vos elégi de mundo (14 May, St. Matthias, p. 549)*

----Sat. AL. *Ascéndit Deus (Ascension Day, p. 343)*

Year II, Weds. AL. *Invéni David (supra, p. 82)*

---Friday AL. *Ego vos elégi de mundo. (14 May, St. Matthias, p. 549)*

OFFERTORY *Iubiláte Deo, univérsa terra*   *Ps. 66: 1, 14*

Cantors

ij.

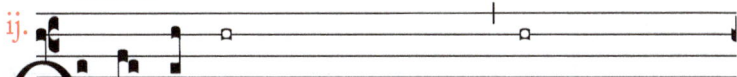

O BE joy- ful in God all ye lands; sing praises

Choir

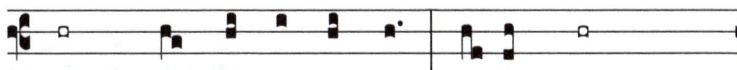

unto the ho- nour of his Name: O come hither and

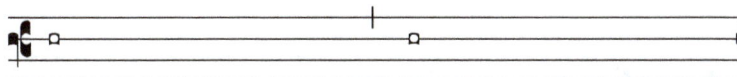

hearken all ye that fear God; and I will tell you

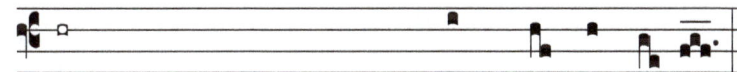

what things he hath done for my soul, al- le- lu- ia.

Sunday, Year A and Weekdays:

COMMUNION *Lætábimur in salutári*   *Ps. 20:5*

Cantors   *Choir*

i.

W E will re- joice in thy sal- va- tion: and tri- umph

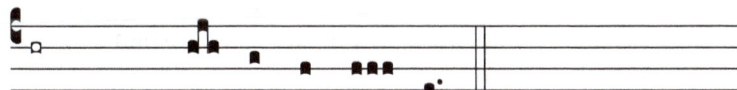

in the NAME of the LORD our God.

Verses from Psalm 20 *may be sung.*

Sunday, Year B:

COMMUNION *Dicit Andréas*   *John 1: 41, 42*

Cantors

i.

AN- DREW saith unto his bro- ther Simon: We

have found the Messiah, which is being in-ter-pre-ted,

Choir

the Christ: and he brought him to Je- sus.

Verses from **Psalm 34:1, 5, 6, 14-20** *may be sung.*

Sunday, Year C:

COMMUNION *Dicit Dóminus: Impléte hýdrias.*   *John 2: 7-11*

Cantors

i.

THE LORD saith unto them, Fill the jars with water

Choir

and take some to the stew-ard of the feast: when the

steward of the feast tasted the water now become wine,

he saith to the bridegroom, Thou hast kept the good

wine until now;   this was the first sign Jesus did

in the presence of his dis - ci - ples.

Verses from **Psalm 66:1-5, 7** *may be sung.*

Thurs. Co. *Multitúdo languéntium (Epiphany V, p. 104)*
Fri. Co. *Ego vos elégi de mundo (Easter VI, p. 337)*

Epiphany III

Sundays Years A and B:

INTROIT *Dóminus secus mare* *Matt. 4:18, 19; Ps. 19:1*

Cantors

vij.

THE LORD, walking by the sea of Galilee, saw two

brethren, Peter and Andrew, and he saith un-to them:

Choir *FINE*

Fol-low me and I will make you fish- ers of men.

Cantors *Choir*

Ps. The hea- vens declare the glo- ry of God: and the

Cantors

firmament show- eth his han- dy-work. Glo- ry be..., *(etc.)*

Choir *Full*

As it was..., *(etc.)* The LORD..., *(etc.)*

Sundays Year C and Weekdays:

INTROIT *Adoráte Deum*   *Cf. Ps. 97:7,8 & 1*

Cantors

vij.

ALL ye Angels of God, fall down, and wor- ship

Choir

be- fore him: Si- on heard, and was exceeding joyful,

FINE   *Cantors*

and the daughters of Ju-dah were glad.   *Ps.* The LORD is

Choir

King, the earth may be glad there- of: yea, the multitude

Cantors

of the isles may be glad there- of.   Glo- ry be..., *(etc.)*

Choir   *Full*

As it was..., *(etc.)*   All ye Angels..., *(etc.)*

GRADUAL *Timébunt gentes* Ps. 102:15 ℣. 16

THE na-tions shall fear thy Name, O LORD: and all the

kings of the earth thy ma- jes- ty. ℣. When the LORD

shall build up Si- on: and when his glo- ry shall ap- pear.

Year I, Weds. GR. *Iurávit Dóminus* (3 Sep. St. Gregory, p. 598)

Year II Mon. GR. *Invéni David* (Common of Martyrs, p. 653)

---Friday GR. *Miserére mei, Dómine* (Weds. Lent III. p. 171)

ALLELUIA *Dóminus regnávit, exsúltet terra* Ps. 97:1

AL- LE- LU- IA. Al - le- lu- ia.

℣. The LORD is King, the earth may be glad there- of:

Choir

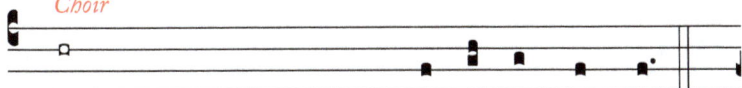

yea, the multitude of the isles may be glad there- of.

All

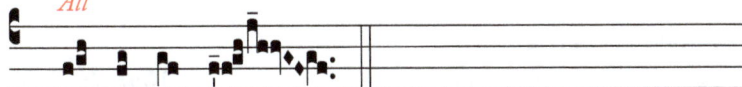

Al - le- lu- ia.

Year I, Weds. AL. *Iurávit Dóminus (Common of Confessors, p. 682)*

Year II Tues. AL. *Invéni David (Baptism of the Lord, p. 82)*

OFFERTORY *Déxtera Dómini*   *Ps. 118:16, 17*

Cantors

ij.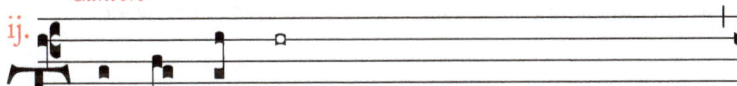

THE right hand of the LORD hath the pre- eminence;

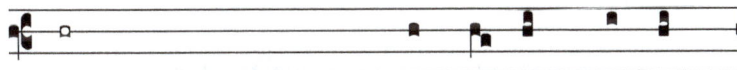

the right hand of the LORD bring- eth migh- ty things

Choir

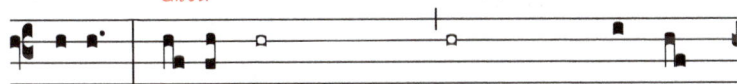

to pass: I shall not die, but live, and declare the works

of the LORD.

Sunday, Years A and B

COMMUNION *Veníte post me*   *Matt. 4: 19-20*

Cantors

i.

FOL- LOW me and I will make you fish- ers of men:

Choir

and they straightway left their nets and fol-low-ed

the Lord.

Verses from Psalm 119:1, 20, 40, 48, 65, 103, 167, 174 *may be sung.*

Sunday, Year C

COMMUNION *Comédite*   *Neh. 8: 10*

Cantors

i.

GO, eat fat meats, drink sweet wine, and send

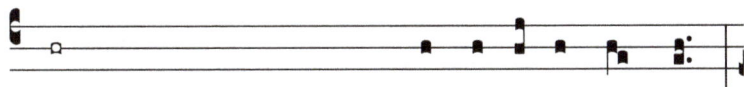

portions to them that have not pre- par- ed for them- selves:

Choir

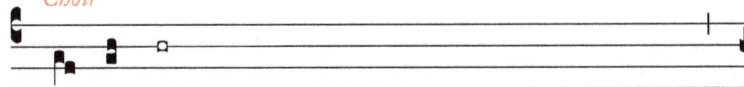

be- cause it is the holy day of the Lord, and be not sad;

for the joy of the LORD is our strength.

Verses from Psalm 81:2-5, 11, 14, 17 *may be sung.*

Weekdays:

COMMUNION *Mirabántur omnes*   *Luke 4:22*

Cantors   *Choir*

i.

ALL won- der- ed at the gra- cious words: which pro-

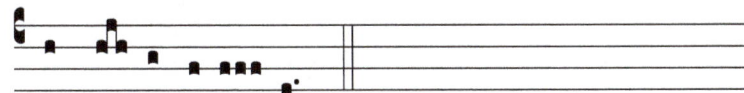

ceed- ed out of his mouth.

Verses from Psalm 97:1, 4-10, 12 *may be sung.*

Epiphany IV

INTROIT *Lætétur cor*   *Ps. 105:3, 4, 1*

Cantors

vij.

LET the heart of them re- joice that seek the LORD:

Choir   *FINE*

seek the LORD and his strength; seek his face ev- er- more.

Cantors

Ps. O give thanks unto the LORD, and call up- on his Name:

Choir   *Cantors*

Tell the people what things he hath done.   Glo- ry be..., *(etc.)*

Choir   *Full*

As it was..., *(etc.)* Let the heart..., *(etc.)*

GRADUAL *Quis sicut Dóminus*   *Ps. 113:5, 6*

Cantors

℣.

W HO is like unto the LORD our God, that hath his

Choir

dwell-ing so high: and yet humbleth himself to behold the

Cantors

things that are in hea-ven and earth? ℣. He tak- eth up

Choir

the simple out of the dust: and lifteth the poor out

of the mire.

Year I, Thurs. GR. *Suscépimus (Candlemas, February 2, p. 516)*

ALLELUIA *Adorábo*   *Ps. 138:2*

Cantors   *All*

vj.

A L- LE- LU- IA. Al - le- lu- ia.

Cantors   *Choir*

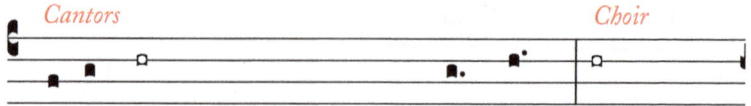

℣. I will worship toward thy holy tem- ple: and will sing

All

praises un-to thy name.   Al - le- lu- ia.

OFFERTORY *Bonum est*   Ps. 92:1

Cantors

ij.

I T is   a good thing to give thanks un-to the LORD:

Choir

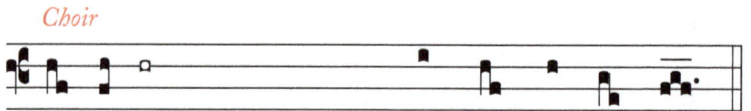

and to sing praises unto thy Name, O Most High-est.

Sunday, Year A

COMMUNION *Beáti mundo corde*   Matt. 5:8, 9, 10

Cantors

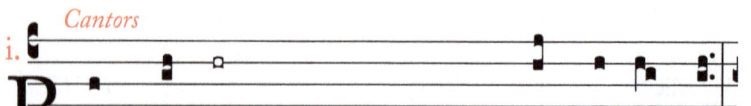

i.

B LESS-ED are the pure in heart, for they shall see God:

Choir

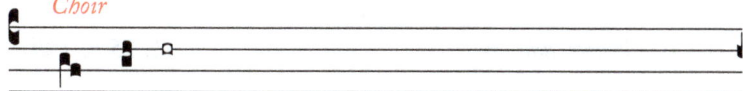

bless-ed are the peacemakers, for they shall be called

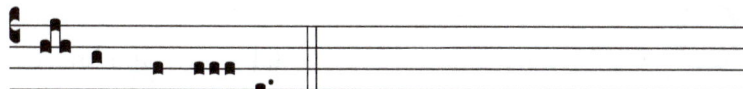

the chil-dren of God.

Verses from Psalm 34:1, 5, 6, 14-20 *may be sung.*
or Psalm 35:1, 3, 16, 18, 23, 27

Sunday, Years B & C and Weekdays

COMMUNION *Illúmina fáciem*   *Ps. 31: 18, 19*

Cantors

i.

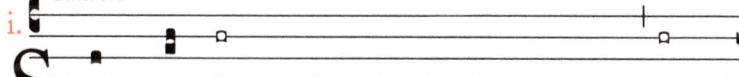

SHOW thy servant the light of thy countenance, and

Choir

save me for thy mer- cy's sake: let me not be confounded,

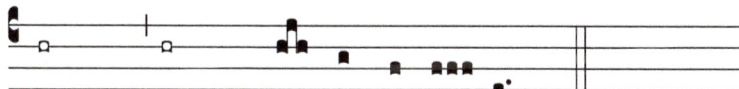

O LORD, for I have cal- led up- on thee.

Verses from Psalm 31:1-6, 8, 16-17 *may be sung.*

Epiphany V

INTROIT *Veníte, adorémus*   Ps. 95:6, 7 & 1

Cantors   *Choir*

vij.

O COME, let us wor- ship and fall down: and kneel

FINE

before the LORD our Maker; for he is the LORD our God.

Cantors   *Choir*

Ps. O come let us sing un- to the LORD: let us heartily

rejoice in the strength of our sal- va- tion.

Cantors   *Choir*   *Full*

Glo- ry be..., *(etc.)*   As it was..., *(etc.)*   O come,..., *(etc.)*

Sunday, Year A

GRADUAL *Dispérsit, dedit*   *Ps. 112:9, ℣. 2*

Cantors

℣.

HE hath dispersed abroad and given to the poor, and

Choir

his righteousness remaineth for ev- er: his horn shall be

Cantors

ex- al- ted with hon- our, ℣. Bles- sed is the man that fear-

Choir

eth the LORD: he hath great delight in his com- mand- ments.

Sunday, Years B & C and Weekdays

GRADUAL *Tollite hóstias*   *Ps. 96:8, 9 ℣. 29:8*

Cantors   *Choir*

℣.

BRING pre- sents, and come in- to his courts: O wor-

ship the LORD in the beau- ty of ho- li- ness.

101

Cantors

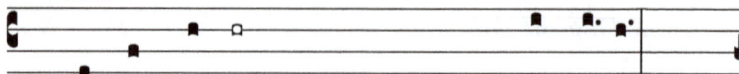

℣. The voice of the LORD strippeth bare the for-ests:

Choir

in his temple doth every thing speak of his ho - nour.

Year I, Tues. GR. *Dómine Dóminus (Trinity IX, p. 413)*

---Saturday GR. *Dómine refúgium (Trinity XXI, p. 460)*

Year II Wed. GR. *Os iusti (1 June, St. Justin, Martyr, p. 556)*

ALLELUIA   *Laudáte Dóminum*   *Ps. 117*

Cantors   *All*

vj.

AL-   LE- LU- IA.   Al - le- lu- ia.

Cantors   *Choir*

℣. O praise the LORD all ye na- tions: praise him, all

All

ye peo- ples.   Al - le- lu- ia.

Year I, Sat. AL. *Dómine refúgium (Trinity XIII, p. 428)*

OFFERTORY *Pérfice gressus meos* Ps. 17:5-6

Cantors

ij.

O HOLD thou up my goings in thy paths, that my

footsteps slip not; incline thine ear unto me, and

Choir

heark- en un- to my words: Show thy marvellous loving-

kindness, O LORD; thou that art the Saviour of them that

put their trust in thee.

Sunday, Years A & C and Weekdays
COMMUNION *Introíbo*   *Ps. 43:4*

I WILL go unto the al- tar of God: e- ven

unto the God of my joy and glad- ness.

Verses from Psalm 43:1, 2, 3, 5 *may be sung.*

Sunday, Year B and Monday Year I
COMMUNION *Multitúdo languéntium*   *Luke 6:17–19*

A GREAT multitude of the sick and those who were

troubled with unclean spi-rits came to him: pow'r

came forth from him, and heal - ed them all.

Verses from Psalm 34:1, 5, 6, 14-20 *may be sung.*

Monday Year II

Co. *Mense séptimo festa*   *Lev. 23:41, 43*

Cantors

IN the seventh month shall ye celebrate the feast, which

I made the children of Is-ra-el to dwell in booths:

Choir

when I brought them out of the land of Egypt,

I the Lord your God.

Verses from Psalm 34 *may be sung.*

Epiphany VI

INTROIT *Esto mihi*   *Ps. 31:3, 4, 2*

Cantors

vij.

BE thou my God and defender, and a place of refuge

Choir

that thou may- est save me: for thou art my upholder, my

refuge, and my Saviour; and for thy Name's sake be

FINE   *Cantors*

thou my leader, and my sus- tai- ner. *Ps.* In thee, O LORD,

have I put my trust: let me never be put to con-fu-sion;

Choir

but deliver me in thy righ- teous- ness and save me.

Cantors   *Choir*   *Full*

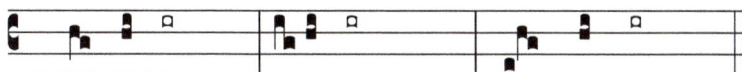

Glo- ry be...*(etc.)* As it was..., *(etc.)* Be Thou my...,*(etc.)*

GRADUAL *Tu es Deus*   *Ps. 77:14, 15*

Cantors   *Choir*

v.

THOU art the God that do- eth won- ders: and hast

Cantors

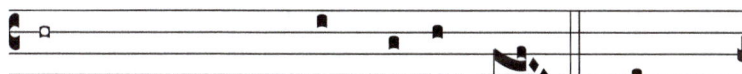

declared thy power a-mong the peo- ples. ℣. Thou

Choir

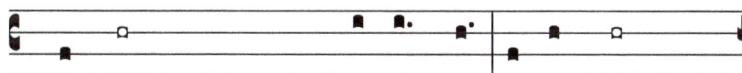

hast mightily delivered thy peo- ple: e- ven the sons of

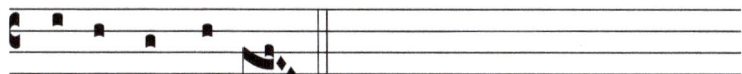

Ja- cob and Jo- seph.

Year I, Fri. GR. *Beáta gens (Trinity XVII, p. 441)*

Year II, Fri. GR. *Beátus vir qui timet (Common of Martyrs, p. 660)*

ALLELUIA *Cantáte Dómino* *Ps. 98:1*

Cantors   *All*

vj.

AL- LE- LU- IA.   Al - le- lu- ia.

Cantors   *Choir*

℣. O sing unto the LORD a new song: for he hath done

All

mar- vel- lous things.   Al - le- lu- ia.

Year II Fri. AL. *Beátus vir qui timet (Common of Confessors, p. 706)*

OFFERTORY *Benedíctus es*   *Ps. 119:12, 13*

Cantors

ij.

BLES- SED art thou, O LORD; O teach me thy

Choir

sta- tutes: with my lips have I been telling of all the

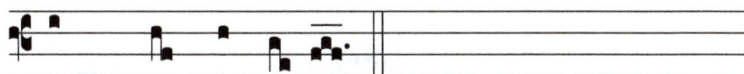

judge- ments of thy mouth.

COMMUNION *Manducavérunt*   *Ps. 78:30*

Cantors

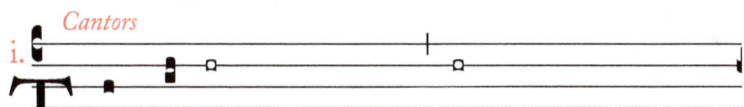

THEY did eat and were filled, for the LORD gave

Choir

them their own de- sire: they were not dis- ap- point-ed

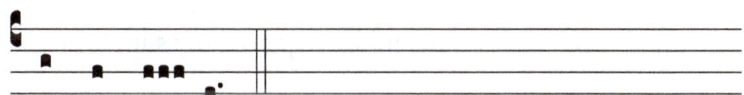

of their hun-ger.

Verses from Psalm 78:1, 3-4, 24, 25, 28, 29 *may be sung.*

Friday CO. *Qui vult veníre (Common of Martyrs, p. 662)*

Saturday CO. *Visionem quam vidístis (Lent II, p. 151)*

THE SUNDAY CALLED SEPTUAGESIMA
OR
Third Sunday before Lent

INTROIT *Circumdedérunt me dolóres mortis*   *Cf. Ps. 18*

Cantors

vij.

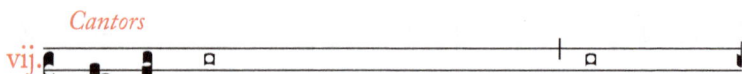

T HE sor - rows of death came about me; the pains of

Choir

hell gat hold up - on me: and in my tribulation I made

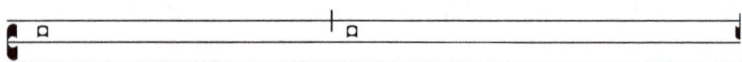

my prayer unto the LORD, and he regarded my supplication

Cantors

out of his ho - ly tem - ple. *Ps.* I will love thee, O LORD,

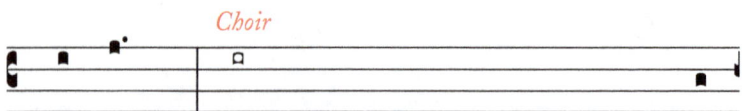

Choir

my strength: The LORD is my stony rock, my fortress, and

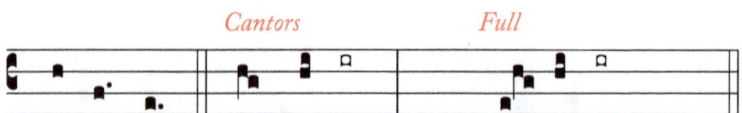

Cantors   *Full*

my Sa - viour. Glo - ry be..., *(etc.)*   The sor-rows..., *(etc.)*

GRADUAL *Adiútor in opportunitátibus* Ps. 9:9,10,18,19

Cantors

THE LORD will be a refuge in the time of trouble; and

they that know thy Name will put their trust in thee:

Choir

for thou, LORD, hast never failed them that seek thee.

Cantors

℣. For the poor shall not always be forgotten;

the patient abiding of the meek shall not perish for ev-er:

Choir

up, LORD, and let not man have the up-per hand.

Sunday only: TRACT *De profúndis*   *Ps 130:1–4*

Cantors

viij.

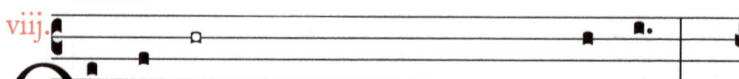

OUT of the deep have I called unto thee, O LORD:

Choir

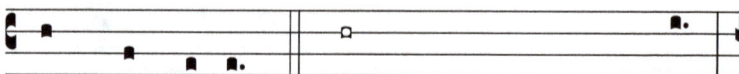

Lord, hear my voice. ℣. O let thine ears consider well:

Cantors

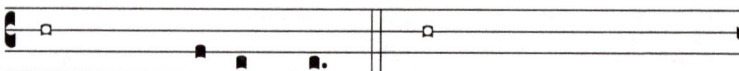

the voice of my com-plaint. ℣. If thou, LORD, wilt be

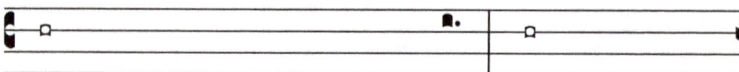

extreme to mark what is done a-miss: O Lord, who may

Choir

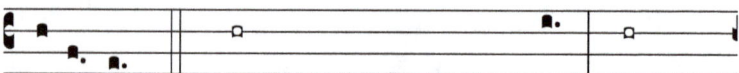

a-bide it?   ℣. For there is mercy with thee: therefore

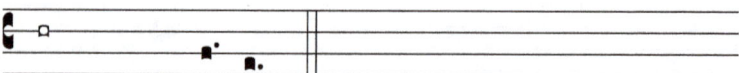

shalt thou be fear-ed.

OFFERTORY *Bonum est*   *Ps 92:1*

Cantors

ij.

IT is a good thing to give thanks un-to the LORD:

Choir

and to sing praises unto thy Name, O Most High - est.

COMMUNION *Illúmina fáciem*   *Ps 31:18,19*

Cantors

i.

SHOW thy servant the light of thy countenance, and

Choir

save me for thy mer-cy's sake: let me not be confounded,

O LORD, for I have cal- led up- on thee.

Verses from Psalm 31:1-6,8, 16-17 *may be sung.*

PROPER of the SEASON
THE SUNDAY CALLED SEXAGESIMA
Second Sunday before Lent

INTROIT *Exsúrge, quare obdórmis*   *Cf. Ps 44:23-26,1*

Cantors

vij.

A-RISE, O LORD, wherefore sleepest thou? Awake,

Choir

and cast us not a-way for ev- er: where-fore hidest thou

thy countenance, and forgettest our adversity and misery?

Our belly cleaveth unto the ground;   arise and save us,

FINE   *Cantors*

O Lord, our helper and our de-li-ver- er.   *Ps.* O God,

Choir

we have heard with our ears: our fa-thers have told us.

114

SEXAGESIMA

Cantors　　　　　*Choir*　　　　　*Full*

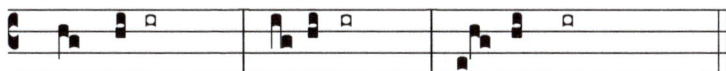

Glo - ry be..., *(etc.)* As it was..., *(etc)* A- rise, O Lord..., *(etc.)*

GRADUAL *Scíant gentes*　　　　　　　　　*Ps. 83:18,13*

Cantors

℣.

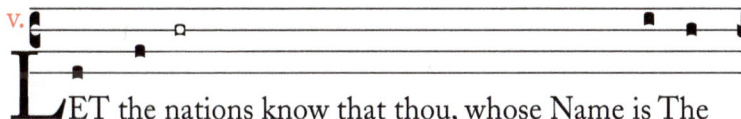

ᴸET the nations know that thou, whose Name is The

Choir

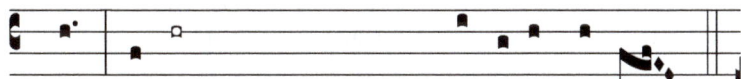

LORD: art only the Most Highest ov-er all the earth.

Cantors

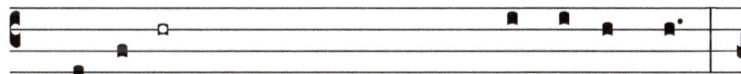

℣. O my God, make them like unto the whir-ling dust:

Choir

and as the stub-ble be-fore the wind.

Sunday only: TRACT *Commovísti*   Ps. 60:2,4b,5

Cantors

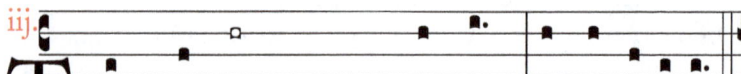

THOU hast moved the land, O LORD: and di-vi-ded it.

Choir

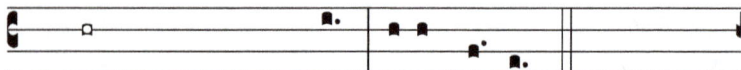

℣. Heal the sores there-of: for it sha-keth.

Cantors

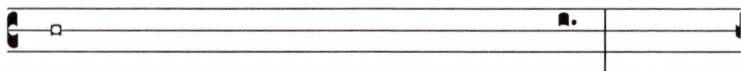

℣. That they may triumph because of the truth:

Full

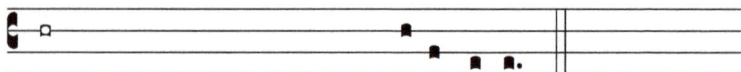

that thy belovèd may may be de-liv-er-ed.

OFFERTORY *Pérfice gressus meos*   Ps. 17:5,6b,7

Cantors

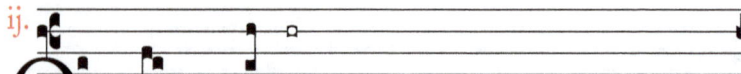

O HOLD thou up my goings in thy paths, that my

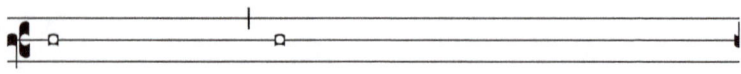

footsteps slip not; incline thine ear to me, and

Choir

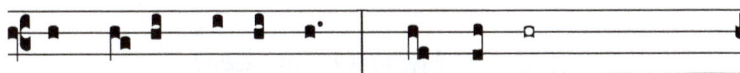

heark- en un- to my words: Show thy marvellous loving-

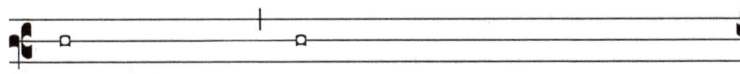

kindness, O LORD; thou that art the Saviour of them that

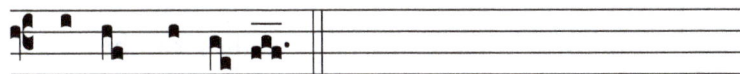

put their trust in thee.

COMMUNION *Introíbo*   *Ps. 43:4*

Cantors   *Choir*

i.

I WILL go unto the al- tar of God: e- ven

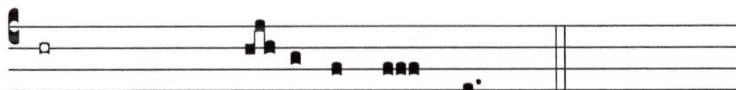

unto the God of my joy and glad- ness.

Verses from Psalm 43:1, 2, 3, 5 *may be sung.*
Verses from Psalm 31:1-6,8, 16-17 *may be sung.*

117

THE SUNDAY CALLED QUINQUAGESIMA

OR

The Sunday next before Lent

INTROIT *Esto mihi* *(Epiphany VI, p. 106)*

GRADUAL *Tu es Deus* *(Epiphany VI, p. 107)*

Sunday only: TRACT *Iubiláte Deo*   *Ps. 100:1,2*

Cantors

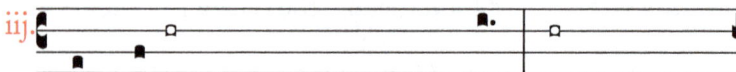

O BE joyful in the LORD, all ye lands: serve the

Choir

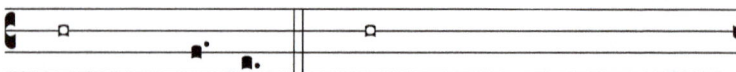

LORD with glad-ness. ℣. Come before his presence

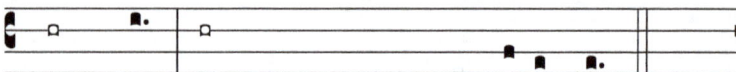

with a song: be ye sure that the LORD he is God.

Cantors

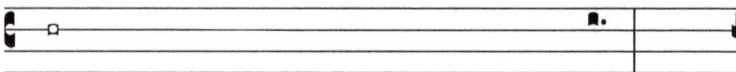

℣. It is he that hath made us, and not we our-selves:

Full

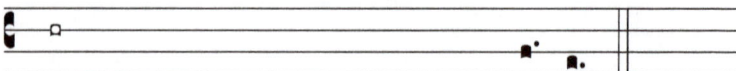

we are his people, and the sheep of his pas-ture.

OFFERTORY *Benedíctus es* *(Epiphany VI, p. 108)*

COMMUNION *Manducavérunt* *(Epiphany VI, p 109)*

ASH WEDNESDAY

SEASON OF LENT

LENT PROSE *Attende, Dómine*

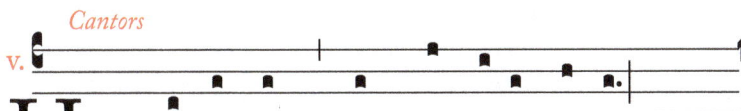

Cantors

HEAR us, O LORD, * have mer- cy up- on us:

Choir

for we have sin- ned a- gainst thee. *(Repeat after each verse)*

1. To thee, Re- deem- er, on thy throne of glo- ry:
2. O Thou chief Cor- ner- stone, Right Hand of the Fa- ther:
3. God, we im- plore thee, in thy glo- ry sea- ted:
4. Sins oft com- mit- ted now we lay be- fore thee:
5. In- no- cent, cap- tive, ta- ken un- re- sis- ting:

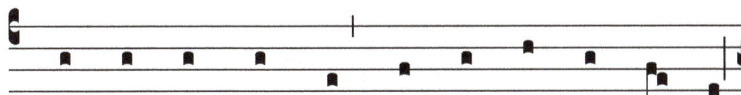

lift we our weep- ing eyes in ho- ly plead- ings:
Way of Sal- va- tion, Gate of Life Ce- les- tial:
bow down and hear- ken to thy weep- ing chil- dren:
with true con- tri- tion, now no more we veil them:
false- ly ac- cused, and for us sin- ners sen- tenced,

119

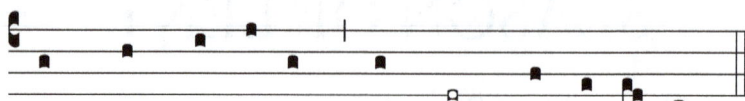

lis- ten O Je- su, to our sup-pli-ca- tions.
cleanse thou our sin- ful souls from all de- file- ment.
pi- ty and par- don all our griev- ous tres- pas- ses.
grant us, Re- dee- mer, lov- ing ab- so- lu- tion.
save us, we pray thee, Je- su our Re- dee- mer.

ASH WEDNESDAY

ANTIPHON *Exáudi nos*   *Ps. 69, 17 & 1*

Cantors

vij.

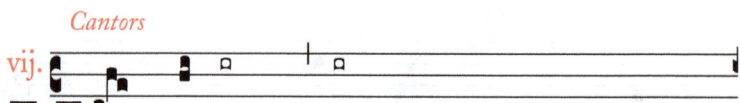

HEAR me, O LORD, for thy loving-kindness is

Choir

com-for-ta-ble: turn thee unto me according to the

Cantors

multitude of thy mer- cies. *Ps.* Save me, O God,

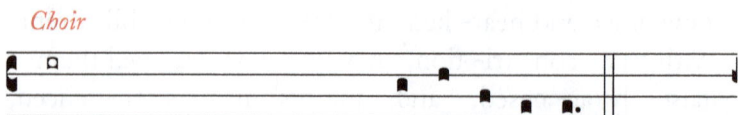

Choir

for the waters are come in ev-en un-to my soul.

120

Cantors   *Choir*   *Full*

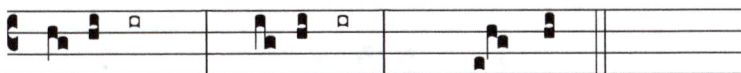

Glo-ry be...,*(etc.)* As it was..., *(etc.)* Hear me.... *(etc.)*

Antiphon *Ne proícias me*   *Ps. 51:11*

viij.

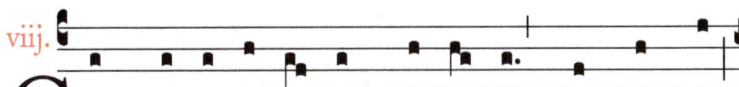

Cast me not a-way from thy pre-sence: and take not

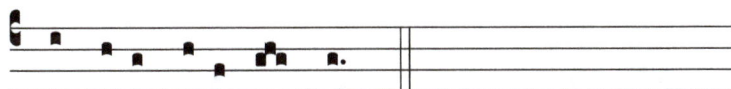

thy Hol-y Spi-rit from me.

Psalm 51 *Miserere mei, Deus* *may be sung to the following tone:*

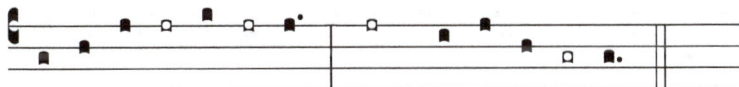

Anthem *Immutémur hábitu*   *Cf. Joel 2:13*

vij.

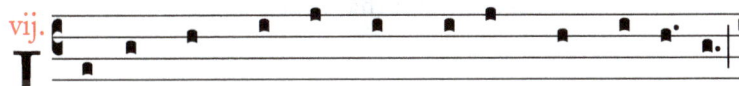

Let us change our rai-ment * for sack-cloth and ash-es:

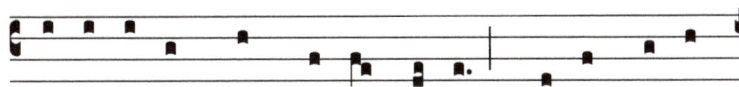

let us fast and mourn be-fore the Lord: for our God is

121

mer-ci-ful   to for-give us our sins.

ANTHEM *Iuxta vestíbulum*   *Cf. Joel 2:17; Esther 4:17*

vij.

LET the priests, * the mi-ni-sters of the LORD, weep

be-tween the porch and the al- tar, And let them say:

Spare, O LORD, spare thy peo- ple;   and shut not up, O

LORD, the mouths of them that praise thee.

RESPONSORY *Emendemus*

ij.

LET us a- mend the sins that in our ignorance we have

com-mit-ted: lest the day of death come upon us sud-

denly, and we find no place for re-pen-tance though we

seek it. R̥. Hear, LORD, and have mer-cy: for we have

sin-ned a- gainst thee. V̥. Help us, O God of our Salva-

tion for the glory of thy Name de-li-ver us, O LORD.

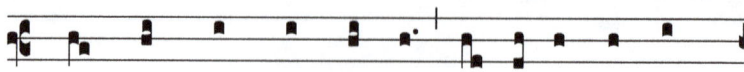

℟. Hear, LORD, and have mer-cy: for we have sin-ned

a- gainst thee. ℣. Glo-ry be to the Father and to the

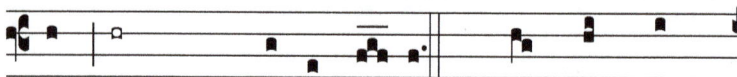

Son; and to the Ho-ly Spi- rit. ℟. Hear, LORD, and

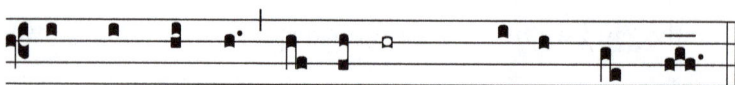

and have mer-cy: for we have sin-ned a- gainst thee.

INTROIT *Miseréris ómnium*   *Wisd. 11:24,25, 27; Ps. 57:1*

Cantors

vij.

THOU hast mercy upon all, O LORD, and abhorrest

Choir

nothing which thou hast made: and for-givest the sins of

men, because they should amend, and sparest them:

FINE   *Cantors*

for thou art the LORD our God. *Ps.* Be mer- ciful unto me,

Choir

O God, be mer-ci- ful un- to me: for my soul trust-eth

Cantors   *Choir*   *Full*

in thee.   Glo-ry be..., *(etc.)* As it was..., *(etc.)* Thou hast...

GRADUAL *Miserére mei Deus* Ps. 57:2, 4

Cantors

v.

BE mer- ciful unto me, O God, be mer- ci- ful un- to me:

Choir *Cantors*

for my soul trust- eth in thee. ℣. He shall send from

Choir

hea- ven: and save me from the reproof of him that

would eat me up.

TRACT *Dómine, non secundum peccáta nostra* Ps. 103:10; 79:8, 9

Cantors

viij.

O LORD, deal not with us after our sins: nor reward

Choir

us according to our wick- ed-ness-es. ℣. O LORD,

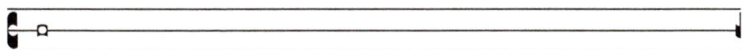

remember not our old sins, but have mercy upon us, and

that soon: For we are come to great mi- se- ry.
(Here genuflect.)

Cantors

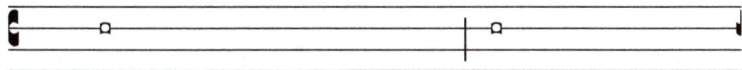

℣. Help us, O God of our salvation, for the glory of thy

Full

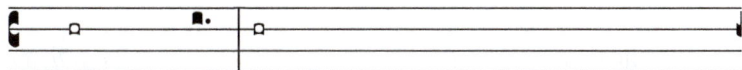

Name, O Lord: O deliver us and be merciful unto our

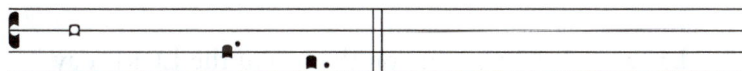

sins, for thy Name's sake.

OFFERTORY *Exaltábo te*   *Ps. 30:1.2*

Cantors

ij.

I WILL mag- nify thee, O LORD, for thou hast set me

Choir

up, and not made my foes to tri- umph o- ver me: O LORD

my God, I cried unto thee, and thou hast heal- ed me.

COMMUNION *Qui meditábitur*   *Ps. 1:2b, 3b*

Cantors

i.

HE who doth meditate on the law of the LORD day

Choir

and night: will bring forth his fruit in due sea- son.

Psalm 1 *may be sung.*

Thursday

INTROIT *Dum clamárem* *(Trinity X, p. 415)*

GRADUAL *Iacta cogitátum tuum* *(Trinity III, P. 391)*

OFFERTORY *Ad te, Dómine, levávi* *(Advent I, p. 13)*

COMMUNION *Acceptábis* *(Trinity X, p. 418)*

Friday and Saturday

INTROIT *Audívit Dóminus*   *Ps 30:11,1*

Cantors ... *Choir*

vij.

HEAR, O LORD, and have mer-cy up-on me: LORD,

FINE   *Cantors*

be thou my hel-per. *Ps.* I will magnify thee, O LORD,

Choir

for thou hast set me up: and not made my foes to

Cantors   *Choir*   *Full*

tri-umph o-ver me. Glo-ry be...,*(etc.)* Hear O Lord,..., *(etc.)*

GRADUAL *Unam pétii* *(Holy Family, p. 64)*

Friday only TRACT *Dómine, non secundum* *(Ash Weds., p. 126)*

OFFERTORY *Dómine, vivifica*   *Cf. Ps 119:25b*

Cantors

QUICK-EN me, O Lord, ac-cord-ing to thy word:

Choir

that I may know thy tes-ti-mo-nies.

COMMUNION *Servíte Dómino*   *Cf. Ps 2:11,12*

Cantors

SERVE the LORD in fear, and rejoice unto him with

Choir

re-verence: take hold of discipline, lest ye per-ish

from the right way.

Psalm 2:1-9 *may be sung.*

Lent I

Introit *Invocábit me*   *Ps. 91:15, 16, & 1*

Cantors

HE shall call upon me, and I will hearken unto him;

Choir

I will deliver him, and bring him to ho- nour: with length of

FINE   *Cantors*

days will I sat-is- fy him. *Ps.* Who- so dwelleth under

Choir

the defence of the Most High: shall abide under the

Cantors

shadow of the Al- migh- ty. Glo-ry be..., *(etc.)*

Full

As it was..., *(etc.)* He shall ..., *(etc.)*

131

Monday IN. *Sicut óculi*   *Ps 123:2,1*

Cantors

vij.

E-VEN as the eyes of servants look unto the hand of

Choir

their mas-ters: ev-en so our eyes wait upon the LORD

Cantors

our God, until he have mer-cy up-on us. *Ps.* Un-to thee

Choir

lift I up mine eyes: O thou that dwellest in the hea-vens.

Cantors   *Choir*   *Full*

Glo-ry be..., *(etc.)* As it was..., *(etc.)* E- ven as..., *(etc.)*

Tuesday IN. *Dómine refugium*   *Ps 90:1,2*

Cantors

vij.

LORD, thou hast been our refuge from one ge-ne-ra-

Choir

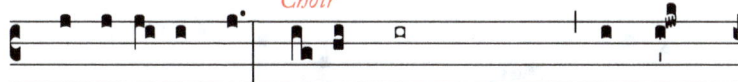

tion to an-o-ther: thou art from everlasting, and world

Cantors

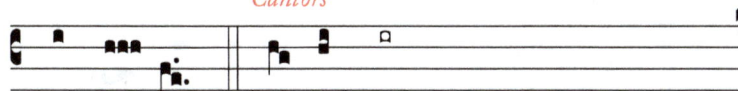

with-out end. *Ps.* Be-fore the mountains were brought

Choir

forth, or ever the earth and the world were made: thou

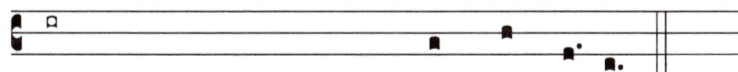

art God from everlasting, and world with-out end.

Cantors *Choir* *Full*

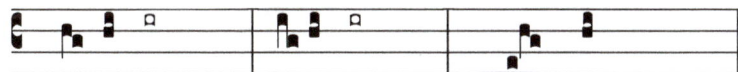

Glo-ry be..., *(etc.)* As it was..., *(etc.)* Lord thou..., *(etc.)*

GRADUAL *Angelis suis* *Ps. 91:11-12*

Cantors *Choir*

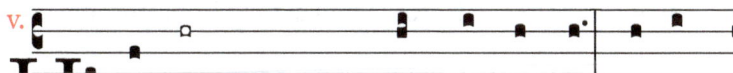

HE shall give his Angels charge o- ver thee: to keep

Cantors

thee in all thy ways. ℣. They shall bear thee in their

Choir

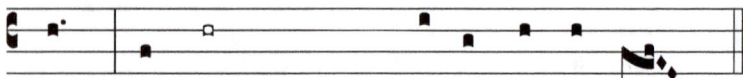

hands: that thou hurt not thy foot a- gainst a stone.

Monday GR. *Protector noster (Trinity V, p. 398)*

Tuesday GR. *Dirigátur (Trinity XIX, p. 452)*

Sunday TRACT *Qui hábitat*   *Ps. 91:1-7, & 11-16*

Cantors

viij

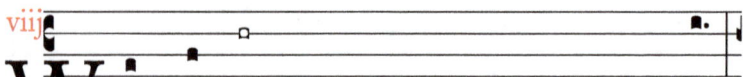

WHO-SO dwelleth under the defence of the Most High:

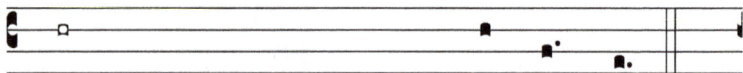

shall abide under the shadow of the Al- migh- ty.

Choir

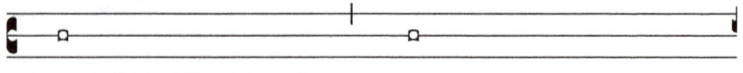

℣. I will say unto the Lord, Thou art my hope and my

Cantors

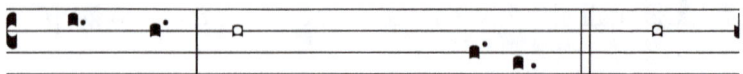

strong- hold: my God, in him will I trust.   ℣. For he

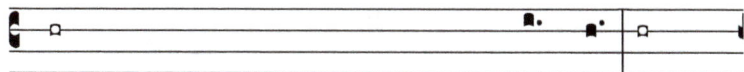

shall deliver thee from the snare of the hun- ter: and from

Choir

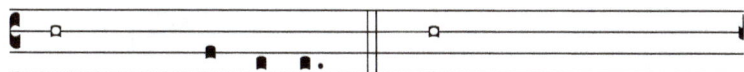

the noisome pes- ti- lence. ℣. He shall defend thee under

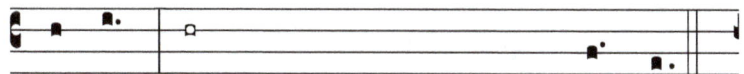

his wings: and thou shalt be safe under his fea- thers.

Cantors

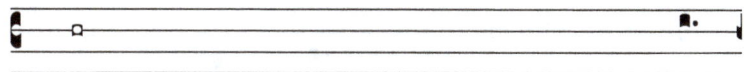

℣. His faithfulness and truth shall be thy shield and buck-

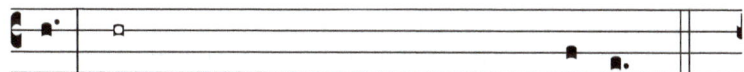

ler: thou shalt not be afraid for any terror by night.

Choir

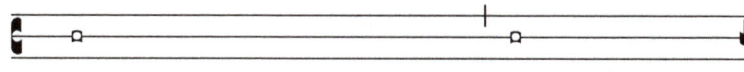

℣. Nor for the arrow that flieth by day; for the pestilence

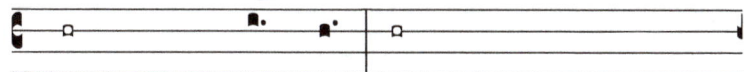

that walketh in dark- ness: nor for the sickness that

Cantors

destroyeth in the noon- day. ℣. A thousand shall fall

beside thee, and ten thousand at thy right hand: but it

Choir

shall not come nigh thee: ℣. For he shall give his Angels

Cantors

charge over thee: to keep thee in all thy ways. ℣. They

shall bear thee in their hands: that thou hurt not thy foot

Choir

a- gainst a stone. ℣. Thou shalt go upon the lion and

ad- der: the young lion and the dragon shalt thou tread

136

Cantors

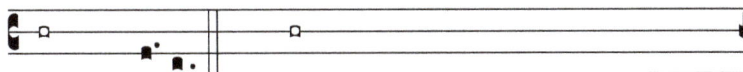

under thy feet. ℣. Because he hath set his love upon me,

therefore will I de- li- ver him: I will set him up, because

Choir

he hath known my Name. ℣. He shall call upon me, and

Cantors

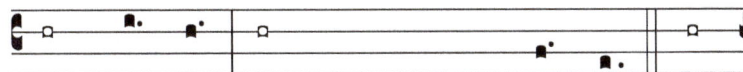

I will hear him: yea, I am with him in trou- ble. ℣. I will

Full

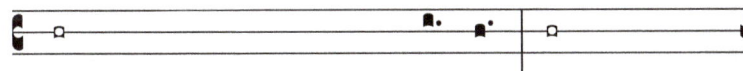

deliver him, and bring him to ho- nour: with long life will

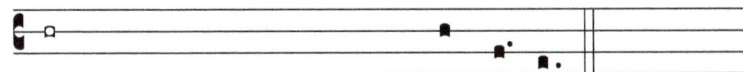

I satisfy him, and show him my sal- va- tion.

Monday Tʀ. *Dómine, non secundum (Ash Weds., p. 126)*

137

OFFERTORY *Scápulis suis*   *Ps. 91:4-5*

Cantors

ij.

H E shall de- fend thee under his wings, and thou shalt

Choir

be safe un- der his fea- thers: his faith- fulness and truth

shall be thy shield and buck- ler.

Monday OF. *Levábo óculos meos*   *Cf. Ps 119:18,26,73*

Cantors

ij.

I WILL lift up mine eyes, O LORD, that I may see

the wondrous things of thy law, that I may learn thy

Choir

judge-ments: O give me understanding that I may

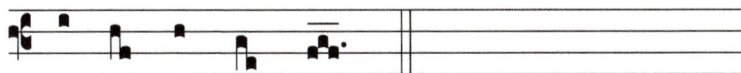

learn thy com-mand-ments.

Tuesday OF. *In te sperávi (Holy Family, p. 65)*

COMMUNION *Scápulis suis*   *Ps. 91:4-5*

Cantors

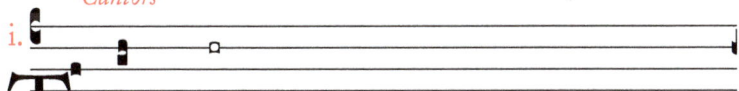

THE LORD shall defend thee under his wings, and

Choir

thou shalt be safe un- der his fea- thers: his faith- fulness

and truth shall be thy shield and buck- ler.

Verses from **Psalm 91:1-3, 11-16** *may be sung.*

Monday CO. *Amen dico vobis (Christ the King, p. 475)*

139

Tuesday Co. *Cum invocárem*   *Ps 4:1*

Cantors

i.

THOU hast heard me when I called , O God of my

Choir

right-eous-ness: Thou hast set me at liberty when I was

in trouble; have mercy upon me and heark-en un-to

my prayer.

Verses from Psalm 4:2-8 *may be sung.*

EMBERTIDE
Ember Wednesday in Lent

INTROIT *Reminíscere*   *Ps 25:5,21,1*

Cantors

vij.

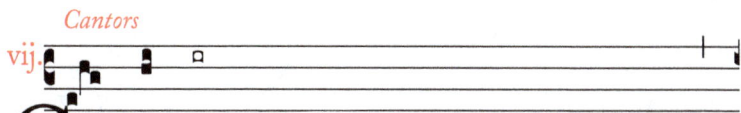

CALL to remembrance, O LORD, thy tender mercies,

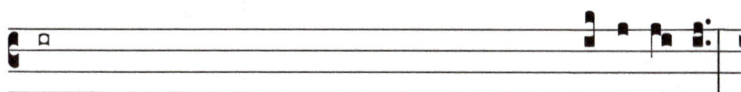

and thy loving-kindnesses, which have been ev-er of old:

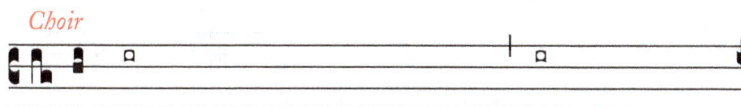

Choir

O let not our enemies triumph over us; deliver us,

FINE   *Cantors*

O God of Israel, out of all our trou-bles. *Ps.* Un-to thee,

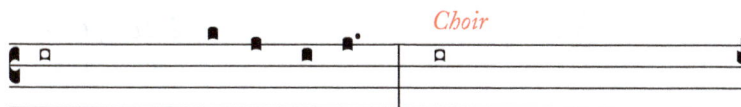

Choir

O LORD, do I lift up my soul: my God, in thee have

Cantors

I trusted, let me not be con-found-ed. Glo-ry be..., *(etc.)*

Choir   *Full*

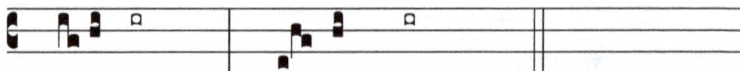

As it was..., *(etc.)* Call to ..., *(etc.)*

GRADUAL *Tribulatiónes cordis mei*   Ps. 25:17, 18

Cantors   *Choir*

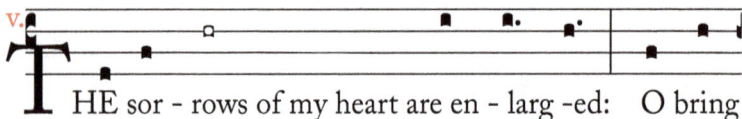

THE sor - rows of my heart are en - larg -ed: O bring

Cantors

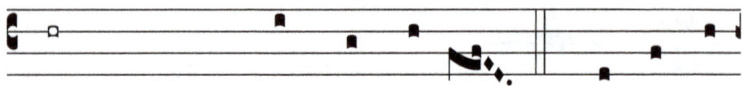

thou me out of my trou - bles, O LORD. ℣. Look up - on

Choir

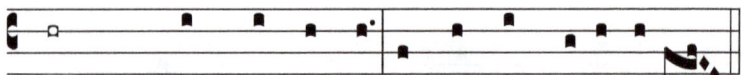

my adversity and mi - se - ry: and for-give me all my sins.

TRACT *De necessitátibus*   Ps. 25:16b,17,1,2

Cantors

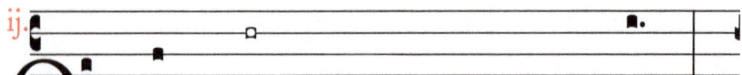

O BRING thou me out of my troubles, O LORD:

Choir

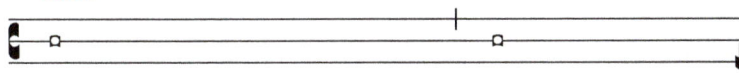

look upon my adversity and misery,   and forgive me

Cantors

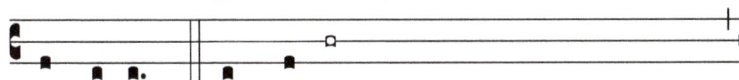

all my sin.   ℣. Un-to thee, O LORD, will I lift up my soul,

Choir

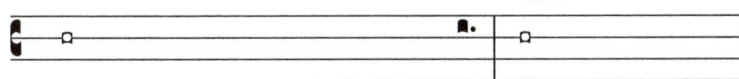

my God, I have put my trust in thee: O let me not be

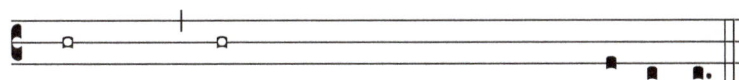

confounded; neither let mine enemies triumph ov-er me.

Cantors

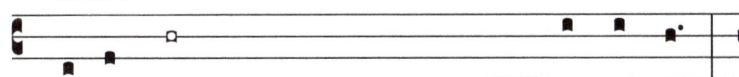

℣. For all they that hope in thee shall not be a-sham-ed:

Choir

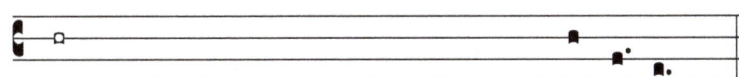

but such as do vain things shall be put to con-fu-sion.

OFFERTORY *Meditábor* *(Lent II, p. 151)*

143

COMMUNION *Intéllege*   *Ps 5:1b,2*

Cantors

i.

CON-si-der my meditation: O hearken thou unto the

Choir

voice of my calling, my King and my God;   for un-to

thee will I make my prayer, O LORD.

Verses from Psalm 5:3-7,12-13 *may be sung.*

Thursday

INTROIT *Conféssio*   *Ps 96:6,1*

Cantors   *Choir*

vij.

GLO-RY and worship are be-fore him: pow-er and

FINE   *Cantors*

and honour are in his sanc-tu- a- ry. *Ps.* O sing unto

Choir

the L<small>ORD</small> a new song: sing unto the L<small>ORD</small>, all the

Cantors   *Choir*   *Full*

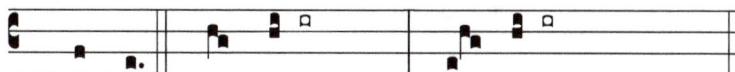

whole earth.   Glo-ry be..., *(etc.)* Glo- ry and..., *(etc.)*

G<small>RADUAL</small> *Custodi me* *(Trinity X, p. 416)*

O<small>FFERTORY</small> *Immíttet ángelus* *(Trinity XIV, p. 432)*

C<small>OMMUNION</small> *Panis, quem ego dédero* *(Trinity XV, p. 435)*

Ember Friday in Lent

I<small>NTROIT</small> *De necessitátibus*   *Ps 25:16b,17,1*

Cantors

vij.

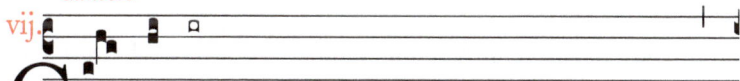

C<small>ALL</small> to remembrance, O L<small>ORD</small>, thy tender mercies,

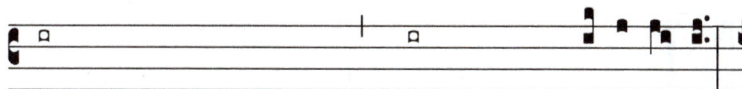

and thy loving-kindnesses, which have been ev-er of old:

Choir

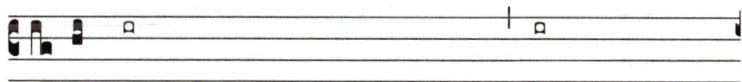

O let not our enemies triumph over us; deliver us,

FINE   *Cantors*

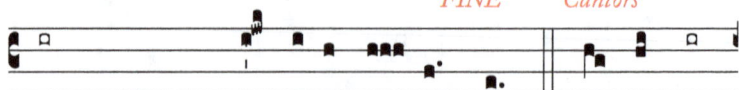

O God of Israel, out of all our trou-bles. *Ps.* Un-to thee,

Choir

O LORD, do I lift up my soul: my God, in thee have

Cantors

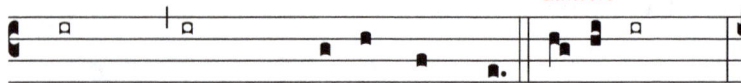

I trusted, let me not be con-found-ed. Glo-ry be..., *(etc.)*

Choir   *Full*

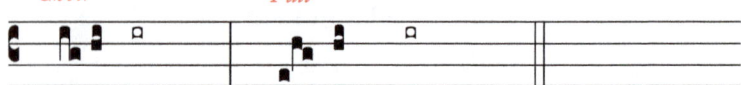

As it was..., *(etc.)* Call to ..., *(etc.)*

GRADUAL *Salvum fac servum tuum*   *Ps. 86:2b,6*

Cantors   *Choir*

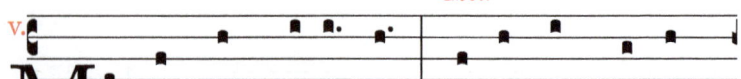

MY God, save thy ser-vant   that put-teth his trust

Cantors   *Choir*

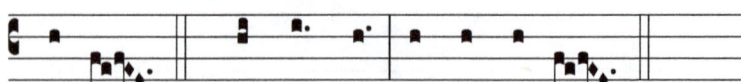

in thee. ℣. Give ear, LORD, un-to my   prayer.

TRACT *Dómine non secúndum* *(Ash Wedsnesday, p. 126)*

EMBERTIDE

OFFERTORY *Bénedic anima mea (Christmas II p. 74)*

COMMUNION *Erubéscant, et conturbéntur* Ps. 6:10

Cantors

i.

ALL mine enemies shall be con-foun-ded and sore vex-ed:

Choir

they shall be turnèd back and put to shame sud-den-ly.

Verses from Psalm 6:1-6 *may be sung.*

Ember Saturday in Lent

INTROIT *Intret orátio* Ps. 88:1b

Cantors

vij.

O LET my prayer enter into thy pre-sence, O LORD:

Choir *FINE* *Cantors*

in-cline thine ear un-to my cal-ling. *Ps.* O LORD God

Choir

of my sal-va-tion, I have cried day and night be-fore thee.

147

Cantors   *Choir*   *Full*

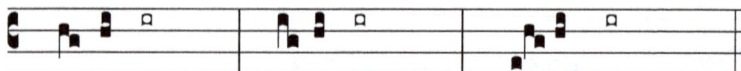

Glo-ry be..., *(etc.)*   As it was..., *(etc.)*   O let my..., *(etc.)*

GRADUAL *Propítius esto*   *(Trinity IV, p. 395)*

TRACT *Laudáte Dóminum*   *Ps. 117:1,2*

Cantors

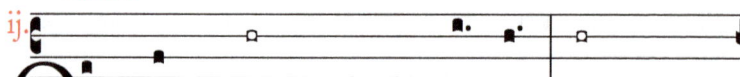

O PRAISE the LORD, all ye na-tions: praise him,

Choir

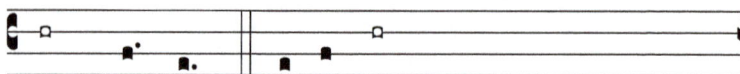

all ye peo-ples. ℣. For his merciful kindness is ever more

Full

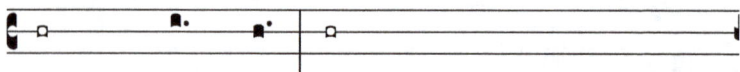

and more toward us: and the truth of the LORD endureth

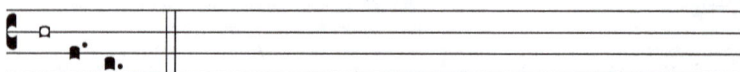

for ev-er.

148

OFFERTORY *Dómine Deus salútis* Ps. 88:1

Cantors

ij.

O LORD God of my salvation, I have cried day and

Choir

night be-fore thee: O let my prayer enter into thy

pre-sence, O LORD.

COMMUNION *Dómine Deus meus*   *Ps 7:1*

Cantors

i.

O LORD my God, in thee have I put my trust:

Choir

save me from all them that persecute me, and de-li-ver me.

Psalm 7:2,8bc,11,18 *may be sung.*

Lent II

INTROIT *Tibi dixit cor meum*   *Ps. 27:8, 9, & 1*

Cantors

vij.

MY heart hath talked of thee, seek ye my face;

Choir   *FINE*

thy face, LORD, will I seek: O hide not thy face from me.

Cantors   *Choir*

Ps. The LORD is my light and sal- va- tion: whom then

Cantors   *Choir*

shall I fear?   Glo- ry be... *(etc.)* As it was... *(etc.)*

All

My heart hath... *(etc.)*

or IN. *Reminíscere (Ember Weds. in Lent, p. 141)*

GRADUAL *Scíant gentes* *(Sexagesima, p. 115)*

TRACT *Commovísti* *(Sexagesima, p. 116)*

OFFERTORY *Meditábor*   *Ps. 119:47, 48*

Cantors

MY de- light shall be in thy commandments,

Choir

which I have lov- ed ex-ceed-ing-ly: my hands also will

I lift up unto thy commandments, which I have lov- ed.

COMMUNION *Visiónem*   *Matt. 17:19*

Cantors

TELL the vision which ye have seen to no man:

Choir

un- til the Son of Man be risen a- gain from the dead.

Verses from Psalms 45:1-8, 18
or 97:1-6, 11-12 *may be sung.*

151

INTROIT *Redíme me*   *Ps. 26:11b,12,1)*

Cantors

vij.

DE-LI-VER me, O LORD, and be merciful un-to me:

Choir

my foot standeth right, I will praise the LORD in the

FINE   *Cantors*

con-gre-ga-tion. *Ps.* Be thou my judge, O LORD,

Choir

for I have walked in-no-cent-ly: my trust hath been

also in the LORD, there-fore I shall not fall.

Cantors   *Choir*   *Full*

Glo- ry be... *(etc.)* As it was... *(etc.)* De-li-ver... *(etc.)*

GRADUAL *Adiútor meus*   *Ps. 70:6,2*

Cantors   *Choir*

THOU art my helper and re-deem-er: O LORD, make

Cantors

no long tar-ry-ing.. ℣. Let mine enemies be ashamèd

Choir

and con-foun-ded: that seek af-ter my soul.

TRACT *Dómine, non secundum peccáta nostra* *(Ash Weds., p. 126)*

OFFERTORY *Benedícam Dóminum* *(Trinity V, p. 399)*

COMMUNION *Dómine, Dóminus noster* *(Christmas II, p. 75)*

Tuesday

INTROIT *Tibi dixit* *(supra, p. 150)*

GRADUAL *Iacta cogitátum tuum* *(Trinity III, p. 391)*

OFFERTORY *Miserére mihi* *Ps. 51:1*

Cantors

ij. HAVE mer-cy upon me, O God, after thy great

Choir

good-ness: O LORD, do a-way mine of-fen-ces.

COMMUNION *Narrábo ómnia mirabília* *(Trinity I, p. 386)*

Wednesday

INTROIT *Ne derelínquas* *Ps. 38:21,22b,1*

Cantors

vij. FOR-SAKE me not, O LORD my God, be not thou

Choir

far from me: haste thee to help me, O Lord God

FINE *Cantors*

of my sal- va- tion. *Ps.* Put me not to rebuke, O LORD,

Choir

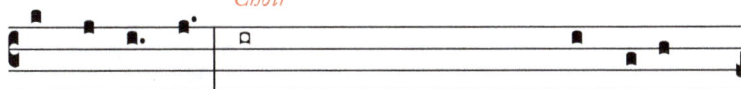

in thine an-ger: nei-ther chasten me in thy hea-vy dis-

Cantors   *Choir*

plea-sure.   Glo- ry be... *(etc.)* As it was... *(etc.)*

Full

For-sake me not... *(etc.)*

GRADUAL *Sálvum fac pópulum*   Ps. 28:10,1

Cantors   *Choir*

℣.

O LORD, save thy peo-ple: and give thy blessing

Cantors

unto thine in-he-ri-tance. ℣. Un-to thee will I cry, O

Choir

LORD my strength: be not deaf to my prayer, lest I

155

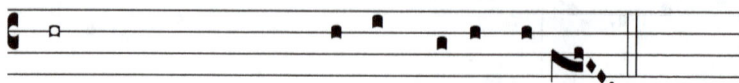

become like them that go down in-to the pit.

TRACT *Dómine, non secundum peccáta nostra* *(Ash Weds., p. 126)*
OFFERTORY *Ad te Dómine levávi* *(Advent I, p. 13)*

COMMUNION *Iustus Dóminus*   *Ps. 11:8*

Cantors

i.

HE righteous LORD lov-eth right-eous-ness:

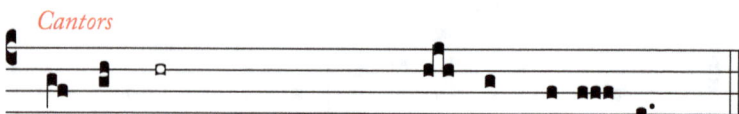

Cantors

his coun-te-nance will behold the thing that is just.

Verses from Psalm 10:1-5 *may be sung.*

Thursday

INTROIT *Deus, in adiutórium* *(Trinity XII, p. 423)*
GRADUAL *Propítius esto* *(Trinity IV, p. 395)*
OFFERTORY *Precátus est Móyses* *(Trinity XII, p. 425)*
COMMUNION *Qui manducat* *(Corpus Christi, p. 488)*

SECOND WEEK of LENT
Friday

INTROIT *Ego autem cum iustítia*   *Ps. 17:16,1*

Cantors

vij.

AS for me, I shall behold thy presence in righ-teous-

Choir

ness: and when I awake up after thy likeness, I shall be

FINE   *Cantors*

sa- tis-fied with it. *Ps.* Hear the right, O LORD:

Choir   *Cantors*

con-si-der my com-plaint. Glo- ry be... *(etc.)*

Choir   *Full*

As it was... *(etc.)* As for me... *(etc.)*

GRADUAL *Ad Dóminum (Trinity II, p. 388)*

TRACT *Dómine, non secundum peccáta nostra (Ash Weds., p. 126)*

OFFERTORY *Dómine in auxílium (Trinity XVI, p. 438)*

157

COMMUNION *Tu Dómine*   *Ps. 12:8*

Cantors   *Choir*

i.

THOU shalt keep us, O LORD: thou shalt preserve us

from this ge-ne-ra-tion for e- ver.

Verses from Psalm 12:1-7 *may be sung.*

Saturday

INTROIT *Lex Dómini*   *Ps. 19:7,1*

Cantors

vij.

THE law of the LORD is an undefiled law, con-ver-

Choir

ting the soul: the tes-timony of the LORD is sure, and

Cantors

giveth wisdom un-to the sim-ple. *Ps.* The hea-vens

Choir

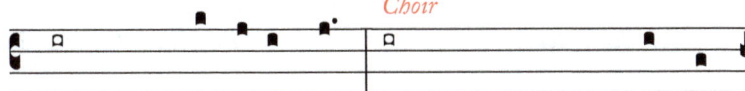

declare the glo-ry of God: and the firmament show-eth

Cantors   *Choir*

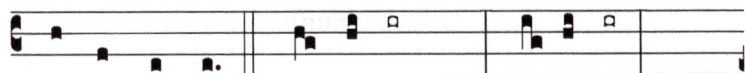

his han-dy-work. Glo- ry be... *(etc.)*   As it was... *(etc.)*

Full

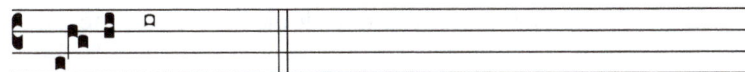

The law of... *(etc.)*

GRADUAL *Bonum est confiteri* *(Trinity XV, p. 434)*

OFFERTORY *Illumína óculos meos* *(Trinity IV, p. 396)*

COMMUNION *Opórtet te filii*   *(Lent IV year C, p. 181)*

Lent III

INTROIT *Oculi mei*   *Ps. 25:15, 16, & 1–2*

Cantors

vij.

MINE eyes are ever looking unto the LORD, for he

Choir

shall pluck my feet out of the net: look thou upon me, and

FINE

have mercy upon me, for I am desolate and in mi- se- ry.

Cantors   *Choir*

Ps. Un- to thee, O LORD do I lift up my soul: my God,

in thee have I trusted, let me not be con- found- ed.

Cantors   *Choir*   *Full*

Glo- ry be..., *(etc.)* As it was..., *(etc.)* Mine eyes..., *(etc.)*

GRADUAL *Exsúrge Dómine*   *Ps. 9:19, ℣. 3*

Cantors

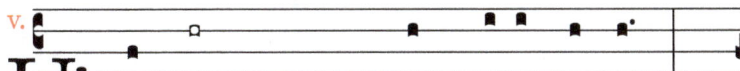

UP, LORD, and let not man have the up- per hand:

Choir   *Cantors*

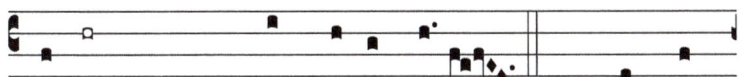

let the heathen be jud- ged in thy sight. ℣. While mine

Choir

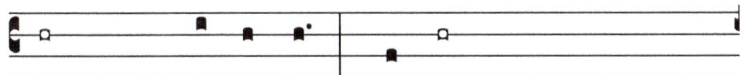

enemies are dri- ven back: they shall fall and perish

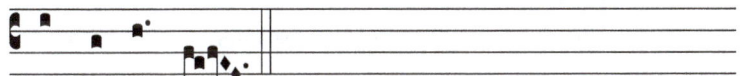

at thy pre- sence.

TRACT *Ad te levávi*   *Ps. 123:1-3*

Cantors

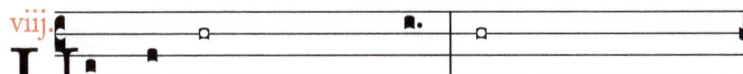

UN- TO thee lift I up mine eyes: O thou that dwellest in

Choir

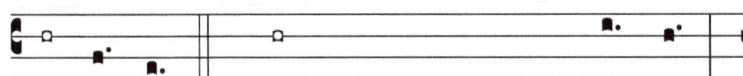

the hea- vens. ℣. Behold, even as the eyes of ser- vants:

Cantors

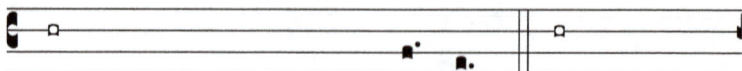

look unto the hand of their mas- ters. ℣. And as the eyes

Choir

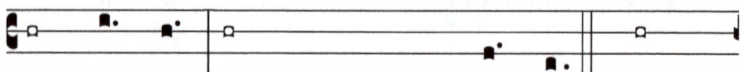

of a mai- den: unto the hand of her mis- tress. ℣. Even so

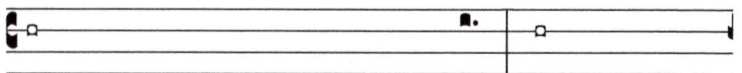

our eyes wait upon the Lord our God: until he have

Cantors   *Full*

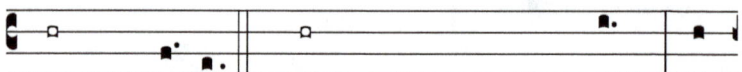

mercy up- on us. ℣. Have mercy upon us, O Lord: have

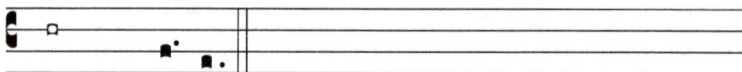

mercy up- on us

OFFERTORY *Iustítiæ Dómini*   *Ps. 19:8, 10, 11*

Cantors

ij.

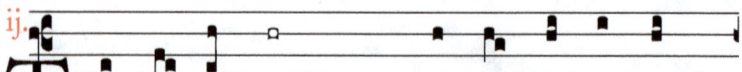

THE   sta- tutes of the Lord are right, and re- joice

162

Choir

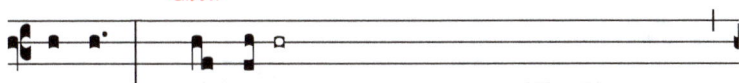

the heart: sweet- er also than honey and the honey-comb;

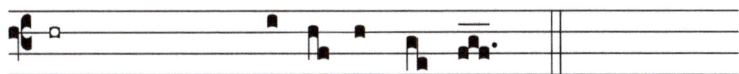

moreover by them is thy ser- vant taught.

Communion *Passer invénit*   *Ps. 84:3,4*

Cantors

i.

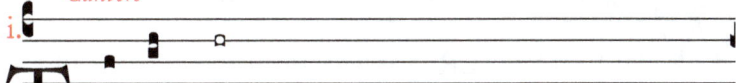

THE spar- row hath found her an house, and the

Choir

swallow a nest where she may lay her young: e- ven

thy altars, O LORD of hosts, my King and my God.

Cantors   *Choir*

Bless- ed are they that dwell in thy house: they will

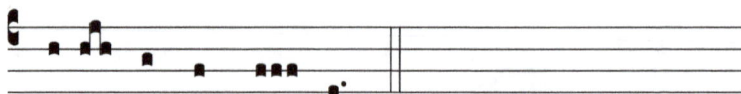

be al- way prais- ing thee.

The First Song of Isaiah, Ecce Deus may be sung. (p. 288)

Sunday Year A:

When the Gospel of the Samaritan Woman is read:

Co. *Qui bíberit aquam*   *John 4: 13–14*

i. *Cantors*

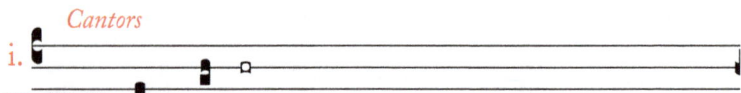

WHO- SO-EVER drinketh the water that I shall

Choir

give him, saith the LORD: it shall be in him a well of

water, springing up unto ev- er- last- ing life.

The First Song of Isaiah, Ecce Deus may be sung. (p.288)

Monday

INTROIT *In Deo laudábo*   *Ps. 56:10,11,1*

Cantors

vij.

IN God's word will I rejoice, in the Lord's word will

Choir

I com-fort me: yea, in God have I put my trust, I will not

FINE   *Cantors*

be afraid what man can do un-to me. *Ps.* Be mer-ci-ful

unto me, O God, for man goeth about to de-vour me:

Choir

he is all the day long fight-ing and troub-ling me.

Cantors   *Choir*   *Full*

Glo- ry be... *(etc.)* As it was... *(etc.)* In God's word... *(etc.)*

165

GRADUAL *Deus vitam meam*   *Ps. 56:8,1*

THOU, O God, tellest my wan-der-ings: put my tears in-to thy bot- tle.. ℣. Be mer-ci-ful unto me, O God, for man goeth about to de-vour me: he is daily fight-ing and troub-ling me.

TRACT *Dómine, non secundum peccáta nostra (Ash Weds., p. 126)*

OFFERTORY *Exáudi Deus*   *Ps. 55:1,2*

HEAR my prayer, O God, and hide not thyself from my pe-ti-tion: take heed un-to me and hear me.

Communion *Quis dabit*   *Ps. 14:8*

Cantors

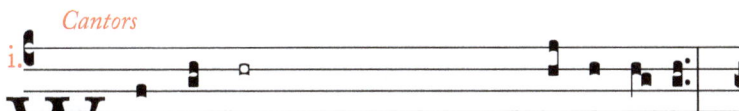

WHO shall give salvation unto Israel out of Si-on?

Choir

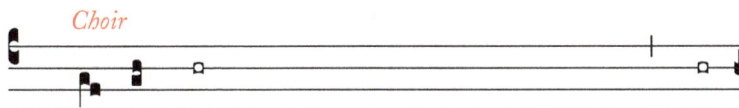

When the LORD turneth the captivity of his people, then

shall Jacob rejoice, and Is-ra- el shall be glad.

Verses from Psalm 14:3-7 *may be sung.*

Tuesday

INTROIT *Ego clamávi*   *Ps. 17: 6, 8 & 1*

Cantors

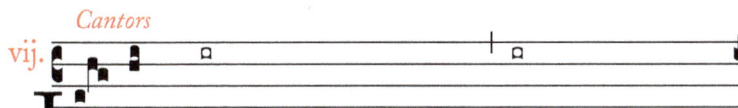

I HAVE called upon thee, O God, for thou shalt

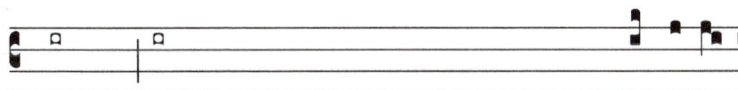

hear me: incline thine ear unto me and hearken un- to my

Choir

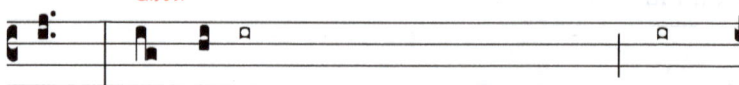

words: Keep me, O LORD, as the apple of an eye. Hide me

FINE *Cantors*

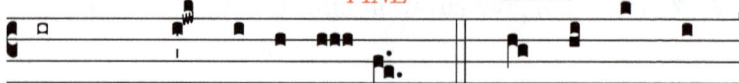

under the sha- dow of thy wings. *Ps.* Hear the right, O

Choir

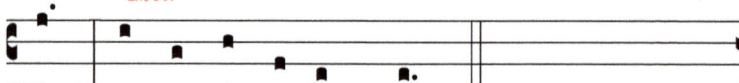

LORD: con- si- der my com- plaint.

Cantors *Choir* *Full*

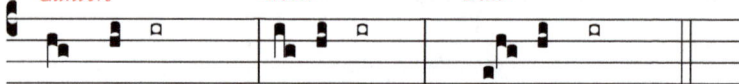

Glo- ry be..., *(etc.)* As it was..., *(etc.)* I have called...,

GRADUAL *Ab occúltis*　　　　　　　　　　　　　Ps. *19:12,13*

Cantors

v.

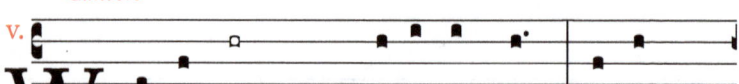

WHO can tell how oft he of-fen-deth?: O cleanse

Cantors

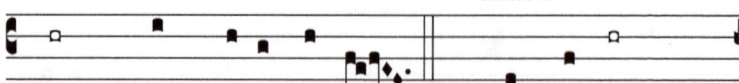

thou me from my se-cret faults. ℣. Keep thy servant also

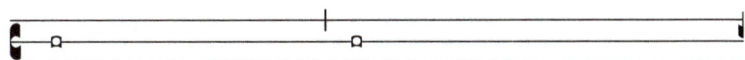

from presumptuous sins, lest they get the dominion

Choir

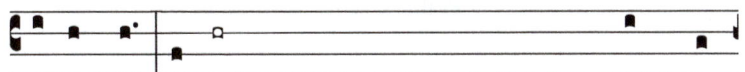

ov-er me: so shall I be undefiled and innocent from the

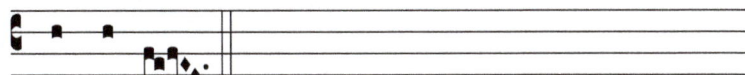

great of-fence.

OFFERTORY *Déxtera Dómini* *(Epiphany III, p. 93)*

COMMUNION *Dómine, quis habitábit?*   *Ps. 15:1,2*

Cantors

i.

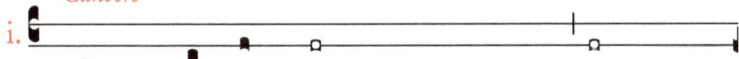

LORD, who shall dwell in thy tabernacle? or who shall

Choir

rest up-on thy ho-ly hill?   Ev- en he that leadeth an

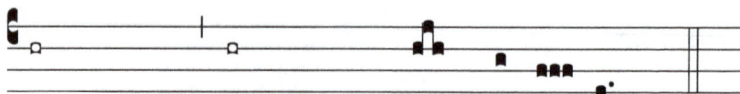

uncorrupt life, and doeth the thing that is right.

Verses from Psalm 15:2b-7 *may be sung.*

Wednesday

INTROIT *Ego autem in Dómino*   *Ps 31:7b,8,1*

Cantors

vij.

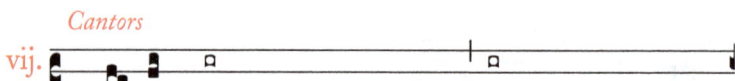

MY trust hath been in the LORD: I will be glad and

Choir

rejoice in thy mer- cy; for thou hast con-sid-er-ed my

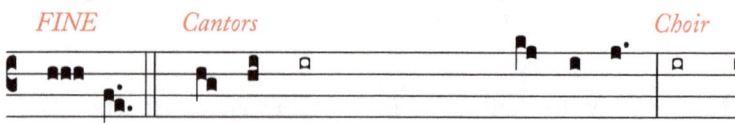

FINE   *Cantors*   *Choir*

trou-ble. *Ps.* In thee, O LORD, have I put my trust: let me

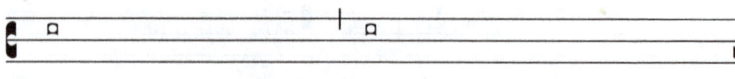

never be put to confusion, deliver me in thy righteous-

Cantors   *Choir*

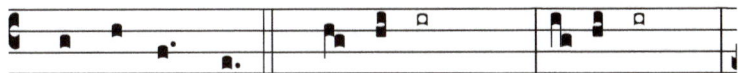

ness and save me.   Glo- ry be... *(etc.)* As it was... *(etc.)*

Full

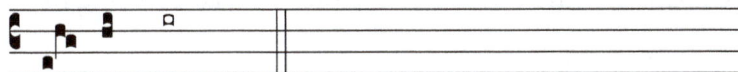

My trust hath... *(etc.)*

GRADUAL *Miserére mei*   *Ps. 6:2,3*

Cantors

℣.

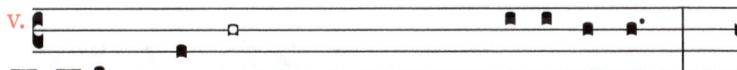

HAVE me-rcy upon me, O LORD, for I am weak:

Choir   *Cantors*

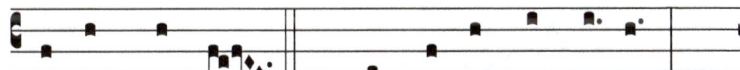

O LORD, heal me.   ℣. For my bones are vex-ed:

Choir

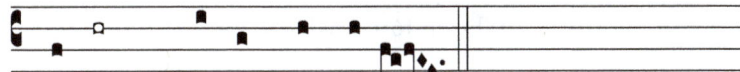

my soul also is sore trou-bl-èd.

TRACT *Dómine, non secundum peccáta nostra* *(Ash Weds., p. 126)*

171

OFFERTORY *Dómine, fac mecum*   *Ps. 109:20*

Cantors

BUT deal thou with me, O Lord God, ac-cor-ding to

Choir

thy Name: for sweet is thy mer- cy.

COMMUNION *Notas mihi fecísti*   *Ps. 16:12*

Cantors   *Choir*

THOU shalt show me the path of life: in thy presence,

O LORD, is the ful-ness of joy.

Verses from Psalm 16:1-3,6-11 *may be sung.*

Thursday

INTROIT *Salus pópuli* *(Trinity XIX, p. 451)*

GRADUAL *Oculi ómnium* *(Corpus Christi, p. 478)*

OFFERTORY *Si ambulávero* *(Trinity XIX, p. 453)*

COMMUNION *Tu mandásti* *(Trinity XIX, p. 454)*

Friday

INTROIT *Fac mecum*   *Ps. 86:17,1*

Cantors

vij.

SHOW some token upon me, O LORD, for good,

that they who hate me may see it and be a-sham-ed:

Choir

be-cause thou, LORD, hast holpen me, and com-fort

FINE   *Cantors*

ed me. *Ps.* Bow down thine ear, O LORD, and hear me:

Choir   *Cantors*

for I am poor and in mis-e-ry.   Glo- ry be... *(etc.)*

Choir   *Full*

As it was... *(etc.)* Show some... *(etc.)*

GRADUAL *In Deo speravit (Trinity XI, p. 420*

TRACT *Dómine, non secundum peccáta nostra (Ash Weds., p. 126)*

OFFERTORY *Intende voci*   *Ps. 5:2*

Cantors

ij.

O hear-ken thou unto the voice of my calling, my King

Choir

and my God: for un-to thee, O Lord, will I make my prayer.

COMMUNION *Qui bíberit aquam (supra, p. 164)*

Saturday

INTROIT *Verba mea*   *Ps. 5:1,2,3*

Cantors

vij.

PON-DER my words, O LORD, consider my me-di-

Choir

ta-tion: O hear-ken thou unto the voice of my calling,

FINE   *Cantors*

my King and my God. *Ps.* For un-to thee will I make

Choir

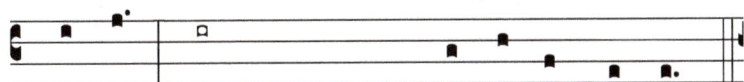

my prayer: my voice shalt thou hear be-times, O LORD.

Cantors   *Choir*   *Full*

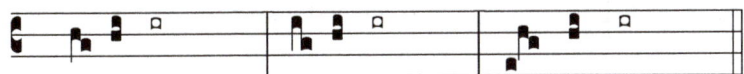

Glo- ry be..., *(etc.)* As it was..., *(etc.)* Pon-der..., *(etc.)*

GRADUAL *Si ámbulem*   *Ps. 23:4*

Cantors

℣.

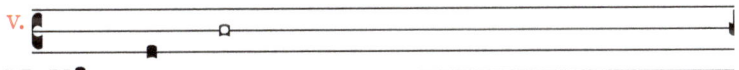

YEA though I walk through the valley of the shadow

Choir

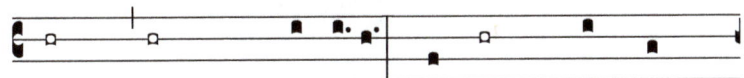

of death, I will fear no ev-il: for thou art with me,

Cantors   *Choir*

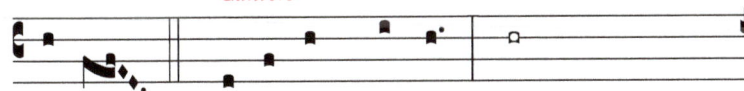

O LORD.. ℣. Thy rod and thy staff: they have

175

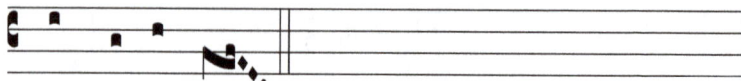

been my com-fort..

OFFERTORY *Gressus meos*   *Ps. 119:133*

Cantors   *Choir*

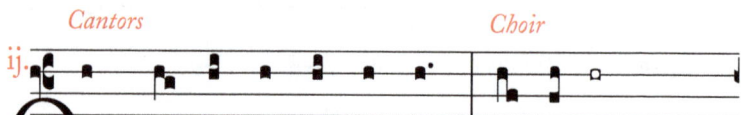

OR-DER my steps in thy word: and so shall no

wickedness have do-min-ion o-ver me, O LORD.

COMMUNION *Nemo te condemnávit (Lent V, p. 194)*

Lent IV

INTROIT *Lætáre Ierúsalem*   *Is. 66: 10,11; Ps. 122:1*

Cantors

vij.

RE- JOICE ye with Jerusalem; and be glad for

Choir

her, all ye that de - light in her: ex-   ult and sing

for joy with her, all ye that in sadness mourn for her:

that ye may suck, and be satisfied with the breasts

FINE   *Cantors*

of her con- so- la- tions. *Ps.* I was glad when they said

Choir

un-to me: we will go into the house of the LORD.

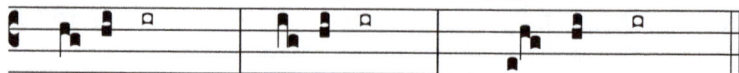

Glo- ry be..., *(etc.)* As it was..., *(etc.)* Re- joice ye..., *(etc.)*

GRADUAL *Lætátus sum*   *Ps. 122:1,7*

Cantors   *Choir*

I WAS glad when they said un- to me: we will go into

Cantors

the house of the LORD.   ℣. Peace be with- in thy walls:

Choir

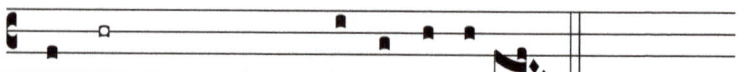

and plenteousness with- in thy pa- la- ces.

TRACT *Qui confídunt*   *Ps. 125:1-2*

Cantors

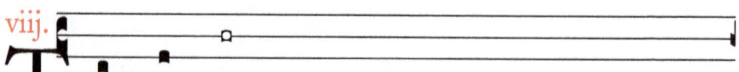

THEY that put their trust in the LORD, shall be even

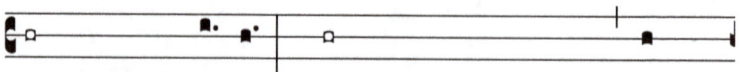

as the mount Si- on: which may not be removed, but

Choir

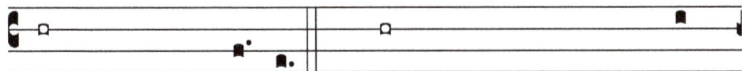

standeth fast for ev-er. ℣. The hills stand about Je- ru-

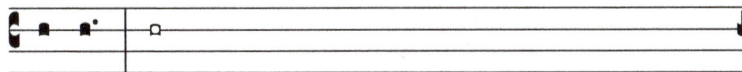

sa- lem; even so standeth the LORD round about his

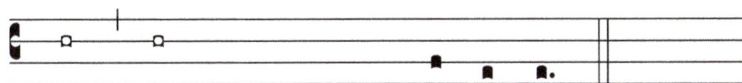

people; from this time forth for ev- er- more.

OFFERTORY *Laudáte Dóminum* *Ps. 135:3-6*

Cantors

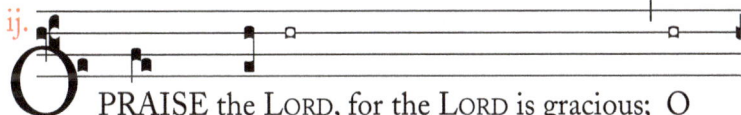

ij. O PRAISE the LORD, for the LORD is gracious; O

Choir

sing praises unto his Name, for it is love-ly: what- so-ever

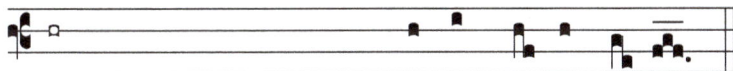

the LORD pleased, that did he in hea- ven and in earth.

179

PROPER of the SEASON

Sunday Year C: *When the Gospel of the Prodigal Son is read:*

OFFERTORY *Illúmina óculos meos*   *Ps. 13:3, 4*

Cantors   *Choir*

LIGHT-en mine eyes, that I sleep not in death; lest

mine enemy say, I have pre - vail - ed a - gainst him.

COMMUNION *Ierúsalem quæ ædificátur*   *Ps. 122: 3,4*

Cantors

JE-RU-SALEM is built as a city, that is at unity in

Choir

it-self: for thi-ther the tribes go up, even the tribes

of the LORD; to give thanks unto the Name of the LORD.

Verses from Psalm 122 *may be sung.*

FOURTH WEEK of LENT

Sunday Year A: *When the Gospel of the Man born blind is read:*
COMMUNION *Lutum fecit*   *John 9:6, 11, 38*

Cantors

HE LORD spat on the ground and made clay of the

Choir

spit- tle, and he anointed mine eyes, and I went and

washed, and I received sight and be- liev-ed in God.

Verses from Psalm 27:1, 4-6, 9-10, 15 *may be sung.*

Sunday Year C: *When the Gospel of the Prodigal Son is read:*
COMMUNION *Opórtet te*   *Lk. 15:2*

Cantors

T is meet that we should be glad, my son, for thy brother

Choir

was dead and is a-live a-gain: and was lost and is found.

Verses from Psalm 27:1, 4-6, 9-10, 15 *may be sung.*

Monday

INTROIT *Deus, in Nómine*   *Ps. 54:1,2,3*

Cantors

vij.

SAVE me, O God, for thy Name's sake, and a-venge me

Choir

in thy strength: hear my prayer, O God, and hearken

FINE   *Cantors*

un-to the words of my mouth. *Ps.* For stran-gers are risen

Choir

up a-gainst me: and tyrants seek af-ter my soul.

Cantors   *Choir*   *Full*

Glo- ry be..., *(etc.)* As it was..., *(etc.)* Save me..., *(etc.)*

GRADUAL *Esto mihi (Trinity VIII, p. 410)*

TRACT *Dómine non secundum (Ash Wednesday, p. 126)*

OFFERTORY *Iubiláte Deo omnis terra*　　　*Ps. 100:1,2*

Cantors　　　　　　　　　　　*Choir*

O BE joy-ful in the LORD, all ye lands; serve the LORD

with gladness: and come before his presence with a song;

be ye sure that the LORD he is God.

COMMUNION *Ab occultis*　　　　　*Ps. 19:12b,13*

Cantors

O CLEANSE thou me from my sec-ret faults:

Choir

keep thy servant also from pre-sump-tuous sins.

Verses from Psalm 19:1-7,14ab *may be sung.*

Tuesday

INTROIT *Exaudi, Deus*   Ps. 55:1,2,3

Cantors

vij.

HEAR my prayer, O God, and hide not thyself from

Choir   *FINE*

my pe-ti-tion: take heed un-to me and hear me.

Cantors   *Choir*

Ps. I mourn in my prayer, and am vex-ed: the enemy crieth

Cantors

so, and the ungodly com-eth on so fast. Glo- ry be..., *(etc.)*

Choir   *Full*

As it was..., *(etc.)* Hear my..., *(etc.)*

GRADUAL *Exsúrge, Dómine, fer opem*   Ps. 44:26,1

Cantors   *Choir*

v.

A-RISE, O LORD, and help us: and deliver us for thy

Cantors

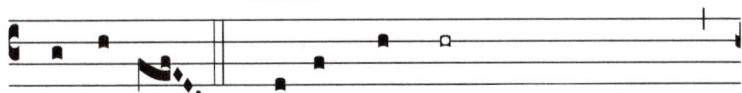

mer-cy's sake. ℣. We have heard with our ears, O God,

Choir

our fathers have told us: what thou hast done in their

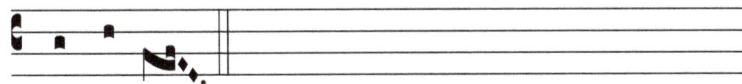

time of old.

OFFERTORY *Exspéctans exspectávi (Trinity XV, p. 435)*

COMMUNION *Lætábimur (Epiphany II, p. 87)*

Wednesday

INTROIT *Dum sanctificátus (Vigil of Pentecost, p. 362)*

GRADUAL *Veníte, fílii (Trinity VII, p. 406)*

TRACT *Dómine non secundum (Ash Wednesday, p. 126)*

OFFERTORY *Benedícite, gentes* Ps. 66:7,8,18

Cantors

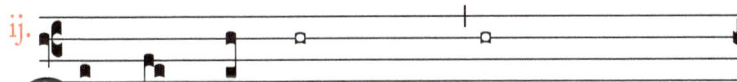

O PRAISE our God, ye peoples, and make the voice

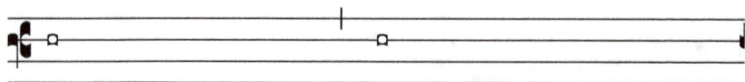

of his praise to be heard; who holdeth our soul in life,

Choir

and suf-fer-eth not our feet to slip: prais-ed be God, who

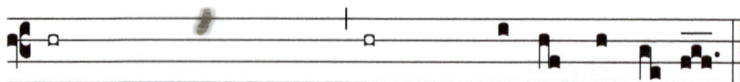

hath not cast out my prayer, nor turned his mer-cy from me.

COMMUNION *Lutum fecit (supra, p. 181)*

Thursday

INTROIT *Lætétur cor (Epiphany IV, p. 96)*

GRADUAL *Respice, Dómine (Trinity XIII, p. 428)*

OFFERTORY *Dómine, ad adiuvándum*   *Ps. 70:1,2*

Cantors   *Choir*

ij.

MAKE haste to help me, O Lord: let them be con-

founded that wish e-vil un-to thy ser-vants.

COMMUNION *Dómine, memorábor (Trinity XVI, p. 438)*

Friday

INTROIT *Meditátio cordis mei (Immaculate Heart of Mary, p. 554)*

GRADUAL *Bonum est confídere (Trinity XIV, p. 431)*

TRACT *Dómine non secundum (Ash Wednesday, p. 126)*

OFFERTORY *Populum húmilem (Trinity VIII, p. 411)*

COMMUNION *Videns Dóminus (Lent V, p. 193)*

Saturday

INTROIT *Sitiéntes (Baptism, p. 712)*

GRADUAL *Tibi, Dómine*   *Ps. 10:16,1,2*

Cantors

℣. HE poor committeth himself unto thee, O LORD:

Choir   *Cantors*

for thou art the helper of the friend-less. ℣. Why stan-

dest thou so far off, O Lord, and hidest thy face in the

Choir

needful time of trou-ble? The ungodly for his own lust

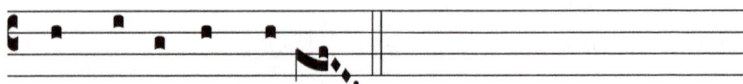

doth per-se-cute the poor.

OFFERTORY *Factus est Dóminus (Baptism, p. 713)*

COMMUNION *Dóminus regit me*   Ps. 23:1,2

Cantors

i.

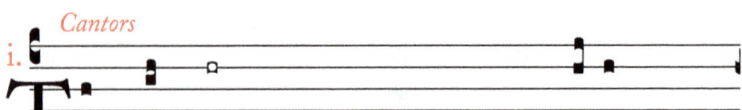

THE LORD is my shepherd, therefore can I lack

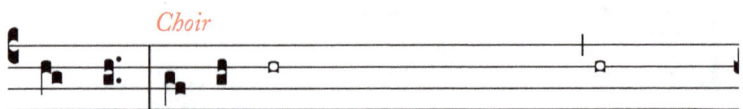

Choir

no-thing: he shall feed me in a green pasture, and lead

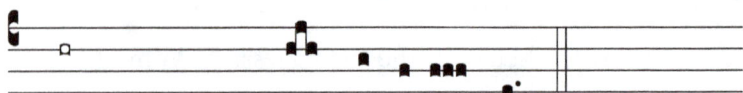

me forth beside the wa- ters of com-fort.

Verses from Psalm 23:3-6 *may be sung.*

Lent V

INTROIT *Iudica me, Deus*   *Ps. 43: 1, 2, 3*

Cantors

vij.

GIVE sen- tence with me, O God, and defend the cause

Choir

of my soul against the un- god- ly peo- ple: de - li - ver

me, and rid me from the deceitful and wicked man; for

FINE

thou, O Lord, art my God, and my strong sal- va- tion.

Cantors

Ps. O send out thy light and thy truth, that they may lead me:

Choir

and bring me unto thy holy hill, and to thy dwell-ing.

Full

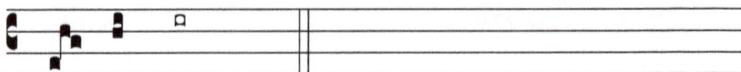

Give sen- tence... *(etc.)*

GRADUAL *Eripe me, Dómine*   *Ps. 143: 9, 10* ℣. *Ps. 18:49*

Cantors

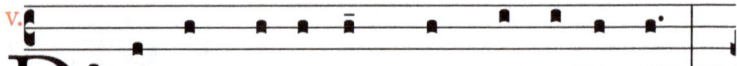

DE-LIV-ER me, O LORD, from mine e- ne- mies:

Choir

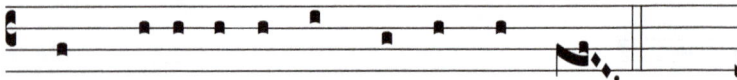

teach me to do the thing that plea- seth thee.

Cantors

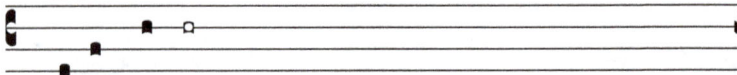

℣. It is the LORD that delivereth me from my cruel

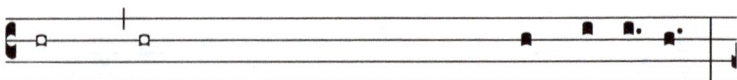

enemies, and setteth me up above mine ad-ver-sa-ries:

Choir

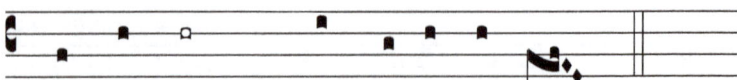

thou shalt deliver me from the wick-ed man.

TRACT *Sæpe expugnavérunt me*   *Ps. 129: 1–4*

Cantors

viij.

MA - NY a time have they fought a - gainst me:

Choir

from my youth up.   ℣. May Israel now say: yea many a

Cantors

time have they vexed me from my youth up.   ℣.   But

they have not prevailed a - gainst me: the ploughers

Choir

ploughed up- on my back.   ℣. And made long fur-rows:

but the righteous LORD hath hewn the snares of the

ungodly in pie- ces.

OFFERTORY *Confitébor tibi... in toto*   *Cf. Ps. 119:7, 10, 17, 25*

Cantors

I WILL give thanks unto the LORD with my whole

heart; O do well unto thy servant, that I may live, and

Choir

keep thy word: quick-en thou me, according to thy

word, O LORD.

COMMUNION *Qui mihi minístrat* John 12:26

Cantors *Choir*

IF a- ny man serve me, let him fol-low me: and where

I am, there shall al- so my ser- vant be.

Verses from Psalm 17:1-2, 9-12, 16 *may be sung.*

When the Gospel of Lazarus is read:

COMMUNION *Videns Dóminus* John 11:33,35,43, 44,39

Cantors

WHEN the LORD saw the sisters of Lazarus weeping

Choir

at the tomb, and the Jews al-so weep-ing, he cri- ed with a

loud voice, Lazarus come forth: and he that was dead came

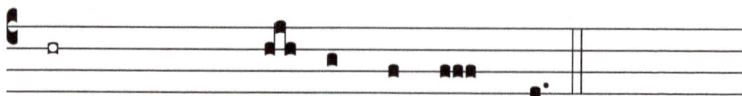

forth bound hand and foot with grave-clothes.

Verses from Psalm 130 *may be sung.*

When the Gospel of the adulterous woman is read:
COMMUNION *Nemo te condemnávit*　　　　　　*John 8: 10, 11*

Cantors

WO- MAN, hath no man condemned thee? No man,

Choir

LORD. Nei- ther do I condemn thee: go, and sin no more.

Verses from Psalm 32:1-3, 5-6, 9 *may be sung.*

Monday

INTROIT *Miserére mihi...conculcávit*　　　　*Ps.　43: 1, 2, 3*

Cantors

BE mer-ci-ful unto me, O God, for man goeth a-bout

194

Choir   *FINE*

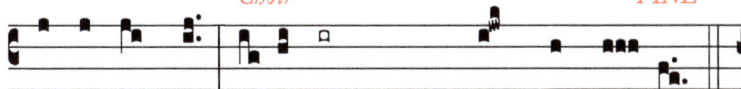

to de-vour me: he is daily fighting, and troub-ling me.

Cantors

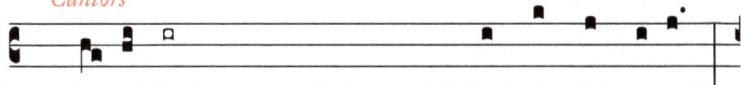

Ps. Mine e-ne-mies are daily at hand to swal-low me up:

Choir

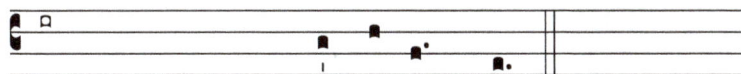

for they be many that fight a-gainst me.

Full

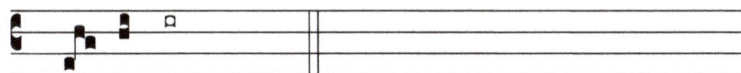

Be mer-ci-ful... *(etc.)*

GRADUAL *Deus, exaudi*   *Ps. 54:2,1*

Cantors   *Choir*

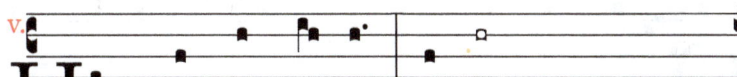

HEAR my prayer, O God: and hearken unto the

Cantors

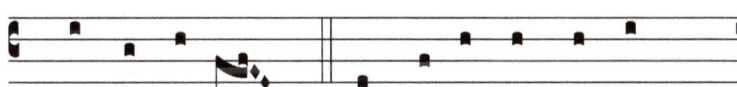

words of my mouth. ℣. Save me, O God, for thy

Choir

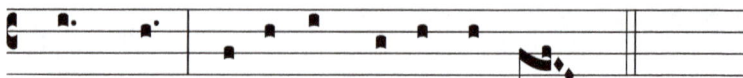

Name's sake: and a-venge me in thy strength

TRACT *Dómine non secundum (Ash Wednesday, p. 126)*
OFFERTORY *Dómine, convértere (Trinity II, p. 389)*

COMMUNION *Dóminus virtútum*   *Ps. 24:10b*

Cantors   *Choir*

THE Lord of hosts: he is the King of glo-ry.

Verses from Psalm 24:1-9 *may be sung.*

Tuesday

INTROIT *Expécta Dóminum*   *Ps. 27:16,1*

Cantors   *Choir*

O TAR-RY thou the Lord's lei-sure: be strong, and

FINE

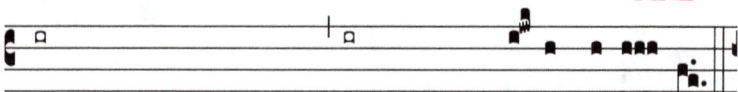

he shall comfort thy heart; and put thou thy trust in the LORD.

Cantors *Choir*

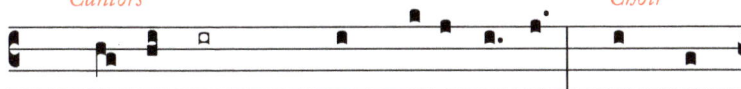

Ps. The LORD is my light and my sal-va-tion: whom then

Full

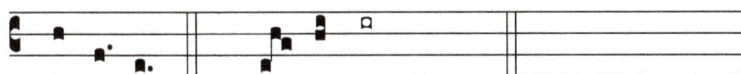

shall I fear?　O　tarry thou... *(etc.)*

GRADUAL *Discérne causam*　　　　　　　　　　*Ps. 43:1b,3*

Cantors　　　　　　　　　　　　　　　*Choir*

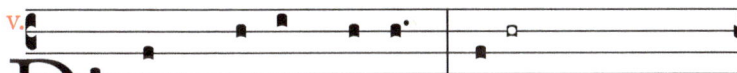

℣. DE-FEND my cause, O LORD: de-liver me from the

Cantors

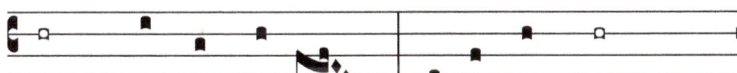

deceitful and wick-ed man.　℣. O send out thy light and

Choir

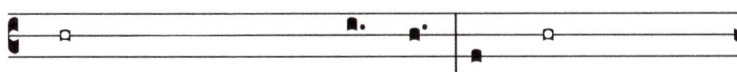

thy truth, that they may lead me:　and bring me

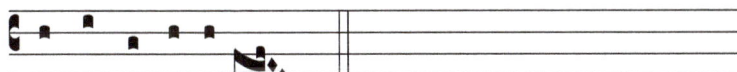

un-to thy ho-ly hill.

197

PROPER of the SEASON

OFFERTORY *Sperant in te* *(Trinity III, p. 392)*

COMMUNION *Redíme me*   *Ps. 24:10b*

Cantors   *Choir*

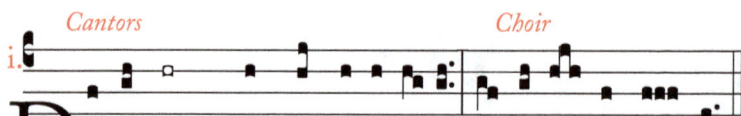

DE-li-ver me, O God of Is-ra-el: out of all my trou-bles.

Verses from Psalm 25:1,2,6,7,16-20 *may be sung.*

Wednesday

INTROIT *Liberátor meus*   *Ps. 18:49,1,2*

Cantors

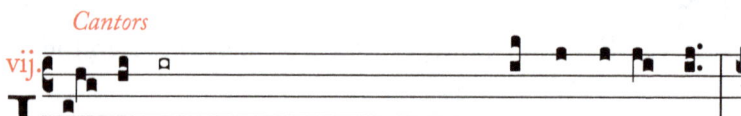

IT is he that delivereth me from my cruel e-ne-mies:

Choir

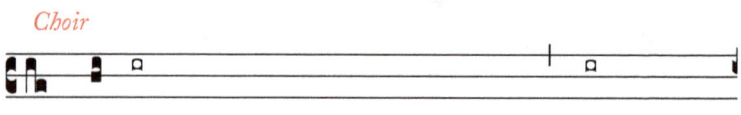

and set-teth me up above mine adversaries; thou shalt rid

FINE   *Cantors*

me from the wick-ed man, O Lord. *Ps.* I will love thee,

Choir

O Lord my strength: the Lord is my stony rock, and my

Full

defence, and my Sav-iour.   It   is he... *(etc.)*

GRADUAL *Exaltabo te*   *Ps. 30:1,2,3*

Cantors

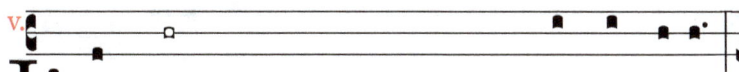

I WILL magnify thee, O LORD, for thou hast set me up:

Choir   *Cantors*

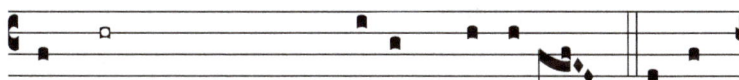

and not made my foes to tri-umph ov-er me.   ℣. O LORD

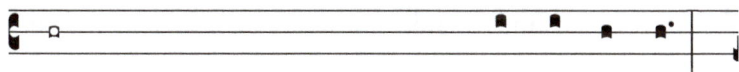

my God, I cried unto thee, and thou hast heal-ed me;

Choir

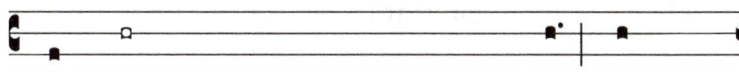

thou, LORD, hast brought my soul out of hell; thou

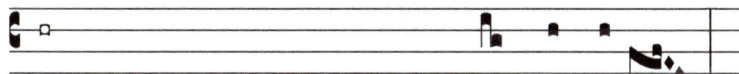

hast kept my life from them that go down to the pit.

TRACT *Dómine non secundum (Ash Wednesday, p. 126)*

199

OFFERTORY *Eripe me* *Ps. 59:1*

Cantors

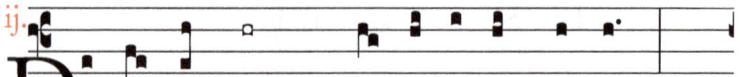

DE-LIV-ER me from mine e-ne-mies, O God:

Choir

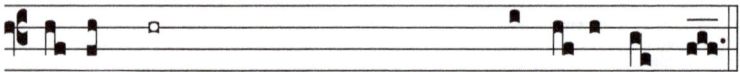

de-fend me, O LORD, from them that rise up a-gainst me.

COMMUNION *Lavábo inter innocéntes* *Ps. 26:6,7*

Cantors

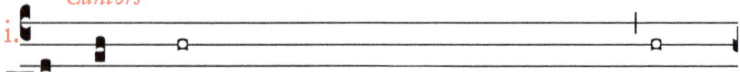

I WILL wash my hands in innocency, O LORD, and so

Choir

will I go to thine al-tar: that I may show the voice of

thanksgiving, and tell of all thy won-drous works.

Verses from Psalm 26:1-3,8-9,11-12 *may be sung.*

PASSION WEEK
Thursday

INTROIT *Omnia quae fecisti (Trinity XX, p. 455)*
GRADUAL *Tollite hóstias (Epiphany V, p. 101)*
OFERTORY *Super flúmina (Trinity XX, p. 458)*
COMMUNION *Meménto verbi tui (Trinity XX, p. 458)*

SAINT MARY IN PASSIONTIDE
Friday in Passion Week

INTROIT *Stabant iuxta crucem*   *Jn. 19:25; Ps. 56:1*

Cantors

vij.

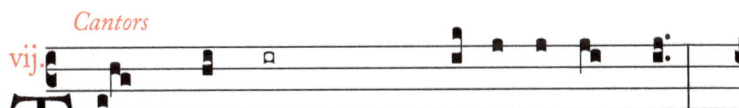

THERE stood by the Cross of Je-sus his Mo-ther:

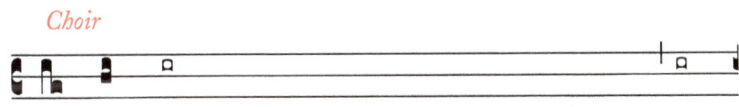

Choir

and his Mother's sister, Mary the wife of Cleophas, and

FINE   *Cantors*

Salome, and Ma-ry Mag-da- lene. *Ps.* Be mer-ci-ful

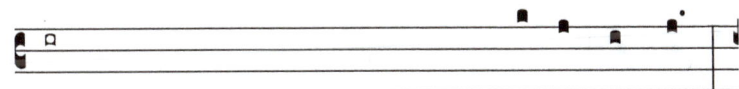

unto me, O God, for man goeth about to de-vour me:

201

Choir

Full

he is daily fight-ing and trou-bling me.　　There stood...

GRADUAL *Dolorósa et lacrimábilis*

Cantors

V.

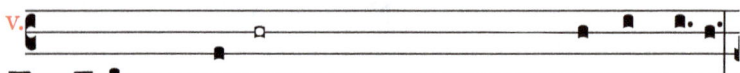

MOURN-ful and weeping art thou, O Vir-gin Ma-ry:

Choir

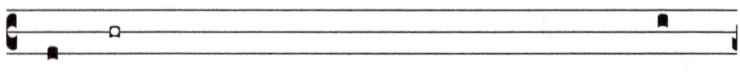

stan-ding by the Cross of the Lord Jesus thy Son, the

Cantors

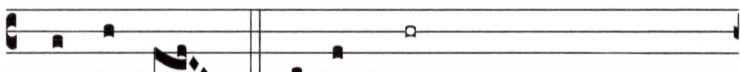

Re-deem-er.　　℣. Vir-gin Mother of God, he whom

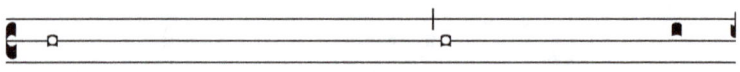

the whole world containeth not;　endureth this tor-ment

Choir

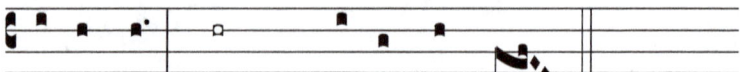

of the Cross: the Author of life made man.

TRACT *Stabat sancta María*   *Cf. Lam 1:12*

Cantors

viij.

THERE stood mournful by the Cross of our Lord Jesus

Christ: holy Mary, Queen of Heaven, and Lady of the world.

Choir

℣. All ye that pass by: behold and see if there be any sorrow

like unto my sor-row.

SEQUENCE *Stabat Mater dolorósa*

The Sequence Stabat Mater may be sung or said. The text given here may be replaced by a prose or musical setting which relies on a different translation of the same Sequence.

AT the Cross her sta-tion keep-ing, Stood the mourn-

ful Mo-ther weep-ing, Where he hung, her dy-ing Son.

Through her soul, of joy be-reav-èd, Torn with an-

guish, deep-ly griev-èd, Lo! the pierc-ing sword hath run.

O, how sad and sore dis-tres-sèd, Then was she,

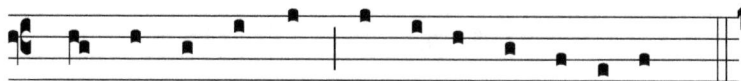

that Mo-ther bles-sèd   Of the sole-be-got-ten One!

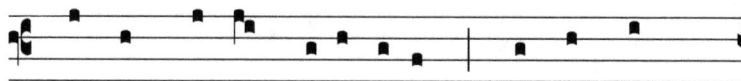

Torn with grief and de-so-la-tion,   Mo-ther meek,

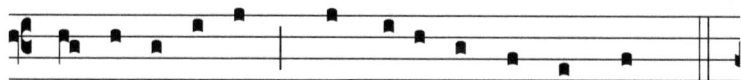

the bit-ter Pas-sion,   Saw she of her glo-rious Son.

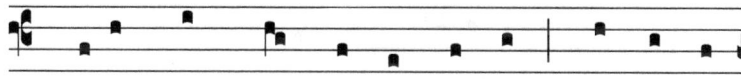

Who, on Christ's dear Mo-ther think-ing, With her Son

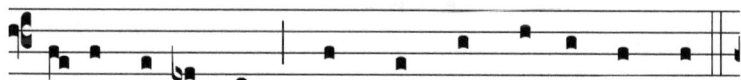

in sor-row sink-ing, Would not share her sad-ness deep?

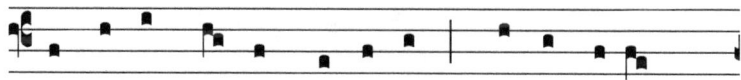

For his peo-ple's sins chas-ti-sèd,   She her Je-sus

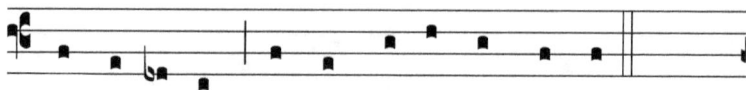

saw des-pis-èd,   Saw him by the scour-ges rent.

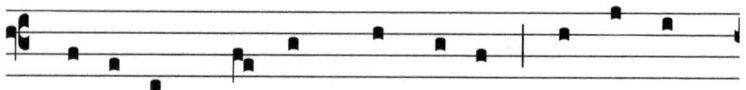

Saw her own sweet Off-spring ta-ken,   And in death

by all for-sa-ken, While his spi-rit forth he sent.

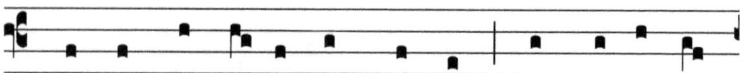

Mo-ther, fount of love o'er-flow-ing,   Ah, that I, thy

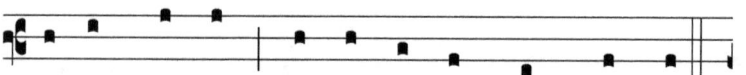

sor-row know-ing,   In thy grief may mourn with thee.

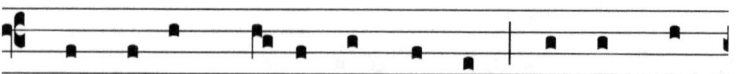

That my heart, fresh ar-dour gain-ing, Love of Christ

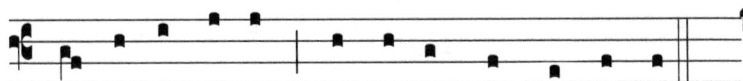

my God at-tain-ing,   Un-to him may pleas-ing be.

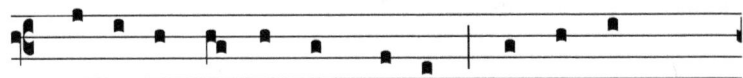

Ho-ly Mo-ther, be there writ-ten   Ev'-ry wound

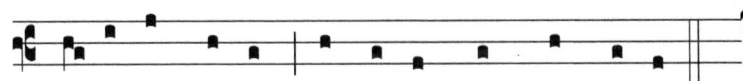

of Je-sus smit-ten,   in my heart, and there re-main

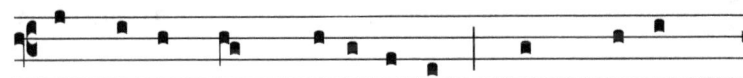

As thy Son through tri-bu-la-tion   Deigned to pur-

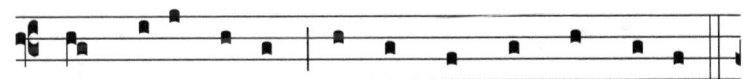

chase my sal-va-tion, Let me share with thee the pain.

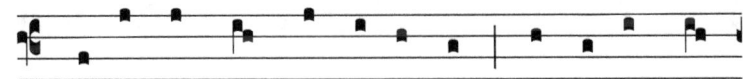

Let me weep with thee be-side him, For the sins which

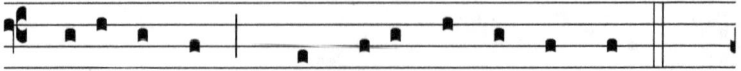

cru-ci-fied him, While my life re-mains in me.

Take be-neath the Cross my sta-tion, Share with thee

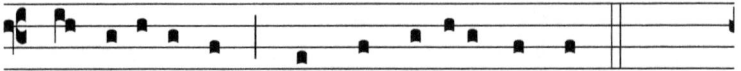

thy de-so-la-tion, Hum-bly this I ask of thee.

Vir-gin, vir-gins all ex-cel-ling, Spurn me not, my

prayer re-pel-ling: Make me weep and mourn with thee.

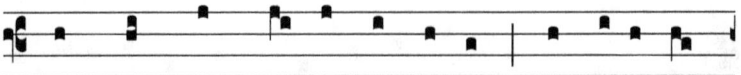

So Christ's death with-in me bear-ing, Let me, in his

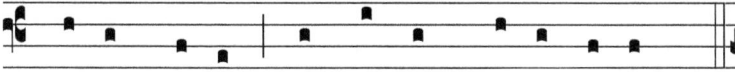

Pas-sion shar-ing, Keep his wounds in me-mo-ry.

Let thy Son's wounds pe-ne-trate me: Let the Cross

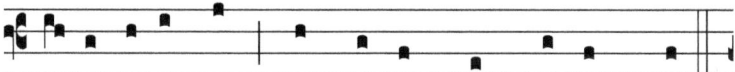

i-ne-bri-ate me, And his own most pre-cious Blood.

Lest in flames I burn and per-ish, On the judge-ment

day, O cher-ish And de-fend me, Vir-gin good.

Christ, when-e'er this world shall leave me, Through

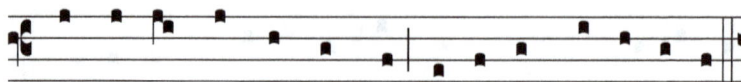

thy Mo-ther then re-ceive me To the palm of vic-to-ry.

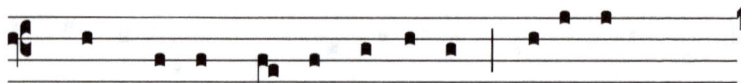

When the bonds of flesh are ri-ven, Glo-ry to

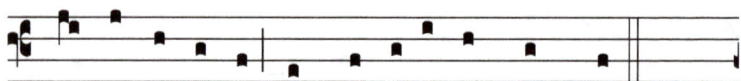

my soul be giv-en   In thy Pa-ra-dise with thee.

A-men.   (Al-le-lu-ia)

OFFERTORY *Recordáre, Virgo Mater*   *Cf. Jer. 18:20*

Cantors

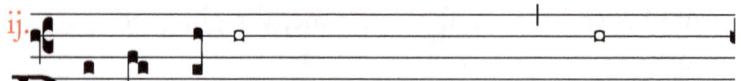

ij.

RE-mem-ber, O Virgin Mother of God, when thou

Choir

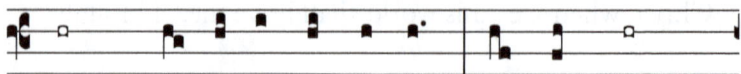

stand-est in the sight of the LORD: that thou speak good

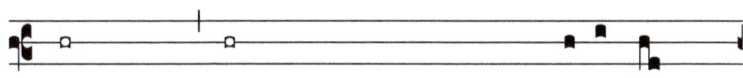

things for us,   and that he may turn away his in-dig-

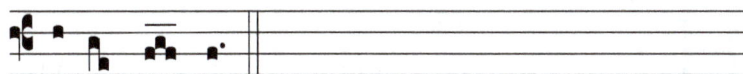

na-tion from us.

COMMUNION *Felíces sensus beátae Maríae*

Cantors

i.

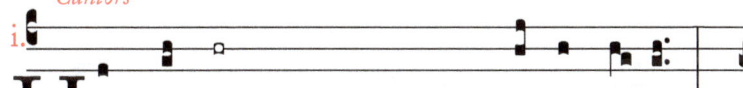

HAP-PY the heart of the Blessèd Vir-gin Ma-ry:

Choir

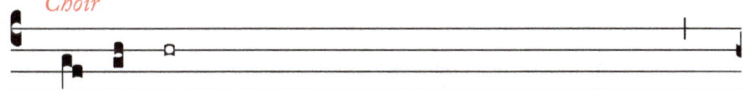

who with-out death gained the palm of martyrdom

beneath the Cross of the Lord.

Verses from Psalm 25:1,2,7,6,16-20 *may be sung.*

or

CO. *Redíme me (above, p. 198)*

INTROIT *Miserére mihi...tríbulor*   *Ps. 31:10,17,19,1*

Cantors

vij.

HAVE mer-cy upon me, O LORD, for I am in trou-ble:

Choir

de-li-ver me from the hand of mine enemies, and from

them that per-se-cute me: let me not be confounded

FINE   *Cantors*

O LORD, for I have call-ed up-on thee. *Ps.* In thee, O

Choir

LORD, have I put my trust: let me never be put to

confusion; deliver me in thy right-eous-ness.

Full

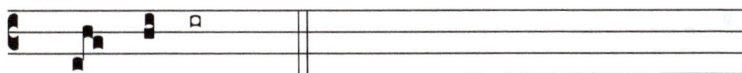

Have mer-cy... *(etc.)*

GRADUAL *Pacífice*   *Ps. 35:20,22*

Cantors   *Choir*

℣.

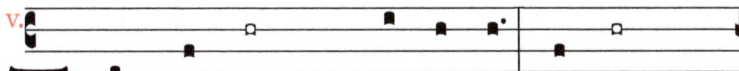

T HEIR com-mun-ing is not for peace: but they imagine

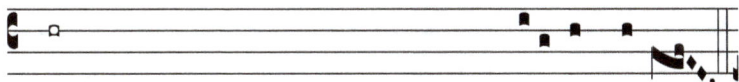

deceitful words against them that are qui-et in the land.

Cantors

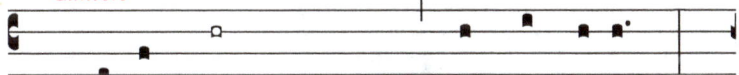

℣. This hast thou seen, O LORD, hold not thy tongue:

Choir

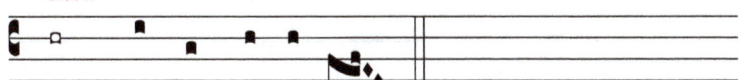

go not far from me, O LORD.

OFFERTORY *Benedíctus es, Domine*   *Ps. 119:12,121b,42*

Cantors

ij.

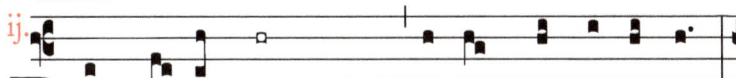

B LESS-ed art thou, O LORD; O teach me thy sta-tutes:

213

Choir

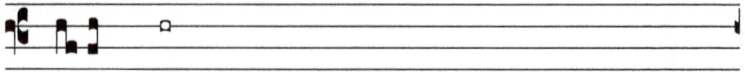

O give me not over unto the proud that are mine op-

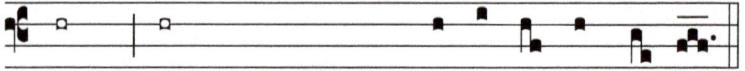

pressors; so shall I make answer un-to my blas-phe-mers.

COMMUNION *Ne tradíderis*   *Ps. 27:14*

Cantors

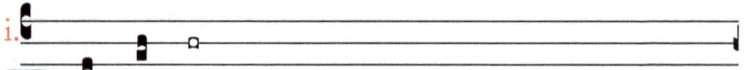

DE-LI-VER me not over into the will of mine ad-ver-

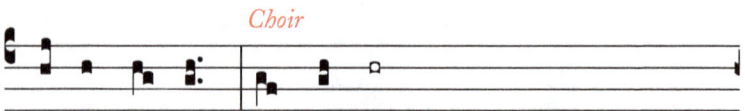

Choir

sa-ries, O LORD: for there are false witnesses risen up

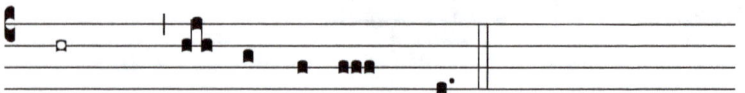

against me, and such as speak wrong.

Verses from Psalm 27:1-3,10,15,16 *may be sung.*

HOLY WEEK

AT THE BLESSING OF PALMS

ANTIPHON *Hosanna fílio David* (F.B.)　　　　　　*Mt. 21:9*

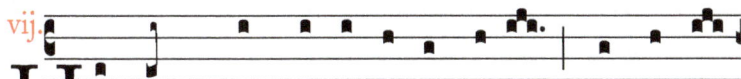

HO- SAN- NA * to the son of Da- vid: bles-sed is

he　　that co- meth in the Name of the LORD: O King

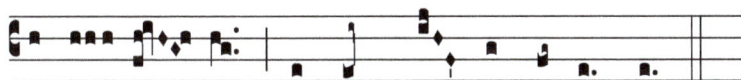

of Is- ra- el: Ho- san- na　in the high- est.

The Distribution of Palms

The following psalm verses, alternating with the antiphons, are sung with the intonation each time, unless the verse is too short, as is the case of verse 23.

PSALM 118　*Confitémini Dómino*

Cantors

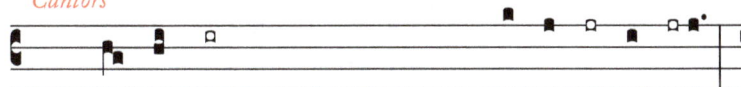

℣. 1. O give thanks unto the LORD, *for* he is gra- cious;

Choir

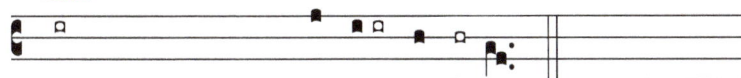

because his mercy en-*dur*-eth for ev-er.　　*Repeat Antiphon.*

215

22 The same stone which the *build*-ers refused, * is become the head-stone *in* the corner. *Repeat Antiphon.*

23 This *is* the LORD'S doing, * and it is *mar*-vel-lous in our eyes. *Repeat Antiphon.*

27 God is the LORD, who hath *show*-ed us light; * bind the sacrifice with cords, | yea, even unto the *horns* of the altar. *Repeat Antiphon.*

28 Thou art my God, and *I* will thank thee; * thou art my God, and *I* will praise thee. *Repeat Antiphon.*

ANTIPHON *Púeri Hebræórum, portántes* (F.B.)

THE chil- dren of the He- brews,* bear-ing bran-ches

of o-live, went out to meet the LORD, cry-ing out

and say- ing, Ho- san- na in the high- est.

PSALM 24 *Dómini est terra*

Cantors   Choir

THE earth is the Lord's, and all that there-*in* is: the

216

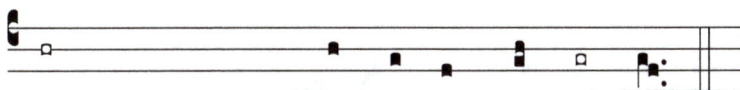

com- pass of the world, and *they* that dwell there- in.

2 For he hath founded it upon *the* seas : and prepared *it* upon the floods. *Repeat Antiphon.*

7 Lift up your heads, O ye gates, | and be ye lift up, ye everlas-*ting* doors : and the King of glo-*ry* shall come in.

8 Who is the King of *glo*-ry : it is the LORD strong and mighty, even the LORD migh-*ty* in battle. *Repeat Antiphon.*

9 Lift up your heads O ye gates, and be ye lift up, ye everlas-*ting* doors : and the King of *glo*-ry shall come in.

10 Who is the King of glo-*ry* : even the Lord of hosts, | he is the *King* of glory. *Repeat Antiphon.*

ANTIPHON *Pueri Hebræorum vestiménta* (F.B.)

HE chil- dren of the He- brews,* spread their gar- ments

in the way   and cri- ed out say- ing, Ho-san-na

to the son of Da- vid: bles- sed is he that

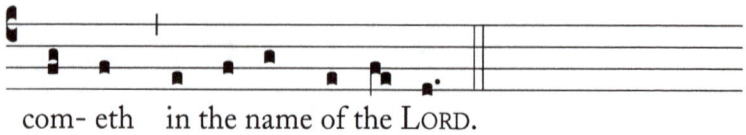

com- eth   in the name of the LORD.

PSALM 47 *Omnes gentes, pláudite*

Cantors

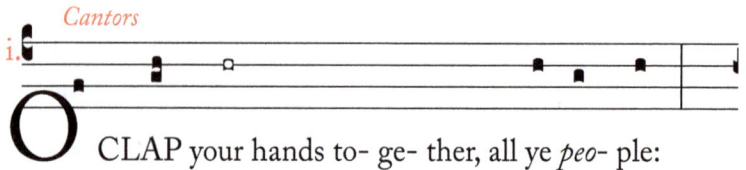

O CLAP your hands to- ge- ther, all ye *peo*- ple:

Choir

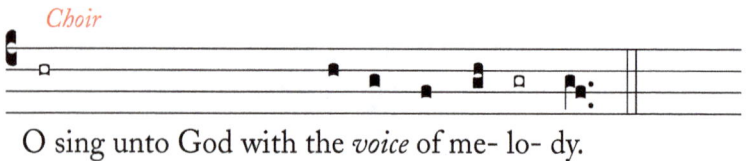

O sing unto God with the *voice* of me- lo- dy.

2   For the LORD is high, and to be *fear*-ed : he is the great
    King *up*-on all the earth.   *Repeat Antiphon.*

3   He shall subdue the people un-*der* us : and the nations
    un-der our feet.

4   He shall choose out an heritage *for* us : even the worship
    of Jacob, *whom* he loved.   *Repeat Antiphon.*

5   God is gone up with a mer-*ry* noise : and the LORD with
    the *sound* of the trump.

6   O sing praises, sing praises unto *our* God : O sing praises,
    sing praises *un*-to our King.   *Repeat Antiphon.*

7   For God is King of all *the* earth : sing ye praises with *un*-
    derstanding.

8   God reigneth over the *na*-tions : God sitteth up-*on* his
    holy seat.   *Repeat Antiphon.*

9 The princes of the people are joined unto the people of the God of A-*bra*-ham : for God, which is very high exalted, | doth defend the earth, as it *were* with a shield.

Repeat Antiphon.

AT THE PROCESSION

Deacon or Priest　　　　　　　　*All*

℣. Let us go forth in peace. ℟. In the Name of Christ. A-men.

During the procession, the following antiphons and hymn may be sung:

I

ANTIPHON *Occúrrunt turbae*

Cantors　　　　　　　　　　　　　　　*Choir*

viij.

THE mul-ti-tudes, with flowers and bran-ches　go

Cantors

forth to meet their Re-dee-mer: and render worthy ho-

Choir

mage to the triumphant con-que-ror: the Gentiles

Cantors

with their lips proclaim the Son of God: and in the praise

of Christ their voices thunder through the sky:

Choir

Hosanna in the high-est.

II

ANTIPHON *Cum angelis* (F.B.)

vij.

WITH the an-gels and the chil-dren * may we be

found faith-ful, cry-ing un-to the van-qui-sher of death:

Ho-san-na in the high-est.

PALM SUNDAY
III

ANTIPHON *Turba multa*

MA-NY peo-ple that were come to the feast

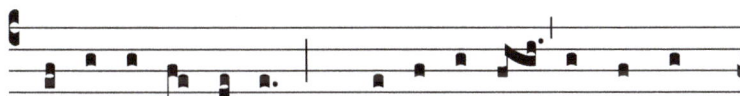

cri-ed un-to the LORD. Bles-sed is he that com-eth

in the Name of the LORD. Ho-san-na in the high- est.

IV

ANTIPHON *Cœpérunt omnes* (F.B.)

THE whole * mul-ti-tude of them that went down

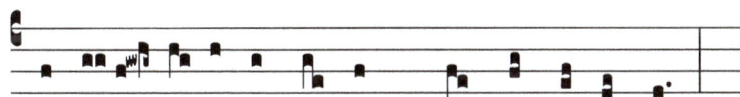

be- gan to re-joice and praise God with a loud voice

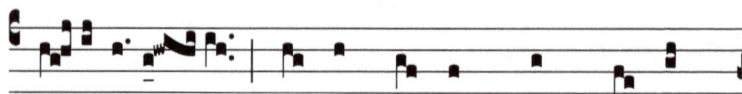

for all the migh-ty works which they had

seen, say-ing: Bles-sed is the King that co-meth in the Name

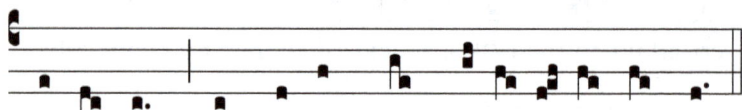

of the Lord; peace on earth, and glo-ry in the high-est.

V

ANTIPHON *Omnes colláudant* (F.B.)

viij.

ALL men * praise thy Name, and say, Bles-sed is he

that com-eth in the Name of the Lord: Ho-san-na

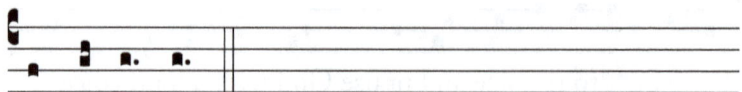

in the high-est.

PSALM 147 *Láuda Ierúsalem*   *Ps. 147:12-20*

viij.

PRAISE the LORD, O Je-*ru*-sa-lem: praise thy

God, O Si-on.

13. For he hath made fast the bars of thy *gates*: and hath blessed thy child-*ren* withín thee.

14. He maketh peace in thy *bor*-ders: and filleth thee *with* the flour of wheat.

15. He sendeth forth his commandment upon *earth*: and his word runneth *ve*-ry swiftly.

16. He giveth snow like *wool*: and scattereth the hoar-*frost* like ashes.

17. He casteth forth his ice like *mor*-sels: who is able *to* abide his frost?

18. He sendeth out his word and *mel*-teth them: he bloweth with his wind *and* the waters flow.

19. He showeth his word unto *Ja*-cob: his statutes and ordi-nances *un*-to Israel.

20. He hath not dealt so with any *na*-tion: neither have the heathen *know*-ledge of his laws.

Repeat Antiphon.

ANTIPHON *Fulgéntibus*

Cantors

viij.

WITH palms bright-ly shin-ing * we fall low

Choir

be-fore the LORD who co-meth: let us all go forth to

meet him with hymns and with songs, glo-ri-fy-ing

him and say-ing: Blessed is he that co-meth.

VII

ANTIPHON *Ave, Rex noster*

Cantors

i.

HAIL, O our King, Son of David, Re-deem-er

Choir

of the world, whom the prophets have foretold to be

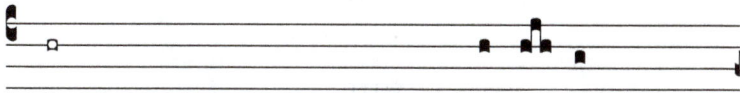

him that cometh as the Saviour of the house of

Cantors

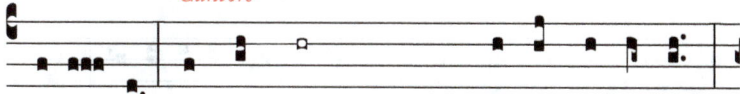

Is- ra- el. For thee the Father hath sent in-to the world,

Choir

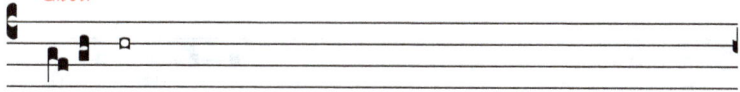

the sa-ving Victim, to whom looked forward all the

Saints which have been since the world be-   gan,

Cantors   *Full*

and now, Hosanna to the Son of Da-vid. Bles-sed is he

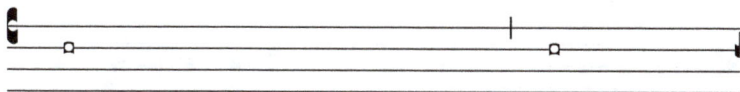

that cometh in the Name of the Lord. Hosanna

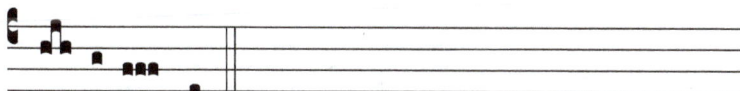

in the high- est.

Here may be sung the hymn, Gloria, laus et honor, *1940 Hymnal 62, English Hymnal: 621, 622.*
When the procession has entered the church, this last antiphon is sung:

VIII

ANTIPHON *Ingrediente*

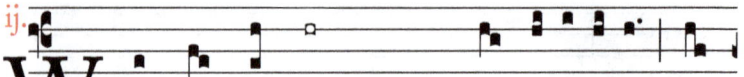

WHEN the LORD entered into the ho-ly ci-ty: the

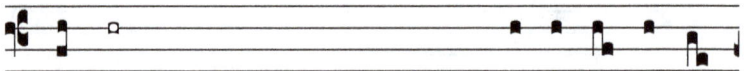

chil-dren of the Hebrews foretold the re-sur-rec-tion of

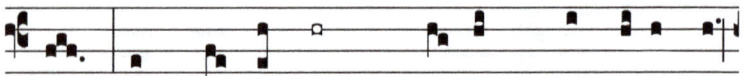

life. † And bear-ing bran-ches of palms, they cri-ed out:

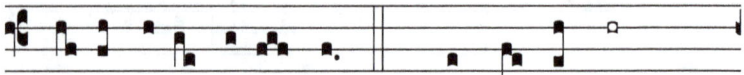

Ho-san-na in the high-est. ℣. When the peo-ple had

heard that Jesus was com-ing to Je-ru-sa-lem, they went

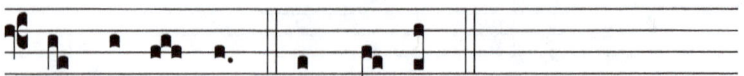

forth to meet him. † And bear-ing... *(etc.)*

PALM SUNDAY
AT THE MASS

INTROIT *Dómine, ne longe*   *Ps. 22:19,21,1*

Cantors

vij.

O LORD, remove not thy succour afar from me;

Choir

have respect to my de-fence, and hear me: de-li-ver

me from the mouth of the lion; yea, from the horns of the

FINE   *Cantors*

unicorns hast thou re-gar-ded my cry. *Ps.* My God, my

Choir

God, look upon me; why hast thou for-sa-ken me: and

art so far from my health, and from the words of my

227

Full

com-plaint?   O   LORD... *(etc.)*

TRACT *Deus, Deus meus*   *Ps. 22:1-8,17b,18,21,23,31,32*

Cantors

viij.

MY God, my God, look upon me: why hast thou

Choir

for-sa-ken me : ℣. And art so far from my health and from

Cantors

the words of my com-plaint? ℣. O my God, I cry in the

daytime, but thou hearest not : and in the night season

Choir

also I take no rest. ℣. And thou continuest ho-ly:

228

Cantors

O thou worship of Is-ra-el. ℣. Our fa-thers hoped in

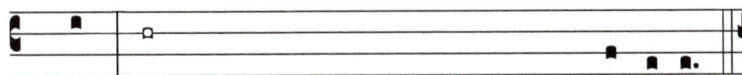

thee : they trusted in thee, and thou didst de-li-ver them.

Choir

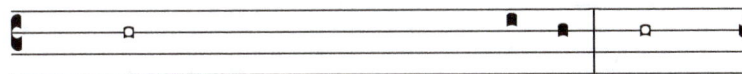

℣. They called upon thee, and were hol-pen : they put

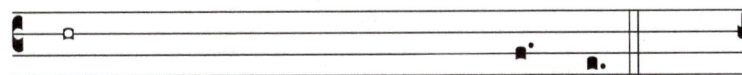

their trust in thee, and were not con-foun-ded.

Cantors

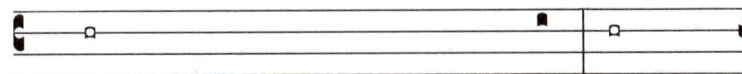

℣. But as for me, I am a worm, and no man : a very

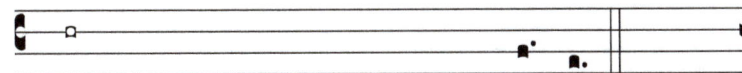

scorn of men, and the outcast of the peo-ple.

Choir

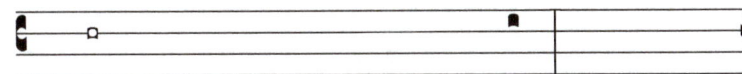

℣. All they that see me laugh me to scorn :

229

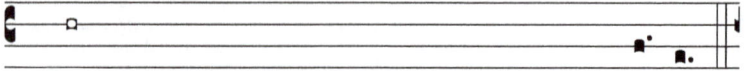

they shoot out their lips, and shake their heads, say-ing,

Cantors

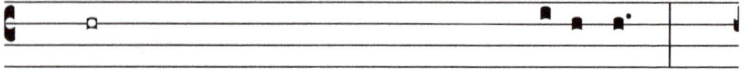

℣. He trusted in God, that he would de-li-ver him :

Choir

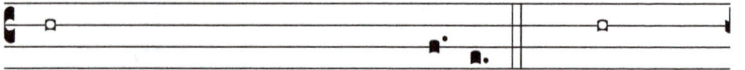

let him deliver him, if he will have him. ℣. They stand

staring and looking upon me : they part my garments

Cantors

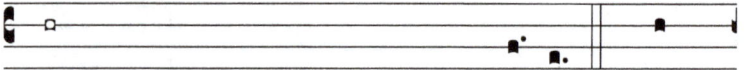

among them, and cast lots upon my ves-ture. ℣. Save

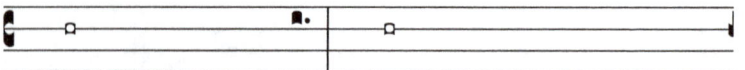

me from the lion's mouth : thou hast heard me also from

Choir

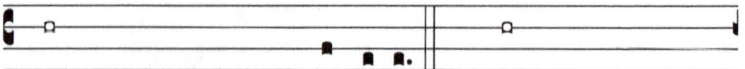

among the horns of the u-ni-corns. ℣. O praise the LORD,

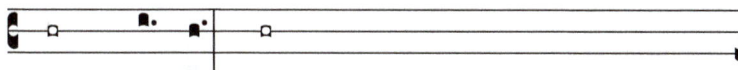

ye that fear him : magnify him all ye of the seed of

Cantors

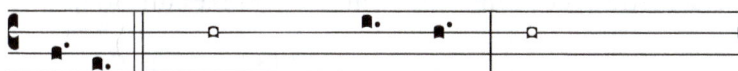

Ja-cob. ℣. My seed shall serve him : they shall be

Choir

counted unto the Lord for a ge-ner-a-tion. ℣. They shall

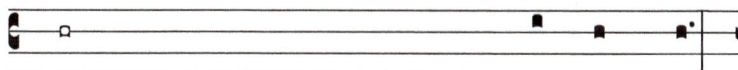

come, and the heavens shall declare his righ-teous-ness:

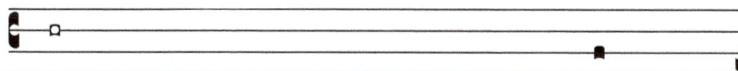

unto a people that shall be born, whom the Lord

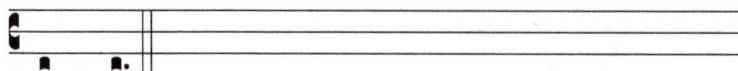

hath made.

TRACT *Christus factus est*   *Phil. 2:8, 9*

Cantors

CHRIST be- came obedient for our sakes un- to death:

Choir

ev- en the death of the Cross. ℣. Where-fore God also

hath highly ex- alt- ed him: and given him a Name

which is a- bove ev - ery name.

OFFERTORY *Impropérium*   *Ps. 69:21, 22*

Cantors

THY re- buke hath broken my heart, and I am full of

heaviness; I looked for some to have pity upon me, but

232

Choir

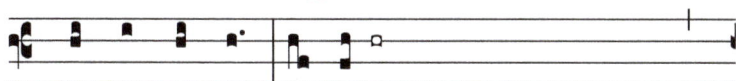

there was no man: nei- ther found I any to comfort me;

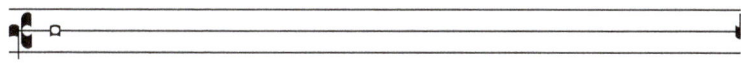

they gave me gall to eat, and when I was thirsty they gave

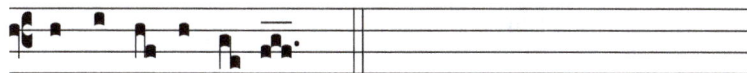

me vi- ne- gar to drink.

COMMUNION *Pater, si non potest* *Matt. 26:42*

Cantors

i.

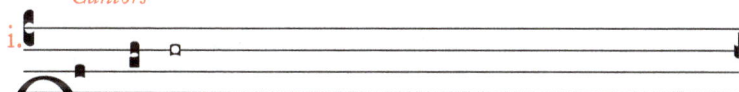

O MY Father, if this cup may not pass away from me,

Choir

ex- cept I drink it: thy will be done.

Verses from Psalm 22:1-2, 4, 6, 16-17, 21-23, 27-32
or 116:10-16 *may be sung.*

233

MONDAY

Introit *Iudica, Dómine*   Ps. 35:1,2,3

Cantors

vij.

PLEAD thou my cause, O Lord, with them that strive

with me; and fight thou against them that fight a-gainst

Choir

me: lay hand upon the shield and buckler, and stand up

FINE

to help me, O Lord, the strength of my sal-va-tion.

Cantors

Ps. Bring forth the spear, and stop the way against them

Choir

that per-se-cute me: say unto my soul, I am thy sal-va-tion.

Full

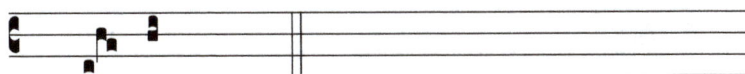

Plead thou..., *(etc.)*

GRADUAL *Exsurge, Domine, et intende*   *Ps. 35:23,3*

Cantors

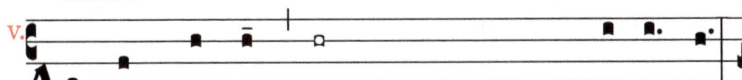

℣. A-WAKE O LORD, and stand up to judge my quar-rel:

Choir   *Cantors*

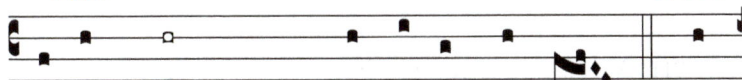

a-venge thou my cause, my God and my Lord. ℣. Bring

Choir

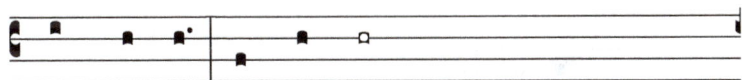

forth the spear: and stop the way against them that

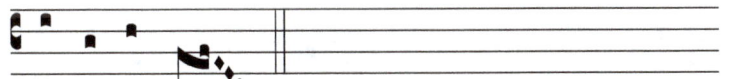

per-se-cute me.

TRACT *Dómine, non secundum (Ash Wednesday, p. 126)*

OFFERTORY *Eripe me, Dómine*   *Ps. 143:9,10*

Cantors

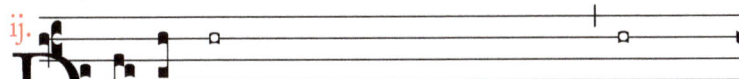

ij. DE-li-ver me, O LORD, from mine enemies, for I flee

Choir

un-to thee to hide me: teach me to do the thing that

pleaseth thee, for thou art my God.

COMMUNION *Erubéscant (Ember Friday in Lent, p. 147)*

TUESDAY

INTROIT *Nos autem gloriári (Maundy Thursday, p. 243)*

GRADUAL *Ego autem, cum infirmaréntur*   Ps. 35:13,1,2

Cantors

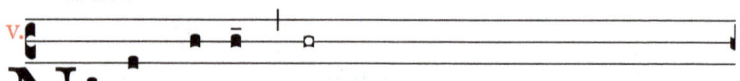

℣. NE-ver-the-less, when they were sick, I put on sack-

Choir

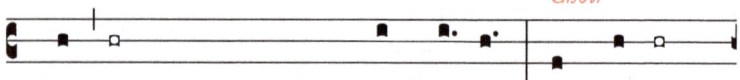

cloth and humbled myself with fast-ing: and my prayers

Cantors

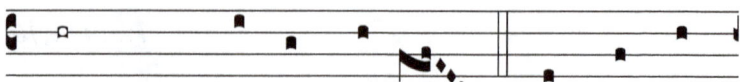

shall turn into mine own bos-om.   ℣. Plead thou my

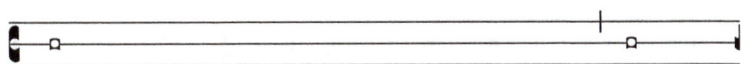

cause, O LORD, with them that strive with me, and fight

Choir

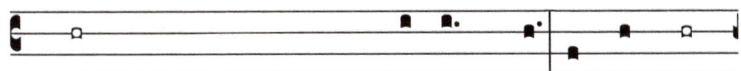

thou against them that fight a-gainst me: lay hand upon

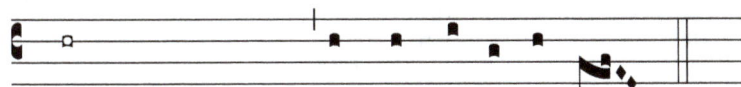

the shield and buckler, and stand up to help me.

OFFERTORY *Custódi me...de mano peccatóris*　　　*Ps. 140:4*

Cantors

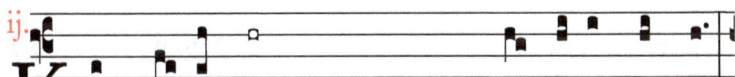

KEEP me, O LORD, from the hands of the un-god-ly:

Choir

pre-serve me from the wick-ed men.

COMMUNION *Advérsum me loquebántur*　　　*Ps. 69:12,13,14*

Cantors

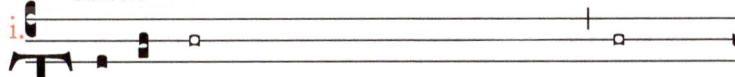

THEY that sit in the gate speak against me, and the

237

Choir

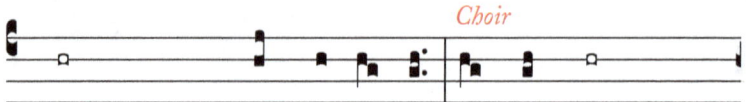

drunkards make songs up-on me: but, LORD, I make

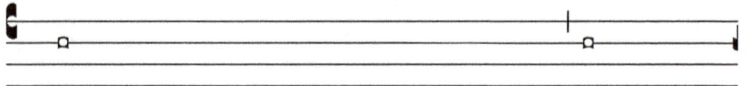

my prayer unto thee, in an acceptable time, hear me, O

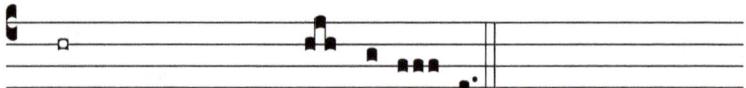

God, in the multitude of thy mer-cy.

Verses from Psalm 69:1-2,13-14,17-18,31,35 *may be sung.*

WEDNESDAY

INTROIT *In Nómine Iesu*   *Phil. 2:10,8,11; Ps. 102:1*

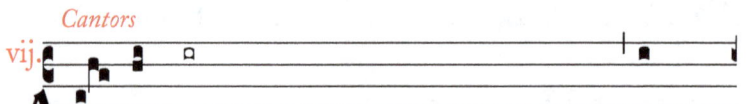

Cantors

vij.

AT the Name of Jesus every knee should bow, of

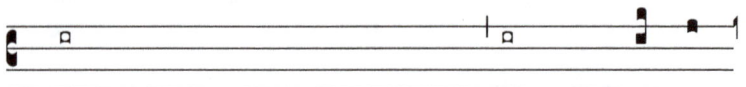

things in heaven and things on earth, and things un-der

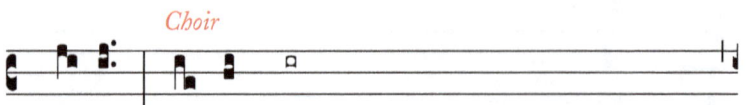

Choir

the earth: for that the LORD became obedient unto death,

238

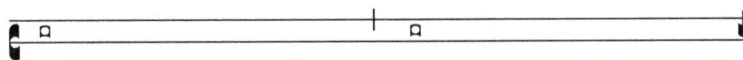

even the death of the Cross; wherefore Jesus Christ is

FINE   *Cantors*

L<small>ORD</small>, in the glory of God the Fa-ther. *Ps.* Hear my

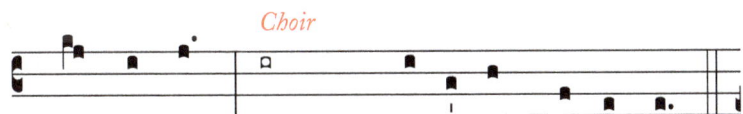

Choir

prayer, O L<small>ORD</small>: and let my cry-ing come un-to thee.

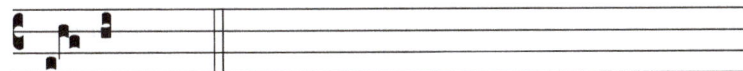

Full

At the..., *(etc.)*

G<small>RADUAL</small> *Ne avértas fáciem*   *Ps. 35:13,1,2*

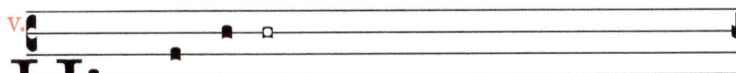

Cantors

H<small>IDE</small> not thy face from thy servant, for I am in

Choir   *Cantors*

trou-ble: O haste thee, and hear me. ℣. Save me, O

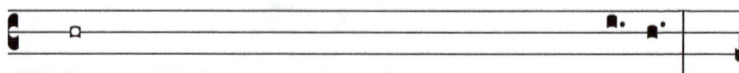

God, for the waters are come in, even unto my soul:

Choir

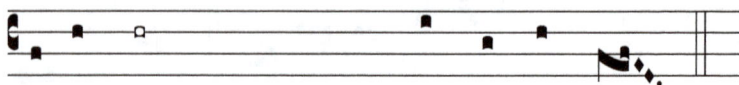

I stick fast in the deep mire, where no ground is.

TRACT *Dómine exáudi*   *Ps 102:1–4,13*

Cantors

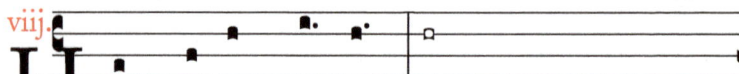

viij. HEAR my prayer, O LORD: and let my crying come

Choir

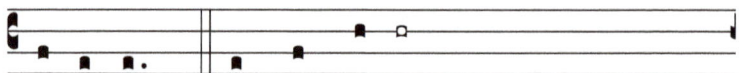

un-to thee. ℣. Hide not thy face from me in the time of

Cantors

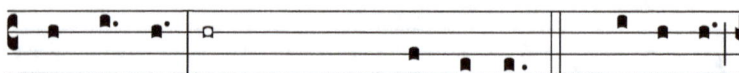

my trou-ble: incline thine ear un-to me. ℣. When I call:

Choir

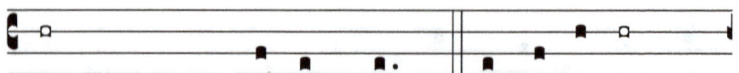

O hear me, and that right soon. ℣. For my days are con-

240

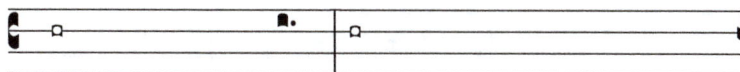

sumed away like smoke: and my bones are burnt up as it

Cantors

were a fire-brand. ℣. My heart is smitten down, and

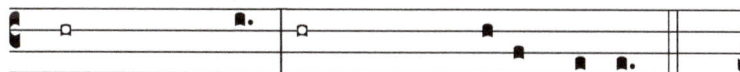

withered like grass: so that I forget to eat my bread.

Choir

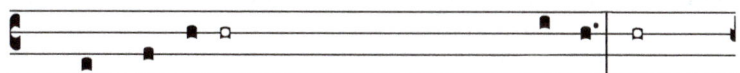

℣. Thou shalt ar-ise and have mercy upon Si-on: for it is

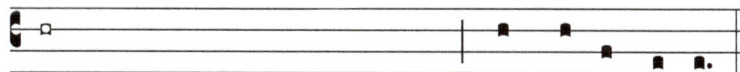

time that thou have mercy upon her, yea, the time is come.
Another version of this tract is the Respond for Good Friday page 255.

OFFERTORY *Dómine, exáudi*   *Ps. 102:1,2*

Cantors

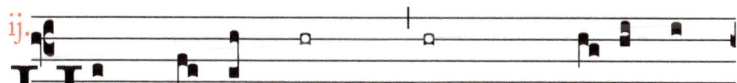

ij. HEAR my prayer, O LORD, and let my cry-ing come

241

Choir

un-to thee: hide not thy face from me.

COMMUNION *Potum meum*   *Ps. 102:9b,10b,11b,12,13*

Cantors

i.

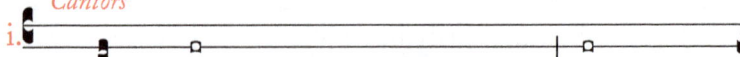

I HAVE mingled my drink with weeping; for thou hast

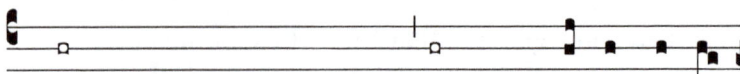

taken me up and cast me down, and I am wi-ther-ed like

Choir

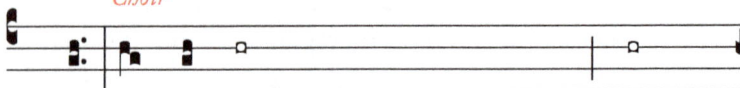

grass: but thou, O LORD, shalt endure for ever; thou shalt

arise and have mercy upon Sion, for it is time that thou

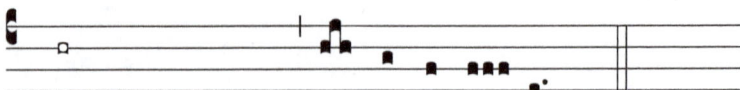

have mercy upon her, yea, the time is   come.

Verses from Psalm 102:1-2,17 *may be sung.*

242

THE MASS of the LORD' SUPPER

INTROIT *Nos autem gloriári*   *Gal. 6:14; Ps. 67:1*

Cantors

vij.

WE should glory in the Cross
or But as for us, it behoveth us to glory in the Cross

Choir

of our LORD Je- sus Christ: In whom is our salvation,

life, and resurrection; through whom we are saved and de-

FINE   Cantors

liv- er- ed. *Ps.* God be merciful unto us and bless us:

Choir

and show us the light of his countenance, and be mer-

Full

ci- ful un- to us.   We should..., *(etc.)*
                       But   as for us, *(etc.)*

The Gloria in excelsis *is sung.*

GRADUAL *Christus factus est* *(Good Friday, p. 256)*

or

GRADUAL *Oculi ómnium*   *Ps. 145:15, 16*

Cantors

THE eyes of all wait up-on thee, O Lord,   and

Choir

thou givest them their meat in due sea- son.   ℣. Thou

o-pen-est thy hand, and fillest all thing liv- ing with

plen- teous- ness.

TRACT *Ab ortu solis*   *Mal. 1:11 & Prov. 9:5*

Cantors

FROM the rising up of the sun, unto the going down of

the same: my Name shall be great among the Gen- tiles.

Choir

℣. And in every place incense shall be offered unto my Name:

Cantors

and a pure of- fer- ing. ℣. Come, eat of my bread, and

Full

drink of the wine: which I have min- gled.

The Creed *is not said.*

THE WASHING OF FEET
Also Called
The Maundy

After the homily there may follow the ceremony of the Maundy.
Meanwhile the choir sings some of the following antiphons, or other
appropriate hymns:

ANTIPHON 1 *Mandátum novum* (F.B.)   *Jn. 13:34; Ps. 119:1*

A NEW com-mand-ment give I   un-to you: * that ye

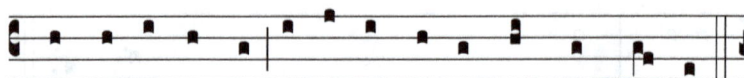

love one a-no-ther as I have lo-ved you, saith the Lord.

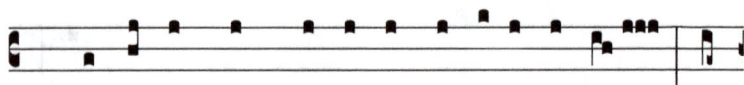

Ps. Bless-ed are those that are un-de-fil-ed in the way: * and

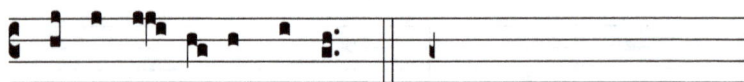

walk in the law of the LORD. *Repeat Antiphon.*

ANTIPHON 2 *Postquam surréxit* (F.B.) *Jn. 13:4,5,15; Ps. 48:1*

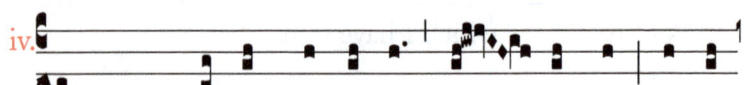

iv.

AF-TER the Lord had ri-sen * from Sup-per he put

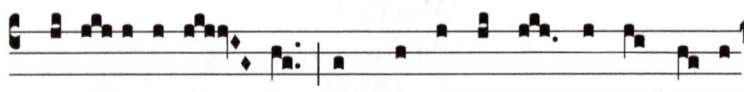

wa-ter in a ba- sin, and be-gan to wash the feet of his

dis-ci-ples: this ex-am-ple left he un-to them.

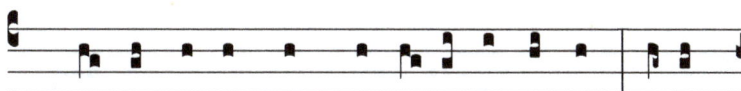

Ps. Great is the LORD, and high-ly to be prai-sed   in the

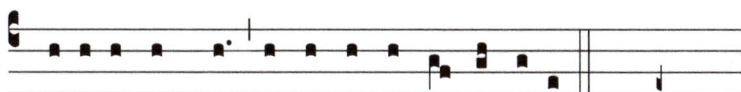

ci-ty of our God: e-ven up-on his ho-ly hill.   *Repeat Ant.*

ANTIPHON 3 *Dóminus Iesus* (F.B.) *Jn. 13:12,13,15; Ps. 85:1*

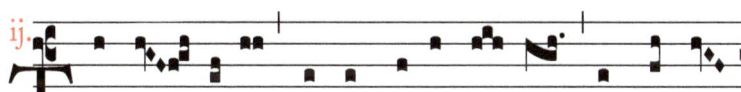

ij.

THE Lord Je-sus, * af-ter he had sup-ped with his dis-

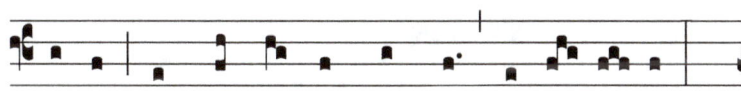

ci-ples,   and had wa-shed their feet, said un- to them:

Know   ye what I, your Lord and Mas-ter, have done

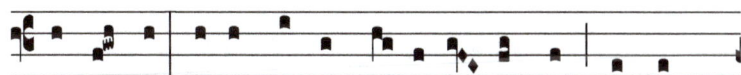

un-to you? I have gi-ven you an ex-am-ple that ye

247

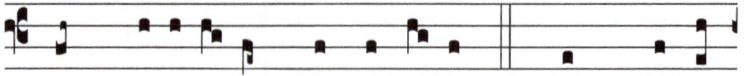

should do as I have done un-to you. *Ps.* LORD, thou art

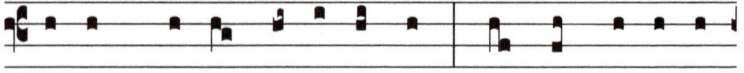

be-come gra-cious un-to thy land: * thou hast tur-ned a-

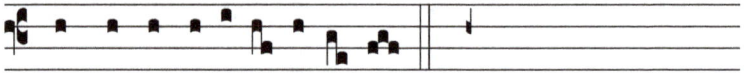

way the cap-ti-vi-ty of Ja-cob. *Repeat Antiphon.*

ANTIPHON 4 *Dómine, tu mihi* (F.B.)　　　　　　*Jn. 13:6,7,8*

LORD, dost thou * wash my feet? Je-sus an-swe-red

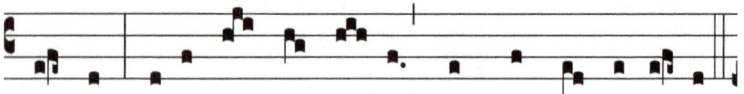

and said: If I wash not thy feet, thou hast no part in me.

℣. He came there-fore un-to Si-mon Pe-ter: and Pe-ter said

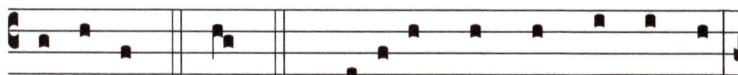

un-to him: Lord. ℣. What I do, thou know-est not now:

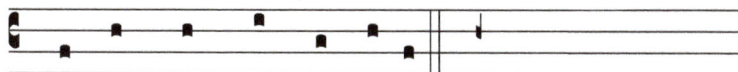

* but thou shalt know here-af-ter. *Repeat Antiphon.*

ANTIPHON 5 *Si ego Dóminus* (F.B.)   *Jn. 13:14; Ps.49:1*

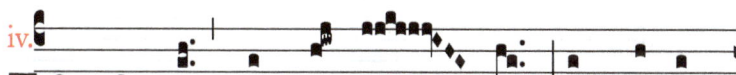

IF I your Lord * and your Mas-   ter   have wa-shed

your feet: how much more ought ye   to wash the feet of

one a- no-ther? *Ps.* O hear ye this, all ye peo-ple: pon-der

it with your ears, all ye that dwell in the world. *Repeat Ant.*

ANTIPHON 6 *In hoc cognóscent* (F.B.)   *Jn. 13:35*

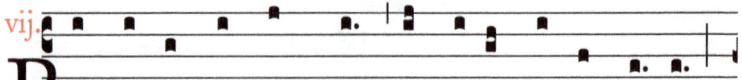

BY this shall all men know that ye are my dis-cip-les:

if ye love one a-no-ther. ℣. Je-sus said un-to his dis-ci-

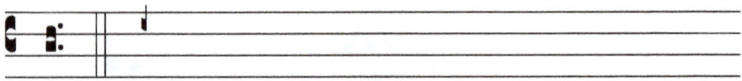

ples: *Repeat Antiphon.*

ANTIPHON 7 *Mandátum novum (above, p. 245 without ps.)*

ANTIPHON 8 *Maneant in vobis* (F.B.)   *1 Cor. 13:13*

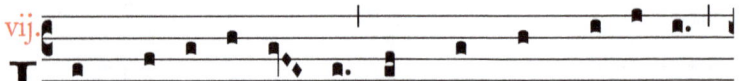

LET there a-bide in you, * faith, hope, and cha-ri-ty,

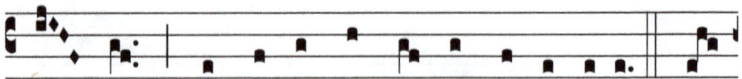

these three: but the grea-test of these is cha-ri-ty. ℣. Now

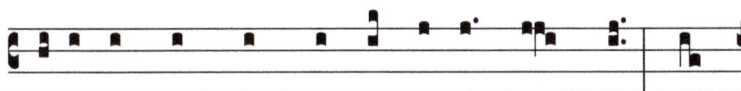

a-bi-deth faith, hope, and cha-rit- y, these three: * but

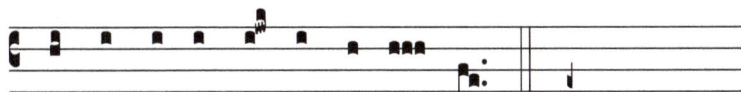

the grea-test of these is cha- ri- ty. *Repeat Antiphon.*

ANTIPHON 9 *Ubi cáritas*

WHERE cha- ri- ty and love are, there is God.

℣. The love of Christ hath joi- ned us in one. ℣. Let us

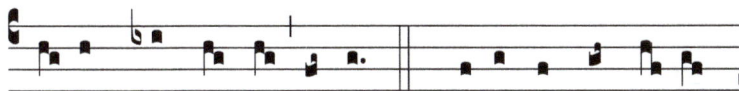

re- joice, and be glad in him. ℣. Let us fear, and let us

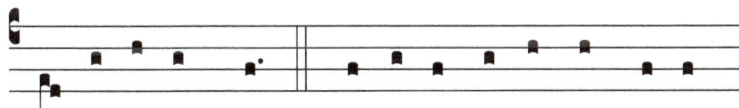

love the li- ving God. ℣. Let us love one a- no- ther in

sin- ce- ri- ty of heart. *Ant.* Where. ℣. When there-

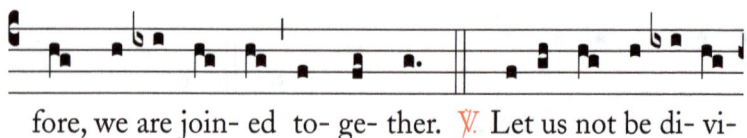

fore, we are join- ed to- ge- ther. ℣. Let us not be di- vi-

ded in spi- rit. ℣. Let all ma- li- cious wrang- ling and

con- ten- tions cease. ℣. And let Christ our God be in

the midst of us. *Ant.* Where. ℣. So may we with the

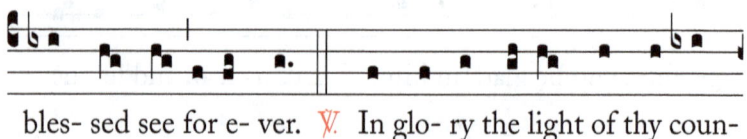

bles- sed see for e- ver. ℣. In glo- ry the light of thy coun-

te- nance, Christ our God. ℣. Joy that is in- fi- nite and

un -de- fi- led. ℣. For e- ver and for e- ver, world with-

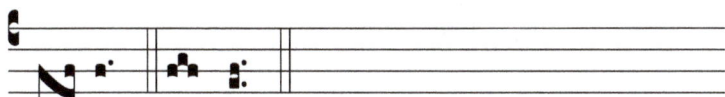

out end.   A- men.

OFFERTORY *Déxtera Dómini*   *(Epiphany III, p. 93)*
or *Ubi Cáritas* *(above p. 251)*

COMMUNION *Dóminus Iesus postquam cenávit*   *Jn. 13:12,13,15*

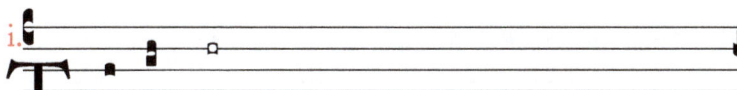

i.

THE Lord Jesus, after that he had supped with his

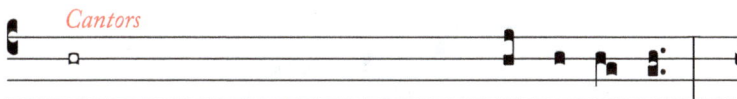

Cantors

disciples, and had washed their feet, said un-to them:

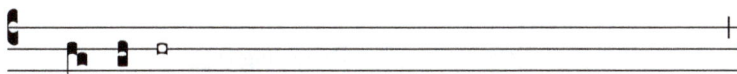

Know ye what I your Lord and Master have done to you?

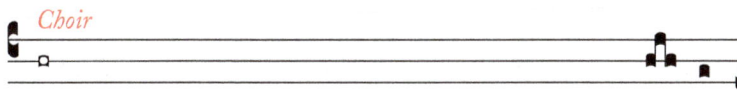

Choir

I have given you an example, that ye should do as I have

253

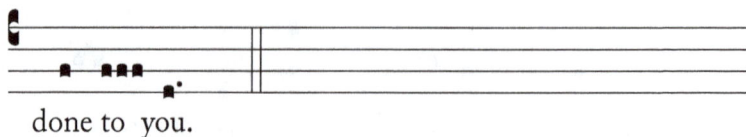

done to you.

During the distribution of Holy Communion, verses from Psalm 23, 72, 104, & 150 *may be sung to Tone ij.1.*

or Co. *Hoc corpus*   *I Cor. 11:24, 25*

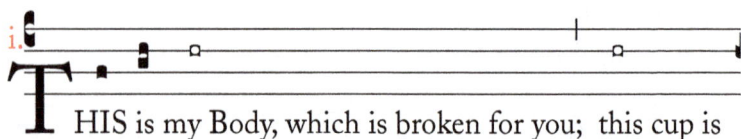

THIS is my Body, which is broken for you; this cup is

Cantors

the new co-ve-nant in my Blood: this do ye, as oft

Choir

as ye drink it, in re- mem- brance of me.

Verses from Psalm 23 *or* 116:10-16 *may be sung.*

At the transfer of the Blessed Sacrament: **Pange língua**, *1940 Hymnal 199, English Hymnal 326.*
The following antiphon and Psalm 22 *(p. 271) may be read in a low voice during the stripping of the Altar.*

ANTIPHON *Dívidunt*

They part my garments among them: and cast lots upon my vesture.

THE LITURGY OF THE WORD
At the Readings

RESPOND *Dómine, exáudi*   *Ps. 102: 2-5, 14*

Cantors

viij.

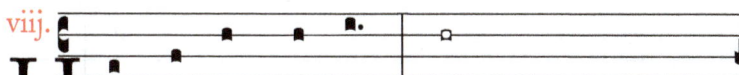

H̲EAR my prayer, O LORD, * and let my crying come

Choir

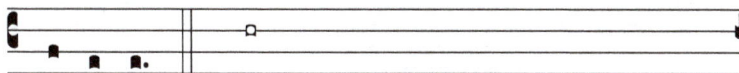

un-to thee. ℣. Hide not thy face from me in the time of

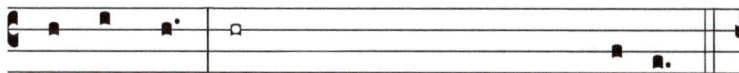

my trou-ble; * incline thine ear unto me when I call;

Cantors

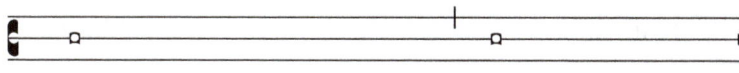

℣. O hear me, and that right soon. For my days are con-

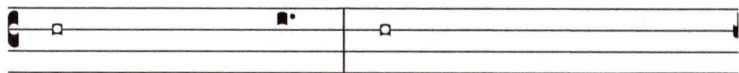

sumed away like smoke, * and my bones are burnt up

Choir

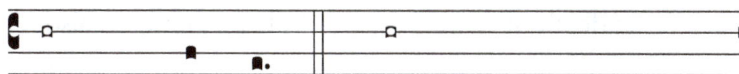

as it were a fire-brand. ℣. My heart is smitten down, and

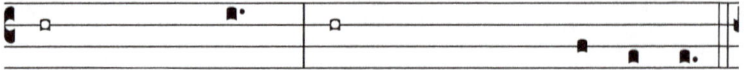

withered like grass; * so that I forget to eat my bread

Cantors

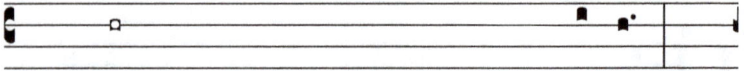

℣. Thou shalt arise, and have mercy upon Zi- on; *

Choir

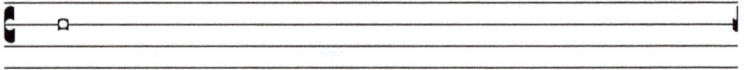

for it is time that thou have mercy upon her,

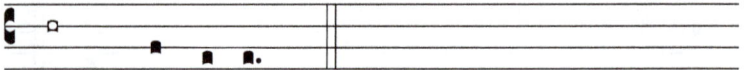

yea the time is come.

GRADUAL *Christus factus est*　　　　　　*Phil. 2:8,9*

Cantors

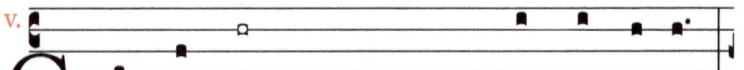

CHRIST be- came obedient for our sakes un- to death:

Choir　　　　　　　　　　　　*Cantors*

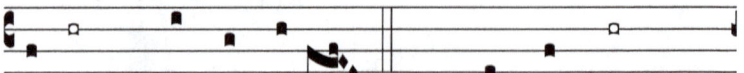

ev-en the death of the Cross. ℣. Where-fore God also

Choir

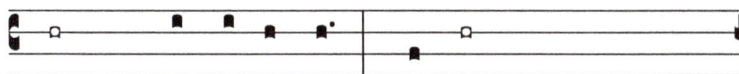

hath highly ex- al- ted him: and given him a Name

which is a- bove ev- ery name.

ADORATION OF THE HOLY CROSS
Invitation

ANTIPHON *Ecce lignum Crucis*

Priest or Cantor

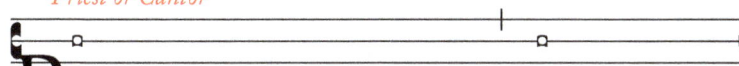

BEHOLD the wood of the Cross, whereon was hung

All

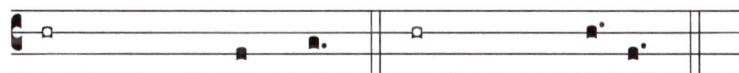

the Saviour of the   world.   O come, let us a-dore.

or this:

Priest or Cantor

vj.

BE-HOLD the wood of the   Cross, where-on was

hung the world's   Sal-va-   tion.

Full

O come, let us a- dore.

Antiphon *Crucem tuam adoramus* Ps. 67:1

Cantors *Choir*

iv.

WE wor-ship * thy ho- ly Cross, O Lord: and praise

and glo- ri- fy thy ho- ly re- sur- rec- tion. For by

vir- tue of the Cross ‡ joy hath come to the whole world.

Ps. God be mer- ci- ful un- to us, and bless us,

‡ *When a relic of the True Cross is used, the following may be substituted.*

vir- tue of this ve- ry wood

258

and show us the light of his coun- te- nance, and be

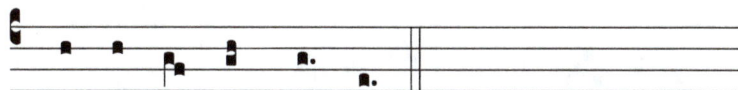

mer- ci- ful un- to   us.

And the antiphon is repeated We worship thy holy Cross.

The Reproaches
I

Two Cantors on the Decani side

℣.

O MY   peo- ple, what have I done un- to thee?

Or where- in   have I wea- ri- ed thee:

Tes- ti- fy 'a- gainst me. ℣. Be- cause I brought thee

forth from the land of E- gypt: thou hast

pre- pa- red a Cross for thy Sa- viour.

Decani Choir

℟. Há- gi- os o The- ós.

Cantoris Choir

Ho- ly God.

Decani Choir

Há- gi- os ís- chy- ros.

Cantoris Choir

Ho- ly, Migh- ty.

Decani Choir

Há- gi- os A- thá- na- tos, e- lé- i- son hi- mas.

Cantoris Choir

Ho- ly and Im- mor- tal, have mer- cy up- on us.

Two Cantors on the Cantoris side

℣. Be- cause I led thee through the de- sert

for - ty years, and fed thee with man- na, and brought thee

in- to   a land ex- cee- ding good: thou hast

pre- par- ed   a Cross for thy Sav- iour.   Hágios, *etc.*

Two Cantors on the Decani side

℣. What more could I have done for thee that I have

not done?   I   in- deed did plant thee,   O my

vine-yard, with ex-cee-ding fair fruit: and thou art be-

come ve- ry bit-ter un- to me: for vi-ne-gar,   min- gled

with gall, thou ga-vest me when thirs-ty, and hast

pierced with a spear the side of thy Sa- viour.

Hágios, *etc. with the remaining alternate choruses.*

II

The following verses may be added, if required:

Two Cantors on the Cantoris side:

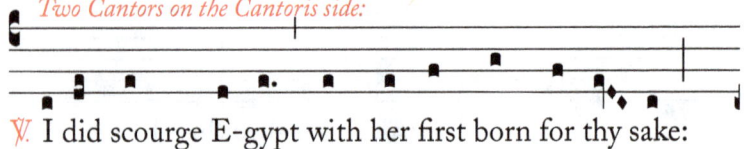

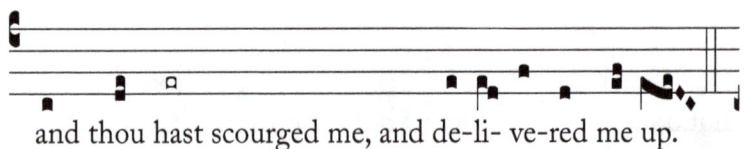

℣. I did scourge E-gypt with her first born for thy sake:

and thou hast scourged me, and de-li- ve-red me up.

Two Cantors

℟. O my peo-ple, . . . me. *(as on p. 259)* ℣. I led thee

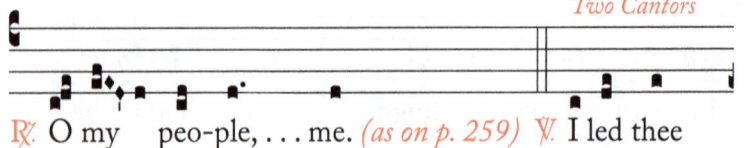

on the Decani side:

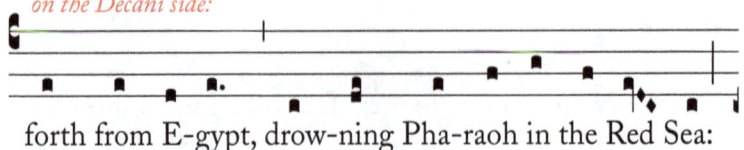

forth from E-gypt, drow-ning Pha-raoh in the Red Sea:

262

Choir

and thou hast delivered me up un-to the chief priests.

Two Cantors on the Cantoris side

℟. O my peo-ple, ... ℣. I did o-pen the sea be-fore thee:

Choir

and thou hast opened my side with a spear: ℟. O my ...

Two Cantors on the Decani side

℣. I did go before thee in the pil-lar of cloud: and thou

hast led me unto the judge-ment-hall of Pi- late

Two Cantors on the Cantoris side

℟. O my peo-ple, ... ℣. I did feed thee with man-na in

the de- sert: and thou hast stricken me with blows and

Two Cantors on the Decani side

scour-ges ℟ O my peo-ple, . . . ℣ I did give thee to

drink the wa-ter of life from the rock: and thou hast

Choir

given me to drink but gall and vi-ne-gar. ℟ O my . . .

Two Cantors on the Cantoris side:

℣ I did smite the kings of the Ca-naan-ites for thy sake:

Choir

and thou hast smit-ten my head with a reed. ℟ O my . . .

Two Cantors on the Decani side

℣. I did give thee a roy-al scep-tre: and thou hast given

Choir

unto my head a crown of thorns. ℟. O my peo-ple, ...

Two Cantors on the Cantoris side:

℣. I did raise thee on high with great power: and thou hast

Choir

hanged me upon the gib-bet of the Cross. ℟. O my ...

HYMN *Crux fidelis*   *Venantius Fortunatus*

i.

Faith-ful Cross, a - bove all o- ther One and on- ly

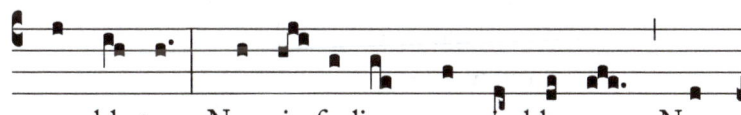

no - ble tree: None in fo-liage, none in blos-som, None

in fruit thy peer may be; Sweet-est wood and sweet-est

i- ron,   Sweet-est weight is hung on thee.

Pange lingua

(Verse 10 is never to be omitted.)

1.   Sing, my tongue, the glorious battle,
       Sing the ending of the fray,
   Now above the Cross, the trophy,
       Sound the loud triumphant lay:
   Tell how Christ, the world's redeemer,
       As a victim won the day.

℟.   Faithful Cross, . . . peer may be.

2.   God in pity saw man fallen,
       Shamed and sunk in misery.
   When he fell on death by tasting
       Fruit of the forbiden tree:
   Then another Tree was chosen
       Which the world from death should free.

℟.   Sweetest wood . . . hung on thee.

3.   Thus the scheme of our salvation
       Was of old in order laid:
   That the manifold deceiver's
       Art by art might be outweighed:
   And the lure the foe put forward,
       Into means of healing made.

℞. Faithful Cross, . . . peer may be.

4. Therefore when the appointed fulness
    Of the holy time was come,
He was sent who maketh all things
    Forth from God's eternal home:
Thus he came to earth incarnate,
    Offspring of a maiden's womb.

℞. Sweetest wood . . . hung on thee.

5. Lo! he lies, an infant weeping,
    Where the narrow manger stands:
While the Mother-maid his members
    Wraps in mean and lowly bands:
And the swaddling clothes is winding
    Round God's helpless feet and hands.

℞. Faithful Cross, . . . peer may be.

6. Thirty years among us dwelling,
    His appointed time fulfil'd,
Born for this, he meets his Passion,
    For that this he freely will'd:
On the Cross the Lamb is lifted
    Where his life-Blood shall be spilled.

℞. Sweetest wood . . . hung on thee.

7. He endur'd the nails, the spitting,
    Vinegar, and spear, and reed;
From that holy Body broken
    Blood and Water both proceed:
Earth, and stars, and sky, and ocean
    By that flood from stain are freed.

℞. Faithful Cross, . . . peer may be.

8.   Bend thy boughs, O tree of glory!
          Thy relaxing sinews bend;
      For awhile the ancient rigour
          That thy birth bestowed suspend:
      And the King of heav'nly beauty
          On thy bosom gently tend.

℟.   Sweetest wood . . . hung on thee.

9.   Thou alone wast counted worthy
          This world's ransom to uphold;
      For a shipwreck'd race preparing
          Harbour, like the Ark of old:
      With the sacred Blood anointed
          From the smitten Lamb that rolled.

℟.   Faithful Cross, . . . peer may be.

10. To the Tri- ni- ty be glo -ry   Ev- er - las - ting as is

meet; E - qual to the Fa - ther, e - qual   To the   Son

and Pa - ra - clete: Tri- nal U- ni- ty, whose prais- es

All cre- a- ted things re - peat.   A - men. ℟ Sweet-est.

THIRD PART:
The Holy Communion
The following antiphons may be sung during the return of the Blessed Sacrament:

ANTIPHON *Adoramus te* (G.H.P.)

i.

WE a-dore thee, * O Christ, and bless thee: for by

thy ho-ly Cross thou didst re-deem the world.

ANTIPHON *Per lignum*

viij.

THrough a tree * were we brought to bon-dage,

through the ho-ly Cross were we brought to free-dom;

the fruit of the tree be-tra-yed us, but the Son of God has

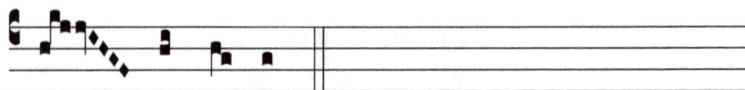

re-   dee-med us.

ANTIPHON *Salvator mundi*

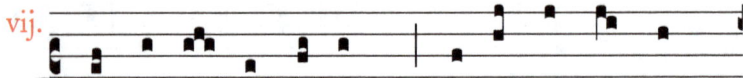

vij.

O Sa-viour of the world, * who by thy Cross and

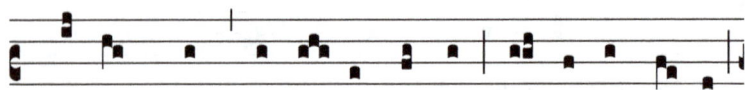

pre-cious Blood hast re-dee-med us; save us and help us,

we hum-bly be-seech thee O LORD.

GOOD FRIDAY

During the distribution of Holy Communion the following may be sung:
PSALM 22 *Deus, Deus meus*

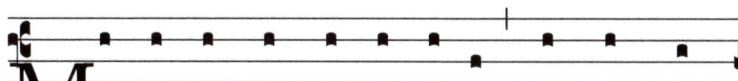

Y God, my God, look up-on me; † why hast *thou*

for-sa-ken me: * and art so far from my health, and

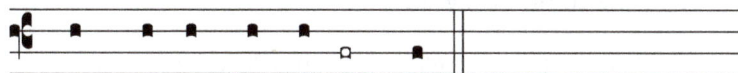

from the words of my *com*-plaint.

2 O my God, I cry in the day-time, but thou *hear*-est not; *
and in the night season also I take *no* rest.

3 And thou conti-*nu*-est holy, * O thou Worship of Is-*ra*-el.

4 Our fathers ho-*ped* in thee; * they trusted in thee, and
thou didst deli-*ver* them.

5 They called upon thee, *and* were holpen; * they put their
trust in thee, and were not confound-*ed*.

6 But as for me, I am a worm, *and* no man; * a very scorn
of men, and the outcast of the peo-*ple*.

7 All they that see me laugh *me* to scorn; * they shoot out
their lips, and shake their heads, say-*ing*,

8 He trusted in the LORD, that he *would* deliver him; * let him deliver him, if he will have *him*.

9 But thou art he that took me out of my *mo*-ther's womb; * thou wast my hope, when I hanged yet upon my mo-*ther's* breasts.

10 I have been left unto thee ever since *I* was born; * thou art my God even from my mo-*ther's* womb.

11 O go not from me; for trouble is *hard* at hand, * and there is none to help *me*.

12 Many oxen are *come* about me; * fat bulls of Bashan close me in on ev-*'ry* side.

13 They gape upon me *with* their mouths, * as it were a ramping and a roaring li-*on*.

14 I am poured out like water, † and all my bones are *out* of joint; * my heart also in the midst of my body is even like mel-*ting* wax.

15 My strength is dried up like a potsherd, † and my tongue cleaveth *to* my gums, * and thou bringest me into the dust *of* death.

16 For many dogs are *come* about me, * and the council of the wicked layeth siege against *me*.

17 They pierced my hands and my feet: † I may tell *all* my bones: * they stand staring and looking upon *me*.

18 They part my gar-*ments* among them, * and cast lots upon my ves-*ture*.

19 But be not thou far from *me,* O LORD; * thou art my succour, haste thee to help *me.*

20 Deliver my soul *from* the sword, * my darling from the power of the *dog.*

21 Save me from the *li*-on's mouth; * thou hast heard me also from among the horns of the u-*ni*-corns.

22 I will declare thy Name un-*to* my brethren; * in the midst of the congregation will I praise *thee.*

23 O praise the LORD, *ye* that fear him: * magnify him, all ye of the seed of Jacob; | and fear him, all ye seed of Is-*ra*-el.

24 For he hath not despised nor abhorred the low estate *of* the poor; * he hath not hid his face from him; | but when he called unto him he heard *him.*

25 My praise is of thee in the great *con*-gregation; * my vows will I perform in the sight of them that fear *him.*

26 The poor shall eat, and be satisfied; † they that seek after the LORD shall praise him: * your heart shall live for e-*ver.*

27 All the ends of the world shall remember themselves, † and be turned un-*to* the LORD; * and all the kindreds of the nations shall worship before *him.*

28 For the kingdom *is* the LORD'S, * and he is the Gover-nor among the na-*tions.*

29 All such as be fat *up*-on earth * have eaten, and wor-
   ship-ped.

30 All they that go down into the dust shall *kneel* before
   him; * and no man hath quickened his own *soul.*

31 My *seed* shall serve him: * they shall be counted unto
   the LORD for a genera-*tion.*

32 They shall come, and shall de-*clare* his righteousness *
   unto a people that shall be born, whom the LORD *hath*
   made.

A Liturgy of the Word for Holy Saturday

ANTIPHON AND PSALM *Sicut cervus*   *Ps. 42: 1-7*

ij. MY soul is a-thirst for God, yea, ev-en for the liv-ing

God: when shall I come to ap-pear be-fore the pre-

sence of God?

1 Like as the hart de-sir-eth the *wa*-ter-brooks: *

so long-eth my soul af-*ter* thee, O God.

2 My soul is athirst for God, yea, even for the *liv*-ing God: *
when shall I come to appear before the pres-*ence* of
God?

3 My tears have been my meat *day* and night: * while they
daily say unto me, Where is *now* thy God?

4   Now when I think thereupon, I pour out my heart *by*
    my-self: * for I went with the multitude, and brought
    them forth into the *house* of God;

5   In the voice of praise and thanks-*giv*-ing: * among such
    as keep *ho*-ly-day.

6   Why art thou so full of heaviness, *O* my soul: * and why
    art thou so disquiet-*ed* with-in me?

7   O put thy *trust* in God: * for I will yet thank him, which
    is the help of my countenance, *and* my God.

The antiphon is repeated.

PSALM *De profundis*   *Ps. 130*

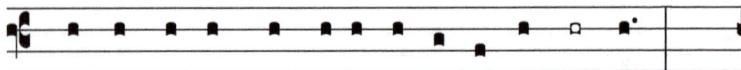

1   Out of the deep have I call-ed *un-to* thee, O LORD: *

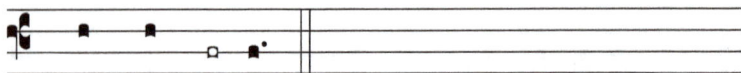

    Lord, *hear* my voice.

2   O let thine ears con-*si-der* well: * the voice of *my* com-
    plaint.

3   If thou, LORD, wilt be extreme to mark what is *done a-*
    miss: * O Lord, who may a-*bide* it?

4   For there is mer-*cy with* thee: * therefore shalt thou be
    fear-ed.

5   I look for the LORD; my soul doth *wait for* him: * in his
    word *is* my trust.

6   My soul fleeth unto the Lord before the *morning* watch: *
    I say, before the morn-*ing* watch.

7   O Israel, trust in the LORD; for with the LORD *there is*
    mercy, * and with him is plenteous re-*demp*-tion.

8   And he shall redeem *Is–ra*-el: * from all *his* sins.

PSALM *Anima mea conturbata*   *Ps. 42:8–15*

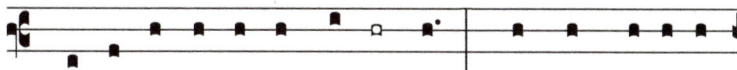

8   My soul is vex-ed with-*in*   me: * there-fore will I re-

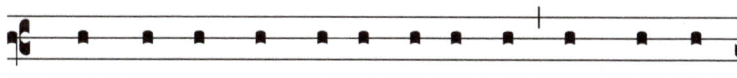

mem-ber thee from the land of Jor-dan, from Her-mon

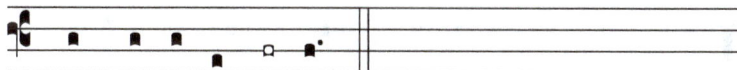

and the *lit*-tle   hill.

9   One deep calleth another, because of the noise of thy
    wa-ter-floods: * all thy waves and storms are gone *o*-ver
    me.

10 The Lord will grant his loving-kindness in the *day*-time: *
    and in the night season will I sing of him, and make my
    prayer unto the God *of* my life.

11 I will say unto the God of my strength, Why hast thou
    for-*got*-ten me? * Why go I thus heavily, while the en-
    emy op-*press*-eth me?

12 My bones are smitten asunder as with *a* sword: * while mine enemies that trouble me cast me *in* the teeth.

13 Namely, while they say daily *un*-to me: * Where is *now* thy God?

14 Why art thou so vexed, O *my* soul: * and why art thou so disquieted *with*-in me?

15 O put thy *trust* in God: * for I will yet thank him, which is the help of my countenance, *and* my God.

At the conclusion of the homily, the following anthem, or another hymn may be said or sung:

ANTHEM *Media víta in mórte súmus* (Merbecke)

IN the midst of life we are in death: of whom may

we seek for suc-cour, but of thee, O LORD, who for

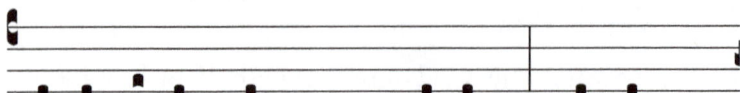

our sins art just- ly dis- pleas-ed? Yet, O

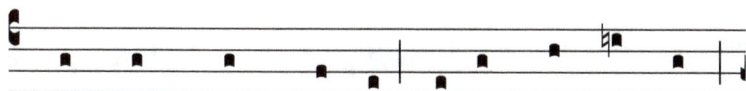

Lord God, most, Ho- ly   O Lord most migh-ty,

O ho-ly and most mer-ci-ful Sav-iour: † de- li- ver us not

FINE

in- to the bit-ter pains of e- ter- nal death. ℣. Thou

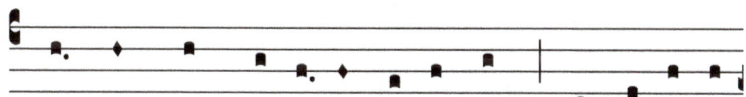

know-est, Lord, the se-crets of our hearts; shut not up thy

mer-ci-ful ears to our prayer: but spare us, Lord most

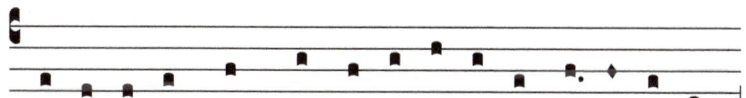

ho-ly, O God most migh-ty, O hol-y and mer-ci-ful Sav-

iour, thou most wor-thy Judge e-ter-nal. Suf-fer us not, at

our last hour, through a-ny pains of death, to fall from thee.

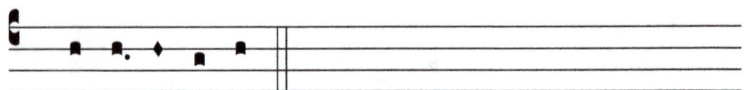

† de- li- ver us not *(etc.)*

SEASON OF EASTER
THE SOLEMN VIGIL OF EASTER

I. The Blessing of the New Fire and Lucernarium

Priest   *Response*

℣. The LORD be with you. ℟. And with thy spi-rit.

Priest   *Response*

Let us pray. . . . ℟. A- men.

During the Solemn Procession the Deacon sings:

Deacon   *Response*

℣. The Light of Christ.   ℟. Thanks be to God.
This is sung three times, each time in a higher tone.

EXSULTET
Deacon

viij.

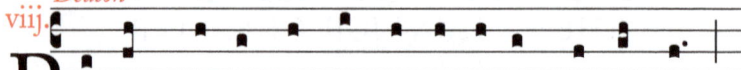

RE- joice now, all ye hea-ven-ly le-gions of An-gels . . .

vj.

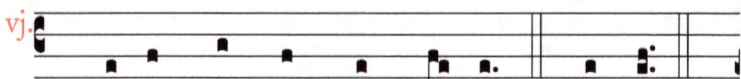

ev- er one God, world with- out end. ℟. A- men.

℣. The LORD be with you. ℟. And with thy spi- rit.

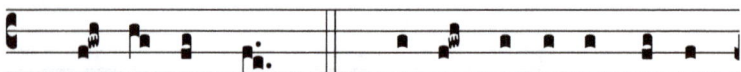

℣. Lift up your hearts. ℟. We lift them up un- to the

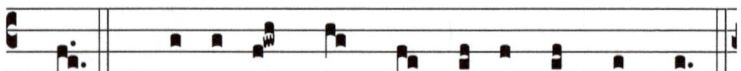

LORD. ℣. Let us give thanks un- to the LORD our God.

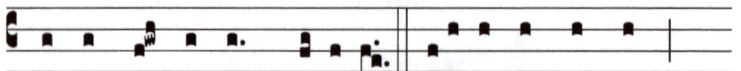

℟. It is meet and right so to do. It is ve-ry meet, right . . .

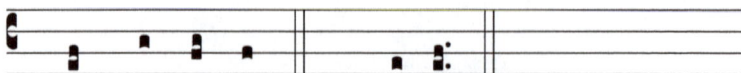

world with-out end. ℟. A-men.

II. The Lessons

After the First Lesson: **The Creation** *(Genesis 1:1-2:2)*

In- to- nation.   Medi- á- tion.   And thîs the én- ding.

PSALM 104: 1-2,5-6,10,12-15,24,30,36 *Benedic, ánima mea.*

PRAISE the LORD, O mý soul: * O LORD my God, thou art become exceeding glorious; thou art clothed with majestŷ and hónour.

2 Thou deckest thyself with light as it were with a gárment, * and spreadest out the heavens lîke a cúrtain.

5 He laid the foundations of thé earth, * that it never should môve at ány time.

6 Thou coveredst it with the deep like as with a gárment; * the waters stând abóve the hills.

10 He sendeth the springs into the rívers, * which rûn amóng the hills.

12 Beside them shall the fowls of the air have their habitátion, * and sing amông the bránches.

13 He watereth the hills from abóve; * the earth is filled with the frûit of thý works.

14 He bringeth forth grass for the cattle, and green herb for the service óf men; * that he may bring food oût of thé earth.

24 O LORD, how manifold are thý works! * in wisdom hast thou made them all; the earth is full ôf thy ríches.

30 When thou lettest thy breath go forth, they shall bé made; * and thou shalt renew the fâce of thé earth.

36 Praise thou the LORD, O mý soul. * Prâise the LÓRD.

283

or

PSALM 33: 4-7,12-13,19-21 *Quia rectum est verbum*

THE word of the LORD ís true: * and all his wôrks are faíthful.

5   He loveth righteousness and júdgment: * the earth is full of the goodnêss of thé LORD.

6   By the word of the LORD were the heavéns made: * and all the host of them by the breâth of hís mouth.

7   He gathereth the waters of the sea together, as it were upon án heap: * and layeth up the deep, as în a treásure-house.

12 Blessed are the people whose God is thé LORD: * and blessed are the folk that he hath chosen to him, to be hîs inhéritance.

13 The LORD looketh down from heaven, and beholdeth all the children óf men: * from the habitation of his dwelling, he considereth all them that dwêll on thé earth.

19 Our soul hath patiently tarried for thé LORD: * for he is our hêlp and oúr shield.

20 For our heart shall rejoice ín him: * because we have-hoped în his hóly Name.

21 Let thy merciful kindness, O LORD, be upón us. * like as we do pût our trúst in thee.

After the Second Lesson: **The Sacrifice of Abraham** *(Genesis 22:1-18)*

In- to- nation. Medi- á- tion. And this thê énd- ing.

PSALM 16:1,6,9-12 *Conserva me, Deus*

PRE-SERVE me, Ó God: * for in thee have I pût mý trust.

6 The LORD himself is the portion of mine inheritance and of my cúp: * Thou shalt maintâin mý lot.

9 I have set the LORD alway befóre me: * for he is on my right hand, therefore I shâll nót fall.

10 Wherefore my heart is glad, and my glory rejoíceth: * my flesh also shall rêst ín hope.

11 For why? thou shalt not leave my soul in héll: * neither shalt thou suffer thy Holy One to see côrrúption.

12 Thou shalt show me the path of life; in thy presence is the fulness of jóy: * and at thy right hand there is pleasure for êvérmore.

After the Third Lesson: **Israel's Deliverance at the Red Sea** *(Exodus 14:10 - 15:1)*

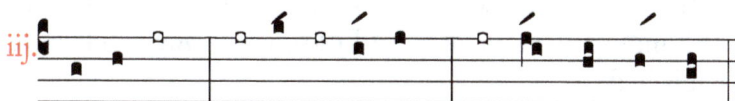

In- to- nation. Mê-di- á- tion. And thîs the énd- ing.

CANTICLE *Cantémus Dómino*   *Exodus 15:1-6,[11-13],17-18*

I WILL sing unto the LORD, for he hath triumphed glôrióusly: * the horse and his rider hath he thrown înto thé sea.

285

The LORD is my strêngth ánd song: * and he is become mŷ salvátion:

He is my God and I will prepare him an hâbitátion: * my father's God and I wîll exált him.

The LORD îs a man óf war: * the LÔRD is hís Name.

Pharaoh's chariots and his host hath he cast întó the sea: * his chosen captains also are drowned în the Réd Sea.

The depths have côveréd them: * they sank into the bôttom as á stone.

Thy right hand, O LORD, is become glôrious in pówer: * thy right hand, O LORD, hath dashed in pieces thê enémy.

[Who is like unto thee, O LÓRD, among thé gods?: * who is like thee, glorious in holiness, fearful in praises, dôing wónders?

Thou stretchedst ôut thy ríght hand: * the earth swâllowéd them.

Thou in thy mercy led forth the people which thôu hast redéemed: * thou hast guided them in they strength unto thy holy hâbitátion.]

Thou shalt bring them în, and plánt them * in the mountain of thine înherîtance,

In the place, O LORD, which thou hast made for theê to dwéll in: * in the sanctuary, O LORD, which thy hands have êstablíshed.

The Lôrd shall reígn * for ever ând for éver.

After the Fourth Lesson: **The New Jerusalem** *(Isaiah 54:5-14)*

In- to- nation. Mê-di- á- tion. And thîs is the énd- ing.

or PSALM 30:1-5,11-13 *Exaltabo te, Domine.*

I WILL magnify thee, O LORD; for thou hast sêt me úp: *
and not made my foes to trîumph ovér me.

2   O LORD my God, I cried ûnto thée: * and thoû hast
healéd me.

3   Thou, LORD, hast brought my soul ôut of héll: * thou
hast kept my life, that I should not go dôwn into thé pit.

4   Sing praises unto the LORD, Ô ye saínts of his: * and
give thanks unto him, for a remembrance ôf his holîness.

5   For his wrath endureth but the twinkling of an eye,
and in his pleasûre is lífe: * heaviness may endure for a night,
but joy comêth in the mórning.

11   Hear, O LORD, and have mercý upón me: * LORD, bê
thou my hélper.

12   Thou hast turned my heaviness înto jóy: * thou hast
put off my sackcloth, and girdêd me with gládness:

13   Therefore shall every good man sing of thy praise
wîthout ceásing: * O my God, I will give thanks untô thee
for éver.

After the Fifth Lesson: **Salvation Freely offrered** *(Isaiah 55:1-11)*

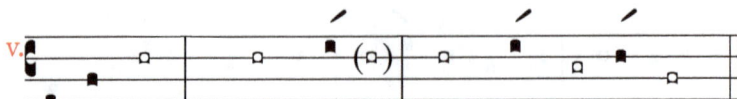

In- to- nation. Me-di- á- tion. And thîs the énd-ding.

CANTICLE *Ecce, Deus. Isaiah 12:2-6*

BEHOLD, God is my salvátion: * I will trust and nôt be áfraid:

For the Lord God is my strength and my sóng: * he also is become mŷ salvátion.

Therefore with joy shall ye draw wáter: * out of the wells ôf salvátion.

And in that day shall ye saý: * Praise the Lord, câll upón his Name;

Declare his doings among the peóple: * make mention that his Name îs exálted.

Sing unto the Lord, for he hath done excellent thíngs: * this is knôwn in áll the earth.

Cry out and shout, thou inhabitant of Zíon: * for great is the Holy One of Israel în the mídst of thee.

After the Sixth Lesson: **The Fountain of Wisdom** *(Bar. 3:9-15,31-4:4)*

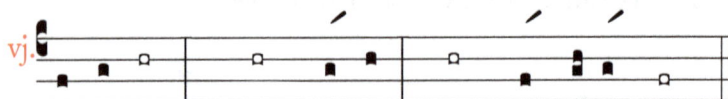

In- to- nation. Me-di- á- tion. And thîs the énd-ing.

PSALM 19:7-10 *Lex Dómini immaculáta*

THE law of the LORD is an undefiled law, converting thé soul: * the testimony of the LORD is sure and giveth wis-dom untô the símple.

8   The statutes of the LORD are right, and rejoice thé heart: *
the commandment of the LORD is pure, and giveth light ûnto
thé eyes.

9   The fear of the LORD is clean, and endureth foréver: *
the judgments of the LORD are true, and righteous âltogéther.

10   More to be desired are they than gold, yea, than much
fíne gold: * sweeter also than honey, ând the hóneycomb.

After the Seventh Lesson: **A new heart and a new spirit** *(Ezekiel 36:24-28)*

In- to- nation.   Mê-di- á- tion.   And thîs the énd- ing.

PSALM 42:1-5;43:3-4 *Sicut cervus*

LIKE as the hart desireth thê watér-brooks: * so longeth
my soul âfter theé, O God.

2   My soul is athirst for God, yea, even for thê lívíng God: *
when shall I come to appear before the prêsence óf God?

3   My tears have been my mêat day ánd night: * while
they daily say unto me, Whêre is nów thy God?

4   Now when I think thereupon, I pour out my heârt by
mýself; * for I went with the multitude, and brought them
forth intô the hoúse of God;

5   In the voice of praise ând thanksgíving: * among such
âs keep hóly-day.

3   O send out thy light and thy truth, that thêy may léad
me, * and bring me unto thy holy hill, and tô thy dwélling.

4   And that I may go unto the altar of God, even unto
the God of my jôy and gládness; * and upon the harp will I
give thanks unto thêe, O Gód, my God.

III. The Liturgy of Holy Baptism

After the last lesson from the Old Testament with its canticle and prayer is sung Gloria in excelsis.

After the Epistle the Celebrant sings Alleluia *thrice, a little higher in pitch each time, and the Choir repeats it each time in the same manner:*

viij.
AL- le lu- ia.

Immediately after the third repetition the Choir proceeds:

Confitémini Dómino

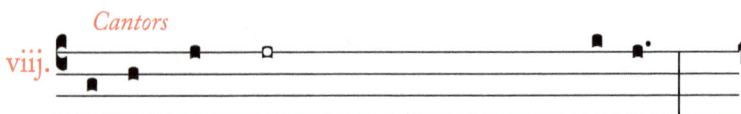

Cantors

viij.

℣. O give thanks unto the LORD, for he is gra-cious:

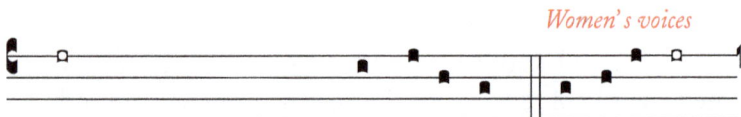

Women's voices

because his mercy endur-eth for ev-er. ℣. Let Is-ra-el now

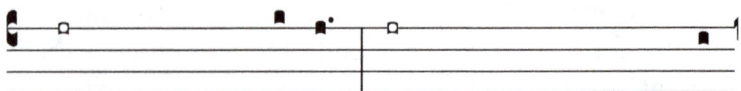

confess that he is grac-ious: and that his mercy endur-eth

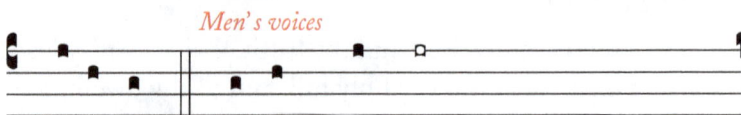

Men's voices

for ev-er. ℣. The right hand of the LORD hath the pre-

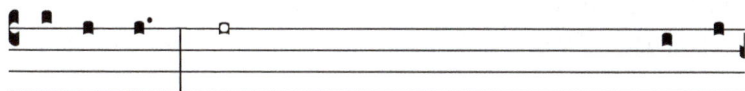

em-i-nence: the right hand of the Lord bringeth migh-ty

Women's voices

things to pass. ℣. I shall not die, but live: and declare the

Men's voices

works of the LORD. ℣. The same stone which the builders

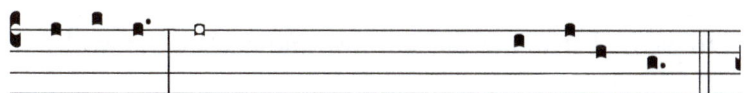

re-fus- ed: is become the head-stone in the cor-ner.

Full

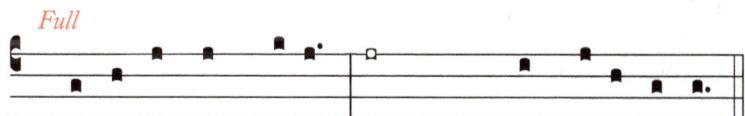

℣. This is the Lord's do-ing: and it is mar-vel-lous in our eyes.
Then the Alleluia *is repeated.*

During the procession to the font, the following may be sung without anti-
phon:

CANTICLE *Sicut cervus, Ps. 42:1-3 (Holy Saturday, p. 275, vs. 1-3)*

Then follows the Gospel and Homily. The Creed is not said. The Litany
of the Saints and Sacrament of Baptism or the Renewal of Baptismal Vows
may follow. During the sprinkling of the people, Vidi aquam, *as found in*
the Common Tones, (page 790) may be sung.

IV. The Liturgy of the Holy Eucharist

OFFERTORY *Déxtera Dómini*   *Ps. 118:16, 17*

Cantors

ij.

THE right hand of the LORD hath the pre-eminence;

the right hand of the LORD bring- eth migh- ty things

Choir

to pass: I shall not die, but live, and declare the works

of the LORD, al- le- lu- ia.

COMMUNION *Pascha nostrum*   *I Cor. 5:7,8*

Cantors

i.

CHRIST our Passover is sacrificed for us, al-le-lu-ia:

Choir

there-fore let us keep the feast with the unleavened bread

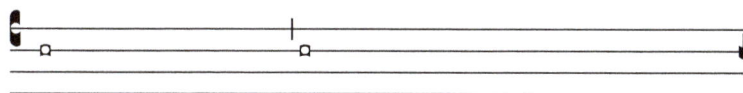

of sincerity and truth, alleluia,

Full

al- le- lu- ia, al- le- lu- ia.

Psalm 118: 1,2,5,8,10,11,13-16, 23-25 *may be sung.*

or

vj.

AL-le- lu- ia, * al- le- lu- ia, al- le- lu- ia.

which may be repeated after singular verses of Psalm 34.

DISMISSAL

Deacon or Priest

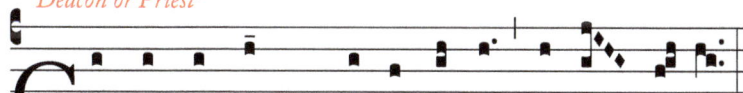

GO-forth in peace, * al- le- lu- ia, al- le- lu- ia.

All

Thanks be to God, * al- le- lu- ia, al- le- lu- ia.

EASTER DAY

INTROIT *Resurrexi*   *Ps. 139:18, 5, 6 & 1-2*

Cantors

vij.

I AM risen, and am still with thee, al-le-lu-ia;

thou hast laid thine hand upon me, al - le - lu - ia:

Choir

thy know-ledge is too wonderful and excellent for me.

FINE

Al- le- lu- ia.   Al- le- lu- ia.   Al - le- lu- ia.

Cantors

Ps. O LORD, thou hast searched me out, and known me:

Choir

thou knowest my down-sitting, and mine up- ris- ing.

Cantors *Choir* *Full*

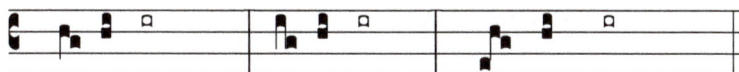

Glo- ry be..., *(etc.)* As it was..., *(etc.)* I am risen...,*(etc.)*

GRADUAL *Hæc dies*   *Ps. 116:24 & 1*

Cantors   *Choir*

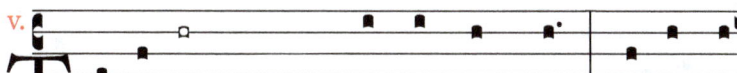

THIS is the day which the LORD hath made: we will be

Cantors

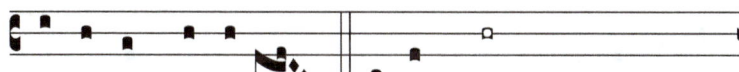

joy-ful and glad in it.   ℣. O give thanks unto the LORD,

Choir

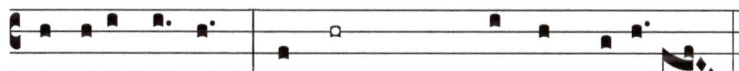

for he is gra-cious: and his mercy en-du-reth for ev-er.

ALLELUIA *Pascha nostrum*   *I Cor. 5:7*

Cantors   *All*

AL- LE- LU-IA. Al - le- lu- ia.

Cantors   *Choir*

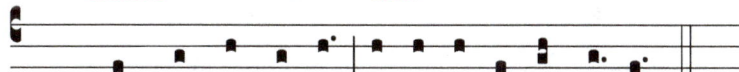

℣. Christ our Pass-o- ver: is sac-ri- fi- ced for us.

295

Then at once, without any repetition of the Alleluia is sung the Sequence,

SEQUENCE *Victimæ pascháli laudes*

Full Choir

i.

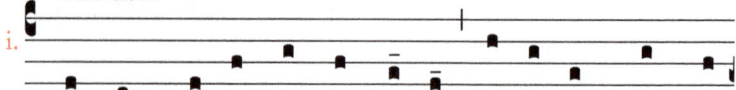

Chris-tians, to the Pas-chal Vic-tim Of-fer your thank-ful

Treble voices

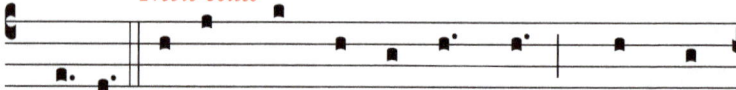

prai-ses. A Lamb the sheep re-deem-eth: Christ, who

on-ly is sin-less, Re-con-cil-eth sin-ners to the Fa-

Full Choir

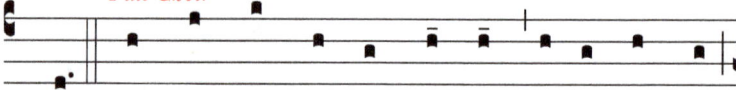

ther. Death and life have con-tend-ed In that com-bat

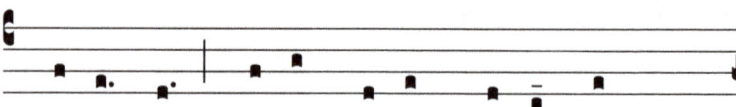

stu-pen-dous: The Prince of Life, who died, reigns

Lower voices

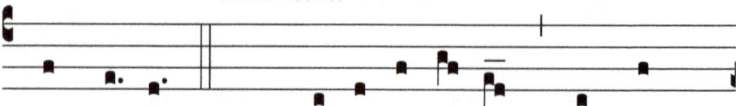

im-mor-tal. Speak, Ma-ry, de-clar-ing What thou

Treble voices

saw- est way-far-ing. 'The Tomb of Christ, who is liv-

ing, The glo-ry of Je-sus' Re-sur-rec-tion: Bright An-

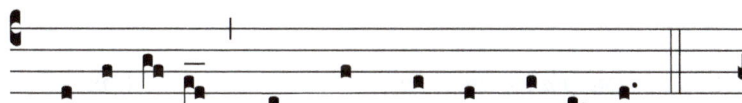

gels at-test-ing, The shroud and nap-kin rest-ing.

Yea, Christ my hope is a- ris- en; To Ga-li-lee he goes

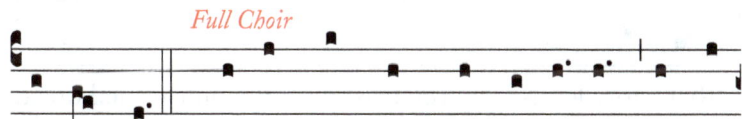

Full Choir

be-fore you.' Christ in-deed from death is ris-en, our new

life ob-tain-ing. Have mer-cy, vic-tor King, ev-er reign-ing!

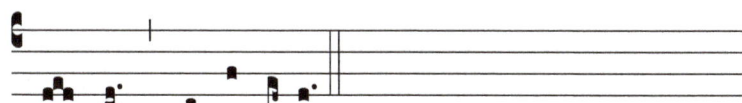

A-men.　Al-le- lu-ia.

297

OFFERTORY *Terra trémuit*   *Ps. 76:8b,9a*

Cantors   *Choir*

THE earth trem- bled and was still: when God

arose to judge- ment, al- le- lu- ia.

COMMUNION *Pascha nostrum*   *I Cor. 5:7,8*

Cantors

CHRIST our Passover is sacrificed for us, al-le-lu-ia:

Choir

there-fore let us keep the feast with the unleavened bread

of sincerity and truth. Alleluia. Allelu- ia. Al- le- lu- ia.

Psalm 118: 1,2,5,8,10,11,13-16, 23-25 *may be sung.*

Monday in the Octave of Easter

INTROIT *Introdúxit vos*   *Ex. 13:5,9; Ps. 105:1*

Cantors

vij.

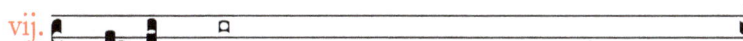

THE LORD hath brought you into a land flowing with

Choir

milk and honey, al-le-lu-ia: that the law of the LORD may

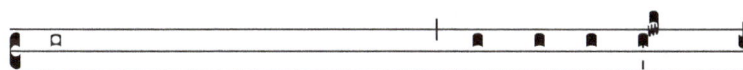

always be in your heart. Alleluia. Al- le- lu- ia.

FINE   *Cantors*

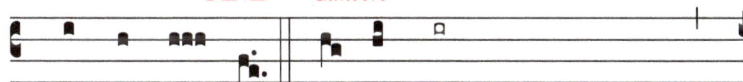

Al - le-   lu- ia. *Ps.* O give thanks unto the LORD,

Choir

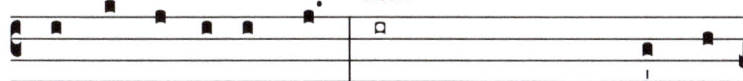

and call up-on his Name: tell the people what things he

Cantors   *Choir*

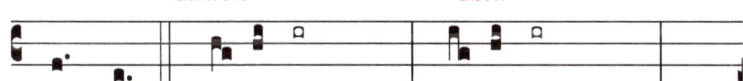

hath done. Glo- ry be..., *(etc.)*   As it was..., *(etc.)*

Full

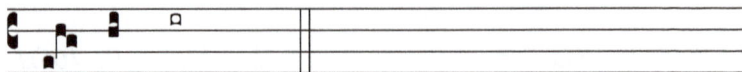

The LORD hath...,*(etc.)*

GRADUAL *Hæc dies...Dicat nunc*   Ps. 118:24,2

Cantors   *Choir*

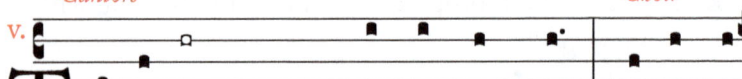

THIS is the day which the LORD hath made: we will be

Cantors

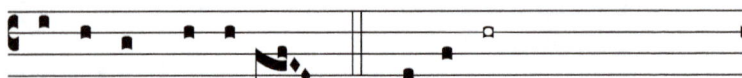

joy-ful and glad in it.   ℣. Let Is-ra-el now confess that

Choir

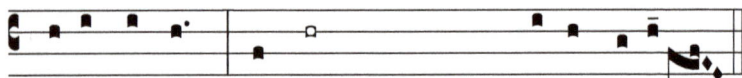

he is gra-cious: and that his mercy en-dur-eth for ev-er.

ALLELUIA *Angelus Dómini*   Mt. 28:2

Cantors   *All*

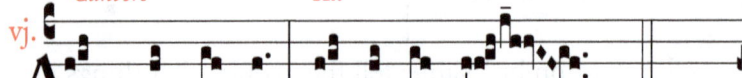

AL- LE- LU-IA. Al - le-lu- ia.

Cantors   *Choir*

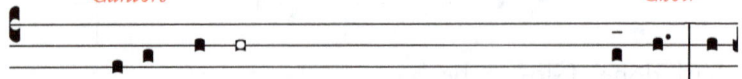

℣. The An-gel of the LORD descended from hea-ven: and

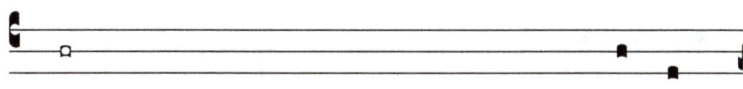

came and rolled back the stone from the door, and sat

All

up-on it.   Al - le- lu- ia.

The Sequence Victimæ paschali laudes, *p. 296 ff, may be said throughout the Octave.*

OFFERTORY *Angelus Dómini (Easter II, p. 318)*

COMMUNION *Surréxit Dóminus (Easter III, p. 323)*

Tuesday in the Octave of Easter

INTROIT *Aqua sapiéntiæ*   *Sir. 15:3,4; Ps. 105:1*

Cantors

vij.

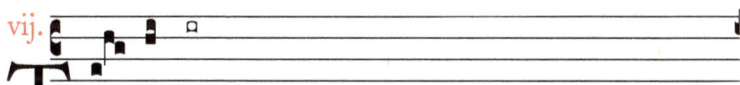

THE wa-ter of wisdom hath he given them to drink,

Choir

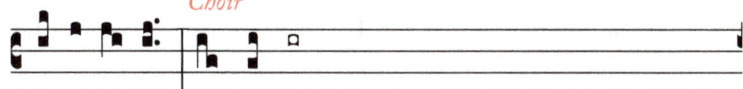

al-le-lu-ia: he shall be stablished in them, and shall not

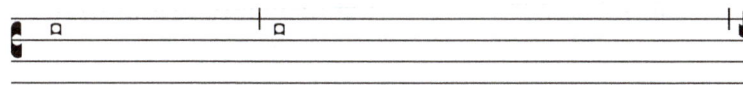

be moved, alleluia: and shall exalt them for ever. Alleluia.

FINE   *Cantors*

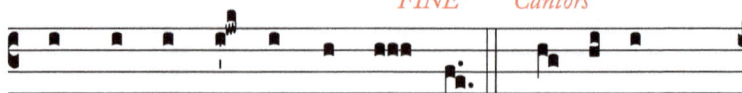

Al- le- lu- ia. Al - le- lu- ia. *Ps.* O give thanks

Choir

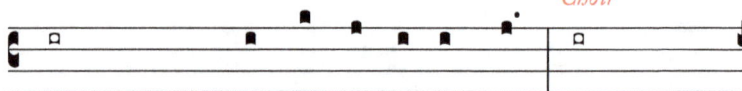

unto the LORD, and call up-on his Name: tell the people

Cantors

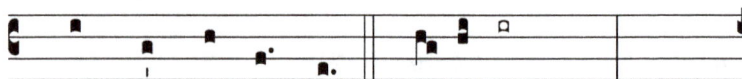

what things he hath done.   Glo- ry be..., *(etc.)*

Choir   *Full*

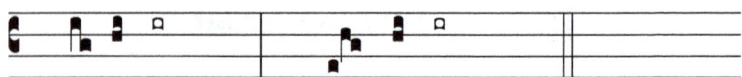

As it was..., *(etc.)*   The wa-ter...,*(etc.)*

GRADUAL *Hæc dies...Dicant nunc*   Ps. 118:24, ℣.107:2

Cantors   *Choir*

v.

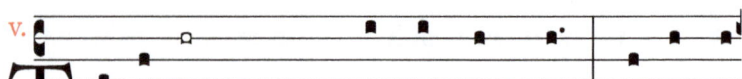

THIS is the day which the LORD hath made: we will be

Cantors

joy-ful and glad in it.   ℣. Let them give thanks whom

302

Choir

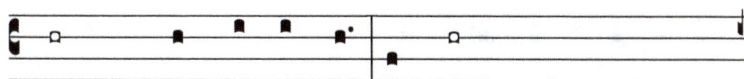

the LORD hath re-deem-ed: and delivered from the hand

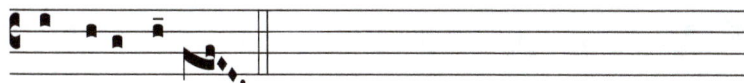

of the e-ne-my.

ALLELUIA *Surréxit Dóminus de sepúlchro*

Cantors   *All*

vj.

AL- LE- LU-IA. Al - le- lu- ia.

Cantors   *Choir*

℣. The LORD hath risen from the tomb: who hung for us

All

up-on the Tree. Al - le- lu- ia.

OFFERTORY *Intónuit de cælo*   *Ps. 18:14,16*

Cantors

ij.

THE LORD thun-dered out of heaven, and the High-

Choir

est ut-ter-ed his voice: and springs of water were seen.

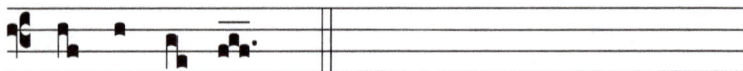

Al- le- lu- ia.

COMMUNION *Si consurrexístis*   *Col. 3:1,2*

Cantors

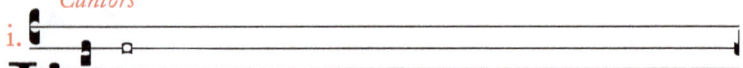

IF ye then be risen with Christ, seek those things which

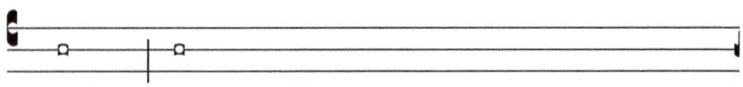

are above, where Christ sitteth on the right hand of God,

Choir

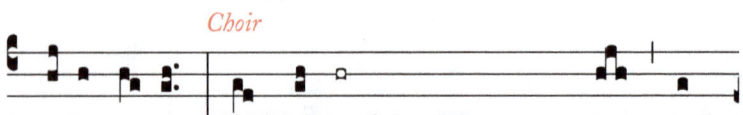

al- le- lu- ia: set your affection on things a-bove. Al-

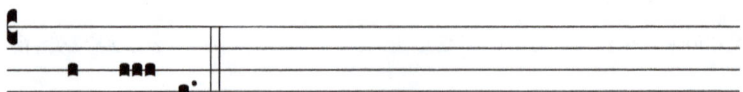

le- lu- ia.

Psalm 105: 1-5,42 *may be sung.*

Wednesday in the Octave of Easter

INTROIT *Veníte benedícti*   *Mt. 25:34; Ps. 96:1*

Cantors

vij.

COME, ye blessed of my Father, inherit the kingdom,

Choir

al-le-lu-ia: which hath been prepared for you from the

foundation of the world. Alleluia.   Al- le- lu- ia.

FINE   *Cantors*

Al - le- lu- ia. *Ps.* O sing unto the LORD a new song:

Choir   *Cantors*

sing unto the LORD, all the whole earth.   Glo- ry be...,

Choir   *Full*

As it was..., *(etc.)*   Come, ye blessed...,*(etc.)*

305

GRADUAL *Hæc dies...Déxtera Dómini*   *Ps. 118:24,16*

Cantors   *Choir*

THIS is the day which the LORD hath made: we will be

Cantors

joy-ful and glad in it. ℣. The right hand of the LORD

Choir

hath the pre-em-i-nence: The right hand of the LORD

bring-eth migh-ty things to pass.

ALLELUIA *Surréxit Dóminus vere*   *Lk. 24:34*

Cantors   *All*

vj.

AL- LE-LU-IA. Al - le- lu- ia.

Cantors   *Choir*

℣. The LORD is risen in-deed: and hath appeared un-to

All

Pe-ter.   Al - le- lu- ia.

OFFERTORY *Portas cæli* *(Corpus Christi, p. 487)*

COMMUNION *Christus resúrgens*   Rom. 6:9

Cantors

i.

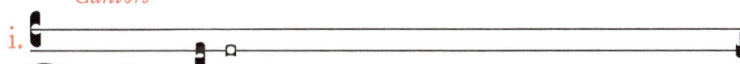

CHRIST be-ing raisèd from the dead, dieth no more,

Choir

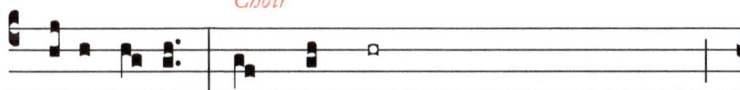

al- le- lu-ia: death hath no more dominion over him.

Allelu- ia.   Al- le- lu- ia.

Psalm 96: 1-4,7-9a *may be sung.*

Thursday in the Octave of Easter

INTROIT *Victrícem manum*   *Wis. 10:20,21; Ps. 98:1*

Cantors

vij.

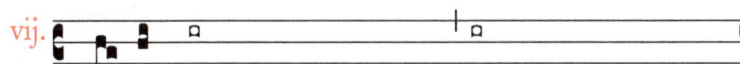

THY vic-torious hand, O LORD, have they magnified

307

Choir

with one accord, al-le-lu-ia: for wis-dom hath opened

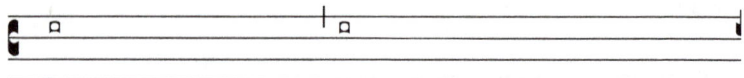

the mouth of the dumb, and made eloquent the tongues

FINE

of babes. Alleluia.   Al- le- lu- ia.   Al - le-   lu- ia.

Cantors   *Choir*

Ps. O sing unto the LORD a new song: for he hath done

Cantors   *Choir*

mar-vel-lous things. Glo- ry be...,   As it was..., *(etc.)*

Full

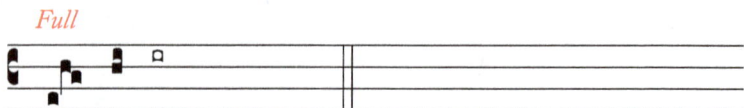

Thy vic-torious..., *(etc.)*

GRADUAL *Hæc dies...Lápidem*   *Ps. 118:24,22,23*

Cantors   *Choir*

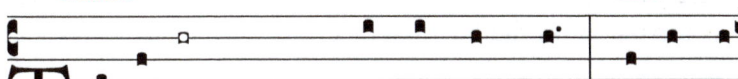

THIS is the day which the LORD hath made: we will be

Cantors

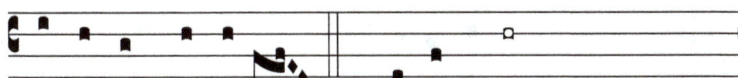

joy-ful and glad in it. ℣. The same stone which the

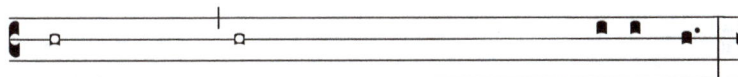

builders refused, is become the headstone in the cor-ner

Choir

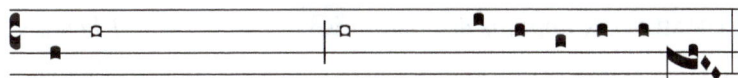

This is the Lord's doing; and it is mar-vel-lous in our eyes.

ALLELUIA *Surréxit Christus, qui creávit*

Cantors   *All*

vj.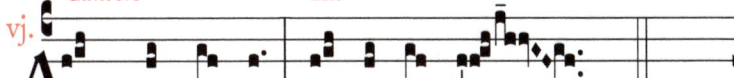

AL- LE- LU-IA. Al - le- lu- ia.

Cantors   *Choir*

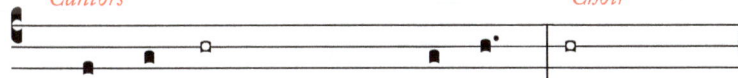

℣. Christ hath risen, who created all things: and hath had

309

All

compassion on the hu-man race. Al - le- lu- ia.

OFFERTORY *In die solemnitátis*   *Ex. 13:5*

Cantors   *Choir*

ij.

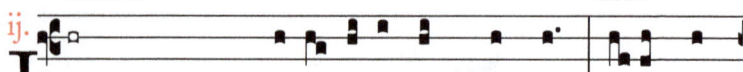

IN the day of your fes-ti-vi-ty, saith the LORD: I will bring

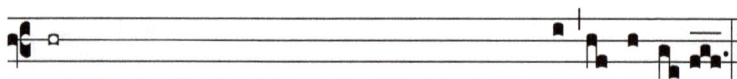

you into a land flowing with milk and hon-ey. al- le- lu- ia.

COMMUNION *Populus acquisitiónis*   *1 Pet. 2:9*

Cantors

i.

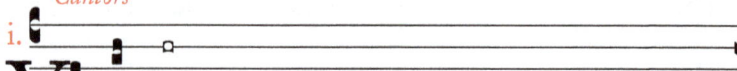

YE are God's own people, that ye should show forth his

Choir

praises, al- le- lu-ia: who hath called you out of dark-

ness into his marvellous light. Al- le- lu- ia.
Psalm 105:1-5,42 *may be sung.*

310

FIRST WEEK of EASTER
Friday in the Octave of Easter

INTROIT *Edúxit eos*   *Ps. 78:54,1*

Cantors

vij.

THE LORD hath brought them out safely, al- le- lu- ia:

Choir

and ov-er-whelmed their enemies with the sea. Alleluia.

FINE   *Cantors*

Al- le- lu- ia.   Al - le-   lu- ia. *Ps.* Hear my law,

Choir

O my peo-ple: incline your ears unto the words of my

Cantors   *Choir*   *Full*

mouth. Glo- ry be..., As it was..., The LORD hath...,

GRADUAL *Hæc dies...Benedíctus*   *Ps. 118:24,26a,27a*

Cantors   *Choir*

THIS is the day which the LORD hath made: we will be

Cantors

joy-ful and glad in it.   ℣. Bles-sed is he that cometh in

Choir

the Name of the LORD: God is the Lord, who hath

show-ed us light.

ALLELUIA *Dicite in gentibus*   *Cf. Ps. 96:10*

Cantors   *All*

vj.

AL- LE- LU-IA. Al - le- lu- ia.

Cantors   *Choir*

℣. Tell it out among the na-tions : that the LORD hath

All

reign-ed from the Tree.   Al - le- lu- ia.

OFFERTORY *Erit vobis*   *Ex. 12:14*

Cantors

ij.

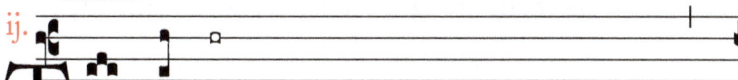

THIS day shall be unto you for a memorial, alleluia;

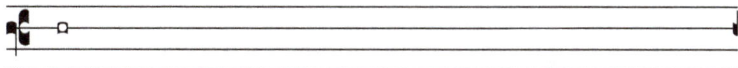

and ye shall keep it for a feast to the Lord throughout

Choir

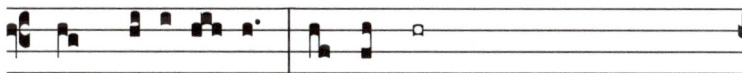

your gen-e-ra-tions: ye shall keep it a feast by an

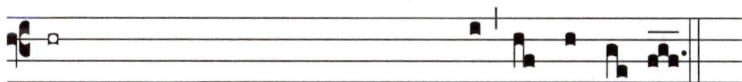

ordinance for ever. Alleluia. Allelu-ia. Al- le- lu- ia.

COMMUNION *Data est mihi (Ascension, p. 344)*

313

Saturday in the Octave of Easter

INTROIT *Edúxit Dóminus*   *Ps. 105:42,1*

Cantors

THE LORD hath brought forth his people with joy,

Choir

al- le- lu- ia: and his chosen with gladness. Alleluia.

FINE   *Cantors*

Al- le- lu- ia.   Al - le- lu- ia.   *Ps.* O   give thanks

Choir

unto the LORD, and call up-on his Name: tell the

Cantors

peoples what things he hath done.   Glo- ry be..., *(etc.)*

Choir   *Full*

As it was..., *(etc.)*   The LORD hath..., *(etc.)*

314

ALLELUIA *Hæc dies*   *Ps. 118:24; 113:1*

vj.

AL- LE- LU-IA.   Al - le- lu- ia.

℣. This is the day which the LORD hath made: we will re-

joice and be glad in it.   Al - le- lu- ia.

℣. Praise the LORD ye ser-vants, O praise the Name of

the LORD.   Al - le- lu- ia.

OFFERTORY *Benedíctus qui venit* (*Baptism of the Lord, p. 83*)

COMMUNION *Omnes qui in Christo baptizáti estis*
(*Baptism of the Lord, p. 83*)

PROPER OF THE SEASON
Second Sunday of Easter
being
Divine Mercy Sunday

INTROIT *Quasi modo géniti infántes*   *I Peter 2:2; Ps. 81:1*

Cantors   *Choir*

vij.

AS new- born babes, al- le- lu- ia: de - sire the

sincere milk of the word. Al- le- lu- ia.

FINE   *Cantors*

Al- le- lu- ia. Al - le- lu- ia. *Ps.* Sing we

Choir

merrily unto God, our hel- per: make a cheerful noise

Cantors

unto the God of Ja- cob. Glo- ry be, *(etc.)*

Choir   *Full*

As   it was, *(etc.)* As new-born babes, *(etc.)And*

316

SECOND WEEK OF EASTER

Thursday In. *Deus, dum egrederéris (Whitsun Week, p. 374.)*
other days In. *Accípite iucunditátem (25 Apr., St. Mark, p. 540)*

Alleluia *In die resurrectiónis*   *Matt. 28:7; John 20:26*

Cantors All

vj.

AL- LE- LU-IA.   Al - le- lu- ia.

Cantors   Choir

℣. In the day of my resurrection, saith the Lord: I will go

All

before you in- to Ga- li- lee.   Al - le- lu- ia.

Cantors   Choir

And af- ter eight days, when the doors were shut: stood

Jesus in the midst of his disciples, and said,

All

Peace be un- to you.   Al - le- lu- ia.

317

Tues. A<small>L</small>. *Dóminus regnávit, decórem (Christmas Dawn, p. 57)*
Saturday A<small>L</small>. *Surréxit Christus qui creávit (above, p. 309)*

O<small>FFERTORY</small> *Angelus Dómini*   *Mt. 28:2, 5, 6*

Cantors

ij.

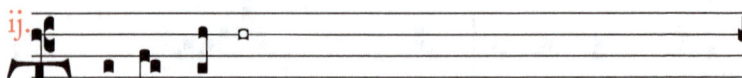

T<small>HE</small> an- gel of the L<small>ORD</small> descended from heaven, and

Choir

said un- to the wo- men: He whom ye seek is risen, as

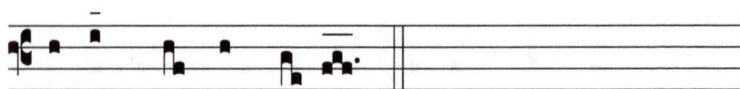

he said. Al- le- lu- ia.

C<small>OMMUNION</small>   *Mitte manum tuam*   *John 20:27*

Cantors

i.

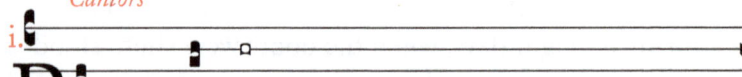

R<small>EACH</small> hi- ther thy hand, and behold the print of the

Choir

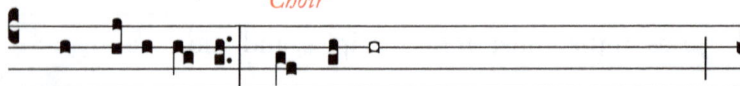

nails, al-le-lu-ia: and be not faithless, but believing.

Al-le-lu- ia, Al- le- lu- ia.

Psalm 118:1-2, 5, 8, 10-11, 13-17, 21-25 *may be sung.*

Mon. & Tues.

Communion *Spíritus, ubi vult spirat*   *John 3:8*

Cantors

i.

THE Spi-rit bloweth where he will; and thou hearest

Choir

the sound thereof, alleluia, al-le-lu-ia: but canst not tell

whence he cometh and whither he goeth. Alleluia.

Allelu- ia.   Al- le- lu- ia.

Psalm 78:1,3-4a,24-26,28 *may be sung.*

319

INTROIT *Iubiláte Deo*   *Psalm 66: 1,2*

Cantors

vij.

O BE joy-ful in God, all ye lands, alleluia; sing

praises unto the honour of his Name, al - le - lu - ia:

Choir

make his praise to be exceeding glorious. Alleluia,

FINE   *Cantors*

Al- le- lu- ia. Al - le- lu- ia. *Ps.* Say un- to God,

O how wonderful art thou in thy works, O LORD:

Choir   *Cantors*

through the great- ness of thy pow- er. Glo- ry be...

Choir   *Full*

As it was..., *(etc.)*   O   be   joy-   ful...,   *(etc.)*

Weds. IN. *Repleátur os meum laude (Whit-Friday, p. 376)*

ALLELUIA *Cognovérunt discípuli*   Luke 24:35, 46

Cantors   *All*

vj.

AL- LE- LU-IA.   Al - le- lu- ia.

Cantors   *Choir*

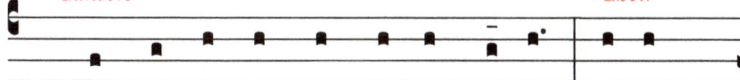

℣. The dis- ci-ples knew the Lord Je- sus: in the

All

break- ing of the bread. Al - le- lu- ia.

Cantors   *Choir*

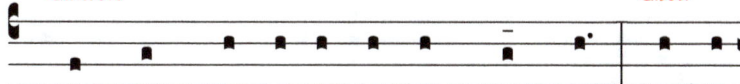

℣. Ought not Christ to have suf-fered these things: and to

All

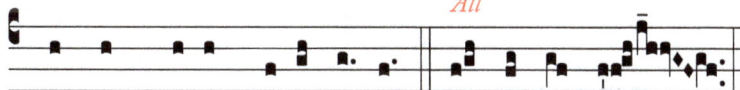

have en-tered in- to his glo- ry? Al - le- lu- ia.

321

Mon. AL. *Loquébar (5 Feb. St. Agatha, p. 521)*
Tues. AL. *In te, Dómine, sperávi (Trinity VI, p. 402)*
Fri. AL. *Caro mea vere (Corpus Christi, p. 478)*
Sat. AL. *Spíritus est qui vivíficat (Easter VII, p. 352)*

OFFERTORY   *Lauda ánima mea*   *Ps. 146:2*

Cantors

PRAISE the LORD, O my soul; while I live will I

Choir

praise the LORD: Yea, as long as I have any being,

I will sing praises unto my God.   Al- le- lu- ia.

Sunday Year B and weekdays:
COMMUNION *Cantáte Dómino*   *Ps. 96:2*

Cantors   *Choir*

O SING unto the LORD, al - le- lu- ia: sing un- to

the LORD, and praise his Name; be telling of his salvation

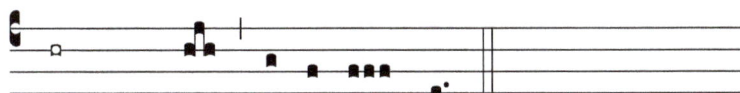

from day to day.　Al- le- lu-　ia.

Verses from Psalm 96:1, 3-4, 7-9, 11-12 *may be sung.*

Sunday Year A: *Surréxit Dóminus*　　　　　　*Luke 24:34*

Cantors　　　　　　*Choir*

THE LORD is ri- sen in-deed,　and hath appeared unto

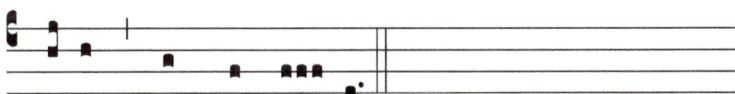

Pe-ter.　Al- le- lu- ia.

Verses from Psalm 96:1, 3-4, 7-9, 11-12 *may be sung.*

Sunday Year C: *Simon Ioannis*　　　　　　*John 21: 15, 17*

Cantors

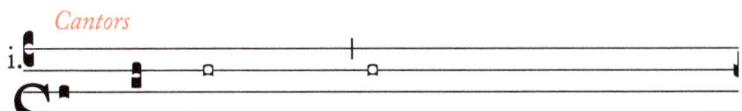

SI- MON, son of Jonas, lovest thou me

Choir

more than these? LORD; thou knowest all things; thou

knowest that I love thee.   Al- le- lu-   ia.

Verses from **Psalm 34** *may be sung.*

Tues. Co. *Vídeo cælos apértos (Dec. 26, S. Stephen, p. 635)*
Thurs. Co. *Panis quem ego dédero (Trinity XV, p. 435)*
Fri. Co. *Qui mandúcat (Corpus Christi, p. 488)*

Easter IV (Good Shepherd Sunday)

INTROIT *Misericórdia Dómini*   *Psalm 33: 5,6*

Cantors

THE lov- ing-kind-ness of the LORD filleth the whole

Choir

world, al - le - lu - ia. By   the word of the LORD the

FINE

heavens were stablished. Al- le- lu- ia. Al- le- lu- ia.

Cantors   *Choir*

Ps. Re- joice in the LORD, O ye right- eous;   for it

Cantors

becometh well the just to be thank- ful. Glo- ry be, *(etc.)*

Choir   *Full*

As it was,... *(etc.)*   The lov- ing-kindness,... *(etc.)*

Thurs. IN. *Deus, dum egrederéris (Whit–Wednesday, p. 374)*

ALLELUIA *Redemptiónem*   *Ps. 111:9;* ℣. *John 10:14*

Cantors   *All*

vj.

AL- LE- LU-IA.   Al - le- lu- ia.

Cantors   *Choir*

℣. The LORD hath sent re- demp- tion   un- to his peo- ple.

All   *Cantors*

Al - le- lu- ia.   ℣. I am the good

Choir

Shep- herd: and I know my sheep and am known of mine.

All

Al - le- lu- ia.

Thurs. AL. *Invéni David (Baptism of the Lord, p. 82)*
Fri. AL. *Cantáte Dómino (Epiphany VI, p. 108)*

OFFERTORY *Deus, Deus meus*   *Ps. 63:2, 5*

Cantors

O GOD, thou art my God, ear- ly will I   seek thee:

Choir

and lift up my hands in thy Name. Al- le- lu- ia.

COMMUNION *Ego sum pastor bonus*   *John 10:14*

Cantors   *Choir*

I AM the good Shepherd, al- le- lu- ia: and know

my sheep, and am known of mine. Allelu- ia.

Al- le- lu-   ia.

Verses from Psalms 23 *or* 33:1, 12-14, 17-21 *may be sung.*

Weekdays. CO. *Cantáte Dómino (Easter III, p. 322)*
Saturday. CO. *Tanto témpore (Easter V, p. 331)*

INTROIT *Cantáte Dómino*   *Psalm 96: 1,2*

Cantors

O SING un- to the LORD a new song, al-le-lu-ia;

for the LORD hath done marvellous things, al - le - lu - ia.

Choir

In   the sight of the nations hath he showed his righteous

FINE

judgments.   Al- le- lu- ia.   Al - le-   lu- ia.

Cantors

Ps. With his own right hand, and with his   ho- ly arm:

Choir   *Cantors*

hath he gotten him- self the vic- to- ry.   Glo- ry be *(etc.)*

Choir   *Full*

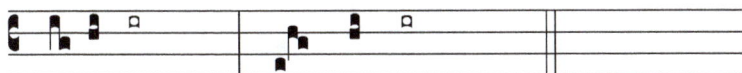

As it was...., *(etc.)* O   sing unto *(etc.)*

Weds. IN. *Repleátur os meum laude (Whit–Friday, p. 376)*

ALLELUIA *Déxtera Dei*   *Ps. 118:16; Rom. 6:9*

Cantors   *All*

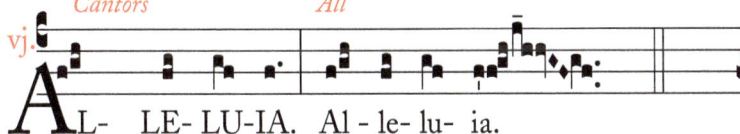

AL-   LE- LU-IA.   Al - le- lu- ia.

Cantors

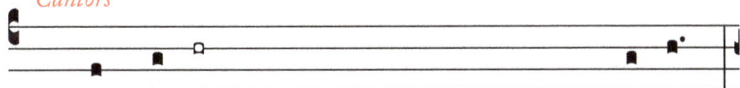

℣. The right hand of the LORD hath the pre-e-mi-nence:

Choir

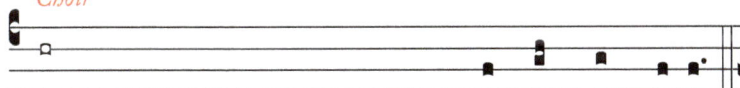

the right hand of the LORD bringeth migh-ty things to pass.

All   *Cantors*

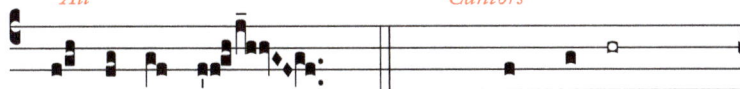

Al - le- lu- ia.   ℣. Christ be-ing raised

Choir

from the dead dieth no more; death hath no more

All

do- mi- nion o- ver him.   Al - le- lu- ia.

Mon. AL. *Spíritus sanctus docébit vos (Whit–Tuesday, p. 373)*
Tues. AL. *Sancti tui, Dómine, benedícent te (22 June, SS. John Fisher & Thomas More, p. 564)*
Weds. AL. *Lætátus sum (Advent II, p. 23)*
Thurs. AL. *Confitémini Dómino et invocáte (Trin. XIX, p. 452)*
Fri. AL. *Ego vos elégi de mundo (13 May, St. Matthias, p. 549)*
Sat. AL. *Iubiláte Deo (Common of Confessors, p. 689)*

OFFERTORY *Iubiláte Deo*   *Ps. 66: 1, 14*

Cantors

ij.

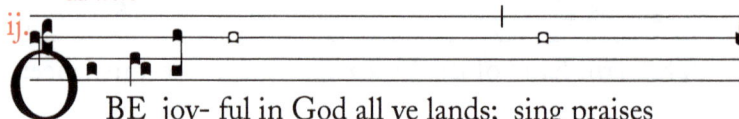

O BE joy- ful in God all ye lands; sing praises

Choir

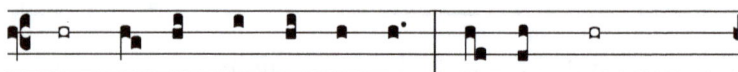

unto the ho- nour of his Name; O come hither and

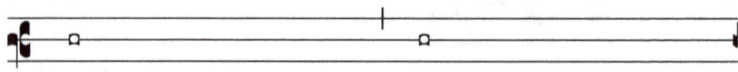

hearken all ye that fear God,   and I will tell you

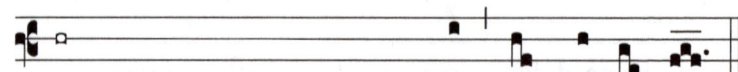

what things he hath done for my soul. Al- le- lu- ia.

330

FIFTH WEEK of EASTER

<small>Communion</small> *Ego sum vitis*   *John 15: 5*

Cantors

I AM the true vine,   ye are the bran- ches;

Choir

he that abideth in me, and I in him, the same bringeth

forth much fruit.   Allelu- ia.   Al- le- lu-   ia.

Verses from Psalm 80:1, 8-11, 14-15, 17-18 *may be sung.*

Sunday Year A: *Tanto témpore*   *John 14:9*

Cantors

HAVE I been so long time with you, and yet hast

Choir

thou not known me, Phi- lip?   He that hath seen me hath

Cantors

seen the Fa- ther, al - le - lu- ia.   Be- liev- est thou

Choir

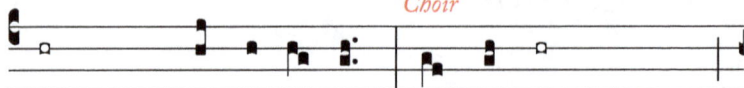

not that I am in the Fa- ther: and the Father in me?

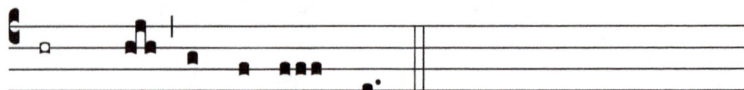

Allelu- ia. Al- le- lu- ia.

Verses from Psalm 33:1-3, 12-13, 17 *may be sung.*

Mon. Co. *Spíritus sanctus docébit vos (Easter VI, p. 337)*

Easter VI (Rogation Sunday)

INTROIT *Vocem iucunditátis*   *Isa. 48:20, Ps. 66*

Cantors

WITH a voice of singing declare ye this, and let it be

Choir

heard, Al- le- lu- ia; ut- ter it even unto the ends of

the earth: the LORD hath delivered his people.

FINE   *Cantors*

Al- le- lu- ia. Al - le- lu- ia. *Ps.* O be joy-ful

Choir

in God, all ye lands: sing praises unto the honour of his

Name; make his praise to be glo- ri- ous.

Cantors   *Choir*   *Full*

Glo- ry   be..., *(etc.)* As it was..., *(etc.)* With a voice..., *(etc.)*

ALLELUIA *Surréxit Christus*   *Joh. 16:28*

Cantors   *All*

vj.

AL- LE- LU- IA.   Al - le- lu- ia.

℣. Christ is risen, and hath showed light un- tô us:

Choir

whom he hath redeemed with hîs möst pre- cious Blood.

All   *Cantors*

Al - le- lu- ia.   ℣. I   came forth from

Choir

the Father, and am come into thê world: again, I leave the

All

world and go tô thë Fa- ther.   Al - le- lu- ia.

SUNDAY:

A 1. ℣. Christ is risen, *as above.*

  2. ℣. I will not leave you com- fôrt- less: I go away
and come again unto you, and yoûr heärt shall rejoice.

B. 1. ℣. I came forth, *as above.*

  2. ℣. I have chosen you out of thê world: that ye
       should go and bring fruit, and that your fruît
       shoüld re-main.

C. 1. ℣. Christ is risen *or* I came forth, *as above.*

  2. ℣. The Holy Ghost shall teâch you: whatsoever
       Î saïd unto you.

Mon. AL. *Cantáte Dómino (Epiphany VI, p. 108)*

OFFERTORY *Benedícite, gentes*   *Ps. 66: 7, 8, 18*

Cantors

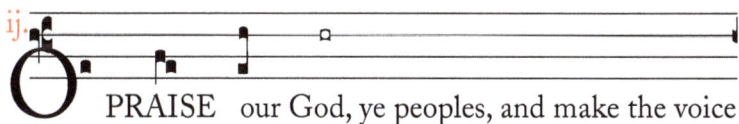

O PRAISE   our God, ye peoples, and make the voice

Choir

of his praise to be heard; who hold-eth our soul in life,

Cantors

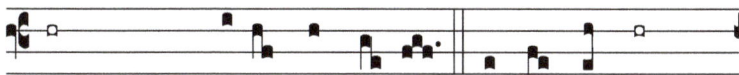

and suffereth not our feet to slip: prais- ed be God, who

335

Choir

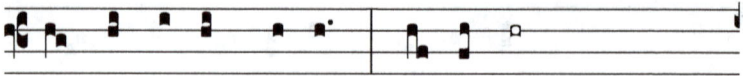

hath not cast out my prayer: nor turn-ed his mercy from

me. Al- le- lu- ia.

COMMUNION
Sunday Year A: *Non vos relínquam*   *John 14:18*

Cantors

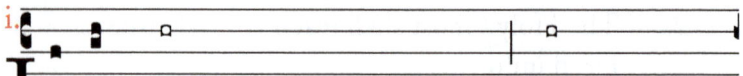

i. I WILL not leave you com- fort- less: I will come

Choir

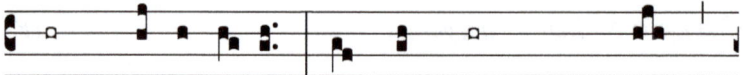

to you, al- le- lu- ia;   and your heart shall re- joice.

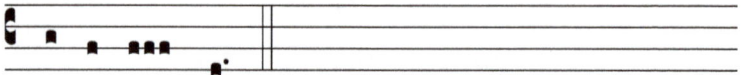

Al- le- lu-   ia.

Verses from Psalm 122 *may be sung.*

Sunday Year B: *Ego vos elégi* — *John 15:16*

Cantors

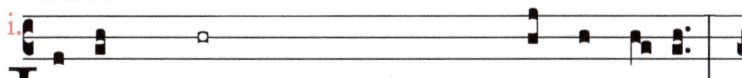

I HAVE chosen you out of the world, al- le- lu- ia:

Choir

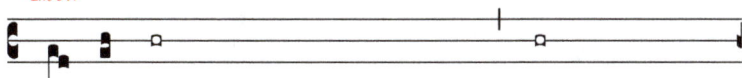

that ye should go and bring forth fruit, and that your fruit

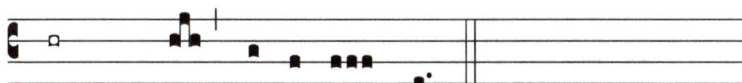

should re-main. Al- le- lu- ia.

Verses from Psalm 122 *may be sung.*

Sunday Year C: *Spíritus Sanctus docebit vos* — *John 14:26*

Cantors

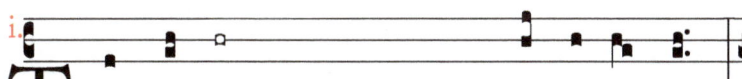

THE Ho- ly Ghost shall teach you, al- le- lu- ia:

Choir

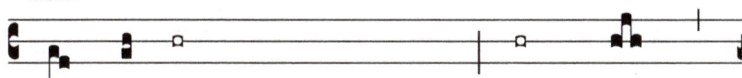

what- so- ev- er I have said unto you. Allelu- ia,

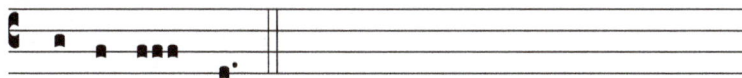

Al- le- lu- ia.

Verses from Psalm 51:1, 7-8, 10-11, 13, 15, 18 *may be sung.*

337

Mon. Co. *Spíritus qui a Patre procédit Jn. 15:26;15:14:17:1,5*

Cantors

THE Spirit who proceedeth from the Father, al- le-

Choir

lu- ia: he shall glorify me. Allelu- ia.

Al- le- lu- ia.

Verses from Psalm 78:1-4,6-7,24-26,30 *may be sung.*

Tues. Co. *Dum vénerit Paráclitus*   *Jn. 16:8*

Cantors

WHEN the Comforter, the Spirit of Truth, is come:

Choir

he will convince the world of sin, and of righteousness,

and of judgment. Allelu- ia. Al- le- lu- ia.

Verses from Psalm 34 *may be sung.*

INTROIT *Exaudívit*   *Ps. 18:7,1,2*

Cantors

vij.

HE hath heard my voice out of his holy temple,

Choir

al- le- lu- ia: and my complaint hath come before

him, it hath entered even into his ears. Al- le- lu- ia.

FINE   *Cantors*

Al - le- lu- ia. *Ps.* I will love thee O LORD my strength:

Choir

the LORD is my stony rock, my fortress, and my Sav-iour.

Cantors   *Choir*   *Full*

Glo- ry be..., *(etc.)* As it was..., *(etc.)* He hath..., *(etc.)*

ALLELUIA *Confitémini Dómino*   *Ps. 118:1*

vj. A̲L‑ LE‑ LU‑ IA.   Al ‑ le‑ lu‑ ia.

℣. O give thanks unto the Lord, for he is gra‑cious: and

his mercy en‑dur‑eth for ev‑er.   Al ‑ le ‑ lu‑ ia.

OFFERTORY *Confitébor Dómino*   *Ps. 109:29,30*

ij. I WILL give great thanks unto the LORD with my mouth:

and praise him a‑mong the mul‑ti‑tude. For he shall

stand at the right hand of the poor: to save his soul

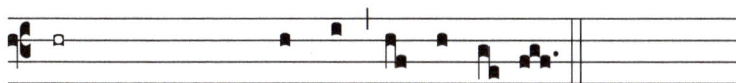

from unrighteous jud-ges.   Al- le- lu- ia.

COMMUNION *Petite et accipiétis Lk.11:9,10; cf.Mt.7:7,8;10:1*

Cantors

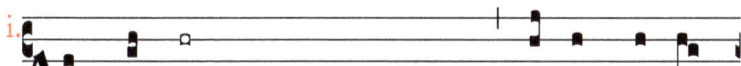

ASK and it shall be given unto you; seek and ye shall

Choir   *Cantors*

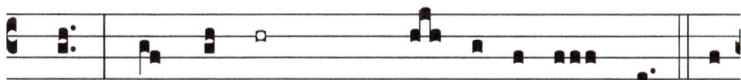

find: Knock, and it shall be o-pen-ed un- to   you.   For

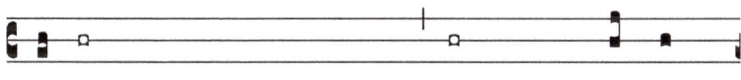

ev-ery one that asketh, receiveth, and he that seek-eth

Choir

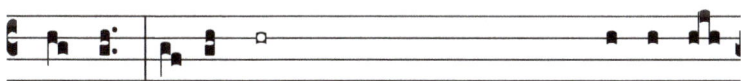

find-eth: and to him that knocketh, it shall be o-pen-ed,

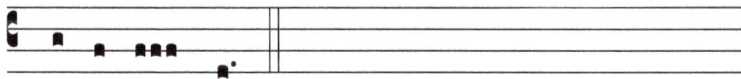

al- le- lu-   ia.

Verses from Psalm 31:1-6,8,27 *may be sung.*

341

VIGIL of the ASCENSION

INTROIT *Vocem iucunditátis* *(supra, Easter VI, p. 333)*
ALLELUIA *Surréxit Christus* *(supra, Easter VI, p. 334)*
OFFERTORY *Benedícite gentes* *(supra, Easter VI, p. 335)*
COMMUNION *Cantáte Dómino* *(supra, Easter III, p. 322)*

ASCENSION DAY

INTROIT *Viri Galilaéi* *Acts 1:11; Ps. 47:1*

Cantors

vij.

YE men of Galilee, why stand ye gazing up into

Choir

heaven? Al- le- lu- ia: in like manner as you have seen

him going up into heaven, so shall he come again. Alleluia.

FINE *Cantors*

Allelu- ia. Al - le- lu- ia. *Ps.* O clap your hands

Choir

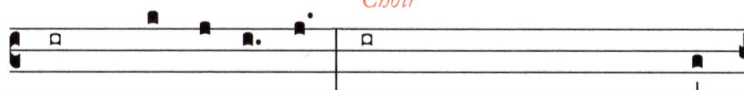

together, all ye peo- ple: O sing unto God with the voice

Cantors & Choir   *Full*

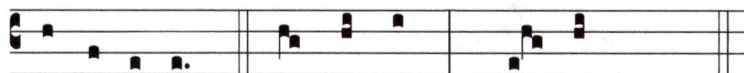

of me- lo- dy.   Glo- ry be *(etc.)* Ye   men *(etc.)*

ALLELUIA *Ascéndit Deus*   *Ps. 47:5; 68:17, 18*

Cantors   *All*

vj.

AL- LE- LU-IA.   Al - le- lu- ia.

Cantors   *Choir*

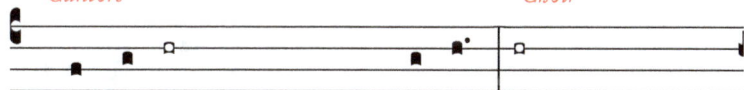

℣. God is gone up with a mer- ry noise: and the LORD with

All

the sound of the trum- pet.   Al- le- lu- ia.

Cantors

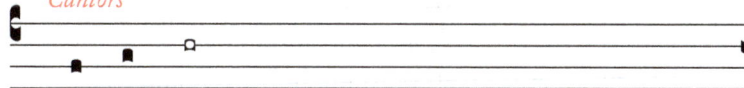

℣. The LORD is among them as in the holy places of Sinai,

Choir

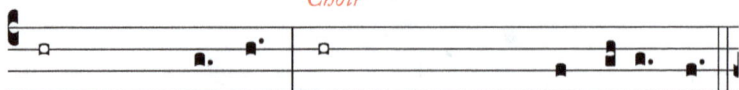

he is gone up on high: he hath led cap- ti- vi- ty cap- tive.

All

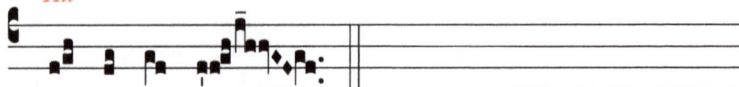

Al - le- lu- ia.

OFFERTORY *Ascéndit Deus*   *Ps. 47: 5*

Cantors   *Choir*

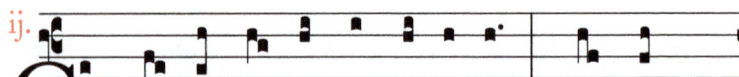

ij.

GOD is gone up with a mer- ry noise: and the

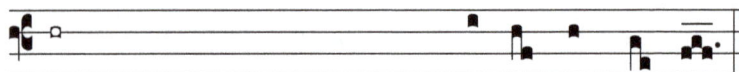

LORD with the sound of the trump-et. Al- le- lu- ia.

COMMUNION
Year A: *Data est mihi*   *Matt. 28: 18, 19*

Cantors

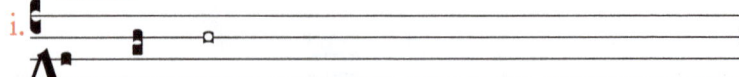

i.

ALL pow- er is given unto me in heaven and in earth

Choir

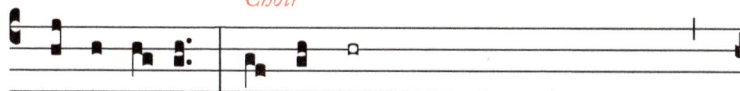

al- le- lu- ia;   go ye therefore and teach all nations,

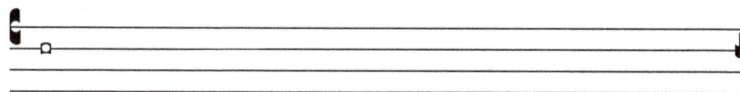

baptizing them in the Name of the Father and of the Son,

and of the Holy Ghost. Al- le- lu- ia. Al- le- lu-   ia.

Verses from Psalm 78:1, 3-4a, 24-26, 28 *may be sung.*

COMMUNION
Year B: *Signa*   *Mark 16:17-18*

Cantors

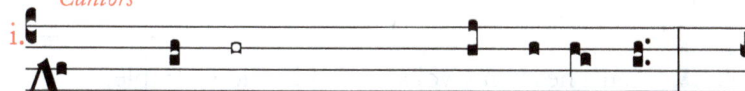

i. AND   these signs shall follow them that be- lieve:

Choir

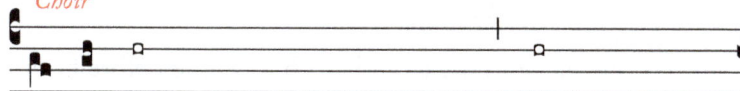

in my Name shall they cast out demons: they shall lay hands

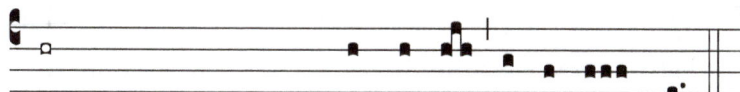

on the sick, and they shall re- co- ver. Al- le- lu-   ia.

Verses from Psalm 34 *may be sung.*

345

Year C: *Psállite Dómino*   *Ps. 68: 32*

Cantors

i.

SING ye to the LORD, who ascended the hea- ven

Choir

of hea- vens: to the sun- ris- ing.   Al- le- lu-   ia.

Psalm 68:1, 4-6, 18-20, 24, 28-29, 32-33 *may be sung.*

Friday and Saturday after Ascension

INTROIT *Exaudívit*   *Ps. 18:7 & 1*

Cantors

vij.

HE hath heard my voice out of his holy temple,

Choir

al- le- lu- ia: and my complaint hath come before him;

FINE

it hath entered even into his ears, al-le-lu-ia, al-le-lu- ia.

346

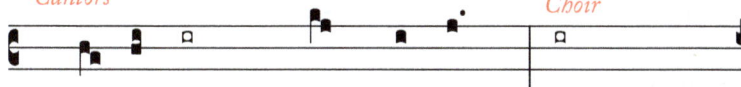

Cantors   *Choir*

Ps.   I will love thee, O Lord, my strength: the Lord is my

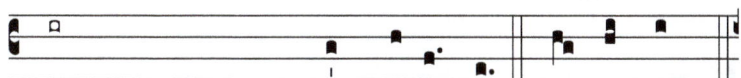

Cantors

stony rock, my fortress and my sav-iour.   Glo- ry   be

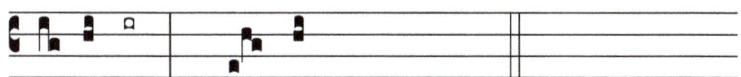

Choir   *Full*

as it was.   He hath heard.

Friday ALLELUIA *Confitémini (Rogationtide, p. 340)*

Saturday ALLELUIA *Exívi a Patre (Easter VII, p. 350)*

OFFERTORY *Confitébor Dómino (Rogationtide, p. 340)*

COMMUNION *Non vos relínquam (Easter VI, p. 336)*

INTROIT *Exáudi, Dómine*   *Ps. 27:8,9,1*

Cantors

vij.

CON-SI-DER, O LORD, and hear me, when I cry unto

thee, alleluia;   unto thee my heart hath said, Thy face,

Choir

LORD, have I sought; thy face, LORD, will I seek: O hide

not thou thy face from thy servant. Al- le- lu- ia.

FINE   *Cantors*

al - le- lu- ia.   *Ps.* The LORD is my light and my sal-

Choir   *Cantors*

va- tion: whom then shall I fear?   Glo- ry be ..., *(etc.)*

Choir   *Full*

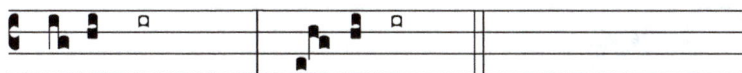

As it was..., *(etc.)* Con-si-der..., *(etc.)*

ALLELUIA *Regnávit Dóminus*   *Ps. 47:8; John. 14:18*

Cantors   *All*

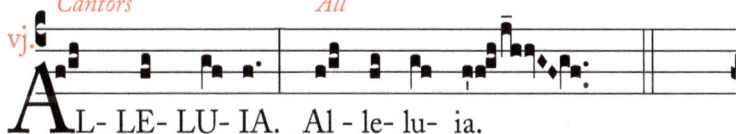

℣. AL- LE- LU- IA. Al - le- lu- ia.

Cantors   *Choir*

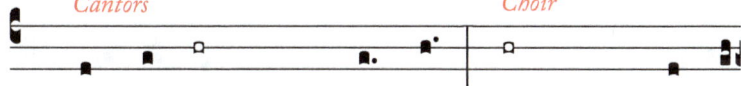

℣. God reign-eth over the hea- then: God sitteth up-on his

All   *Cantors*

ho- ly seat. Al - le- lu- ia.   ℣. I will

Choir

not leave you com- fort- less: I go away and come again

All

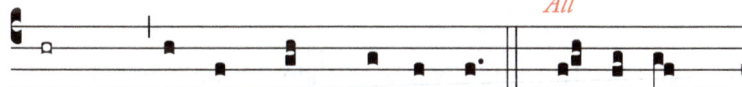

unto you, and your heart shall re- joice. Al - le- lu-

349

ia.

Sunday Year A: *Regnavit Dóminus* *as above and then the verse:*
Exívi a Patre   *John 16:28*

℣. I came forth from the Father, and am come into

the world: again, I leave the world and go to the Fa- ther.

Al - le- lu- ia.

OFFERTORY *Ascéndit Deus* *(Ascension Day, p. 344)*

COMMUNION *Pater, cum essem*   *John 17:12,13,15*

FA- THER, while I was with them in the world, I kept

Choir

those that thou gavest me, al- le- lu- ia; and now I come

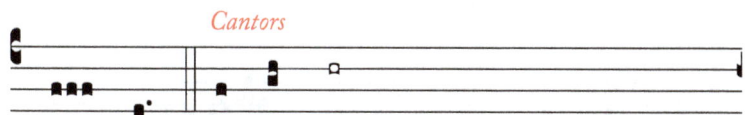

Cantors

to thee: I pray thee not that thou shouldest take

Choir

them out of the world; but that thou shouldest keep them

from the evil. Allelu- ia. Al- le- lu- ia.

Verses from Psalm 122 *may be sung.*

Monday and Thursday

IN. *Accípite iucunditátem (25 April, St. Mark, p. 540)*

AL. *Spíritus Sanctus docébit vos (Tues. Whitsun Week, p. 373)*

OF. *Lauda ánima mea (Easter III, p. 322)*

CO. *Spíritus qui a Patre procédit (Easter VI, p. 338)*

IN. *Deus, dum egrederéris (Ember Weds., p. 374)*

ALLELUIA *Spíritus est qui vivíficat*   *Jn. 6:64*

Cantors *All*

AL- LE- LU- IA.   Al - le- lu- ia.

Cantors *Choir*

℣. It is the Spirit that quick-en-eth: the flesh pro-fi-teth

All

no-thing.   Al - le- lu- ia.

OF. *Meditábor (Lent II, p. 151)*

CO. Tues. *Spíritus sanctus docébit vos (Easter VI, p. 337)*
   Fri. *Simon Ioánnis (Easter III, p. 323)*

Wednesday, and Saturday Morning

IN. *Repleátur os meum (Whit–Friday, p. 376)*

ALLELUIA *Non vos relínquam*　　　　　　　　*Jn. 14:18*

Cantors　　　　　　*All*

vj.

AL- LE- LU- IA.　Al - le- lu- ia.

Cantors　　　　　　　　　　　*Choir*

℣. I will not leave you com-fort-less:　I go away and come

again unto you, and your heart shall re-joice.

All

Al - le- lu- ia.

OF. *Ascéndit Deus (Ascension, p. 344)*

CO. **Weds.** *Pater, cum essem cum eis (above p. 350)*

　　　Sat. *Spíritus ubi vult spirat (Easter II, p. 319)*

PROPER of the SEASON

WHITSUNDAY

Saturday Afternoon or Evening

I. The Lessons

After the First Lesson On Babel *(Genesis. 11:1-9)*

TRACT *Dóminus dissolvit*   *Ps. 33:10,11,12*

Cantors

THE LORD bringeth the counsel of the hea-then to

Choir

nought: and maketh the devices of the people to be of

none effect, and casteth out the coun-sels of prin-ces.

Cantors

℣. The coun-sel of the LORD shall endure for ev-er:

Choir

and the thoughts of his heart from generation to gen-er-

Cantors

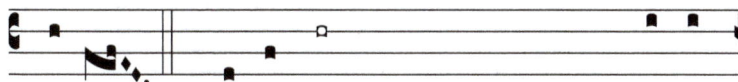

a-tion. ℣. Bles-sed are the people whose God is the

Choir

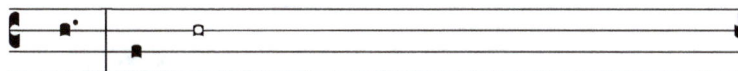

LORD: and bles-sed are the folk that he hath chosen to

him, to be his in-he-ri-tance.

After the Second Lesson On God's Descent on Mount Sinai
(Ex 19:3-8,16-20)

Tract *Lex Dómini*   *Ps. 19:7-10*

Cantors

viij.

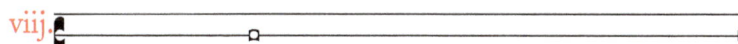

THE The law of the LORD is an undefiled law, convert-

Choir

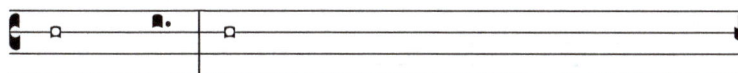

ing the soul: the testimony of the LORD is sure, and

Cantors

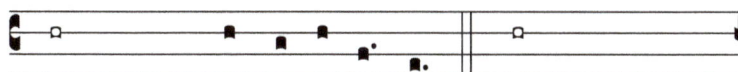

giveth wisdom un-to the sim-ple. ℣. The statutes of the

Choir

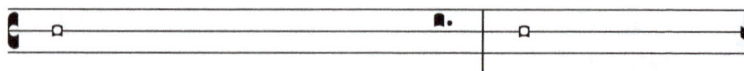

LORD are right, and rejoice the heart: the commandment

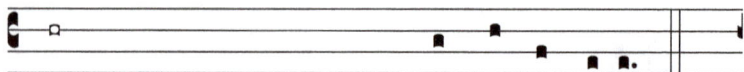

of the LORD is pure, and giveth light un-to the eyes.

Cantors

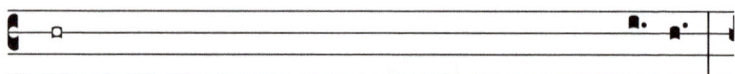

℣. The fear of the LORD is clean, and endureth for ev-er:

Choir

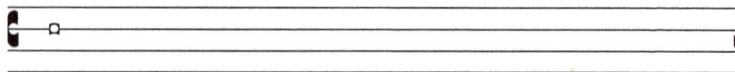

the judgements of the LORD are true, and righteous

Cantors

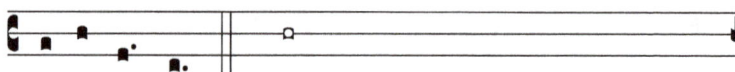

al-to-ge-ther. ℣. More to be desired are they than gold,

Choir

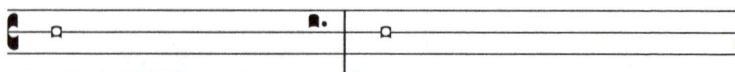

yea, than much fine gold: sweeter also than honey,

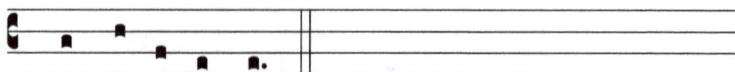

and the ho-ney-comb.

After the Third Lesson On the Dry Bones and God's Spirit
(Ezek 37:1-14)

TRACT *Confitémini Dómino (Ps. 107:1-6,8,9)*

Cantors

iv.

O GIVE thanks unto the LORD, for he is gra-cious:

Choir   *Cantors*

and his mercy endur-eth for ev-er. ℣ Let them give

Choir

thanks whom the LORD hath re-dee-med: and deliverèd

Cantors

from the hand of the e-ne-my; ℣ And gathered them

Choir

out of the lands, from the east, and from the west: from

Cantors

the north, and from the south. ℣ They went astray in the

357

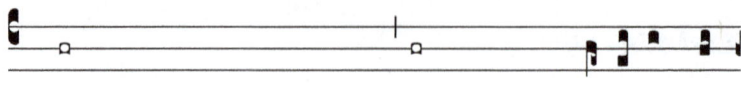

the wilderness out of the way, and found no ci-ty to dwell

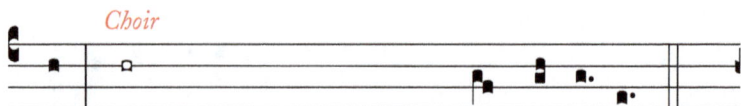

Choir

in: hungry and thirsty, their soul fain-ted in them.

Cantors   *Choir*

℣. So they cried unto the LORD in their trou-ble: and he

Cantors

delivered them from their dis-tress. ℣. O that men would

Choir

therefore praise the LORD for his good-ness: and declare

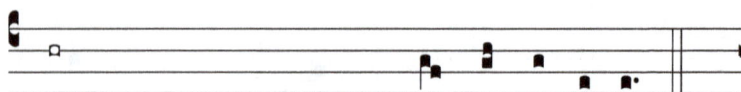

the wonders that he doeth for the chil-dren of men.

Cantors

℣. For he sa-tis- fi-eth the emp-ty soul: and filleth the

(musical notation)

hungry soul with good-ness.

After the Fourth Lesson On the Outpouring of the Spirit
(Joel 2:28-32)
TRACT *Benedic, anima mea*   *Ps. 104:1,2,24,27-30*

Cantors

(musical notation)

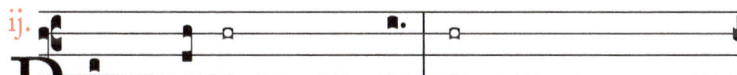

ij. PRAISE the LORD, O my soul: O LORD my God, thou

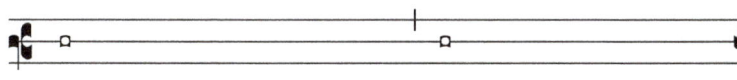

(musical notation)

art become exceeding glorious; thou art clothed with

Choir

(musical notation)

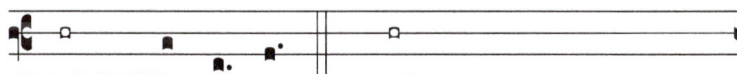

majesty and hon-our. ℣. Thou deckest thyself with

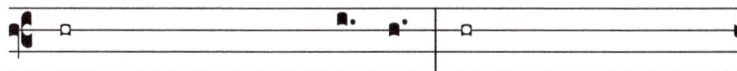

(musical notation)

light as it were with a gar-ment: and spreadest out the

Cantors

(musical notation)

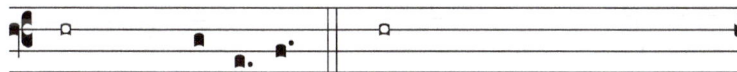

heavens like a cur-tain. ℣. O LORD, how manifold are

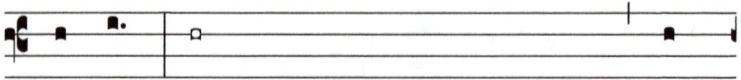

thy works: in wisdom hast thou made them all; the

Choir

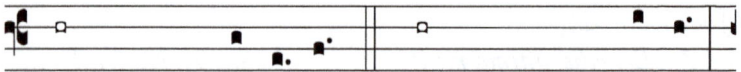

earth is full of thy rich-es. ℣. These wait all up-on thee:

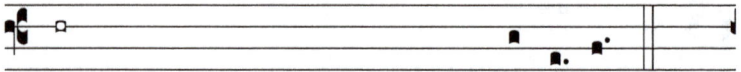

that thou mayest give them meat in due sea-son.

Cantors

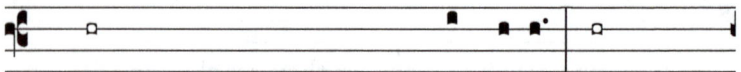

℣. When thou givest it them, they ga-ther it: and when

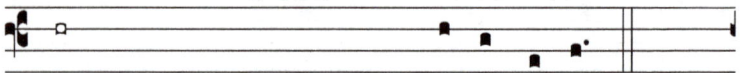

thou openest thy hand, they are fil-led with good.

Choir

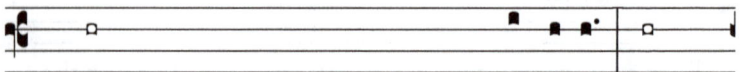

℣. When thou hidest thy face, they are troublèd: when

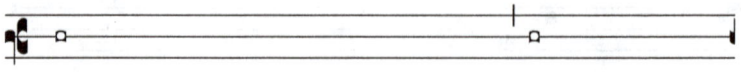

thou takest away their breath, they die, and are turned

Cantors

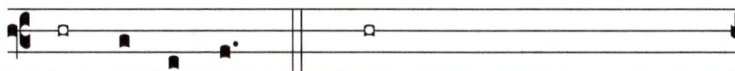

again to their dust. ℣. When thou lettest thy Spirit go

Full

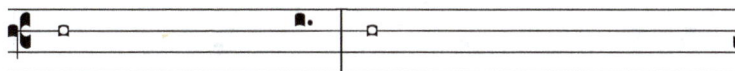

forth, they shall be made: and thou shalt renew the face

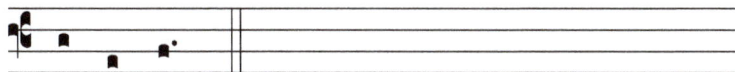

of the earth.

INTROIT *Cáritas Dei*   *Rom. 5:5; Ps 103:1*

Cantors

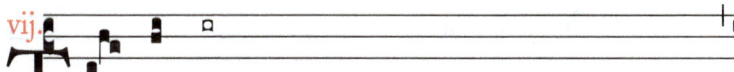

HE love of God hath been poured out in our hearts,

Choir

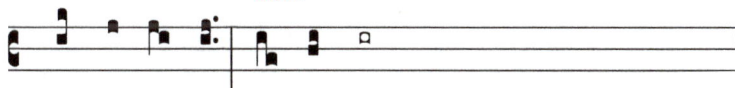

al- le- lu- ia;   by the Holy Ghost who dwelleth in us,

FINE   *Cantors*

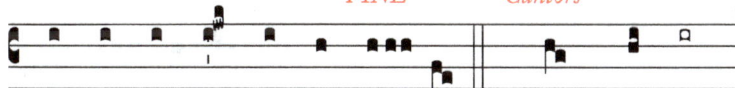

al- le- lu- ia, al - le- lu- ia. *Ps.* Praise the LORD,

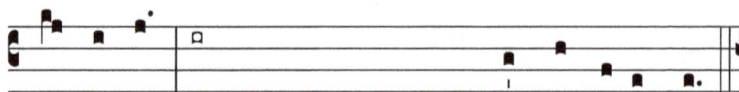

O my soul: and all that is within me praise his ho-ly Name.

Cantors   *Choir*   *Full*

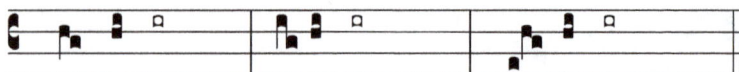

Glo- ry be..., *(etc.)* As it was..., *(etc.)* The love of..., *(etc.)*

or IN. *Dum Sanctificátus*   *Ezek. 36:23–26, Ps. 34:1*

Cantors

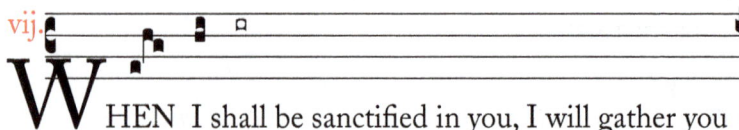

WHEN I shall be sanctified in you, I will gather you

Choir

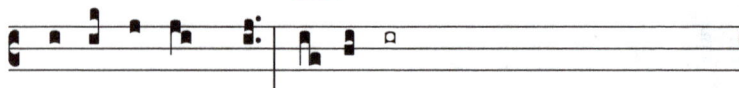

out of all coun-tries: and I will sprinkle clean water upon

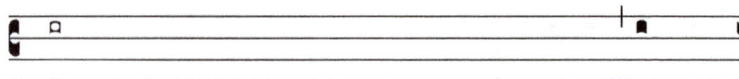

you, and ye shall be clean from all your filthiness; and a new

FINE

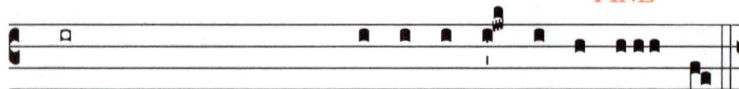

spirit will I put within you. al- le- lu- ia, al - le- lu- ia.

362

Cantors / *Choir*

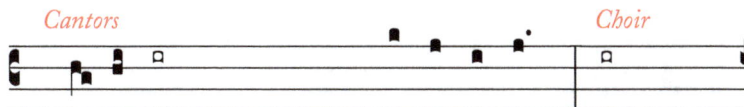

Ps. I will always give thanks un-to the LORD: his praise

Choir / *Cantors*

shall ever be in my mouth. Glo- ry be..., *(etc.)*

Choir / *Full*

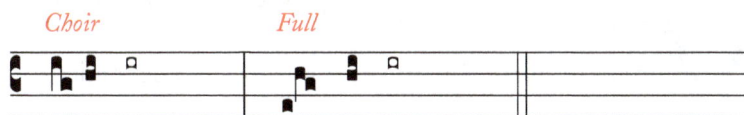

As it was..., *(etc.)* When I shall..., *(etc.)*

ALLELUIA *Emítte Spíritum*   *Ps. 104:30*

Cantors / *All*

AL - LE- LU- IA.   ℟. Al - le- lu- ia.

Cantors

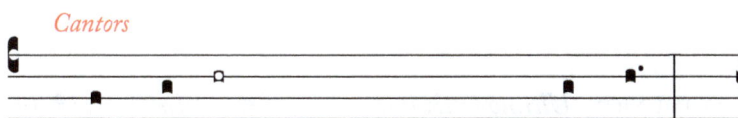

℣. O   send forth thy Spirit and they shall be made:

Choir / *Cantors*

and thou shalt renew the face of the earth. ℟. Al - le- lu-

363

ia.

OFFERTORY *Emítte Spíritum*   *Ps. 104:30*

Cantors

ij. O SEND forth thy Spirit, and they shall be made:

Choir

and thou shalt renew the face of the earth. al- le-

lu- ia.

COMMUNION *Ultimo festivitátis*   *Jn. 7:37,38,39*

Cantors

i. ON the last day of the feast, Jesus said, He that

beieveth on me, out of his heart shall flow rivers of liv-ing

Choir

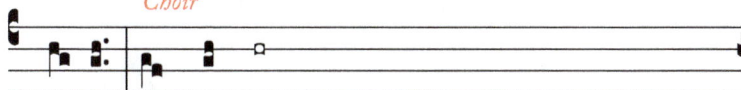

wa-ter: now this he spake of the Spirit which they that

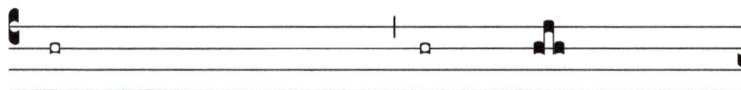

believe on him should receive. Al-le-lu - ia,

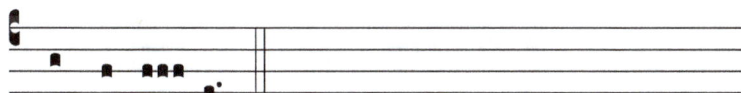

Al - le - lu - ia.

Verses from Psalm 104:1,30,31,33,34 *may be sung.*

THE DAY OF PENTECOST
Commonly called
Whitsunday

INTROIT *Spíritus Dómini*   *Wisd. 1:7; Ps. 68:1*

Cantors

vij.

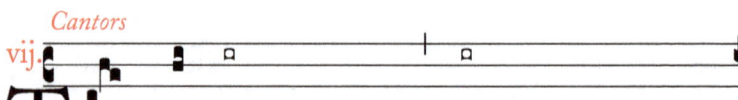

THE   Spi- rit of the LORD * hath filled the whole

Choir

world, al- le- lu- ia; and that which containeth all things

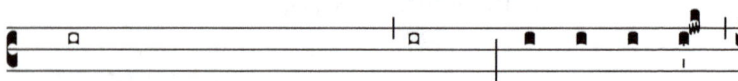

hath knowledge of the voice. Alleluia. Al-   le- lu- ia,

FINE   *Cantors*

Al - le-   lu- ia. *Ps.* Let God arise and let his

Choir

e-ne- mies be scat- ter- ed: let them also that hate him

Cantors & Choir   *Full*

flee be- fore him. Glo- ry be..., *(etc.)* The Spi- rit..., *(etc.)*

366

ALLELUIA *Emítte Spíritum*   *Ps. 104:30*

Cantors   *All*

vj.

AL - LE- LU- IA.   ℞. Al - le- lu- ia.

Cantors

℣. O   send forth thy Spirit and they shall be made:

Choir

and thou shalt renew the face of the earth. ℞. Al - le- lu-

Cantors   *Here genuflect*

ia.   ℣. Come, Ho- ly Ghost, and fill the hearts

Choir

of thy faithful peo- ple: and kindle in them the

All

fire of thy love.   *   ℞. Al - le- lu- ia.

* Alleluia *is not repeated on Whitsunday; the Sequence is begun*
  immediately. On other days, if the Sequence is omitted,the Alleluia
  is repeated.

367

SEQUENCE *Veni, Sancte Spíritus*

1940 Hymnal 109
English Hymnal 155

i.

COME thou Ho-ly Pa-ra-clete, And from thy ce- les-

tial seat, Send thy light and bril- lian-cy,   Fa-ther of the

poor draw near, Gi-ver of all gifts, be here, Come, the

soul's true ra-dian-cy. 2. Come, of com-for-ters the

best, Of the soul the sweet-est guest, Come in toil re-

fresh-ing-ly: Thou in la-bour rest most sweet, Thou art

sha-dow from the heat, Com-fort in ad- ver- si- ty.

3. O thou Light, most pure and blest, Shine with-in the

in-most breast Of thy faith-ful com-pa-ny. Where thou

art not, man hath nought; Ev-'ry ho-ly deed and

thought Comes from thy Di-vi- ni- ty. 4. What is soil-

ed, make thou pure; What is woun-ded, work its cure;

What is par-ched, fruc-ti-fy; What is ri-gid, gent-ly

bend; What is fro-zen, warm-ly tend; Streng-then what

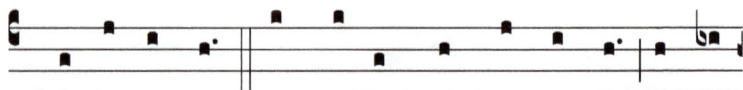

goes err-ing-ly. 5. Fill thy faith-ful, who con-fide In thy

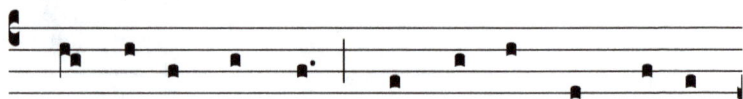

pow'r to guard and guide, With thy sev'n-fold Mys-te-

ry. Here thy grace and vir-tue send; Grant sal-va-tion in

the end. And in heav'n fe-li-ci-ty. A-men. Al-le-lu-ia.

OFFERTORY *Confirma hoc*   *Ps. 68: 28, 29*

Cantors

ij.

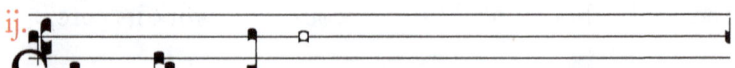

STA- BLISH the thing, O God, that thou hast wrought

Choir

in us, for thy temple's sake at Je-ru-sa-lem: so shall

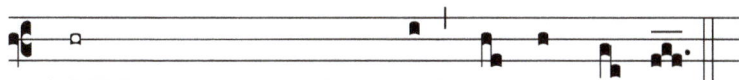

kings bring presents un- to thee. Al- le- lu- ia.

COMMUNION *Factus est repénte*   *Acts 2: 2,4*

Cantors

i.

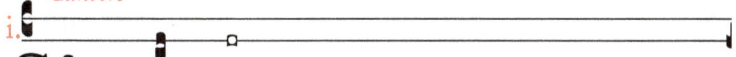

SUD- DEN- LY there came a sound from heaven as a

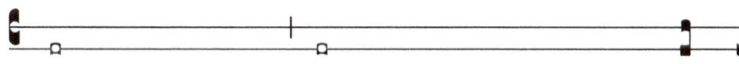

rushing mighty wind, and it filled the house where they

Choir

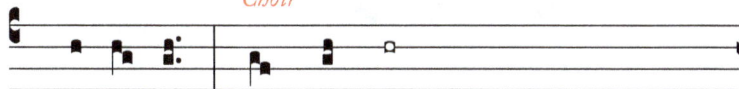

were sit- ting: and they were all filled with the Holy

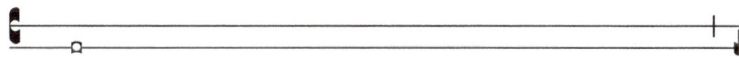

Ghost, and began to speak the wonderful works of God.

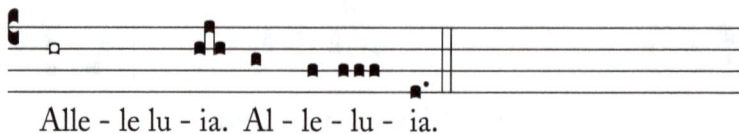

Alle - le lu - ia. Al - le - lu - ia.

Verses from Psalm 68:1,3-5, 7-8, 28, 35 *may be sung.*

Monday

IN. *Cibávit eos (Corpus Christi, p. 477)*

ALLELUIA *Loquebántur váriis linguis*   *Acts 2:4*

AL - LE- LU- IA. ℟. Al - le- lu- ia.

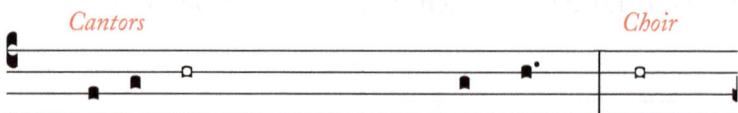

℣. The A-pos-tles spake with di-vers tongues: the won-

der-ful works of God.   ℟. Al - le- lu- ia.

℣. Come, Holy Ghost, *etc. (above, p 367)*
The Sequence Veni, Sancte Spíritus, *pp. 368–370, may be said.*
OF. *Intónuit de caelo (Tuesday in the Octave of Easter, p. 303)*
CO. *Spíritus Sanctus (Easter VI, p. 337)*

IN. *Accípite iucunditátem* *(25 April, St. Mark, p. 540)*

ALLELUIA *Spíritus Sanctus docébit vos*　　　　　　　*Jn. 14:26*

Cantors　　　　　　　*All*

vj.

AL - LE- LU- IA.　℞. Al - le- lu- ia.

Cantors　　　　　　　　　　　*Choir*

℣. The Ho-ly Ghost shall teach you: whatsoever

All

I have said un-to you.　℞. Al - le- lu- ia.

℣. Come, Holy Ghost, *etc. (supra, p 367)*
The Sequence Veni, Sancte Spíritus, *pp. 368–370 may be said.*

OF. *Portas cǽli* *(Corpus Christi, p. 487)*

CO. *Spíritus qui a Patre* *(Easter VI Mon., p. 338)*

Ember Wednesday

INTROIT *Deus, dum egrederéris*   *Ps. 68:7,8,1*

Cantors

vij.

O GOD when thou wentest forth before the people,

when thou wentest through the wilderness, al- le-lu-ia:

Choir

the earth shook and the heavens dropped. Al- le- lu- ia.

FINE   *Cantors*

Al - le- lu- ia. *Ps.* Let God arise and let his

Choir

e-ne- mies be scat- ter- ed: let them also that hate him

Cantors & Choir   *Full*

flee be- fore him. Glo- ry be..., *(etc.)* O God when...,

ALLELUIA *Verbo Dómini*   *Ps. 33:6*

vj.

Cantors   *All*

AL -LE- LU- IA.   ℟. Al - le- lu- ia.

Cantors

℣. By the word of the LORD were the hea-vens made:

Choir

and all the hosts of them by the breath of his mouth.

All

℟. Al - le- lu- ia.

℣. Come, Holy Ghost, *etc. (above, p 367)*
The Sequence **Veni, Sancte Spíritus**, *pp. 368–370, may be said.*
OF. *Meditábor (Lent II, p. 151)*

COMMUNION *Pacem relinquo vobis*   *Jn. 14:27*

Cantors   *Choir*

i.

PEACE I leave with you, al - le- lu - ia: my peace I

375

give unto you. Al-le - le lu - ia. Al - le - lu - ia.

Verses from Psalm 122 *may be sung.*

Thursday

IN. *Spíritus Dómini* *(above, p. 366)*

AL. *Emítte Spíritum* *(above, p. 367)*

The Sequence Veni, Sancte Spíritus, *pp. 368–370, may be said.*

OF. *Confírma hoc* *(above, p. 370)*

CO. *Factus est repénte* *(above, p. 371)*

Ember Friday

INTROIT *Repleátur os meum*   Ps. 71:7,22,1

Cantors

vij.

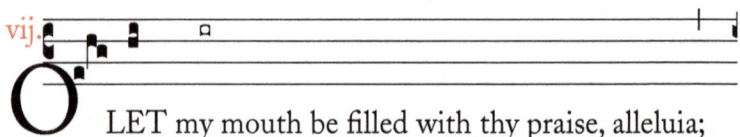

O LET my mouth be filled with thy praise, alleluia;

Choir

that I may sing, al- le-lu-ia: my lips will rejoice when I

FINE

sing unto thee. Al- le-lu- ia, Al - le- lu- ia.

Cantors

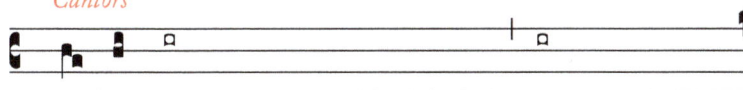

Ps. In thee, O LORD, have I put my trust; let me never be

Choir

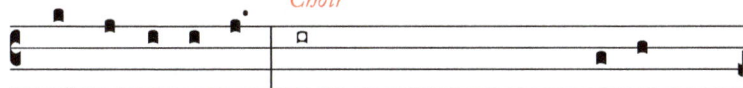

put to con-fu-sion: deliver me and rescue me in thy

Cantors & Choir

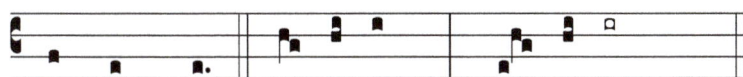

right-eous-ness.   Glo- ry be..., *(etc.)* O   let my..., *(etc.)*

ALLELUIA *O quam bonus*   *Wis. 12:1*

Cantors   *All*

vj.

AL - LE- LU- IA.   ℟. Al - le- lu- ia.

Cantors   *Choir*

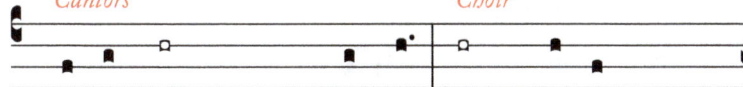

℣. O how good and sweet, O Lord, is thy Spi- rit

All

with-in us.   ℟. Al - le- lu- ia.

℣. Come, Holy Ghost, *etc. (supra, p 367)*

or Ad libitum AL. *Lauda ánima mea*   *Ps.146:1*

Cantors / *All*

AL - LE- LU- IA.   ℟. Al - le- lu- ia.

Cantors

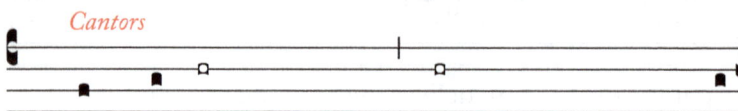

℣. Praise the LORD, O my soul; while I live will I praise the

Choir

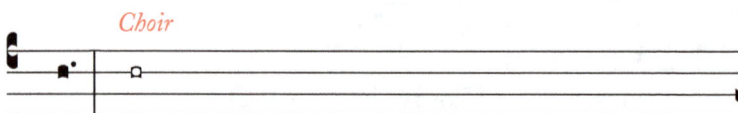

Lord: yea, as long as I have any being, I will sing praises

All

un-to my God.   ℟. Al - le- lu- ia.

℣. Come, Holy Ghost, *etc. (supra, p 367)*

The Sequence Veni, Sancte Spíritus, *pp. 368–370, may be said.*

OF. *Lauda ánima mea (Easter III, p. 322)*

CO. *Non vos relínquam (Easter VI, p. 336)*

Ember Saturday

IN. *Cáritas Dei (Vigil of Pentecost, p. 361)*

AL. *Laudate Dóminum (Epiphany V, p. 102)*
    ℣. Come, Holy Ghost, *etc. (supra, p 367)*

The Sequence Veni, Sancte Spíritus, *pp. 368–370, may be said.*

OF. *Dómine, Deus salútis (Ember Sat. in Lent, p. 149)*

CO. *Dómine, Deus meus (Ember Sat. in Lent, p. 149)*

TRINITYTIDE

Trinity Sunday

INTROIT *Benedícta sit*   *Tob. 12:6, Ps. 8*

Cantors

vij.

BLES-SED be the Holy Trinity, and the un-di-vi-ded

Choir

U -ni - ty: we will praise and glorify him, because he

FINE   *Cantors*

hath showed his mer - cy up - on us. *Ps.* O LORD our

Choir

Go-ver-nor: how excellent is thy Name in all the world.

Cantors   *Choir*   *Full*

Glo- ry be..., *(etc.)* As it was..., *(etc.)* Bles - sed be..., *(etc.)*

GRADUAL *Benedíctus es*   *Dan. 3:55,56*

Cantors

v.

BLESS-ED art thou, O LORD, who beholdest the

Choir

great deep: and sit - test up-on the Che-ru-bim.

Cantors

℣. Bless - ed art thou, O Lord, in the firmament of hea- ven:

and above all to be praised and glo-ri-fi-ed for ev - er.

The Canticle Benedíctus es *may replace the Gradual.*

ALLELUIA *Benedíctus es*   *Dan. 3:52*

Cantors   *All*

vj.

AL- LE- LU- IA. Al - le- lu- ia.

Cantors

℣. Bless - ed art thou, O Lord God of our fa - thers:

380

Choir

and worthy to be prais - ed for ev - er - more.

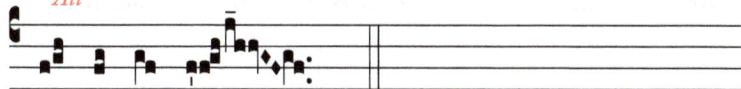

All

Al - le- lu- ia.

OFFERTORY *Benedíctus sit*   *Tob. 12:6*

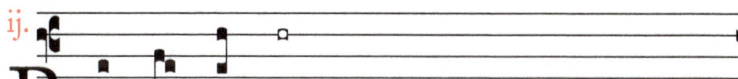

Cantors

ij.

BLES-SED be God the Father, and the only begotten

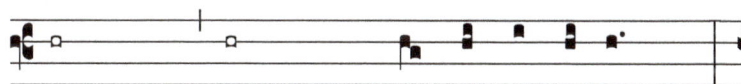

Son of God; and blessed be the Ho - ly Spi -rit:

Choir

for the mer - cy he hath done un - to   us.

COMMUNION *Benedícimus Deum*   *Job. 12:6*

Cantors

i.

LET us bless the God of heaven; and in the sight of

Choir

all living will we give thanks un - to him: be - cause

he hath done unto us after his lov - ing-kind - ness.

Verses from Tobit 13:1, 3, 5-6, 8-10 *may be sung.*

FIRST SUNDAY after TRINITY

INTROIT *Dómine, in tua misericórdia*   *Ps. 13:6 & 1*

Cantors

vij.

O LORD my God, in thy loving-kindness and mercy

have I trusted; and my heart is joyful in thy sal- va- tion:

Choir

I will sing unto the LORD, because he hath dealt so

FINE   *Cantors*

lov- ing- ly with me. *Ps.* How long wilt thou forget me, O

Choir

Lord, for e- ver: how long wilt thou hide thy face from me?

Cantors   *Choir*   *Full*

Glo- ry be...*(etc.)* As it was..., *(etc.)* O LORD ..., *(etc.)*

GRADUAL *Ego dixi*   *Ps. 41:5, ℣. 2*

Cantors   *Choir*

℣. I SAID, LORD, be mer- ci- ful un- to me: heal my

Cantors

soul, for I have sinned a- gainst thee.   ℣. Bless- ed is

Choir

he that considereth the poor and nee- dy: the LORD

shall deliver him in the time of trou- ble.

ALLELUIA *Verba mea*   *Ps. 5:1*

vj. AL- LE- LU- IA. Al - le - lu- ia.

Cantors   *All*

℣. Pon- der my words, O LORD: consider my me- di- ta- tion.

Cantors   *Choir*

Al - le - lu- ia.

All

OFFERTORY *Inténde voci*   *Ps. 5:2,3*

O HEAR- KEN thou unto the voice of my calling,

Cantors

my King and my God: for un- to thee will I make my prayer.

Choir

385

COMMUNION *Narrábo ómnia mirabília*   *Ps. 9:1,2*

Cantors

i.

I WILL speak of all thy marvellous works; I will be

Choir

glad, and re- joice in thee: yea, my songs will I make of thy

Name, O thou most High- est.

Verses from Psalm 9:7-12 *may be sung.*

SECOND SUNDAY after TRINITY

INTROIT *Factus est Dóminus* Ps. 18:19b,20,1

Cantors

vij.

THE LORD was my refuge and my upholder; and he

Choir

brought me forth into a place of li- ber- ty: he de- livered

FINE *Cantors*

me, because he de- light- ed in me. *Ps.* I will love

Choir

thee, O LORD, my strength: the LORD is my rock,

my fortress and my Sa- viour.

Cantors *Choir* *Full*

Glo- ry be...*(etc.)* As it was..., *(etc.)* The LORD ..., *(etc.)*

387

GRADUAL *Ad Dóminum* Ps. 120:1, ℣. 2

Cantors

WHEN I was in trouble I called up- on the LORD:

Choir *Cantors*

and he heard me. ℣. De- li- ver my soul, O LORD, from

Choir

ly- ing lips: and from a de-ceit-ful tongue.

ALLELUIA *Dómine Deus meus* Ps. 7

Cantors *All*

AL- LE- LU- IA. Al - le- lu- ia.

Cantors *Choir*

℣. O LORD my God, in thee have I put my trust: save me

from them that persecute me and de- li- ver me.

All

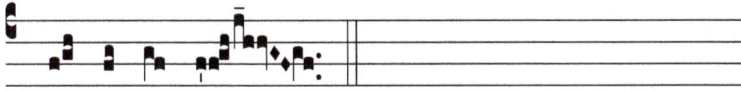

Al - le- lu- ia.

OFFERTORY *Dómine convértere*   *Ps. 6:4*

Cantors

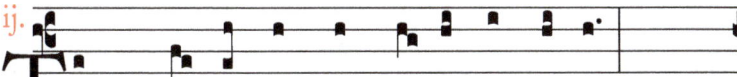

TURN thee, O LORD, and de- li- ver my soul:

Choir

O save me for thy mer-cy's sake.

COMMUNION *Cantábo Dómino*   *Ps. 13:6*

Cantors

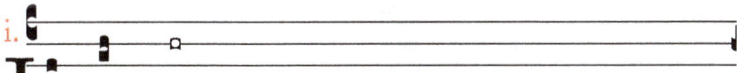

I WILL sing of the Lord, because he hath dealt so

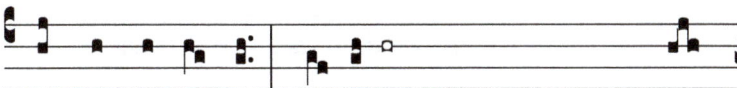

lov- ing- ly with me: yea, I will praise the Name of the

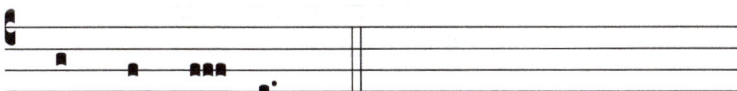

Lord Most High- est.

Verses from Psalm 13:3-6 *may be sung.*

THIRD SUNDAY after TRINITY

Introit *Réspice in me*   *Ps. 25:15, 17, & 1*

Cantors

vij.

TURN thee unto me, and have mercy upon me, O Lord;

Choir

for I am desolate and in tri- bu- la- tion: look thou on mine

affliction, and my travail; and forgive me all mine

FINE   *Cantors*

i- ni- qui- ties, O my God. *Ps.* Un- to thee, O Lord,

Choir

do I lift up my soul: my God, in thee have I trusted;

let me never be con- found- ed.

390

Cantors *Choir* *Full*

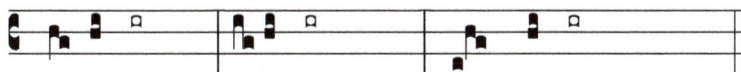

Glo- ry be...*(etc.)* As it was..., *(etc.)* Turn thee unto me...,*(etc.)*

GRADUAL *Iacta cogitátum tuum* *Ps. 55:23,17,19*

Cantors *Choir*

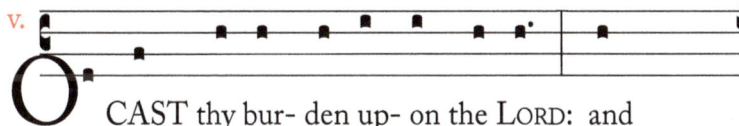

O CAST thy bur- den up- on the LORD: and

Cantors

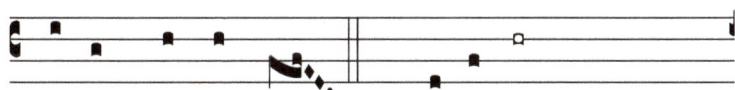

he shall nou- rish thee. ℣. When I cried unto the LORD,

Choir

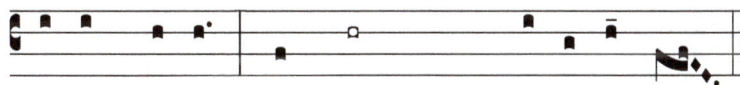

he heard my voice: from the battle that was a- gainst me.

ALLELUIA *Deus iudex iustus* *Ps. 7:12*

Cantors *All*

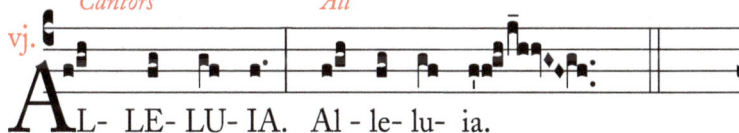

vj. AL- LE- LU- IA. Al - le- lu- ia.

391

Cantors   *Choir*

℣. God is a righteous Judge, strong and pa- tient: and

God is pro- vok- ed ev- ery day.

All

Al - le- lu- ia.

OFFERTORY *Sperent in te*   *Ps. 9:10, 11, 12*

Cantors

ij.

THEY that know thy Name will put their trust in thee;

for thou, LORD, hast never fail- ed them that seek thee:

Choir

O praise the LORD which dwelleth in Sion, for he forgetteth

392

not the com- plaint of the poor.

COMMUNION. *Dico vobis gáudiam*   *Lk. 15:10*

I SAY unto you, There is joy in the presence of the

An-gels of God: o- ver one sin-ner that re-pent-eth.

Verses from Psalm 32 *may be sung.*

FOURTH SUNDAY after TRINITY

INTROIT *Dóminus illuminátio mea*   *Ps. 27:1, 2, 3*

Cantors

vij.

THE LORD is my light, and my salvation, whom then

shall I fear? The LORD is the stronghold of my life, of

Choir

whom shall I be a - fraid? When mine enemies pressed

FINE   *Cantors*

sore against me, they stum - bled and fell. *Ps.* Though an

Choir

host of men were laid a - gainst me: yet shall not my

Cantors   *Full*

heart be a -fraid. Glo - ry be..., *(etc.)* The LORD..., *(etc.)*

GRADUAL *Propítius esto* Ps. 79:9, 10

Cantors *Choir*

BE mer - ci - ful unto our sins, O LORD: where-fore

Cantors

do the heathen say, Where is now their God? ℣. Help

Choir

us, O God of our sal - va - tion: and for the glory of

thy Name, de - li - ver us, O LORD.

ALLELUIA *Deus, qui sedes* Ps. 9: 4, 9

Cantors *All*

AL- LE- LU- IA. Al - le- lu- ia.

Cantors

℣. Thou, O God, art set in the throne that judg - est

395

Choir

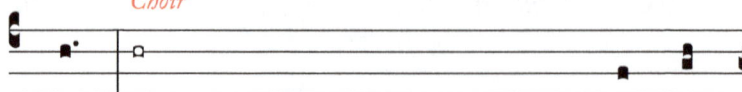

right: be thou the refuge of the opprest in due time of

All

trou - ble. Al - le- lu- ia.

OFFERTORY *Illúmina óculos meos*   *Ps. 13:3*

Cantors   *Choir*

ij.

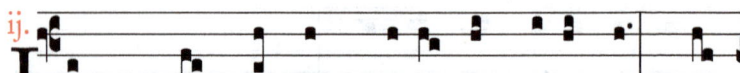

LIGHT - EN mine eyes, that I sleep not in death: lest

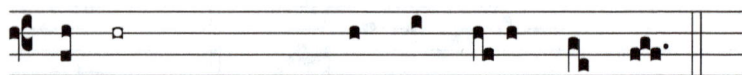

mine enemy say, I have pre - vail - ed a - gainst him.

COMMUNION *Dóminus firmaméntum meum*   *Ps: 18:3*

Cantors

i.

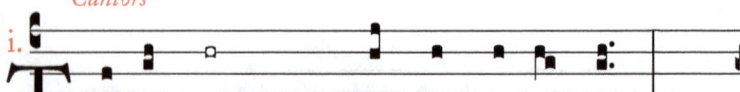

THE LORD is my strong rock, and my de - fence:

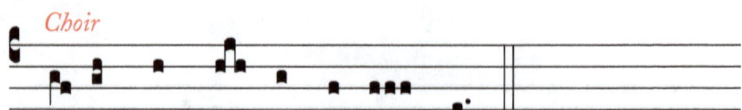

Choir

my Sa - viour, my God, and my might.

Verses of Psalm 18:3, 4, 7, 28, 29, 32, 33, 36 *may be sung.*

FIFTH SUNDAY after TRINITY

INTROIT *Exáudi, Dómine*   *Ps. 27:8,10,11,1*

Cantors

vij.

CON- SI- DER, O LORD, and hear me, when I cry

Choir

un- to thee: be thou my succour, O cast me not away,

FINE

neither forsake me utterly, O God of my sal- va- tion.

Cantors

Ps. The LORD is my light, and my sal- va- tion:

Choir   *Cantors*

whom then shall I fear?   Glo- ry be..., *(etc.)*

Full

Con- si- der, O LORD..., *(etc.)*

GRADUAL *Protéctor noster*   *Ps. 84: 10. 9*

Cantors   *Choir*

BE- HOLD, O God, our de- fen- der: and look

Cantors

up- on thy ser- vants.   ℣. O LORD God of hosts:

Choir

hear the prayers of thy ser- vants.

ALLELUIA *Dómine, in virtúte tua*   *Ps. 21:1*

Cantors   *All*

AL- LE- LU- IA.   Al - le- lu- ia.

Cantors

℣.   The   King shall rejoice in thy strength, O LORD:

Choir

exceeding glad shall he be of thy sal- va- tion.

All

Al - le- lu- ia.

OFFERTORY *Benedícam Dóminum*   *Ps. 16: 8, 9*

ij. *Cantors*

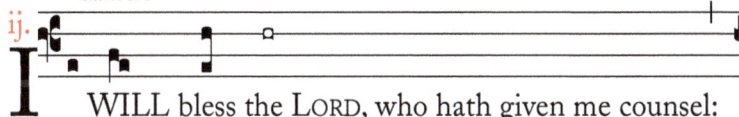

I WILL bless the LORD, who hath given me counsel:

Choir

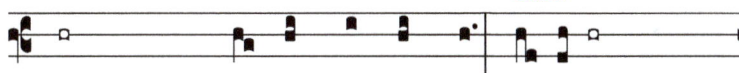

I have set God al- ways be- fore me;   for he is on my

right hand, there- fore I shall   not fall.

COMMUNION *Unam pétii a Dómino*   *Ps. 27:4*

i. *Cantors*

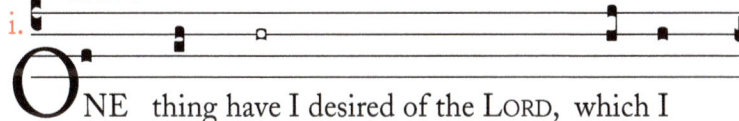

ONE   thing have I desired of the LORD, which I

Choir

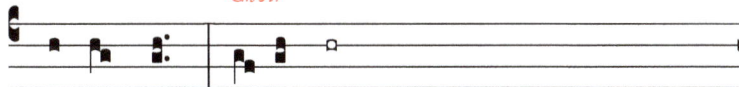

will re- quire: e- ven that I may dwell in the house

399

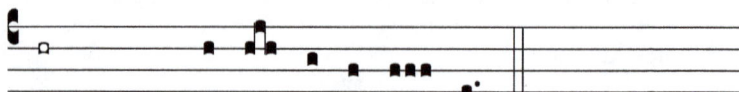

of the LORD all the days of my life.

Verses of Psalm 27:1, 2, 3, 10, 13, 15, 16 *may be sung.*

SIXTH SUNDAY after TRINITY

INTROIT *Dóminus fortitúdo*   *Ps. 28:8, 9, 1*

Cantors

vij.

THE LORD is the strength of his people, and a strong-

Choir

hold of salvation to his A- noint- ed One: O LORD,

save thine own people, and give thy blessing unto thine

FINE

inheritance; O feed them also, and set them up for ev- er.

Cantors

Ps. Un- to thee will I cry, O LORD; my God, be not

Choir

si- lent un-to me: lest, if thou make as though thou

401

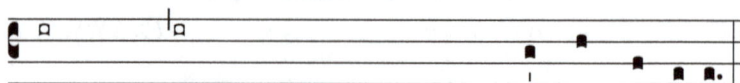

hearest not, I become like them that go down in- to the pit.

Cantors   *Choir*   *Full*

Glo- ry be..., *(etc.)* As it was..., *(etc.)* The LORD..., *(etc.)*

GRADUAL *Convértere*   *Ps. 90:13, 1*

Cantors   *Choir*

℣. TURN thee a-gain, O LORD, at the last: and be gra-

Cantors

cious un- to thy ser-vants. ℣. LORD, thou hast been our

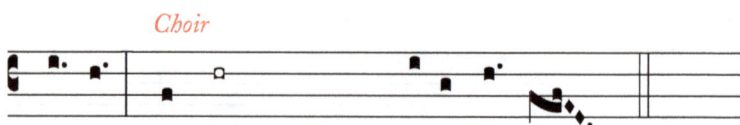

Choir

re-fuge: from one generation to an- o- ther.

ALLELUIA *In te, Dómine, speravi*   *Ps. 31:2,3*

Cantors   *All*

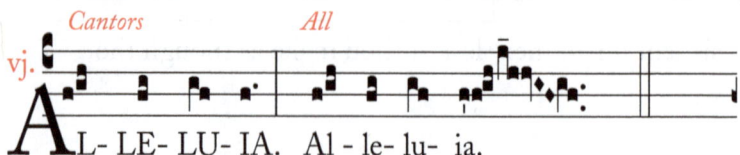

vj. AL- LE- LU- IA. Al - le- lu- ia.

Cantors

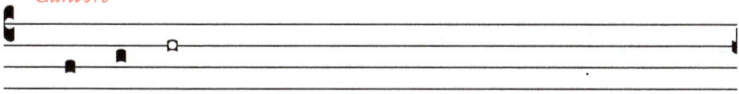

℣. In thee, O Lᴏʀᴅ, have I put my trust, let me never

Choir

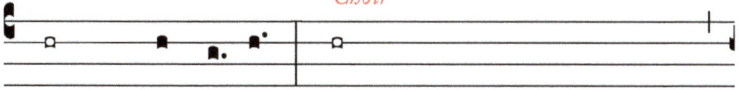

be put to con- fu- sion: deliver me in thy righteousness;

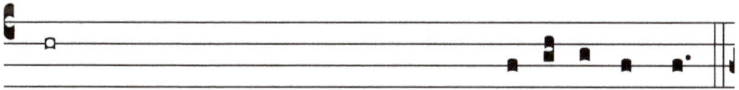

bow down thine ear to me, make haste to de- li- ver me.

All

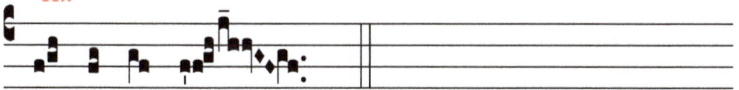

Al - le- lu- ia.

OFFERTORY *Pérfice gressus meos* Ps. 17:5-6

Cantors

ij.

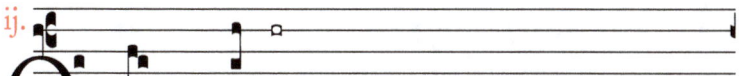

O HOLD thou up my goings in thy paths, that my

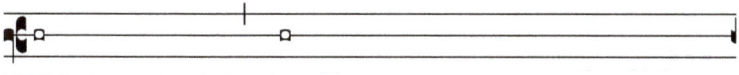

footsteps slip not; incline thine ear unto me, and

Choir

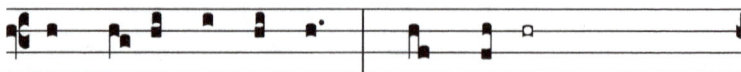

heark- en un- to my words: Show thy marvellous loving-

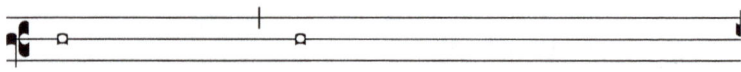

kindness, O Lord; thou that art the Saviour of them that

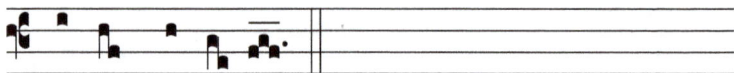

put their trust in thee.

COMMUNION *Circuíbo*   *Ps. 27:7*

Cantors

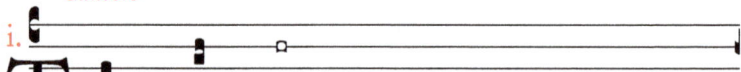

i. THERE-FORE I will offer in his dwelling an oblation

Choir

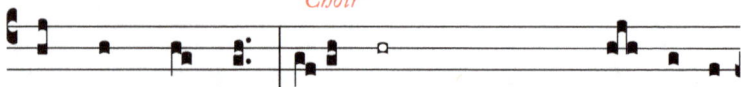

with great glad-ness: I will sing and speak prai-ses un-to

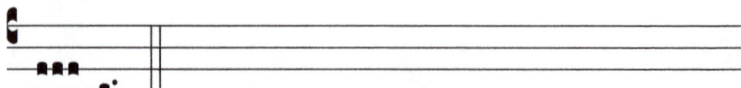

the Lord.

Verses from Psalm 27:1-5 *may be sung.*

404

SEVENTH SUNDAY after TRINITY

INTROIT *Omnes gentes pláudite*   *Ps. 47:1,2*

Cantors

O CLAP your hands together, all ye peo- ple:

Choir

O sing unto God with the voice of joy and tri- umph.

Cantors

Ps. For the Lord is high, and to be fear - ed:

Cantors

he is the great King up- on all the earth.

Cantors   *Choir*   *Full*

Glo- ry be..., *(etc.)* As it was..., *(etc.)* O clap..., *(etc.)*

GRADUAL *Veníte fílii* Ps. *34:11,5*

Cantors

COME, ye children, and heark - en un - to me:

Choir

I will teach you the fear of the LORD.

Cantors

℣. Come un-to me and be en- light - en - ed:

Choir

and your faces shall not be a - sham - ed.

ALLELUIA *Omnes gentes pláudite* Ps. *47:1*

Cantors *All*

AL- LE- LU- IA. Al - le- lu- ia.

Cantors

℣. O clap your hands together, all ye peo - ple:

Choir

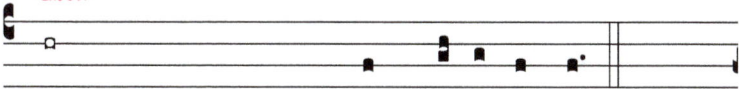

O sing unto God with the voice of me- lo - dy.

All

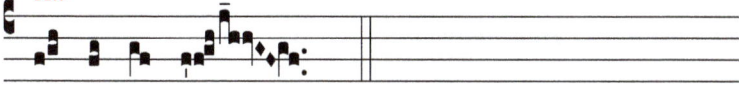

Al - le- lu- ia.

OFFERTORY *Sicut in holocáusto* Dan. 3:40

Cantors

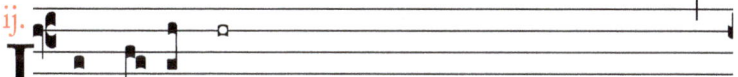

ij.

LIKE as in the burnt-offerings of rams and bullocks;

Choir

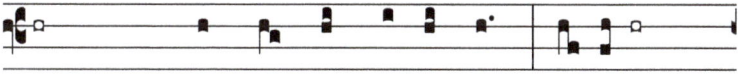

and like as in ten thou- sands of fat lambs: so let our sac-

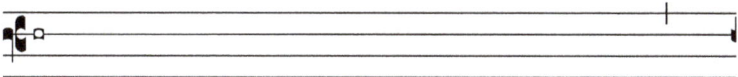

rifice be in thy sight this day, that it may please thee;

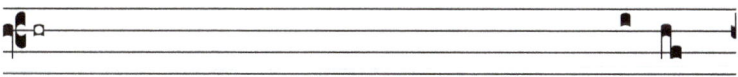

for they shall not be confounded that put their trust in

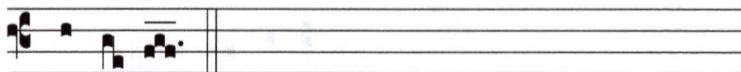

thee, O LORD.

COMMUNION *Inclína aurem tuam* *Ps. 31*

Cantors *Choir*

i.

BOW down thine ear to me: make haste to de-li- ver me.

Verses from Psalm 31:1-2, 6-9, 21-22, 26-27 *may be sung.*

EIGHTH SUNDAY after TRINITY

INTROIT *Suscépimus*   *Ps. 48:8,9,& 1*

Cantors

vij.

WE have waited, O God, for thy loving-kindness in

the midst of thy temple; according to thy Name, O God,

Choir

so is thy praise un- to the world's end: thy right hand

FINE   *Cantors*

is full of righ- teous- ness. *Ps.* Great is the LORD, and

Choir

highly to be prais- ed: in the city of our God,

Cantors   *Full*

even up- on his ho - ly hill. Glo- ry be *(etc.)* We have, *(etc.)*

409

GRADUAL *Esto mihi*   *Ps. 71:2, 1*

Cantors

BE thou my strong rock, and house of de- fence:

Choir   *Cantors*

that thou may- est save me.   ℣.   In thee, O Lord,

Choir

have I put my trust: let me never be put to con-fu-sion.

ALLELUIA *Magnus Dóminus*   *Ps. 48*

Cantors   *All*

AL-   LE-LU- IA.   Al - le- lu- ia.

Cantors   *Choir*

℣. Great is the LORD, and highly to be prais - ed: in the

city of our God, even up - on his ho - ly hill.

All

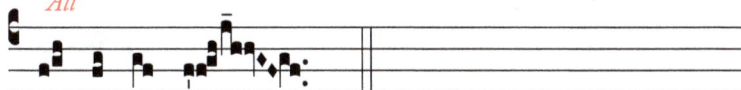

Al- le- lu- ia

OFFERTORY *Pópulum húmilem*   *Ps. 18:28, 32*

Cantors

ij.

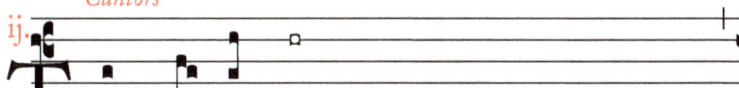

THOU shalt save the people that are in adversity, O LORD,

and shall bring down the high looks of the proud:

Choir

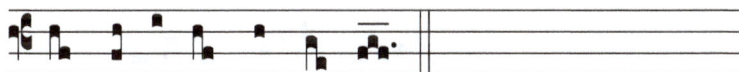

for who is God, but the LORD?

COMMUNION   *Gustáte et vidéte*   *Ps. 34:8*

Cantors

i.

O TASTE and see how gra- cious the LORD is:

Choir

bless - ed is he that put - teth his trust in   him.

Verses from Psalm 34:1, 5, 6, 14-20 *may be sung.*

NINTH SUNDAY after TRINITY

Introit *Ecce Deus*   Ps. 54:4,5,1

Cantors

vij.

B E- HOLD, God is my helper; the Lord is he that up-

Choir

hold - eth my soul: re - ward thou evil unto mine

enemies; destroy them in thine anger, for thy righteous-

FINE

ness' sake, O Lord my strength and my de- fend - er.

Cantors   *Choir*

Ps. Save me, O God, for thy Name's sake: and avenge

Cantors   *Full*

me in thy strength. Glo- ry be..., *(etc.)* Be-hold..., *(etc.)*

GRADUAL *Dómine, Dóminus noster*   *Ps. 8:1*

Cantors   *Choir*

O LORD, our Go- vern -or: how excellent is thy

Cantors

Name in all the world. ℣. Thou hast set thy glo- ry:

Choir

a- bove the hea- vens.

ALLELUIA *Eripe me de inimícis meis*   *Ps. 59*

Cantors   *All*

AL- LE-LU- IA. Al - le- lu- ia.

Cantors   *Choir*

℣. De- li- ver me from mine enemies, O God: defend me

from them that rise up a- gainst me.

All

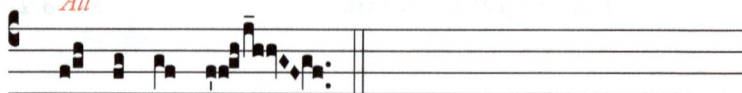

Al- le- lu- ia.

OFFERTORY *Iustítiæ Dómini*   *Ps. 19:8, 10, 11*

Cantors

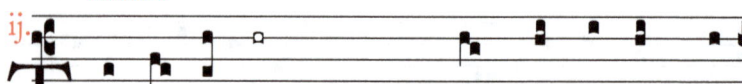

THE sta- tutes of the LORD are right, and re- joice the

Choir

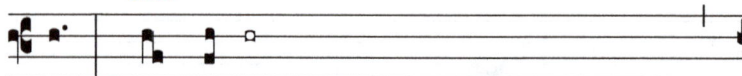

heart: sweet- er also than honey, and the honey - comb;

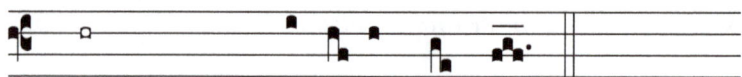

moreover, by them is thy ser- vant taught.

COMMUNION *Qui manducat*   *Jn. 6:56*

Cantors

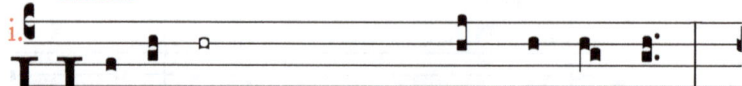

HE that eateth my Flesh and drink-eth my Blood:

Choir

dwel-leth in me and I in him, saith the LORD.

Psalm 119:1,2,11,49,50,72,103,105,162 *may be sung.*

414

TENTH SUNDAY after TRINITY

INTROIT *Dum clamárem*   *Ps. 55:19,20,23,1,2*

Cantors

WHEN I called upon the LORD, he heard my voice,

Choir

even from the battle that was a-gainst me: yea, ev-en

God that endureth for ever shall hear me, and bring them

down: O cast thy burden upon the LORD, and he shall

FINE   *Cantors*

nou - rish thee. *Ps.* Hear my prayer, O Lord, and hide

Choir

not thyself from my pe- ti- tion: take heed unto me, and

PROPER of the SEASON

hear me. Glo- ry be *(etc.)* As it was *(etc.)* When I *(etc.)*

GRADUAL *Custódi me*   *Ps. 17:8 & 1*

KEEP me, O LORD, as the ap-ple of an eye: hide me

under the sha- dow of thy wings. ℣. Let my

sentence come forth from thy pre- sence: and let thine

eyes look upon the thing that is e- qual.

ALLELUIA *Te decet hymnus*   *Ps. 65*:1

AL- LE- LU- IA. Al - le- lu- ia.

416

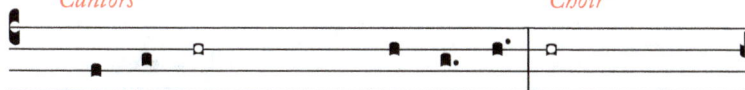

℣. Thou, O God, art praised in Si- on: and unto thee

shall the vow be performed in Je- ru- sa- lem.

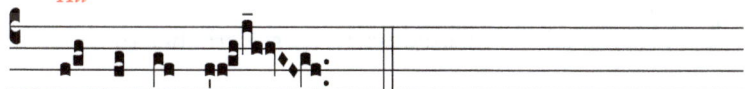

Al- le- lu- ia.

OFFERTORY *Ad te, Dómine, levávi*   *Ps. 25:1-3*

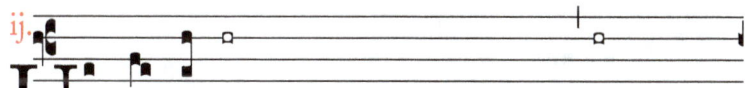

UN- TO thee O LORD, lift I up my soul; O my God,

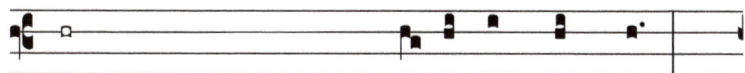

in thee have I trusted, let me not be con- foun- ded:

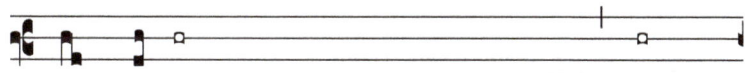

nei- ther let mine enemies triumph over me;   for all

417

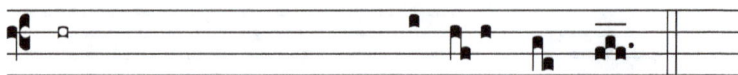

they that hope in thee shall not be a- sham- ed.

COMMUNION   *Acceptábis*   *Ps 51:19*

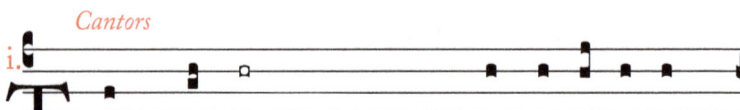

THOU shalt be pleased with the sa- cri- fice of righ-

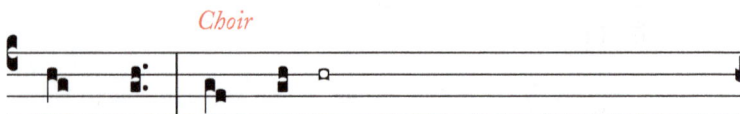

teous - ness: with the burnt offerings and oblations upon

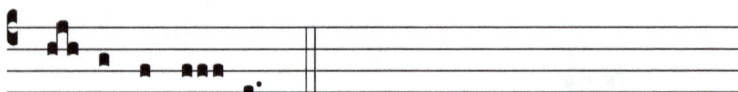

thine al- tar, O LORD.

Verses from Psalm 51:1a, 8, 10-13, 15, 17, 18 *may be sung.*

ELEVENTH SUNDAY after TRINITY

INTROIT *Deus in loco sancto*   *Cf. Ps. 68: 5, 6, 35, 2*

Cantors

vij.

GOD in his holy habitation; it is he that maketh

Choir

brethren to be of one mind in an house: He will give the

dominion and pre-eminence un- to his peo- ple.

Cantors

Ps. Let God arise, and let his e- ne- mies be scat- ter- ed:

Choir

let them also that hate him flee be- fore him.

Cantors   *Full*

Glo- ry be..., *(etc.)*   God in his holy habitation:..., *(etc.)*

GRADUAL *In Deo sperávit* Ps. 28:8b,1

Cantors

℣.

MY heart hath trusted in God, and I am help-ed:

Choir

therefore my heart danceth for joy, and in my song will I

Cantors *Choir*

praise him. ℣. Un- to thee will I cry, O LORD: be not

silent, O my God, nor de- part from me.

ALLELUIA *Exsultáte Deo* Ps. 81:1, 2

Cantors *All*

℣.

AL- LE- LU- IA Al - le- lu- ia.

Cantors

℣. Sing we merrily unto God our strength; make a

Choir

cheerful noise unto the God of Ja- cob: take the psalm,

All

bring hi- ther the ta- bret.   Al - le- lu- ia.

OFFERTORY *Exaltábo te*   *Ps. 30: 1,2*

Cantors

I WILL magnify thee, O LORD, for thou hast set me up:

Choir

and   not   made my foes to tri- umph ov- er me.

Cantors   *Choir*

O LORD, my God, I cri- ed un- to thee: and thou hast

heal- ed me.

COMMUNION *Honóra Dóminum*   *Prov. 3: 9–10*

Cantors

i.

HO- NOUR the LORD with thy substance, and with the

Choir

first-fruits of all thine in- crease: so shall thy barns be

filled with plenty, and thy presses shall burst out with

new wine.

Verses from Psalms 112:1-9 *or* 128 *may be sung.*

TWELFTH SUNDAY after TRINITY

INTROIT *Deus in adiutórium*   *Ps. 70:1,2*

Cantors

HASTE thee, O God, to deliver me; make haste to

Choir

help me, O LORD: let mine enemies be ashamed and con-

FINE   *Cantors*

founded that seek af-ter my soul. *Ps.* Let them be turned

Choir

backward and put to con- fu- sion: that wish me e- vil.

Cantors   *Choir*   *Full*

Glo- ry be..., *(etc.)* As it was..., *(etc.)* Haste thee,..., *(etc.)*

GRADUAL *Benedícam Dóminum* Ps. 34:1, 2

Cantors *Choir*

I WILL al- ways give thanks un - to the LORD: his praise

Cantors

shall ever be in my mouth. ℣. My soul shall make her boast

Choir

in the Lord: The humble shall hear thereof, and be glad

ALLELUIA *Dómine Deus salútis meæ* Ps. 88

Cantors *All*

AL- LE- LU- IA. Al - le- lu- ia.

Cantors *Choir*

℣. O LORD God of my sal- va- tion: I have cried day and

All

night be- fore thee. Al - le- lu- ia.

OFFERTORY *Precátus est Móyses*   *Ex. 32:11, 15, 13, 14*

Cantors

MO - SES be- sought the LORD his God and said:

Choir

Why, O Lord, doth thy wrath wax hot a- gainst thy

Cantors

peo- ple?   Turn from thy fierce wrath; remember

Choir

Abraham, Is- aac, and Ja- cob: to whom thou swarest to

Cantors

give a land flow- ing with milk and ho- ney; and the Lord

Choir

re- pen- ted of the e- vil: which he thought to do

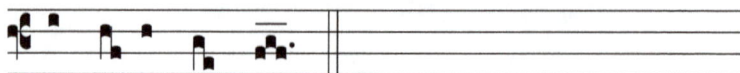

un- to his peo- ple.

COMMUNION *De fructu óperum*   *Ps. 104:13b,14,15*

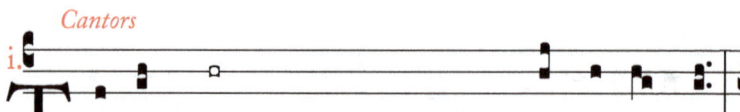

Cantors

i.

T HE earth, O Lord, is filled with the fruit of thy works:

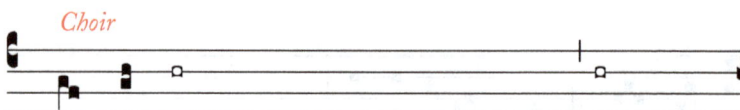

Choir

that thou mayest bring food out of the earth, and wine

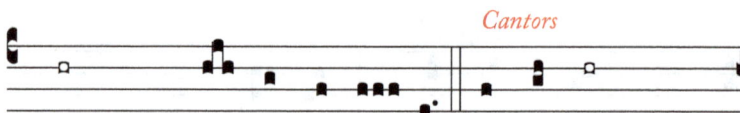

Cantors

that maketh glad the heart of man: and oil to make him

Choir

a cheer-ful coun- te-nance; and bread to strength-en

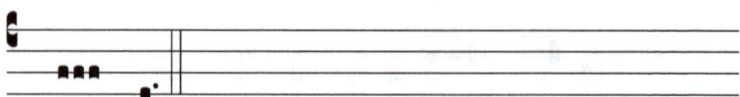

man's heart.

Verses from Psalm 104:1-2,24,30-31,33-34 *may be sung.*

THIRTEENTH SUNDAY after TRINITY

INTROIT *Respice, Dómine*   Ps. *74:21, 20, 23, & 1*

Cantors

vij.

LOOK, O LORD, graciously upon thy covenant, and

forsake not the congregation of the poor for ev- er:

Choir

a- rise, O LORD, maintain thine own cause; and be not

FINE

unmindful of the voices of them that seek thee.

Cantors

Ps. O God, wherefore art thou absent from us so long:

Choir

why is thy wrath so hot against the sheep of thy pas- ture?

Cantors   *Choir*   *Full*

Glo- ry be...*(etc.)*   As it was... *(etc.)* Look, O LORD,...*(etc.)*

GRADUAL *Respice, Dómine*   *Ps. 74:21,20b,23*

Cantors   *Choir*

LOOK up- on thy cove- nant, O LORD: and forget

                                                 Cantors

not the congregation of the poor for ev- er.   ℣. A- rise,

                                    Choir

O LORD, maintain thine own cause: re- member how

the foolish man blas- phe- meth thee dai- ly.

ALLELUIA *Dómine, refúgium*   *Ps. 90:1*

Cantors   *All*

AL- LE-LU- IA. Al - le- lu- ia.

428

Cantors *Choir*

℣. LORD, thou hast been our re- fuge: from one gener-

All

ation to a- no - ther. Al - le- lu- ia.

OFFERTORY *In te sperávi* *Ps. 31:16, 17*

Cantors *Choir*

ij. MY hope hath been in thee, O LORD: I have said,

Thou art my God, my times are in thy hand.

COMMUNION *Panem de cælo* *Wisd. 16:20*

Cantors

i. THOU hast given us bread from hea- ven, O LORD:

Choir

hav- ing every delight, and ev- ery taste of sweet- ness.

Verses from Psalm 78:1-4, 24-26, 28-30 *may be sung.*

429

FOURTEENTH SUNDAY after TRINITY

INTROIT *Protéctor noster*   *Ps. 84:9,10,1,2*

Cantors

vij.

BE-HOLD, O God, our defender, and look upon the

Choir

face of thine A- noint- ed: for one day in thy courts is

FINE   *Cantors*

bet- ter than a thou- sand. *Ps.* O how amiable are thy

Choir

dwell- ings, thou LORD of hosts: my soul hath a desire

and longing to enter into the courts of the Lord.

Cantors   *Choir*   *Full*

Glo- ry be..., *(etc.)*   As it was..., *(etc.)* Be- hold,..., *(etc.)*

GRADUAL *Bonum est confídere* *Ps. 118:8, 9*

Cantors   *Choir*

IT is better to trust in the LORD: than to put any con- fi-

Cantors

dence in man. ℣. It is better to trust in the LORD:

Choir

than to put any con- fi- dence in prin- ces.

ALLELUIA *Veníte, exsultémus* *Ps. 95:1*

Cantors   *All*   *Cantors*

AL- LE- LU- IA. Al - le- lu- ia. ℣. O

Choir

come, let us sing unto the LORD: let us heartily rejoice in

All

the strength of our sal-va-tion. Al - le- lu- ia.

OFFERTORY *Immíttet ángelus*   *Ps. 34:7, 8*

Cantors

ij.

T HE An- gel of the LORD tarrieth round about them

Choir

that fear him, and de- li- ver- eth them: O taste and

see how gra- cious the LORD   is.

COMMUNION *Prímum quǽrite*   *Matt. 6:33*

Cantors   *Choir*

i.

S EEK ye first the king- dom of God: and all these

things shall be added un- to you, saith the LORD.

Verses from Psalm 37:1, 3, 16, 18, 28, 30, 35 *may be sung.*

FIFTEENTH SUNDAY after TRINITY

INTROIT *Inclína, Dómine*   *Ps. 86:1,2,3,4*

Cantors

Bow down, O LORD, thine ear to me, and hear me:

Choir

O my God, save thy servant that trusteth in thee;

have mercy upon me, O LORD, for I have called dai- ly

FINE   *Cantors*

up- on thee.   *Ps.* Com- fort the soul of thy ser- vant:

Choir

for unto thee, O Lord, do I lift up my soul.

Cantors   *Choir*   *Full*

Glo- ry be..., *(etc.)* As it was..., *(etc.)* Bow down..., *(etc.)*

433

GRADUAL *Bonum est confitéri* Ps. 92:1,2

Cantors

IT is a good thing to give thanks un- to the LORD:

Choir

and to sing praises unto thy Name, O Most High- est.

Cantors

℣. To tell of thy loving-kindness early in the morn- ing:

Choir

and of thy truth in the night sea- son.

ALLELUIA *Quóniam Deus magnus* Ps. 95:3

Cantors   *All*

AL- LE- LU- IA. Al- le- lu- ia.

Cantors   *Choir*

℣. For the Lord is a great God: and a great King

434

All

o- ver all the earth.   Al - le- lu- ia.

OFFERTORY *Exspéctans expectavi*   *Ps. 40: 2,3,4*

Cantors

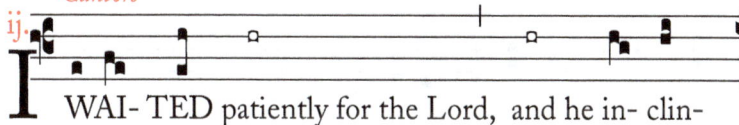

I WAI- TED patiently for the Lord, and he in- clin-

Choir

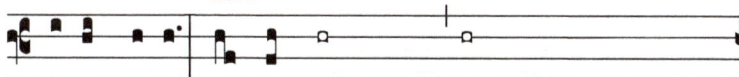

ed un- to me: he heard my calling, and hath put a new

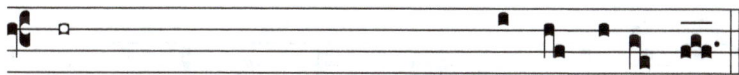

song in my mouth, even a thanks-giv-ing un-to our God.

COMMUNION *Panis quem ego dédero*   *Jn. 6:51*

Cantors

T HE bread that I will give is my Flesh: which I will

Choir

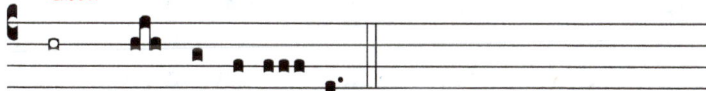

give for the life of the world.

Verses from Psalm 111 *may be sung.*

SIXTEENTH SUNDAY after TRINITY

Introit *Miserére mihi*   *Ps. 86:3,5,1*

Cantors

vij.

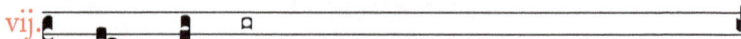

HAVE mer- cy upon me, O Lord, for I have called

Choir

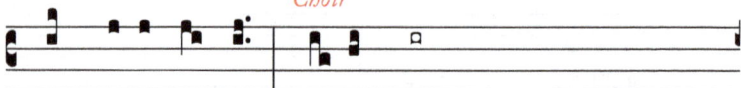

dai- ly up- on thee: for thou, O Lord, art gracious and

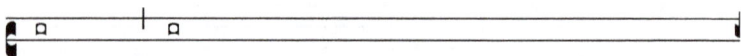

merciful, and plenteous in thy loving-kindness toward

Cantors

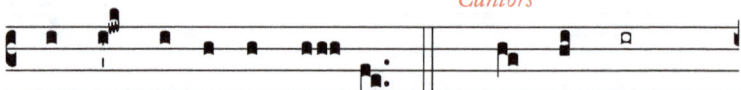

all them that call up- on thee. *Ps.* Bow down thine ear,

Choir

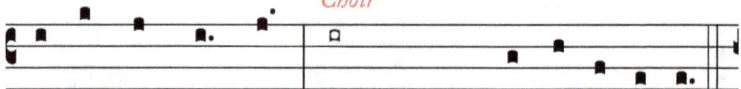

O Lord, and hear me: for I am poor and in mi- se- ry.

Cantors   *Choir*   *Full*

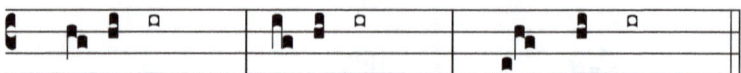

Glo- ry be...*(etc.)* As it was..., *(etc.)* Have mer-cy...,*(etc.)*

GRADUAL *Timébunt gentes*   *Ps. 102:15,16*

Cantors   *Choir*

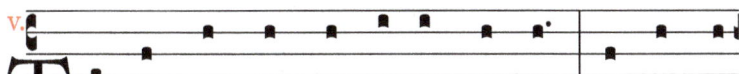

THE na-tions shall fear thy Name, O LORD: and all the

Cantors

kings of the earth thy ma- jes- ty. ℣. When the LORD

Choir

shall build up Si- on: and when his glo- ry shall ap- pear.

ALLELUIA *Cantáte Dómino*   *Ps. 98:1*

Cantors   *All*

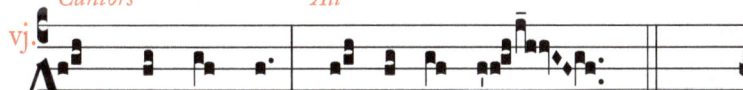

AL- LE- LU- IA. Al- le- lu- ia.

Cantors   *Choir*

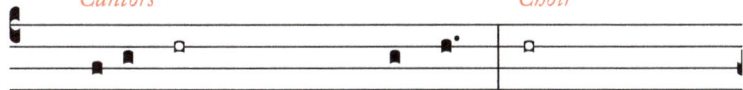

℣. O sing unto the LORD a new song: for he hath done

All

mar- vel- lous things. Al - le- lu- ia.

OFFERTORY *Dómine, in auxílium*   *Ps. 40:14,15*

Cantors

ij.

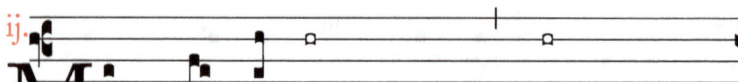

MAKE haste, O LORD, to help me;   let them be

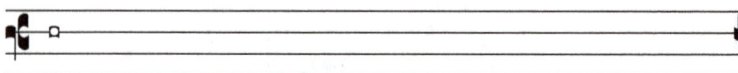

ashamed, and confounded together, that seek after my

Choir

soul to des- troy it: make haste, O LORD, to help me.

COMMUNION *Dómine, memorábor*   *Ps. 71:16,17,18*

Cantors

i.

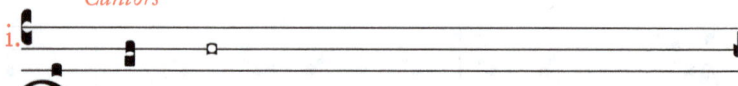

O LORD, I will make mention of thy righteousness

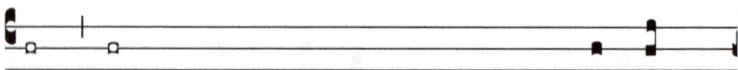

only; thou, O God, hast taught me from my youth up

Choir

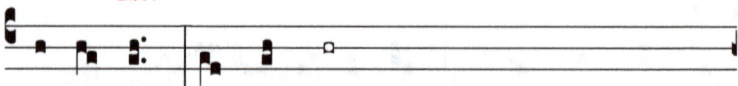

un-til now: for- sake me not, O God, in mine old age,

when I am grey - head - ed.

Verses from **Psalm 71:1-5, 8, 11, 13, 22** *may be sung.*

SEVENTEENTH SUNDAY after TRINITY

INTROIT *Iustus es Dómine*   *Ps. 119:137,124,1*

Cantors

RIGH- TEOUS art thou, O LORD, and true is thy

Choir

judge- ment: deal with thy servant according unto thy

FINE   *Cantors*

mer- ci- ful kind- ness. *Ps.* Bless- ed are those that are

Choir

un- de- fil- ed in the way: and walk in the law of the LORD.

Cantors   *Choir*   *Full*

Glo- ry be..., *(etc.)* As it was..., *(etc.)* Righ- teous art..., *(etc.)*

GRADUAL *Beáta gens*   *Ps. 33:12,6*

Cantors   *Choir*

BLESS- ED is the people whose God is the LORD: and

blessed are the folk that he hath chosen to him to be his

Cantors

in- he- ri- tance.   ℣. By the Word of the LORD were the

Choir

hea- vens made; and all the hosts of them by the

breath of his mouth.

ALLELUIA *Dómine, exáudi*   *Ps. 102:2*

Cantors / *All*

AL- LE- LU- IA.   Al- le- lu- ia.

Cantors / *Choir*

℣. Hear my prayer, O LORD;   and let my cry come

All

un- to thee.   Al - le- lu- ia.

OFFERTORY   *Orávi Deum meum*   *Dan. 9:4,17,19*

Cantors

I, DAN-IEL, prayed unto the LORD my God, and said:

Choir / *Cantors*

Hear, O our God, the prayer of thy ser- vant.   Cause

Choir

thy face to shine upon thy sanc- tu- a- ry: and be- hold,

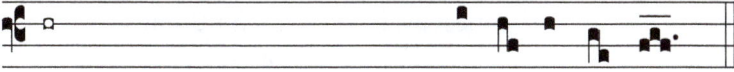

O God, this thy people, who are call-ed by thy Name.

COMMUNION *Vovéte*   *Ps. 76:12,13*

Cantors

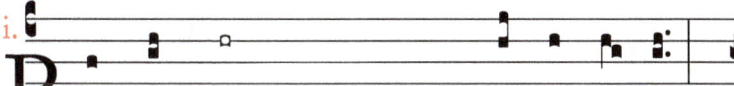

PRO- MISE unto the LORD your God, and keep it:

Choir

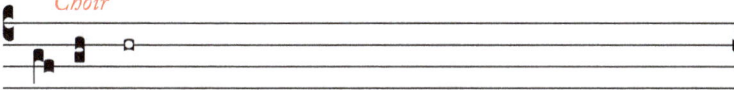

all ye that are round about him bring presents unto him

Cantors

that ought to be fear- ed.   He shall re-frain the spi- rit

Choir

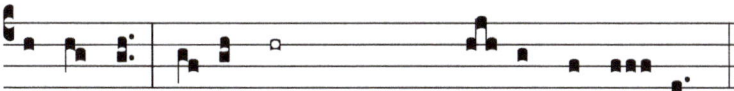

of prin-ces: and is wonderful among the kings of the earth.

Verses from Psalm 76:1-5, 8-9 *may be sung.*

443

The Autum Ember Days

Being the Wednesday, Friday, and Saturday after
Holy Cross Day (14 September)

Ember Wednesday in September

INTROIT *Exsultáte Deo*   *Ps. 81:1-5*

Cantors

vij.

SING we merrily unto God our strength; make a

Choir

cheerful noise unto the God of Ja-cob: take the psalm,

bring hither the tabret, the merry harp with the lute;

blow up the trumpet in the new moon, for this was a

FINE

statute for Israel, and a law of the God of Ja- cob.

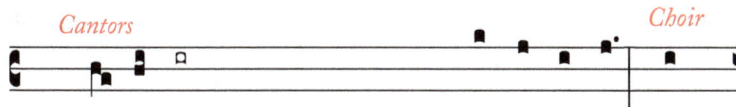

Ps. This he ordained in Joseph for a tes-ti-mo-ny: when

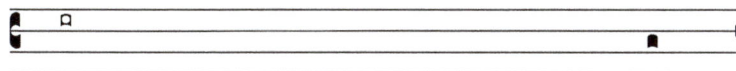

he came out of the land of Egypt, and had heard a

strange lang-uage. Glo- ry be... *(etc.)*   Sing we... *(etc.)*

GRADUAL *Quis sicut Dóminus (Epiphany IV, p. 97)*

OFFERTORY *Meditábor (Lent II, p. 151)*

COMMUNION *Comédite (Epiphany III, p. 94)*

Ember Friday in September

INTROIT *Lætétur cor (Epiphany IV, p. 96)*

GRADUAL *Convértere (Trinity VI, p. 402)*

OFFERTORY *Bénedic ánima mea (Christmas II, p. 74)*

445

COMMUNION *Aufer a me*   *Ps. 119:22-24*

Cantors

i.

O TURN from me shame and rebuke, for I have kept

Choir

thy sta-tutes, O LORD: for thy testimon-ies are my de- light.

Psalm 119: 1, 2, 39, 45, 99, 100, 143 *may be sung.*

Ember Saturday in September

INTROIT *Veníte. adorémus (Epiphany V, p. 100)*

TRACT *Laudáte Dóminum (Ember Saturday in Lent, p. 148)*

OFFERTORY *Dómine, Deus salútis (Ember Sat. in Lent, p. 149)*

COMMUNION *Mense séptimo festa (Epiphany V, p. 105)*

EIGHTEENTH SUNDAY after TRINITY

INTROIT *Da pácem*   *Sir. 36:16,17; Ps. 122:1*

Cantors

GIVE peace, O LORD, to them that wait for thee,

Choir

and let thy Prophets be found faith- ful: re- gard the

FINE

prayers of thy servant, and of thy peo- ple Is- ra-   el.

Cantors   *Choir*

Ps. I was glad when they said un- to me: we will go

Cantors

into the house of the Lord.   Glo - ry be..., *(etc.)*

Choir   *Full*

As it was..., *(etc.)*   Give peace..., *(etc.)*

447

GRADUAL *Lætátus sum*   *Ps. 122:1,7*

Cantors   *Choir*

I WAS glad when they said un- to me: we will go into

Cantors

the house of the LORD.   ℣. Peace be with- in thy walls:

Choir

and plenteousness with- in thy pa- la- ces.

ALLELUIA *Timébunt gentes*   *Ps. 102:16*

Cantors   *All*

AL- LE- LU- IA.   Al- le- lu- ia.

Cantors

℣. The na-tions shall fear thy Name, O LORD:

Choir

and all the kings of the earth thy ma- je- sty.

Al - le- lu- ia.

Offertory   *Sanctificávit Móyses*   *Ex. 24:4,5*

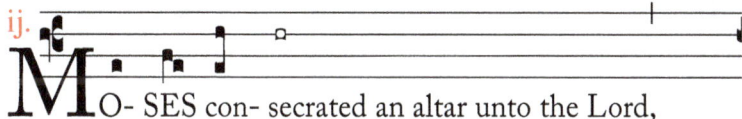

MO- SES con- secrated an altar unto the Lord,

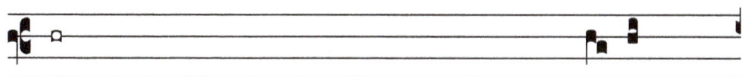

offering burnt offerings upon it, and sa- cri- fi- cing

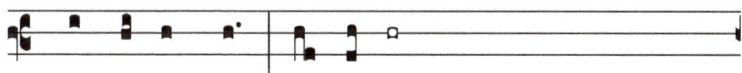

peace of- fer- ings: and he made an evening sacrifice

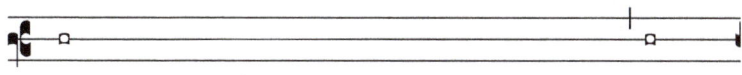

for a sweet- smelling savour unto the Lord God, in the

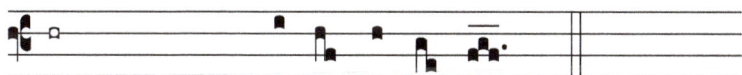

sight of the chil- dren of   Is- ra-   el.

449

COMMUNION *Tóllite hóstias*   *Ps. 96:8, 9*

Cantors

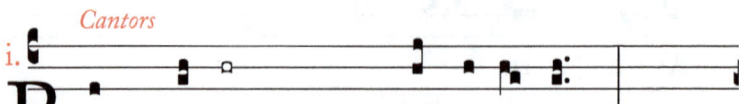

BRING pre-sents, and come in- to his courts:

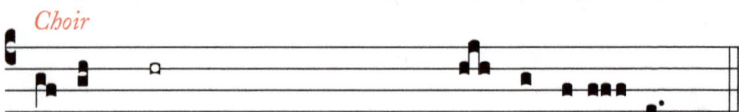

Choir

O wor- ship the LORD in the beau- ty of ho- li- ness.

Verses from Psalm 96:1-8a, 11-13 *may be sung.*

NINETEENTH SUNDAY after TRINITY

INTROIT *Salus pópuli*   *Cf. Ps. 37:40,28;78:1*

Cantors

vij.

I AM the saving health of my peo-ple, saith the

Choir

LORD: out of whatsoever tribulation they shall pray

to me, I will surely help them, and I will be their God

FINE   *Cantors*

for ev- er and ev- er. *Ps.* Hear my law, O my peo-ple:

Choir

incline your ears unto the words of my mouth.

Cantors   *Choir*   *Full*

Glo- ry be... *(etc.)* As it was..., *(etc.)* I   am the..., *(etc.)*

GRADUAL *Dirigátur* Ps. 141:2

Cantors · *Choir*

LET my prayer be set forth in thy sight: as the in-cense

Cantors

O LORD. ℣. And let the lift- ing up of my hands:

Choir

be an eve- ning sa- cri- fice.

ALLELUIA *Confitémini Dómino* Ps. 105:1

Cantors · *All*

AL- LE- LU- IA. Al - le- lu- ia.

Cantors

℣. O give thanks unto the LORD, and call upon his Name:

Choir

tell the people what things he hath done.

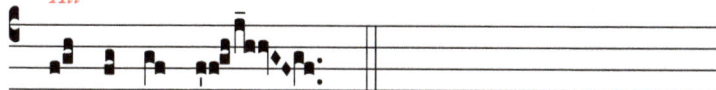

Al - le- lu- ia.

OFFERTORY *Si ambulávero*   *Ps. 138:7*

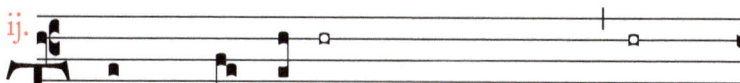

THOUGH I walk in the midst of trouble, yet shalt

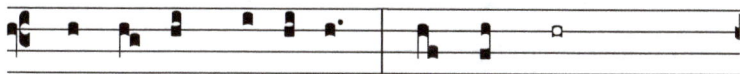

thou re- fresh me, O LORD: thou shalt stretch forth thy

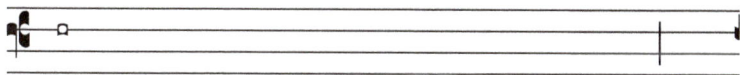

hand upon the furiousness of mine enemies,

and thy right hand shall save me.

COMMUNION *Tu mandásti*   *Ps. 119:4,5*

Cantors

i.

THOU hast charged that we shall diligently keep thy

Choir

com- mand- ments: O that my ways were made so direct

that I might keep thy sta- tutes.

Psalm 119:1, 2, 3, 8, 9, 26, 59, 60, 134, 168 *may be sung.*

TWENTIETH SUNDAY after TRINITY
INTROIT *Omnia quæ fecísti* *Dan. 3:31,29,30,43,42; Ps. 119:1*

Cantors

vij.

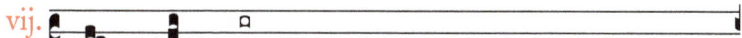

EV - ERY-THING that thou hast brought upon us,

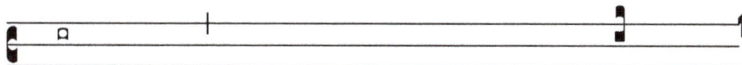

O LORD God, thou hast done in righ- teous-ness

Choir

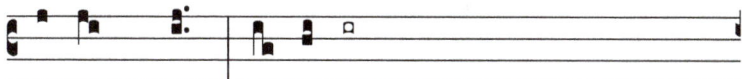

and judge- ment: for we have trespassed against thee, and

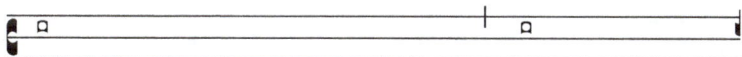

have not obeyed thy commandments; but give glory and

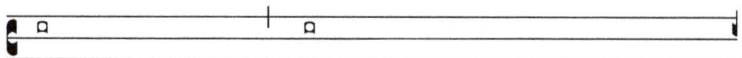

honour to thy Name, and deal with us according to the

FINE   *Cantors*

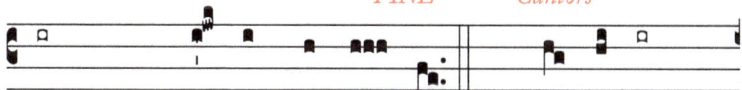

multitude of thy ten- der mer- cies. *Ps.* Bless- ed are

Choir

those that are unde- fil- ed in the way: and walk

Cantors

in the law of the LORD. Glo- ry be..., *(etc.)*

Choir *Full*

As it was..., *(etc.)* Ev - 'ry - thing...,*(etc.)*

GRADUAL *Oculi ómnium* *Ps. 145:15,16*

Cantors *Choir*

℣. THE eyes of all wait up-on thee, O LORD, and thou

Cantors

givest them their meat in due sea- son. ℣. Thou

Choir

o-pen-est thy hand: and fillest all things liv-ing with

456

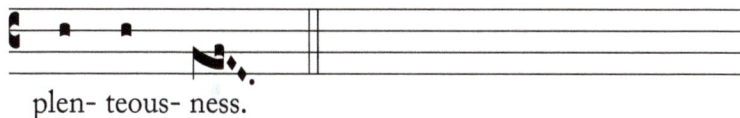

plen- teous- ness.

ALLELUIA *Parátum cor meum* Ps. 108:2

Cantors *All*

AL- LE- LU- IA. Al- le- lu- ia.

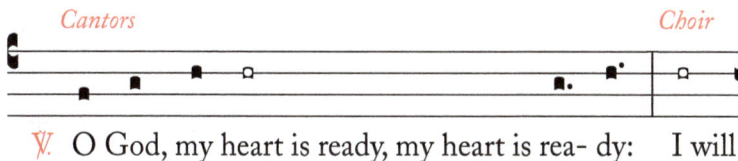

Cantors *Choir*

℣. O God, my heart is ready, my heart is rea- dy: I will

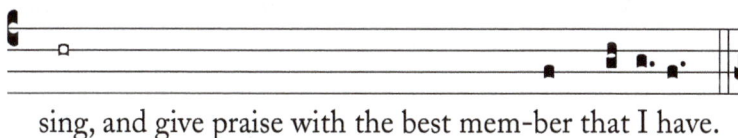

sing, and give praise with the best mem-ber that I have.

All

Al - le- lu- ia.

OFFERTORY *Super flúmina*   *Ps. 137:1*

Cantors

ij.

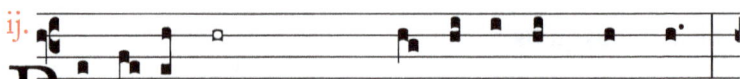

BY the wa- ters of Ba- by- lon we sat down, and wept:

Choir

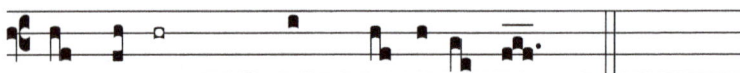

when we re- mem- bered thee, O Si- on.

COMMUNION *Meménto verbi tui*   *Ps. 119:49, 50*

Cantors

i.

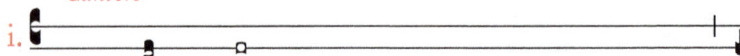

RE- MEM- BER thy word unto thy servant, O LORD,

Choir

wherein thou hast caused me to put my trust: the same

is my comfort   in my af-   flic- tion.
or is my comfort in my af-flic-tion. Al- le-   lu- ia. *

Psalm 119:1, 2, 25, 28, 41, 74, 76, 81, 82, 114 *may be sung.*

* when this Communion is used during Eastertide in a Votive Mass, such as
the Mass In Any Necesity, p. 759

TWENTY-FIRST SUNDAY after TRINITY

INTROIT *In voluntáte tua*　　　　　　　　*Est. 13:9–11;Ps. 119:1*

Cantors

O LORD Almighty, everything is in subjection unto

thee; and there is no man that is able to re- sist thy power:

Choir

for thou hast created everything; heaven and earth, and all

the wonders which under heaven's vault are contained;

FINE　　　　*Cantors*

thou art the LORD and King of all things. *Ps.* Bless- ed

are those that are unde- fil -ed in the way: and walk in the

Cantors & Choir *Full*

law of the LORD. Glo- ry be..., *(etc.)* O Lord..., *(etc.)*

GRADUAL *Dómine, refúgium* *Ps. 90:1, 2*

Cantors *Choir*

℣. LORD, thou hast been our re- fuge; from one generation

Cantors

to a - no - ther. ℣. Be - fore the mountains were brought

Choir

forth, or ever the earth and the world were made: thou

art God from everlasting, and world with - out end.

ALLELUIA *In éxitu*   *Ps. 114:1*

Cantors   *All*

vj.

AL- LE- LU- IA.   Al- le- lu- ia.

Cantors   *Choir*

℣. When Is- rael came out of E- gypt: and the house

of Jacob from among the strange peo- ple.

All

Al - le- lu- ia.

OFFERTORY *Vir erat*   *Job 1:1; 2:7*

Cantors

ij.

THERE was a man in the land of Uz, whose name was

Choir

Job: per - fect and upright, and one that fear - ed God.

461

Cantors   *Choir*

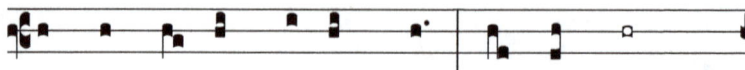

And Sa - tan sought to tempt him: and power was given

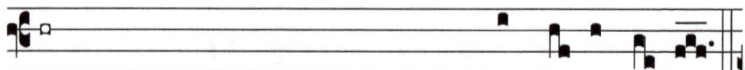

him by the Lord over his possessions, and o-ver his flesh.

Cantors

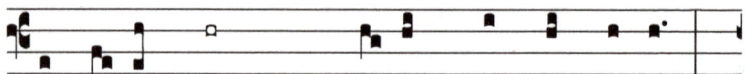

And he de - stroy - ed all his sub - stance and his sons:

Choir

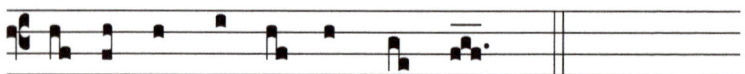

and he smote his flesh with sore boils.

COMMUNION *In salutári tuo*   *Ps. 119:81,84b,86b*

Cantors

i.

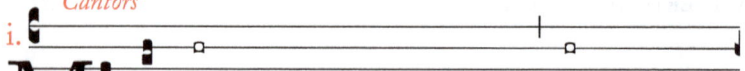

My soul hath longed for thy salvation; and I have a

Choir

good hope in thy word: when wilt thou be avenged of

Cantors

them that per - se - cute me? They per - se - cute me

Choir

false - ly: O be thou my help, O LORD my God.

Psalm 119:1, 41, 85, 113, 123, 157, 161, 166, 174 *may be sung.*

TWENTY-SECOND SUNDAY after TRINITY

INTROIT *Si iniquitátes*   *Ps. 130:3,4,1*

Cantors

vij.

IF thou, O Lord, wilt be extreme to mark iniquities,

Choir

Lord, who may a-bide it: for un-to thee belongeth

FINE   *Cantors*

mercy, O God of Is-ra-   el.   *Ps.* Out of the deep have

I called un-to thee, O Lord: Lord, hear my voice.

Cantors   *Choir*   *Full*

Glo-ry be..., *(etc.)* As it was..., *(etc)* If thou, O Lord,..., *(etc.)*

464

GRADUAL *Ecce quam bonum*   Ps. 133: 1,2

Cantors

℣.

B E- HOLD, how good and joyful a thing it is:

Choir

bre- thren, to dwell to-ge-ther in u - ni- ty.

Cantors

℣. It is like the precious ointment up- on the head:

Choir

that ran down unto the beard, ev-en un- to Aa- ron's beard.

ALLELUIA *Qui timent Dóminum*   Ps. 114: 11

Cantors   *All*

vj.

A L- LE - LU- IA. Al - le- lu- ia.

Cantors

℣. Ye that fear the LORD, put your trust in him:

Choir

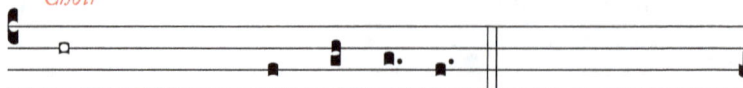

He is their helper and de- fend-er.

All

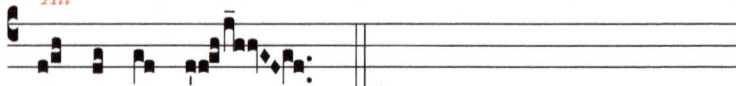

Al - le- lu- ia.

OFFERTORY *Recordáre mei*   *Est.14: 12, 13*

Cantors

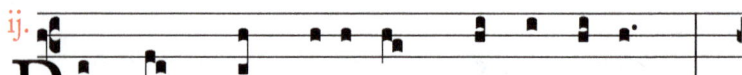

RE- MEM- BER me, O LORD, King of all power:

Choir

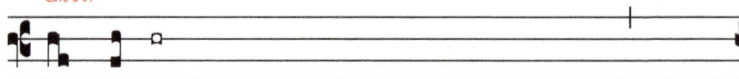

and put a well - ordered speech in my mouth,

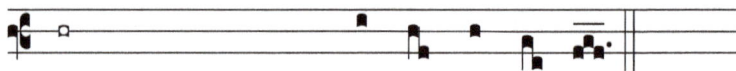

that my words may be pleas- ing in thy sight.

COMMUNION *Ego clamávi*   *Ps. 17:6*

Cantors

i.

I HAVE called upon thee, O God, for thou shalt hear me:

Choir

in- cline thine ear unto me, and hear- ken un- to my words.

Verses from Psalm 16:1, 2, 5, 7-9, 16 *may be sung.*

Introit *Dicit Dóminus* *Jer. 29:11,12,14; Ps. 85:1*

Cantors

vij.

THUS saith the LORD, I know the thoughts that I think

towards you, thoughts of peace, and not of af - flic - tion:

Choir

ye shall call upon me, and I will hearken unto you, and

FINE

will bring again your captivity from ev-ery na - tion.

Cantors

Ps. LORD, thou art become gracious un - to thy land:

Choir

thou hast turned away the cap- ti - vi - ty of Ja - cob.

Cantors   *Choir*   *Full*

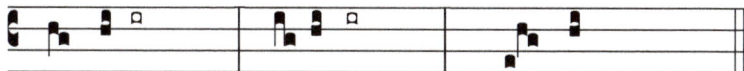

Glo- ry be..., *(etc.)*   As it was..., *(etc.)* Thus saith..., *(etc.)*

GRADUAL *Liberásti nos*   *Ps. 44:8,9*

Cantors

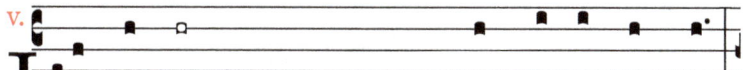

IT is thou, O LORD, that savest us from our e - ne - mies:

Choir

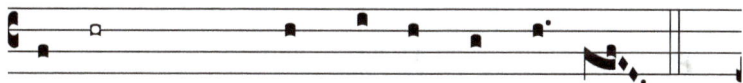

and puttest them to con - fu - sion that hate us.

Cantors

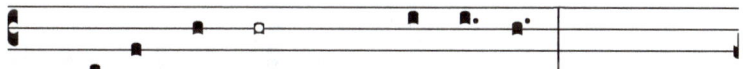

℣. We make our boast in God all day long:

Choir

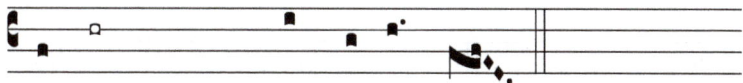

and will praise thy Name for ev - er.

469

ALLELUIA *De profúndis*   *Ps. 130:1*

Cantors   *All*

vj.

AL- LE- LU- IA.   Al- le- lu- ia.

Cantors

℣. Out of the deep have I called unto thee, O LORD;

Choir   *All*

LORD, hear my voice.   Al- le- lu- ia.

OFFERTORY *De profúndis*   *Ps. 130:1*

Cantors

ij.

OUT of the deep have I call - ed un - to thee, O LORD:

Choir

LORD, hear my voice.

COMMUNION *Amen dico vobis: quidquid*   *Mk. 11:24*

Cantors

i.

VE-RI-LY I say unto you, what things soever ye

470

Choir

de - sire, when ye pray: be - lieve that ye receive them,

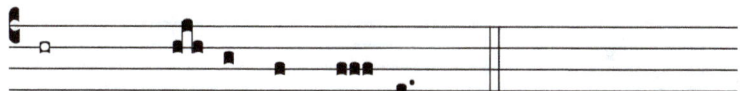

and it shall be done un - to you.

Verses from **Psalm 61** *may be sung.*

Year A of the last Sunday after Trinity

Co. *Dómine, quinque talénta*   *Mt. 25:20,21*

Cantors

i.

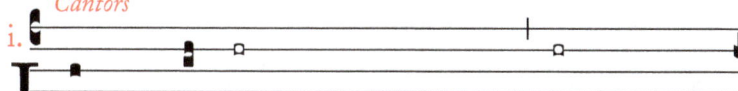

LORD, thou gavest me me five talents: behold I have

Choir

gained five ta-lents more. Well done, thou good and faith-

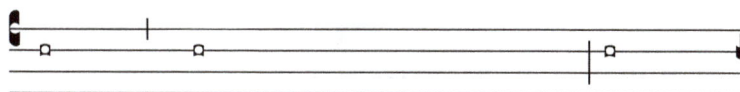

ful servant; thou hast been faithful over a little; I will set

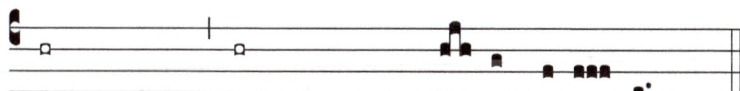

thee over much. Enter thou in-to the joy of the Lord.

Psalm 119:1,2,24,30,48,99,100,129,130 *may be sung.*

SOLEMNITY OF OUR LORD JESUS CHRIST, KING OF THE UNIVERSE

INTROIT *Dignus est* Rev. 5:12; 1:6; Ps. 72

Cantors

vij.

WOR- THY is the Lamb that was slain to receive pow-

er, and riches, and wisdom, and strength, and ho- nour:

Choir *FINE*

to him be glory and dominion for ev- er and ev- er.

Cantors *Choir*

Ps. Give the King thy judge-ments, O God: and thy

righteousness un- to the King's son.

Cantors *Choir* *Full*

Glo- ry be..., *(etc.)* As it was..., *(etc.)* Wor- thy is..., *(etc.)*

472

GRADUAL *Dominábitur*   *Ps. 71:8, 11*

Cantors

HIS do- minion shall be also from the one sea to

Choir

the o- ther: and from the river un- to the world's end.

Cantors   *Choir*

℣. All kings shall fall down be- fore him: all nations

shall do him ser- vice.

ALLELUIA *Potéstas eius*   *Dan. 7:14*

Cantors   *All*

AL- LE- LU- IA. Al - le- lu- ia.

Cantors

℣. His do- minion is an everlasting dominion, which

Choir

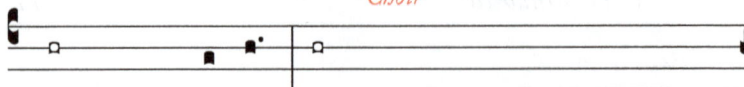

shall not pass a- way: and a kingdom that which shall

All

not be des-troy-ed.   Al - le- lu- ia.

OFFERTORY *Póstula a me*   *Ps. 2:8*

Cantors

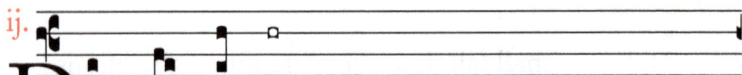

ij. D E- SIRE of me, and I shall give thee the nations

Choir

for thine in- he- ri- tance: and the utmost parts of the

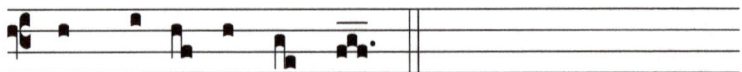

earth for thy pos- ses- sion.

474

CHRIST THE KING

COMMUNION *Sedébit Dóminus Rex*   *Ps. 29:9b, 10b*

Cantors

THE LORD remaineth a King for ev - er:

Choir

The LORD shall give his people the bles- sing of peace.

Year A: CO. *Amen dico vobis*   *Matt. 25:40, 34*

Cantors

VER- I- LY I say unto you: Inasmuch as ye have done it

unto one of the least of these my brethren, ye have done it

Choir

un- to me: come, ye blessed of my Father, inherit the king-

dom prepared for you from the be- gin- ning of the world.

Verses from Psalm 29:1-5, 7-10 *may be sung.*

475

The following Propers are used for the weekdays between Christ the King and the First Sunday of Advent.

from Sundays: Trinity 23–26

In. *Dicit Dóminus (p. 468)*

Gr. *Liberásti nos (p. 469)*

Al. *De profúndis (p. 470)*

Of. *De profúndis (p. 470)*

Co. *Amen dico vobis (p. 470)*

CORPUS CHRISTI
THE MOST HOLY BODY
AND BLOOD OF CHRIST
Being the Thursday after Trinity Sunday,
or as appointed on the First Sunday after Trinity

INTROIT *Cibávit eos*   *Ps. 81: 17, 2,3,11*

Cantors

vij.

HE fed them with the finest wheat flour, al- le-

Choir

lu- ia: and with honey from the rock hath he satisfied

FINE   *Cantors*

them. Al- le- lu- ia. Al - le- lu- ia. *Ps.* Sing we

Choir

merrily unto God our hel- per: make a cheerful noise

Cantors & Choir

unto the God of Ja- cob.   Glo- ry be..., *(etc.)*

Full

He fed them..., *(etc.)*

GRADUAL *Oculi ómnium*   *Ps. 145: 15, 16*

Cantors   *Choir*

THE eyes of all wait upon thee, O LORD: and thou

Cantors

givest them their meat in due sea- son. ℣. Thou

Choir

o-pen-est thine hand: and fillest all things liv-ing with

plen- teous - ness.

ALLELUIA *Caro mea vere*   *Jn. 6: 55,56*

Cantors   *All*

AL- LE- LU-IA. Al - le- lu- ia.

478

Cantors

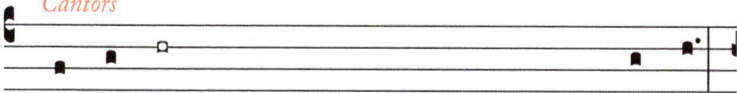

℣. My Flesh is meat indeed, and my Blood is drink in-deed:

Choir

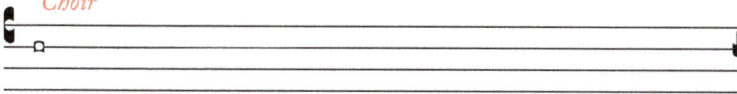

he that eateth my Flesh and drinketh my Blood,

All

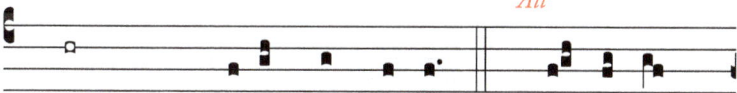

dwelleth in me, and I in him. *℟. Al - le- lu-

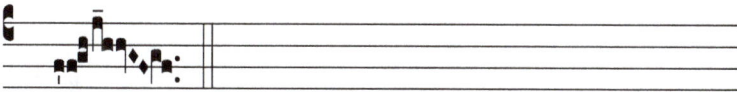

ia.

If the Sequence is to be sung, the Alleluia is not repeated, and the Sequence is begun immediately.
SEQUENCE *Lauda Sion Salvatórem*

Cantors   *Full*

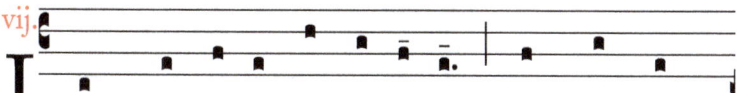

vij. LAUD, O Si- on, thy sal-va-tion, Laud, with hymns

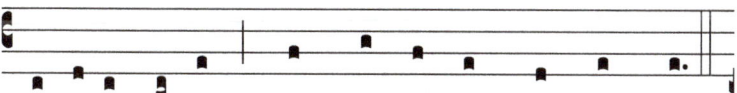

of ex- ul- ta-tion Christ, thy King and Shep-herd true:

Men

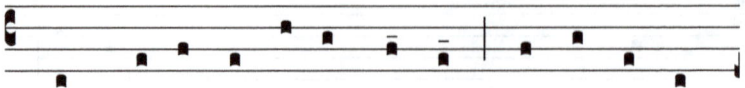

Spend thy-self, his ho-nour rais-ing; Who sur-pass-eth

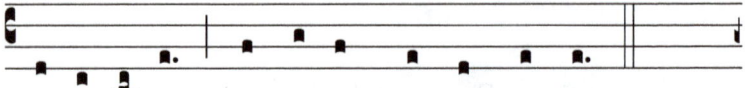

all thy prais-ing; Ne- ver canst thou reach his due.

Trebles

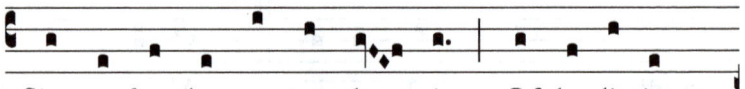

Sing to-day, the mys-tery show- ing   Of the liv-ing,

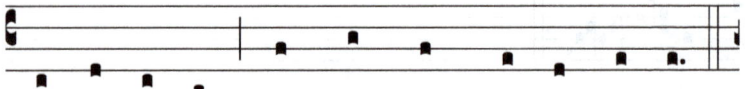

life-be-stow-ing   Bread from heav'n be- fore thee set;

Men

E'en the same of old pro- vi- ded, Where the twelve,

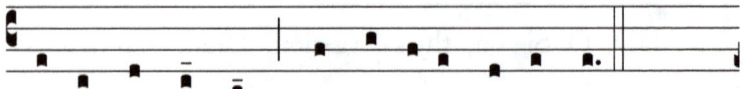

di-vine-ly guid-ed,   At the ho-ly Ta-ble met.

Trebles

Full and clear ring out thy chant-ing, Joy nor sweet-est

480

CORPUS CHRISTI

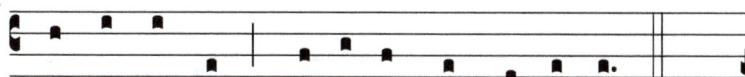

grace be want-ing To thy heart and soul to-day;

Men

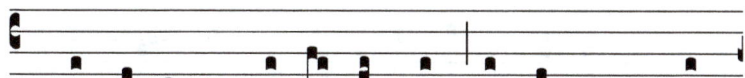

When we ga-ther up the mea-sure of that Sup-per and

it's trea-sure, Keep-ing feast in glad ar-ray

Trebles

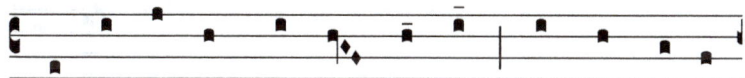

Lo! the new King's Ta- ble grac-ing, This new Pass-o-

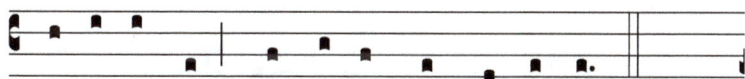

ver of bless-ing Hath ful-fill'd the eld-er rite:

Men

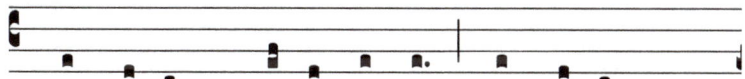

Now the new the old ef- fa- ceth, Truth re-veal'd the

sha-dow chas-eth, Day is break-ing on the night.

Trebles

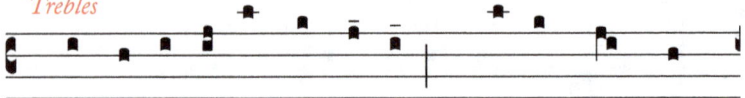

What he did at Sup-per seat-ed, Christ or-dained to

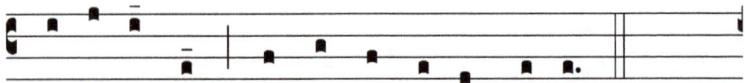

be re-peat-ed, His me-mo-rial ne'er to cease:

Men

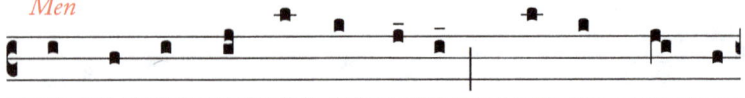

And, his word for guid-ance tak-ing, Bread and wine we

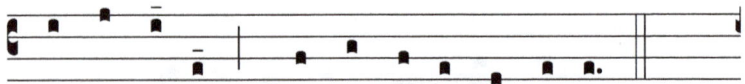

hal-low, mak-ing Thus our Sac-ri- fice of peace.

Trebles

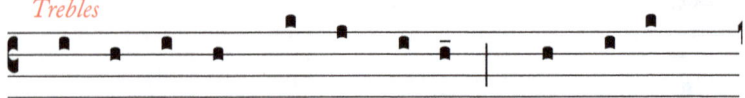

This the truth to Chris-tians giv-en— Bread be-comes

his Flesh from hea-ven, Wine be-comes his ho-ly Blood.

482

Men

Doth it pass thy com-pre-hend-ing? Yet by faith thy

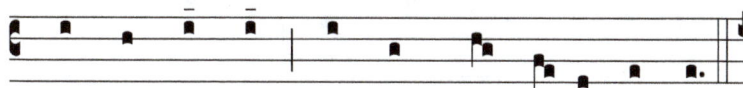

sight trans-cend-ing, Won-drous things are un-der-stood.

Trebles

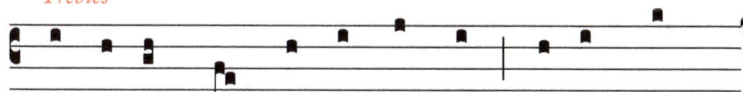

Yea, be-neath these signs are hid-den   Glo-rious things

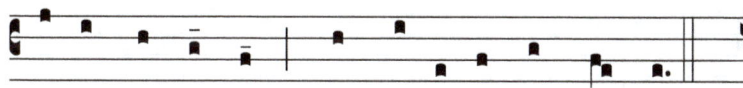

to sight for-bid-den: Look not on the out-ward sign.

Men

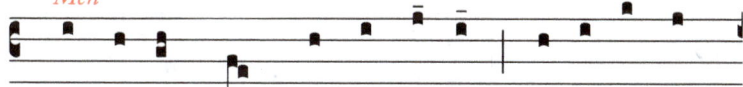

Wine is poured and Bread is bro-ken,   But in ei-ther

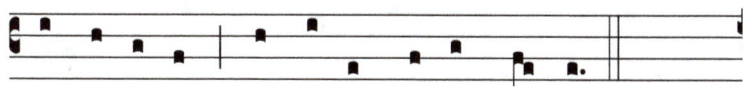

sa-cred to-ken Christ is here by power di- vine.

Trebles

Who-so of this Food par-tak-eth,   Rend-eth not the

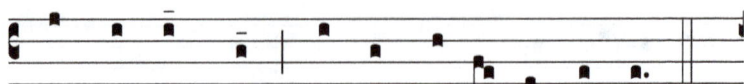

Lord nor break-eth: Christ is whole to   all that taste.

Men

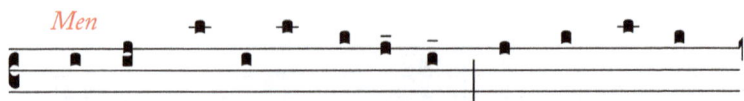

Thou-sands are, as one, re-ceiv-ers   One, as thou-sands

of be-liev-ers,   Takes the Food that can-not waste.

Trebles

Good and e-vil men are shar-ing   One re-past, a

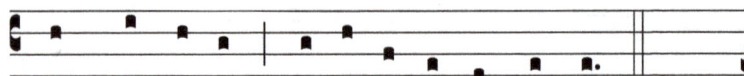

doom pre-par- ing   Va-ried as the heart of man;

Men

Doom of life or death a-ward- ed,   as their days shall

be re-cord-ed Which from one be-gin-ning ran.

Trebles

When the Sac-ra-ment is bro-ken, Doubt not in each

sev-ered to-ken, Hal-low'd by the word once spo-ken,

Men

Rest-eth all the true con-tent Nought the pre-cious Gift

di-vi-deth, Break-ing but the sign be-ti-deth, He him-

self the same a-bi-deth, No-thing of his ful-ness spent.

Trebles

Lo! the An-gels' Food is giv-en To the pil-grim

who hath striv-en; See the chil-dren's Bread from hea-ven.

Men

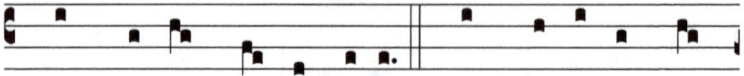

Which to dogs may not be cast; Truth the an-cient types

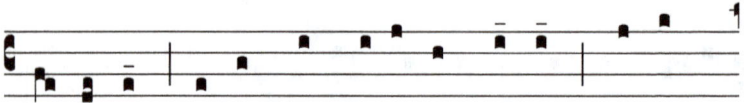

ful-fill-ing   I-saac bound a vic-tim will-ing, Pas-chal

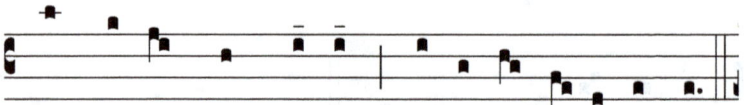

lamb, its life-blood spill-ing, Man-na sent in a-ges past.

Trebles

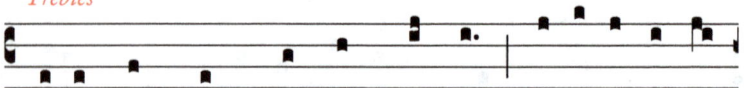

Ve-ry Bread, good Shep-herd, tend us,   Je-su, of thy love

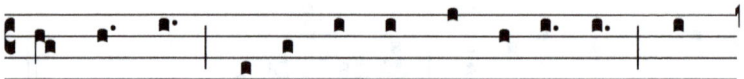

be-friend us, Thou re-fresh us, thou de-fend us,   Thine

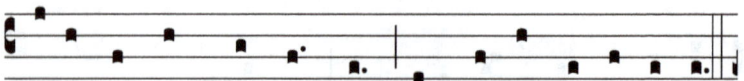

e-ter-nal good-ness send us   In the Land of life to see;

Men

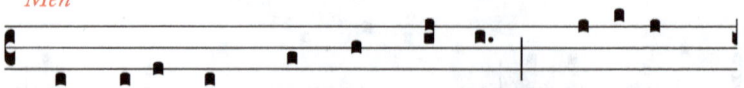

Thou who all things canst and know-est, Who on earth

486

such Food be-stow-est, Grant us with thy Saints, though

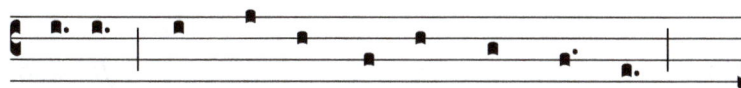

low-est Where the heav'n-ly Feast thou show- est,

Full

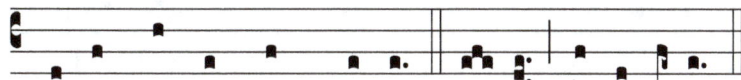

Fel-low heirs and guests to be. A-men, Al-le- lu-ia.

OFFERTORY *Portas cæli*   *Ps. 78: 24-26*

Cantors

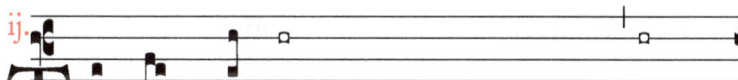

ij. THE LORD o- pened the doors of Heaven, and

Choir

rained down manna also up- on them for to eat: He

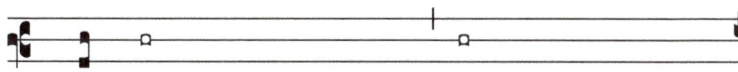

gave them bread from heaven; so men did eat Angels'

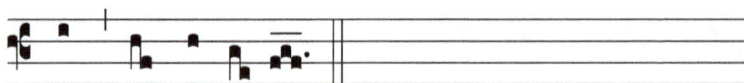

food. Al- le- lu- ia.

or OF. *Sanctificávit Móyses (Trinity XVIII, p. 449)*

COMMUNION   *Qui manducat*   *Jn. 6:56*

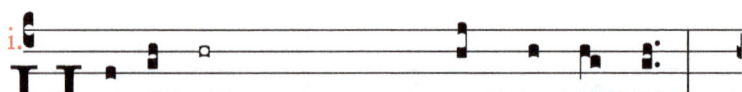

i. HE that eateth my Flesh and drink-eth my Blood:

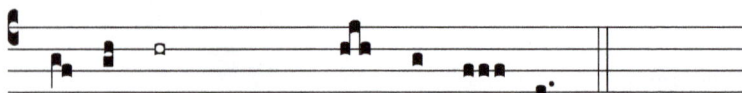

dwel-leth in me and I in him, saith the LORD.

Psalm 23 *or* 119:1,2,11, 49-50, 72, 103, 105, 162 *may be sung.*

Sunday Year C CO. *Hoc corpus (Maundy Thursday, p. 254)*

THE MOST SACRED HEART OF JESUS
Friday after the the First Sunday after Trinity

INTROIT *Cogitationes*   *Ps. 33:11b,18,1*

Cantors

THE thoughts of his heart are from generation to

Choir

ge-ne-ra- tion: to de-li-ver their soul from death,

FINE   *Cantors*

and to feed them in the time of dearth, *Ps.* Re-joice

Choir

in the LORD, O ye righ-teous: for it becometh well the

Cantors & Choir

just to be thank-ful.   Glo- ry be..., *(etc.)*

Full

The thoughts of ..., *(etc.)*

489

GRADUAL *Dulcis et rectus*   *Ps. 25:7,8*

Cantors   *Choir*

GRA-CIOUS and righteous is the LORD: there-fore

Cantors

will he teach sin-ners in the way. ℣. Them that are meek

Choir

shall he guide in judge-ment: and such as are gentle,

them shall he teach his way.

ALLELUIA *Tollite iugum*   *Matthew 11: 29*

Cantors   *All*

AL- LE- LU-IA. Al - le- lu- ia.

Cantors

℣. Take my yoke upon you, and learn of me,   for I am

Choir

meek and lowly of heart: and ye shall find rest

All

un-to your souls.   Al - le- lu- ia.

OFFERTORY *Impropérium (Palm Sunday, p. 232)*

COMMUNION *Unus mílitum*   *John 19:34*

Cantors

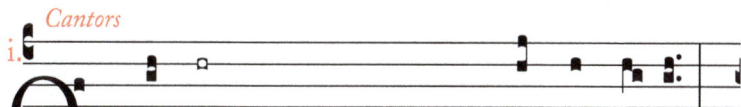

ONE of the sol - diers with a spear pier-ced his side:

Choir

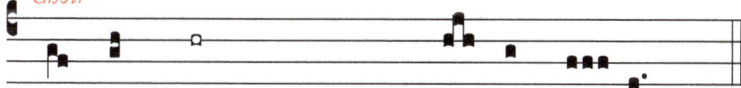

and forth-with came there out blood and wa- ter.

Psalm 89:1, 2, 5, 15, 18, 25, 29, 33, 34a *may be sung.*

PROPERS OF SAINTS
AND HOLY DAYS

2 January, Saints Basil the Great & Gregory Nazianzen

From the Common of Confessors: For a Bishop (pp. 618-684); or from the Common of Doctors of the Church (pp. 693-695).

3 January, The Most Holy Name of Jesus

INTROIT *In Nómine Iesu (Weds. in Holy Week, p. 238)*

GRADUAL *Salvos fac nos*   *Ps. 106:45; Is. 63:16*

Cantors

v.

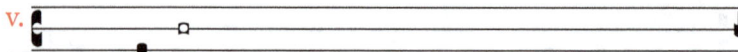

DE-LI-VER us, O LORD our God, and gather us from

Choir

among the na-tions: that we may give thanks unto thy

Cantors

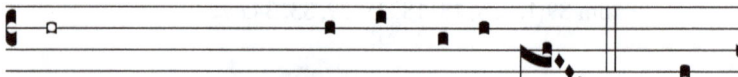

holy Name, and make our boast of thy praise . ℣. Thou,

Choir

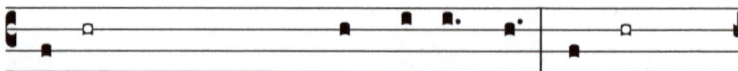

O LORD, art our Father, our Re-dee-mer: thy Name is

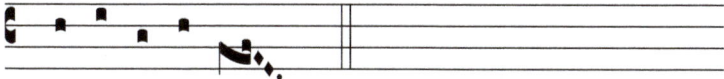

from ev-er-last-ing.

ALLELUIA *Laudem Dómine*

AL- LE- LU- IA.   Al - le- lu- ia.

℣. My mouth shall speak the praise of the Lord:

and let all flesh give thanks un-to his ho-ly Name.

Al - le- lu- ia.

493

OFFERTORY *Confitébor tibi... Deus*   *Ps. 86:12,5*

Cantors

ij.

I WILL thank thee, O Lord my God, with all my heart,

Choir

and will praise thy Name for e-ver-more: for thou, O

Lord, art good and gracious, and of great mercy

unto all them that call upon thee. Al- le- lu- ia.

COMMUNION *Omnes gentes*   *Ps. 86:9,10*

Cantors

i.

ALL na-tions whom thou hast made shall come and

worship thee, O LORD, and shall glo-ri-fy thy Name:

Choir

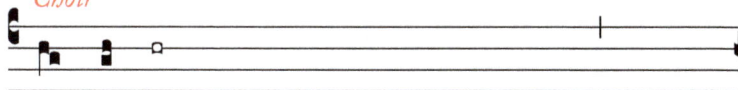

for thou art great, and dost wondrous things;

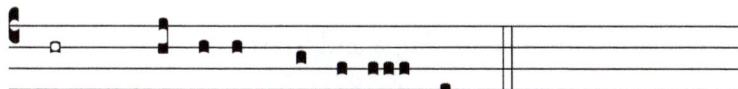

thou art God a-lone. Al-le- lu- ia.

Verses from **Psalm 86:1-8** *may be sung.*

CSP: 4 January, Saint Elizabeth Ann Seton, Religious
From the Common of Holy Men and Women: For Any Matron or Holy Woman (pp. 702-705), or For Religious (pp. 705-708), or For an Educator (p. 711).

CSP (US only): 5 January, Saint John Neumann, Bishop,
From the Common of Confessors: For a Bishop (pp. 678-684).

CSP: 6 January, Saint André Bessette, Religious
From the Common of Holy Men and Women: For Religious (pp. 705-708).

7 January, Saint Raymond of Penyafort, Priest
From the Common of Confessors: For a Priest (pp. 685-687).

12 January, Saint Benedict Biscop, Abbot
From the Common of Holy Men and Women: For an Abbot or Abbess (pp. 708-710).
OLW: Saint Aelred of Rievaulx, Abbot
From the Common of Holy Men and Women: For an Abbot or Abbess (pp. 708-710).

13 January, Saint Hilary, Bishop and Doctor of the Church
From the Common of Confessors: For a Bishop (pp. 618-684); or from the Common of Doctors of the Church (pp. 693-695).
OLSC, OLW: Saint Kentigern (Mungo), Bishop
From the Common of Confessors: For a Bishop (pp. 618-684).

17 January, Saint Anthony, Abbot
From the Common of Holy Men and Women: For an Abbot or Abbess (pp. 708-710).

OLSC, OLW: 19 January, Saint Wulfstan, Bishop
From the Common of Confessors: For a Bishop (pp. 618-684).

20 January, Saint Fabian, Pope and Martyr
From the Common of Martyrs: For a Martyr Pope or Bishop (pp. 652-655); or from the Common of Confessors: For a Holy Pope (pp. 675-678).

Saint Sebastian, Martyr
From the Common of Martyrs: For One Martyr (pp. 659-662).

21 January, Saint Agnes, Virgin and Martyr
From the Common of Martyrs: For a Virgin Martyr (pp. 670-674).

INTROIT *Me expectavérunt*   *Ps. 119:95,96,1*

Cantors

THE un-godly laid wait for me to destroy me, but I will consider thy test-i-mo-nies, O LORD: *Choir* I see that all things come to an end, but thy commandment is

FINE   *Cantors*

ex-ceed-ing broad. *Ps.* Bles-sed are those that are

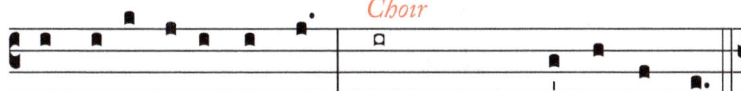

un-de-fil-ed in the way: and walk in the law of the Lord.

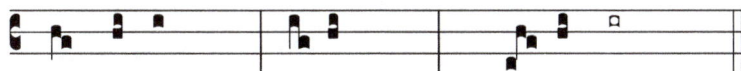

Glo-ry be..., *(etc.)* As it was..., *(etc.)* The un-..., *(etc.)*

ALLELUIA *Quinque prudentes virgines*   Mt. 25:4,6

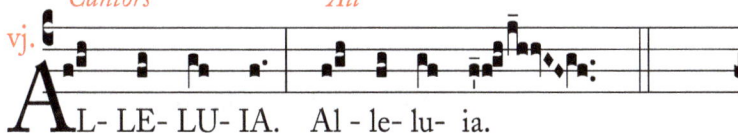

L- LE- LU- IA.   Al - le- lu- ia.

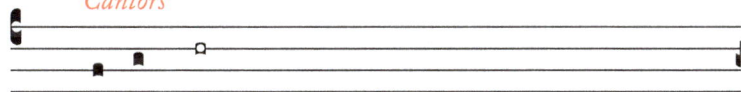

℣. The five wise virgins took oil in their vessels with

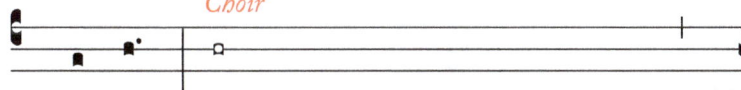

their lamps: and at midnight there was a cry made,

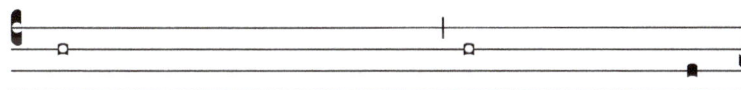

Behold the Bridegroom cometh; go ye out to meet him,

All

Christ the LORD. Al - le- lu- ia.

After Septuagesima, the following is said in place of the Alleluia:
TRACT *Veni, sponsa Christi (Common of Saints, p. 672)*

CSP (Canada only), OLSC, OLW
22 January, Saint Vincent, Deacon and Martyr
From the Common of Martyrs: For One Martyr (pp. 659–662).
CSP (US only)(23 January, when 22 January falls on a Sunday)
Day of Prayer for the Legal Protection of Unborn Children
Minor Propers may be taken from the Mass In any Necessity (pp. 756–759).

CSP (US only) 23 January, Saint Vincent, Deacon and Martyr
Vide supra, 22 January

24 January, Saint Francis de Sales, Bishop and Doctor of
the Church
From the Common of Confessors: For a Bishop (pp. 618–681); or from Common of Doctors of the Church (pp. 692–695).

25 January, The Conversion of Saint Paul the Apostle

INTROIT *Gaudeamus ...Paulus*

Cantors

RE-JOICE we all, and praise the Lord, devoutly keeping

Choir

this festival with due so-lem-ni-ty: where-in Paul, the

blessed Apostle, by his wonderful conversion did greatly

FINE　*Cantors*

illumine this pre-sent world.　*Ps.* For the light of his

Choir

ho-ly preach-ing: and for the con-ver-sion of ho-ly Paul.

Cantors　　　*Choir*　　　*Full*

Glo-ry　be..., *(etc.)* As it was..., *(etc.)* Re-joice..., *(etc.)*

or INTROIT *Scio cui credidi*   *2 Tim. 1:12; Ps. 139:1*

Cantors   *Choir*

vij.

I KNOW whom I have be-liev-ed: and am persuaded

that he is able to keep that which I have committed unto

FINE   *Cantors*

him against that day, a just Judge. *Ps.* O LORD, thou

Choir

hast searched me out and known me: thou knowest my

Cantors

down-sitting and mine up-ris-ing. Glo-ry   be..., *(etc.)*

Choir   *Full*

As it was..., *(etc.)* I know whom..., *(etc.)*

GRADUAL *Qui operatus est* *Gal. 2:8,9; 1 Cor. 15:10*

Cantors

℣.

HE that wrought effectually in Peter to the apostleship,

Choir

was also mighty in me toward the Gen-tiles: and they

Cantors

perceived the grace that was giv-en un-to me. ℣. The

grace of God which was bestowed upon me was not in

Choir

vain: but his grace ever a- bi-deth in me.

501

ALLELUIA *Magnus sanctus Paulus*

Cantors   *All*

vj.

AL- LE- LU- IA.   Al - le- lu- ia.

Cantors

℣. Great and holy is Paul, the chosen vessel of God:

Choir

meet indeed to be glorified, and to in-he-rit the twelfth

All

throne.   Al - le- lu- ia.

After Septuagesima, the following is sung in place of the Alleluia:

TRACT   *Tu es vas electionis*

Cantors

viij.

THOU art the chosen vessel, O holy Paul the Ap-os-tle:

Choir

meet indeed to be glo-ri-fied.   ℣. Preacher of truth: and

Cantors

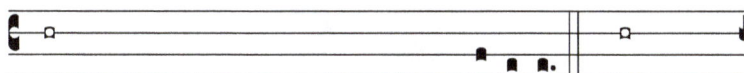

teacher of the Gentiles in faith and ver-i-ty. ℣. By thee

Choir

all nations have known: the grace of God. ℣. Pray for us

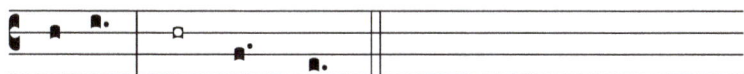

to God: who chose thee.

OFFERTORY *Mihi autem nimis*   *Ps. 139:17*

Cantors

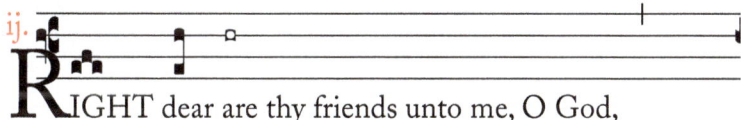

RIGHT dear are thy friends unto me, O God,

Choir

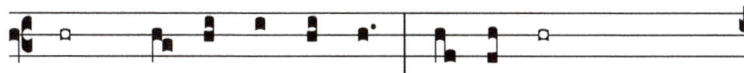

and held in high-est ho-nour: their rule and governance

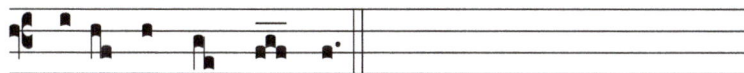

is ex-ceed-ing stead-fast.

COMMUNION *Signa eos* *(Ascension, Year B, p. 345)*

503

PROPER of SAINTS and HOLY DAYS

CSP, OLW: **26 January, Saints Timothy and Titus, Bishops**
From the Common of Confessors: For a Bishop (pp. 678-684).

27 January, Saint Angela Merici, Virgin
From the Common of Virgins (pp. 696-701); or from the Common of Holy Men and Women: For an Educator (p. 711).
OLSC: **Saints Timothy and Titus, Bishops**
Vide supra, 26 January

28 Jan., St. Thomas Aquinas, Priest and Doctor of the Church
From the Common of Confessors: For a Priest (pp. 685-687); or from the Common of Doctors of the Church (pp. 693-695).
ALLELUIA *Spíritus Sanctus docébit vos (Whit Tuesday, p. 373)*
After Septuagesima, the following is sung in place of the Alleluia:
Tract *Beatus vir qui timet (Common of Martyrs, p. 657)*

31 January, Saint John Bosco, Priest
From the Common of Confessors: For a Priest (pp. 685-681); or from the Common of Holy Men and Women: For an Educator (p. 711).

INTROIT *Dispersit, dedit*   *Ps. 112:9,1*

Cantors

vij. HE hath dispersed abroad, and given to the poor;

his righteousness re-main-eth for ev-er: *Choir*   his horn

shall be ex-al-ted with ho-nour. *Ps.* Bless-ed is the man

504

Choir

that fear-eth the LORD: he hath great delight in his

Cantors & Choir　　*Full*

com-mand-ments. Glo-ry be..., *(etc.)* I know He...,

GRADUAL *Veníte fílii (Trinity VII, p. 406)*

COMMUNION, *Amen dico vobis (Christ the King, p. 475)*

OLSC, OLW: 1 February, Saint Brigid of Kildare, Abbess

From the Common of Holy Men and Women: For an Abbot or Abbess (pp. 708-710).

2 February
THE PRESENTATION OF THE LORD
(Candlemas)

At the blessing of the Candles

CANTICLE *Nunc dimittis*   Lk. 2:29-32

ANTIPHON *Lumen*

Cantor   *All*

viij. I

O be a light * to ligh-ten the Gen-tiles: and to be

the glo- ry of thy peo-ple Is- ra- el.

Cantor

LORD, now lettest thou thy servant de- part in peace,

Choir   *All*   *Cantor*

ac-cord-ing to thy word.   To be a light.   For mine eyes

506

Choir *All* *Cantor*

have seen: thy sal- va- tion; To be a light. Which thou

Choir

hast pre- pa- red   before the face of all peo- ple.

All *Cantor*

To be a light. Glo- ry be to the Father, and to the Son,

Choir *All* *Cantor*

and to the Ho- ly Ghost. To be a light. As it was in

Choir

the beginning, is now and ever shall be,   world with- out

All

end. A - men. To be a light.

ANTIPHON *Exurge Dómine* (F.B.)   Ps 44:26,1

Cantor   *Choir*

ij.

O LORD, a-rise, * help us, and de-liv-er us for

Cantor

thy Name's sake. ℣. O God, we have heard with our ears: *

Choir   *Cantor*

our fa-thers have de-clar-ed un- to us. Glo-ry be to

the Fa-ther, and to the Son, and to the Ho-ly Ghost;

Choir

as it was in the be-gin-ning, is now, and e-ver shall be.

Full

world with-out end. A-men.   O LORD, a-rise... *(etc.)*

FEBRUARY

*Towards the end of the distribution, the servers light the candles of the
Ministers, the candles of the congregation, and the candles on the altar.
While the candles are lighted, the following antiphon may be sung:*

ANTIPHON *Ecce Dóminus*   *Cf. Is 35:4,5*

B E-HOLD, * the LORD shall come to us with might-y

power, bring-ing light to eyes of those who serve him well.

*If the time of the lighting of candles requires it, verses of
Psalm 119:105-108, 111-112 may be added to the antiphon.*

In- to- nation. Me-di- á- tion. And thîs the énd- ing.

PSALM *Lucérna pédibus meis.*

T HY word is a lantern unto my féet, * and a light ûnto
mý paths.

106 I have sworn, and am stedfastly púrposèd, * to keep
thy rîghteous júdgments.

107 I am troubled above meásure: * quicken me, O LORD,
accôrding tó thy word.

108 Let the free-will offerings of my mouth please thee,
O LÓRD; * and teach mê thy júdgments.

509

111   Thy testimonies have I claimed as mine heritage for éver; * and why? they are the very jôy of mý heart.

112   I have applied my heart to fulfil thy statutes álway, * even ûnto thé end. GLORY. ANT.

At the beginning of the Procession:

Deacon or Priest   *All*

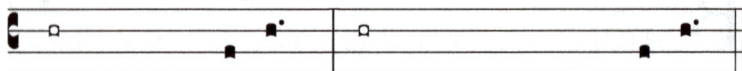

Let us go forth in Peace. In the Name of Christ. A- men.

During the procession, the following antiphons may be sung, or such hymns as are suitable.

ANTIPHON I. *Adorna thalamum*

O SI-ON,* a-dorn thy bride-cham-ber, and re-ceive

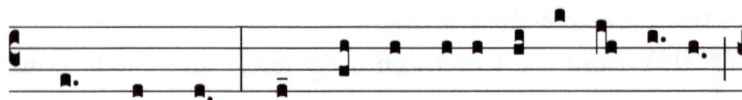

Christ thy King: greet Ma-ry who is the gate of hea-ven:

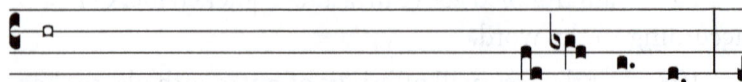

for she bear-eth the King of the glo-ry of the new light:

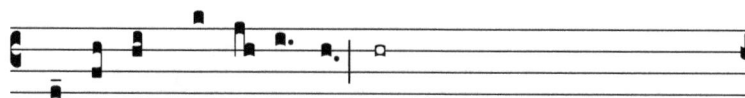

she re-main-eth a Vir-gin, yet beareth in her arms a Son

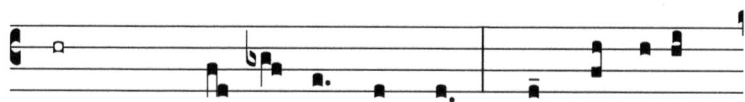

begotten be-fore the mor-ning star: Whom Si-me-on

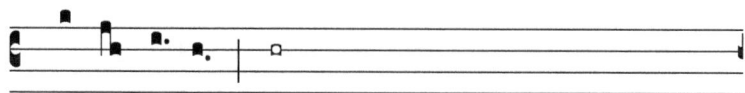

took in his arms, declaring to all nations that he is the

LORD of life and death, and Sa-viour of the world.

ANTIPHON II. *Respónsum accépit Símeon*   *Cf.* Lk 2:26-29

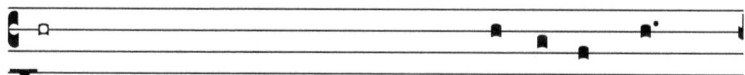

IT was revealed * un-to Simeon by the Ho-ly Ghost,

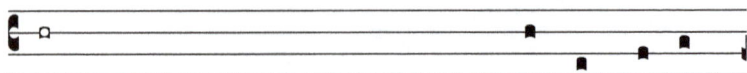

that he should not see death, before he had seen the Lord's

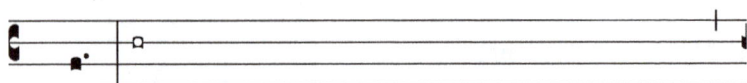

Christ: and when they brought the Child into the temple,

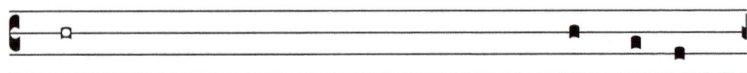

then took he him up in his arms, and bles-sed God, and

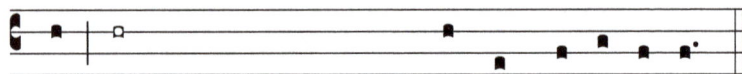

said: Lord, now lettest thou thy ser-vant de-part in peace.

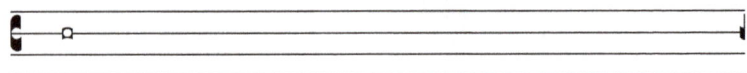

℣. When his parents brought in the Child Jesus, to do for

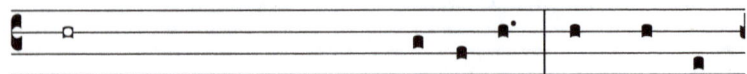

him according to the custom of the law: then took he

512

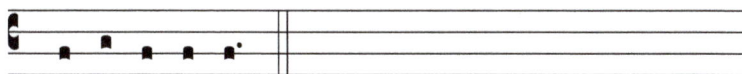

him up in his arms.

When the procession re-enters the church the following is sung:

RESPONSORY *Obtulérunt*   *Cf. Lk 2:22-24*

iv.

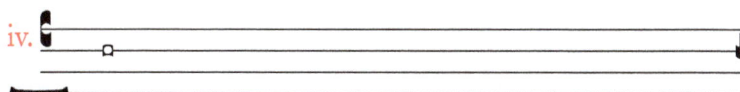

THEY offered,* for him unto the Lord a pair of turtle

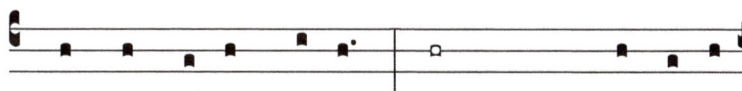

doves, or two young pi-geons: † as it is written in the law

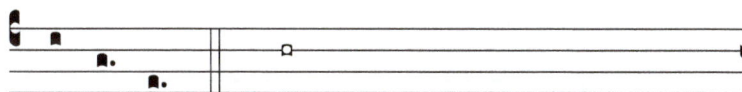

of the Lord. ℣. When the days of Mary's purification

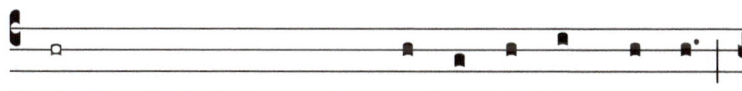

according to the Law of Mo-ses were ac-com-plish-ed,

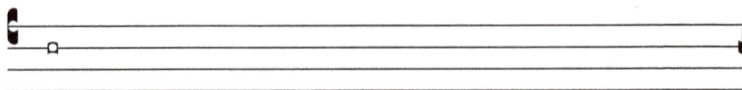

they brought Jesus to Jerusalem, to present him to the

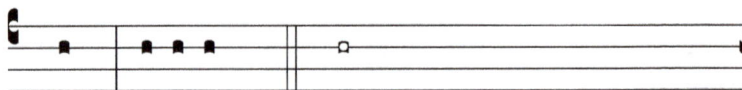

Lord: † as it is ... ℣. Glory be to the Father, and to the

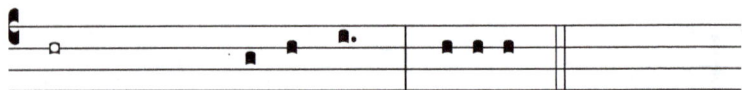

Son: and to the Ho-ly Ghost: † as it is ...

The Procession being ended, the Mass proceeds as usual, begining with the Introit.

INTROIT *Suscépimus*   *Ps. 48:10, 11 & 2*

Cantors

vij.

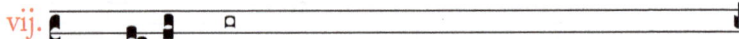

WE have waited, O God, for thy loving- kindness

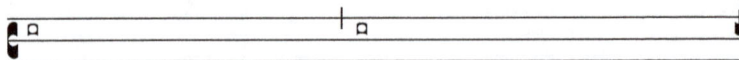

in the midst of thy temple; according to thy Name, O God,

Choir

so is thy praise un- to the world's end: Thy right hand

FINE   *Cantors*

is full of right- eous- ness. *Ps.* Great is the LORD, and highly

Choir

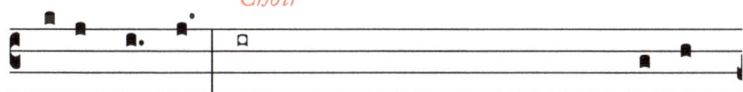

to be prais- ed: in the city of our God, even up- on his

Cantors

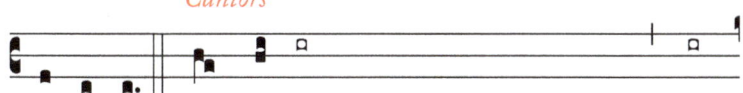

ho- ly hill.   Glo- ry be to the Father, and to the Son, and

Choir

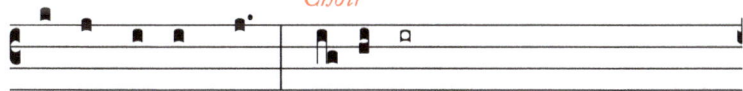

to the Ho- ly Ghost;   As it was in the beginning, is now,

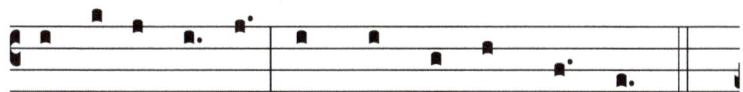

and ev- er shall be, world with- out end.   A- men.

Full

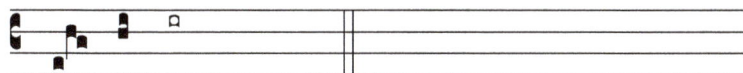

We have waited..., *(etc.)*

GRADUAL *Suscépimus*   *Ps. 48:8, 9, ℣. 7*

Cantors

℣.

WE have waited, O God, for thy loving-kindness

Choir

in the midst of thy tem- ple: ac- cording to thy Name, O

Cantors

God, so is thy praise un-to the world's end. ℣. Like as

we have heard, so have we seen in the ci- ty of our God:

Choir

e-ven up-on his ho- ly hill.

ALLELUIA *Senex púerum*

Cantors   *All*

vj.

AL- LE- LU- IA.   Al - le- lu- ia.

Cantors *Choir*

℣. The old man carried the Child: but the Child

All

govern- ed the old man.   Al - le- lu- ia.

After Septuagesima, instead of Alleluia and the verse folloing, is sung:

TRACT *Nunc dimittis*   *Lk 2:29–32*

Cantors

viij.

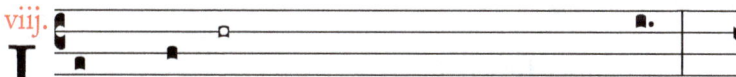

LORD, now lettest thou thy servant depart in peace:

Choir

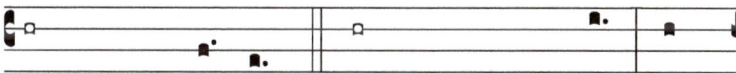

according to thy word. ℣. For mine eyes have seen: thy

Cantors

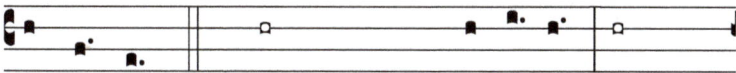

sal-va-tion,   ℣. which thou hast pre-par-ed: before the

Choir

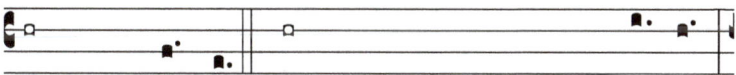

face of all peo-ple ℣. To be a light to lighten the Gen-tiles:

517

and the glory of thy people Is-ra- el.

OFFERTORY *Diffúsa est grátia*   *Ps. 45:2*

Cantors

FULL of grace are thy lips: be- cause God hath

Choir

bless- ed thee for ev- er.

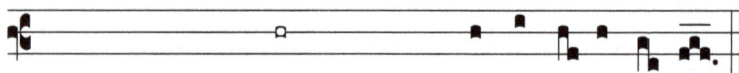

(or in Eastertide) blessèd thee for ev- er, al- le- lu- ia

COMMUNION *Respónsum accépit Símeon*   *Luke 2:26*

Cantors

IT was revealed unto Simeon by the Ho- ly Spi- rit:

Choir

that he should not see death, before he had seen

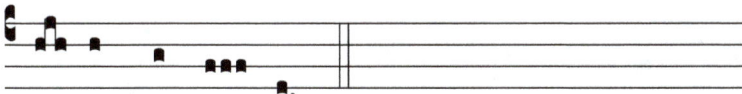

the Lord's a- noin- ted.

The Nunc dimittis *and* Psalm 48:1-2, 7-10, 13 *may be sung.*

3 February, Saint Blaise, Bishop and Martyr
From the Common of Martyrs: For a Martyr Pope or Bishop (pp. 652-655), or For a Martyr Bishop (pp. 655-659).

Saint Ansgar, Bishop
From the Common of Confessors: For a Missionary (pp. 688-692), or For a Bishop (pp. 678-684).

4 February, Saint Gilbert of Sempringham, Religious
From the Common of Holy Men and Women: For Religious (pp. 705-708).

5 February, Saint Agatha, Virgin and Martyr

INTROIT *Gaudeámus ...Agathæ* Ps. 45:1

Cantors

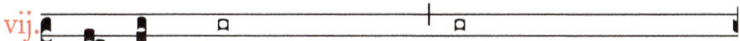

RE-JOICE we all in the LORD, keeping feast day in

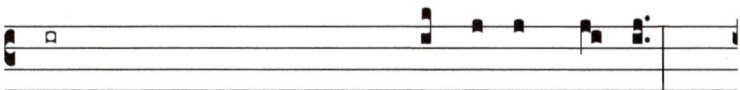

honour of blessed Agatha, the Vir-gin and Mar-tyr:

Choir

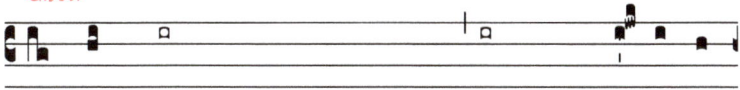

in whose passion the Angels rejoice, and glo-ri-fy the Son

FINE   *Cantors*

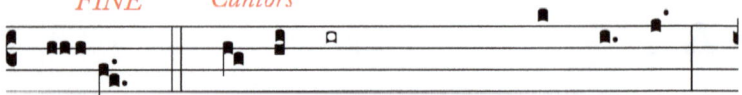

of God   *Ps.* My heart is inditing of a good mat-ter:

Choir

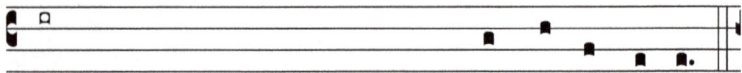

I speak of the things which I have made un-to the King.

Cantors   *Choir*   *Full*

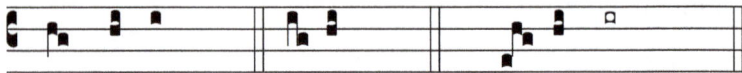

Glo-ry   be..., *(etc.)* As it was..., *(etc.)* Re-joice..., *(etc.)*

GRADUAL *Adiuvábit eam*   *Ps. 46:5,4*

Cantors   *Choir*

GOD shall help her with his coun-te-nance: God is in

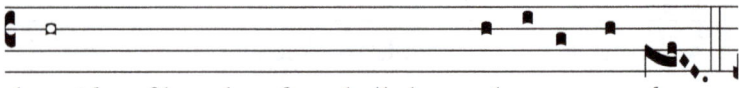

the midst of her, therefore shall she not be re-mov-ed.

Cantors

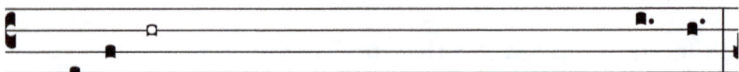

℣. The ri-vers of the flood shall make glad the ci-ty of God:

Choir

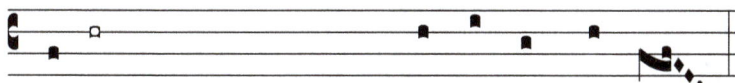

the holy place of the tabernacle of the Most High-est.

ALLELUIA *Loquébar*   *Ps. 119:46*

Cantors   *All*

AL- LE- LU- IA.   Al - le- lu- ia.

Cantors

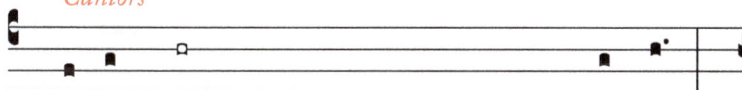

℣. I have spoken of thy testimonies, even be-fore kings:

Choir   *All*

and was not a-sham-ed..   Al - le- lu- ia.

After Septuagesima, the following is said in place of the Alleluia:
TRACT, *Qui séminant in lácrimis (Common of Martyrs, p. 668)*

OFFERTORY, *Afferéntur (Common of Martyrs, p. 674)*

COMMUNION *Feci iudícium*   *Ps. 119:121,122,128*

Cantors

i.

I DEAL with the thing that is lawful and right, O LORD,

Choir

let the proud do me no wrong: I hold straight all thy

commandments, and all false ways I ut- ter- ly   ab- hor.

Verses of Psalm 119:1,78,81,113,115,120,163,166 *may be sung.*

6 February, Saint Paul Miki and Companions, Martyrs

INTROIT *Iusti epuléntur*   *Ps. 68:3,1*

Cantors

vij.

LET the righteous be glad and re-joice be-fore God:

Choir   *FINE*   *Cantors*

and let them be mer-ry   and joy- ful. *Ps.* Let God arise,

522

Choir

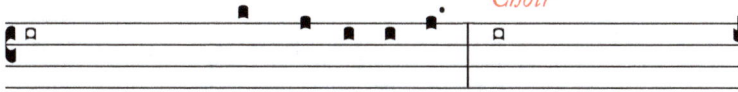

and let his e-ne-mies be scat-ter-ed: let them also that

Cantors

hate him flee be-fore him.   Glo-ry be..., *(etc.)*

Choir   *Full*

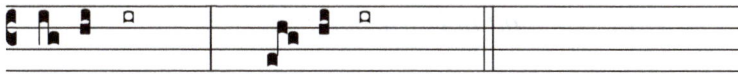

As it was..., *(etc.)* Let the righteous..., *(etc.)*

GRADUAL, *Gloriósus Deus (Common of Martyrs, p. 667)*

ALLELUIA *Iustórum ánimæ*   *Wis. 3:1,2,3*

Cantors   *All*

vj.

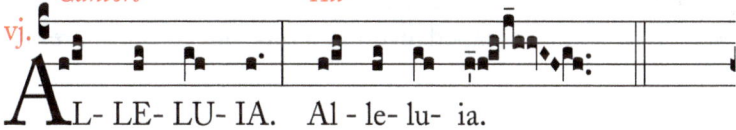

AL- LE- LU- IA.   Al - le- lu- ia.

Cantors

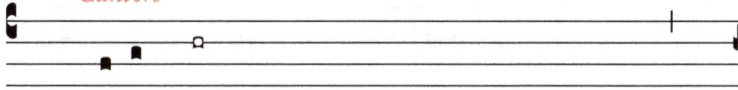

℣. The souls of the righteous are in the hand of God,

Choir

and no torment shall touch them: in the eyes of the

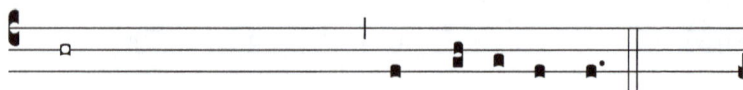

foolish they seemed to die, but they are in peace.

All

Al - le- lu- ia.

After Septuagesima, the following is said in place of the Alleluia:
TRACT, *Qui séminant in lácrimis (Common of Martyrs, p. 668)*

OFFERTORY *Anima nostra sicut passer*   *Ps. 124:6*

Cantors

ij.

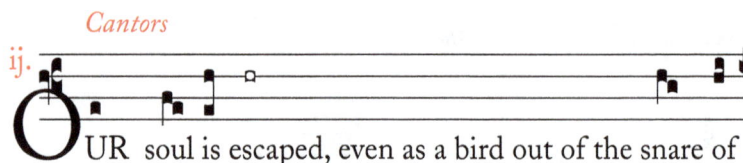

OUR soul is escaped, even as a bird out of the snare of

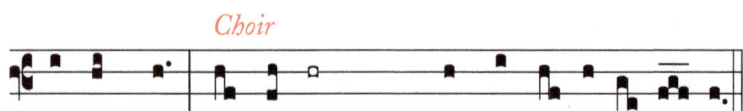

Choir

the fow-ler: the snare is broken, and we are de-liv-er- ed.

COMMUNION *Dico autem vobis*   *Lk. 12:4*

Cantors   *Choir*

i.

I SAY un-to you, my friends: be not afraid of them that

[musical notation]

per-se-cute you.

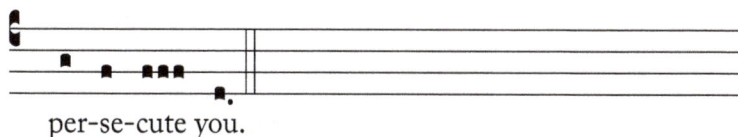

Verses of Psalm 34:1,5,15,17-22 *may be sung.*

8 February, Saint Jerome Emiliani, Priest
From the Common of Holy Men and Women: For an Educator (p. 711).
Saint Josephine Bakhita, Virgin
From the Common of Virgins (pp. 696-701).

OLW (Wales only): 9 February, Saint Teilo, Bishop
From the Common of Confessors: For a Bishop (pp. 678-684).

10 February, Saint Scholastica, Virgin
From the Common of Virgins (pp. 696-701); or from the Common of Holy Men and Women: For an Abbot or Abbess (pp. 708-710).

11 February, Our Lady of Lourdes

INTROIT *Vultum tuum deprecabúntur (Masses of St. Mary, p.752)*

GRADUAL *Benedícta es tu*   *Jud. 13:18; 15:9*

Cantors

[musical notation]

BLES-SED art thou, O Virgin Mary, of the LORD,

Choir

[musical notation]

the Most High God: a-bove all the wo-men up-on earth.

Cantors

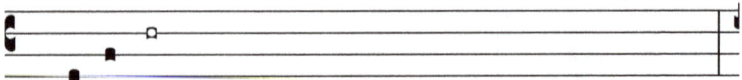

℣. Thou art the glory of Jerusalem, thou art the joy of

Choir

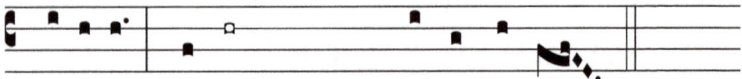

Is-ra-el: thou art the honour of our peo-ple.

ALLELUIA *Tota pulchra es (Immaculate Conception, Dec. 8, p.630)*
After Septuagesima, the following is said in place of the Alleluia:
TRACT *Gaude María (Common of the BVM, p. 649)*
OFFERTORY *Ave María (Advent IV, p. 37)*

COMMUNION *Gloriósa dicta sunt (Dec. 8, Conception, p.630)*

14 February, Saints Cyril, Monk, and Methodius, Bishop Patrons of Europe

INTROIT *Sacerdótes tui (Common of Confessors, p. 681)*

GRADUAL *Sacerdótes eius (Common of Confessors, p. 682)*

ALLELUIA *Laudáte Dóminum (Epiphany V, p. 102)*
After Septuagesima, the following is said in place of the Alleluia:
TRACT *Beátus vir qui timet (Common of a Martyr Bishop, p. 657)*

OFFERTORY *Pópulum húmilem (Trinity VIII, p. 411)*

COMMUNION *Quod dico vobis in ténebris (June 1, Justin, Martyr, p. 557)*

17 February, The Seven Holy Founders of the Servite Order
From the Common of Holy Men and Women: For Religious (pp. 705-708).

21 February, Saint Peter Damian, Bishop and Doctor of the Church
From the Common of Doctors of the Church (pp. 693-695);
or from the Common of Confessors: For a Bishop (pp. 678-684).

February 22
THE CHAIR OF SAINT PETER THE APOSTLE

INTROIT *Státuit ei Dóminus*   *Sir. 45, 30; Ps. 132*

Cantors

THE LORD hath established a covenant of peace with

Choir

him, and made him a chief of his peo-ple: that he should

FINE

have the priestly dignity for ev - er and ev - er.

Cantors   *Choir*

Ps. LORD, re-mem-ber Da-vid: and all his trou-ble.

527

Cantors   *Choir*   *Full*

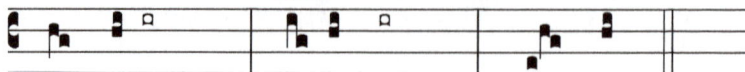

Glo - ry be..., *(etc.)* As it was..., *(etc.)* The LORD..., *(etc.)*

GRADUAL *Exáltent eum*   *Ps. 107:31,32*

Cantors

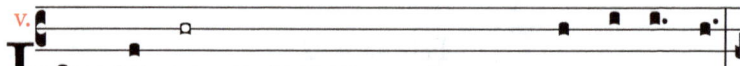

v. LET them exalt him in the congregation of the peo-ple:

Choir   *Cantors*

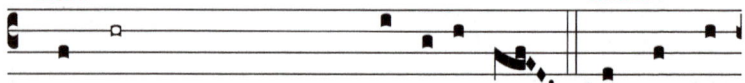

and praise him in the seat of the el- ders. ℣. O that men

Choir

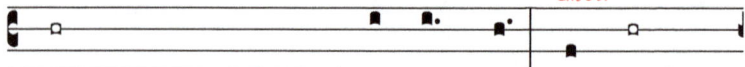

would praise the LORD for his good-ness: and declare the

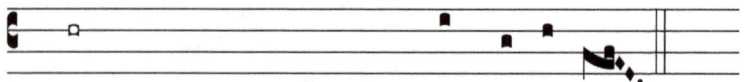

wonders that he doeth for the chil-dren of men.

TRACT *Tu es Petrus*   *Matt. 16:18-19*

Cantors

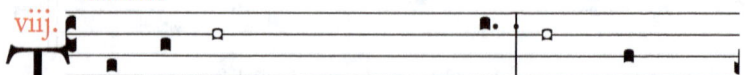

viij. THOU art Pe-ter and upon this rock: I will build

528

Choir

my Church. ℣. And the gates of hell shall not prevail

a-gainst it: And I will give unto thee the keys of the

Cantors

kingdom of hea- ven. ℣. Whatsoever thou shalt bind

Choir

on earth: shall be bound in hea-ven. ℣. And whatsoever

thou shalt loose on earth: shall be loosed in hea-ven.

OFFERTORY *In omnem terram*   Ps 19:4

Cantors   *Choir*

THEIR sound is gone out in-to all lands: * and their

words un-to the ends of the world.

COMMUNION *Tu es Petrus*　　　　　　　　　　　*Matt 16:18*

Cantors　　　　　　　　　　　　　*Choir*

THOU art Pe-ter, and up-on this rock:　I　will build

my　Church.

Psalm 80:1,7-11,14-15,17-18 *may be sung.*

23 February, Saint Polycarp, Bishop and Martyr, Memorial

From the Common of Martyrs: For a Martyr Pope or Bishop (pp. 652–655), or For a Martyr Bishop (pp. 655–659).

MARCH
1 March
Saint David, Bishop
Patron of Wales

INTROIT *Statui ei (Common of Martyrs, p. 652)*

GRADUAL *Ecce sacerdos magnus (Common of Confessors, p. 679)*

TRACT *Beátus vir qui timet (Common of a Martyr Bishop, p. 657)*

OFFERTORY *Inveni David (Common of a Martyr Bishop, p. 658)*

COMMUNION *Fidelis servus et prudens (Common of Confessors, p. 680)*

3 March, Katherine Drexel, Virgin *(Common of Virgins, p 696-701)*

4 March, Saint Casimir
(From the Common of Holy Men and Women: For any holy man, p. 702).

5 March Saint Piran, Abbot
(From the Common for an Abbot or Abbess, p. 708-710)

7 March Saints Perpetua and Felicitas, Martyrs
(From the Common of Martyrs: For Several Martyrs, p. 666-670)

GRADUAL *Anima nostra sicut passer*   Ps 124:6,7

Cantor   *Choir*

℣. OUR soul is escaped, even as a bird: out of the snare of

Cantor

the fow-ler. ℣. The snare is broken, and we are de-liv-ered:

Choir

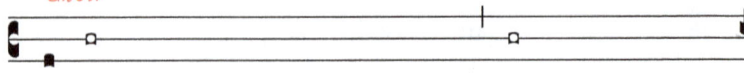

our help is in the name of the Lord, who hath made

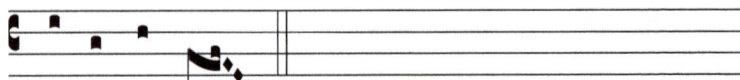

hea-ven and earth.

TRACT *Veni sponsa Chrsti (Common of a Virgin Martyr, p. 672)*

8 March, Saint John of God
(From the Common of Holy Men and Women: For Religious, pp. 702-708).

9 March, Saint Frances of Rome, Religious
(From the Common for any Matron or Holy Woman, or for Relgious, pp. 702-708).

17 March
Saint Patrick, Bishop
Patron of Ireland

INTROIT *Statui ei (Common of Martyrs, p. 652)*

GRADUAL *Ecce sacerdos magnus (Common of Confessors, p. 679)*

TRACT *Beátus vir qui timet (Common of a Martyr Bishop, p 657)*

OFFERTORY *Inveni David (Common of a Martyr Bishop, p. 658)*

COMMUNION *Fidelis servus et prudens (Common of Confessors, p. 680)*

18 March, Saint Cyril of Jerusalem, Bishop and Doctor of the Church
(From the Common of Confessors: For a Bishop (pp 678-689); or from the Common of Doctors of the Church (pp. 693-695).

19 March
SAINT JOSEPH
Spouse of the Blessed Virgin Mary

INTROIT *Iustus ut palma* *(Common for Religious, p. 705)*

GRADUAL *Dómine prævenísti eum* *(Common for an Abbot or Abbess, p. 708)*

TRACT *Beátus vir qui timet* *(Common of a Martyr Bishop, p. 657)*

OFFERTORY *Véritas mea* *(Common of Confessors, p. 683)*

COMMUNION *Ioseph fili David*   Matt. 1:20

Cantor

i.

JO- SEPH, thou son of David, fear not to take unto

Choir

thee Ma- ry thy wife; for that which is conceived in her

is of the Ho- ly Ghost.

When the Gospel, "His parents went to Jerusalem" is read:
Co. *Fili, quid fecísti*   *(Holy Family, p. 65)*

Verses from Psalm 112:1-9 *may be sung.*

23 March, Saint Turibius de Mogrovejo, Bishop *(From the Common of Confessors: For a Bishop (pp 678-681)*

25 March
THE ANNUNCIATION OF THE LORD
(LADY DAY)

INTROIT *Roráte, cæli* *(Fourth Sunday in Advent, p. 35)*

or IN. *Vultum tuum deprecabuntur* *(Masses of St. Mary, p. 753)*

Gradual *Tóllite portas* *(Masses of St. Mary, p. 752)*

or GR. *Diffusa est gratia* *(St. Mary, Mother of God, p. 69)*

TRACT *Audi, fília* *(Common of Virgins, p. 698)*

or TRACT *Et ingressus Angelus*   *Cf. Lk. 1:28*

Cantor

viij.

AND the Angel came in unto her, and said: Hail, Mary

Choir

full of grace; the Lord is with thee. ℣. Blessed art thou

among wo-men: and blessed is the fruit of thy womb.

Cantor

℣. The Holy Ghost shall come up-on thee: and the power

Choir

of the highest shall o-ver-sha-dow thee. ℣. Therefore that

holy thing that shall be born of thee: shall be called the

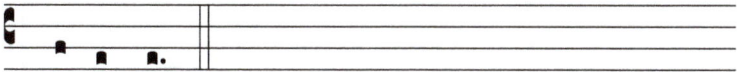

Son of God.

When the Annunciation occurs within Eastertide, the Gradual and Tract are omitted and the following is sung:

ALLELUIA   *Ave María*   St. Luke 2:28
             Virga Iesse flóruit   Num. 17:8

Cantor   *All*

vj.

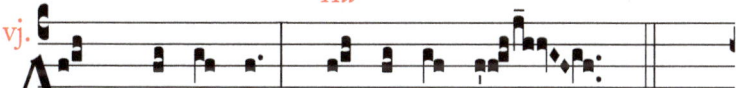

AL- LE- LU- IA.   Al- le- lu- ia.

Cantor

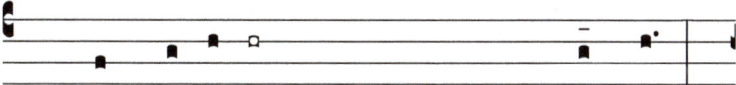

℣. Hail, Ma- ry, full of grace, the LORD is with thee:

Choir   *All*

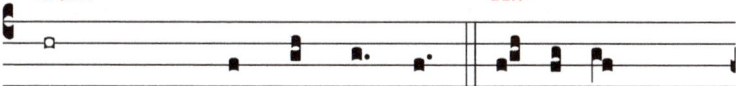

blessed art thou a- mong wo- men: Al - le- lu-

535

Cantors

ia. ℣. The rod of Jesse hath blossomed;

Choir

a Virgin hath begotten God and Man: God hath restored

peace, reconciling in himself the lowest with the high- est.

All

Al - le- lu- ia.

---

or ALLELUIA   *Et ingressus Angelus*   *Luke 1:28*

Cantor   *All*

vj. AL- LE- LU- IA.   Al- le- lu- ia.

Cantor   *Choir*

℣. And the An-gel came in unto her, and said: Hail,

536

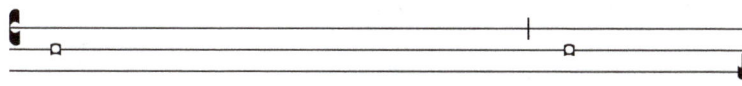

Mary, full of grace; the Lord is with thee: blessed art thou

All   *Cantor*

a-mong wo-men, Al - le- lu- ia.   ℣. Christ, our

Choir   *All*

Pas-so-ver is sac-ri-ficed for us. Al - le- lu- ia.

OFFERTORY *Ave María, grátia plena*
(Common of the Blessed Virgin Mary, p. 651)

COMMUNION *Ecce virgo*   *Isa. 7:14*

i.

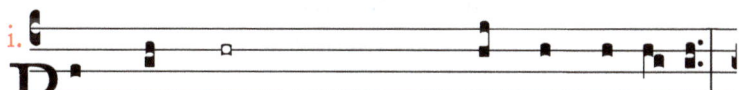

BE - HOLD, a Virgin shall con - ceive, and bear a Son:

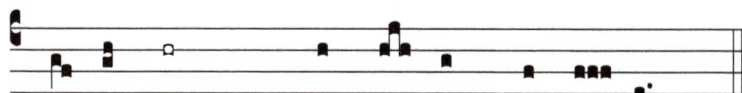

and his Name shall be call - ed Em- ma - nu - el.
or ....Emmanuel.   Al- le-   lu- ia.
Verses from Psalm 19:1-6 *may be sung.*

537

2 April, Saint Francis of Paola, Hermit

From the Common of Holy Men and Women: For Religious (pp. 705-708).

4 April, Saint Isidore, Bishop and Doctor of the Church

(From the Common of Confessors: For a Bishop (pp. 678-684);
or from the Common of Doctors of the Church (pp. 693-695).

5 April, Saint Vincent Ferrer, Priest

(From the Common of Confessors: For a Missionary (pp. 688-692).

7 April, Saint John Baptist de la Salle, Priest

(From the Common of Confessors: For a Priest (pp. 685-687);
or from the Common of Holy Men and Women: For an Educator (p. 711).

11 April, Saint Stanislaus, Bishop and Martyr

(From the Common of Martyrs: For a Martyr Pope or Bishop (pp. 652-
655), or For a Martyr Bishop (pp. 655-659).

13 April, Saint Martin I, Pope and Martyr

From the Common of Martyrs: For a Martyr Pope or Bishop (pp. 652-655);
or from the Common of Confessors: For a Holy Pope (pp. 675-678).

16 April, Saint Magnus of Orkney, Martyr *(OLSC, OLW)*

From the Common of Martyrs: For One Martyr (pp.659-662 or, during
Eastertide, pp. 632-665).

17 April, Saint Kateri Tekakwitha, Virgin *(CSP Canada only)*

Vide infra, 14 July

19 April, Saint Alphege, Bishop and Martyr *(OLSC, OLW)*

From the Common of Martyrs: For a Martyr Pope or Bishop (pp. 652-
655), or For a Martyr Bishop (pp. 655-659).

20 April, Saint Beuno, Abbot *(OLW Wales only)*

From the Common of Holy Men and Women: For an Abbot or Abbess
(pp. 708-710).

APRIL

21 April
Saint Anselm of Canterbury,
Bishop and Doctor of the Church
(OLSC Memorial)

INTROIT *Lex Dómini* *(Lent II, Saturday, p. 158)*

From the Common of Confessors: For a Bishop (pp. 678-684); or from the Common of Doctors of the Church (pp. 693-695).)

23 April
Saint George, Martyr
Patron of England
Memorial (OLW Solemnity)

INTROIT *Protexísti* *(Common of Martyrs, p. 662)*

ALLELUIA *Confitebúntur cæli* *(Common of Martyrs), p. 663*

OFFERTORY *Confitebúntur cæli* *(Common of Martyrs, p. 664)*

COMMUNION *Lætábitur iustus* *(Common of Martyrs, p. 665)*

24 April, Saint Fidelis of Sigmaringen, Priest and Martyr
From the Common of Martyrs: For One Martyr in Eastertide (pp. 662-665); or from the Common of Confessors: For a Priest (pp. 685-687).

Saint Adalbert, Bishop and Martyr
From the Common of Martyrs: For One Martyr in Eastertide (pp. 662-665).

Saint Mellitus, Bishop *(OLW)*
From the Common of Confessors: For a Bishop (pp. 668-684).

25 April
Saint Mark, Evangelist
Feast

(CSP, OLW)

I<small>NTROIT</small> *Accípite iucunditátem*   *4 Esd. 2:36,37; Ps. 78:1*

Cantor

vij.

R<small>E</small>-CEIVE the joyfulness of your glory, al- le- lu- ia:

Choir

giv-ing thanks unto God, alleluia; who hath called you

FINE

to the heavenly kingdom. Al- le-lu- ia. Al- le- lu- ia.

Cantor   *Choir*

Ps. Hear my law, O my peo-ple: incline your ears unto

Cantors

the words of my mouth. Glo-ry be ..., *(etc.)*

Choir   *Full*

As it was ..., *(etc.)* Re-ceive ..., *(etc.)*

540

ALLELUIA *Confitebúntur cæli (Common of Martyrs, p. 663)*

OFFERTORY *Confitebúntur cæli (Common of Martyrs, p. 664)*

COMMUNION *Data est mihi (Ascension, p. 344)*

26 April
Saint Mark, Evangelist
(OLSC)

Vide supra, 25 April

27 April, Saint Louis Grignion de Montfort, Priest *(OLSC)*
Vide infra, 28 April

28 April, Saint Peter Chanel, Priest and Martyr *(OLSC: Memorial) From the Common of Martyrs: For One Martyr in Eastertide (pp. 662-665); or from the Common of Confessors: For a Missionary (pp. 688-692).*

Saint Louis Grignion de Montfort, Priest *(CSP, OLW)*
(From the Common of Confessors: For a Priest (pp. 685-687); or from the Common of Holy Men and Women: For an Educator (p. 711).

29 April
Saint Catherine of Siena,
Virgin and Doctor of the Church
(Patron of Europe)
Memorial (OLW:Feast)

INTROIT *Dilexísti (Common of Virgins, p. 696)*

ALLELUIA *Adducentur* *Cf. Ps. 45:14,15,4*

AL- LE- LU- IA. Al- le- lu- ia.

Cantor

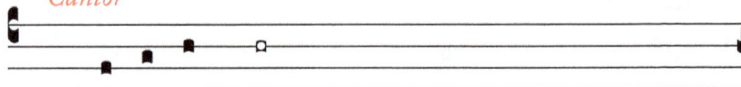

℣. The vir-gins that be her fellows shall bear her

Choir

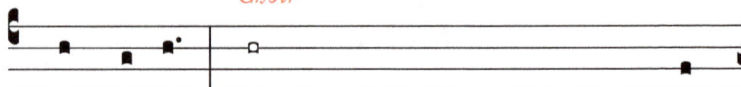

com-pa-ny: they shall be brought unto thee with joy

All

and glad-ness.   Al - le- lu- ia.

Cantor   *Choir*

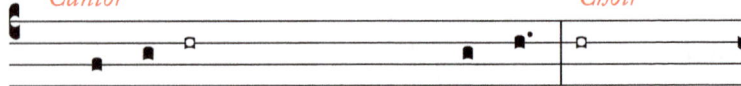

℣. In thy comeliness and in thy beau-ty: go forth, ride

All

pros-per-ous-ly, and reign.   Al - le- lu- ia.

OFFERTORY *Filiæ regnum* *(Common of Virgins, p. 700)*

COMMUNION *Quinque prudentes vírgines (Common of Virgins, p. 700)*

30 April, Saint Pius V, Pope
From the Common of Confessors: For a Holy Pope (pp. 675–678).

1 May
Saint Joseph the Worker

INTROIT *Ecce óculi Dómini*　　　　　　*Ps. 33:17,18,19,1*

Cantor

vij.

B E-HOLD, the eye of the LORD is upon them that fear

him, and put their trust in his mercy, al- le- lu- ia:

Choir

to de-liver their soul from death; for he is our help and

FINE　　　*Cantors*

our shield. Al- le-lu- ia. Al- le- lu- ia. *Ps.* Re- joice in

Choir

the LORD, O ye righ-teous: for it becometh well the

Cantor

just to be thank-ful. Glo-ry be ..., *(etc.)*

543

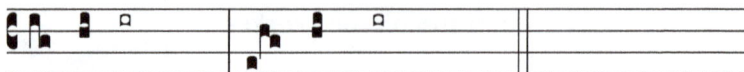

As it was ..., *(etc.)* Be-hold the eys ..., *(etc.)*

ALLELUIA *De quacúmque*   *Cf. Ps. 45:14,15,4*

AL- LE- LU- IA.   Al- le- lu- ia.

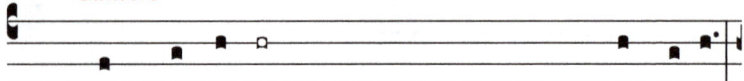

℣. From what-so-ev-er tribulation they shall cry un-to me:

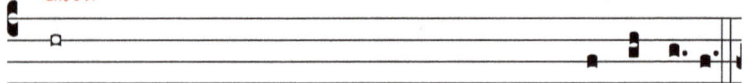

I will hear them, and I will be their de-fen-der for ev-er.

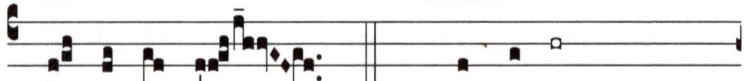

Al - le- lu- ia.   ℣. Grant us, O Joseph, to

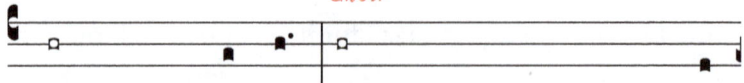

lead an in-no-cent life: and may it ever be safe under thy

All

pro-tec-tion. Al - le- lu- ia.

OFFERTORY *In te sperávi* *(Holy Family, p. 65)*

COMMUNION *Dóminus firmaméntum meum* *(Trinity IV, p. 396)*

2 May, Saint Athanasius Bishop and Doctor of the Church
(From the Common of Confessors: For a Bishop (pp. 678-684);
or from the Common of Doctors of the Church (pp. 693-695).

3 May
Saints Philip and James, Apostles
Feast

INTROIT *Exclamavérunt ad te*   *2 Esd. 9:27; Ps. 33:1*

Cantor

vij.

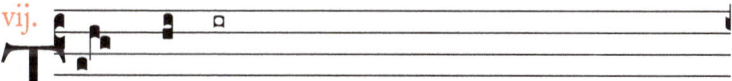

HEY cried unto thee, O LORD, in the time of their

Choir

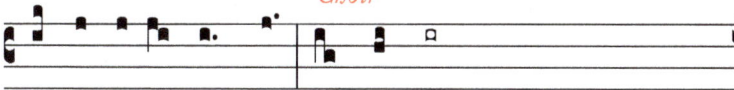

mi-se-ry and trou-ble: and thou didst hear them from

FINE

thy holy heaven. Al- le-lu- ia. Al- le- lu- ia.

Cantor / *Choir*

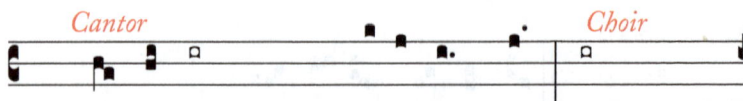

Ps. Re-joice in the Lᴏʀᴅ, O ye right-eous: for it becmeth

Cantor

well the just to be thank-ful.   Glo-ry be ..., *(etc.)*

Choir / *Full*

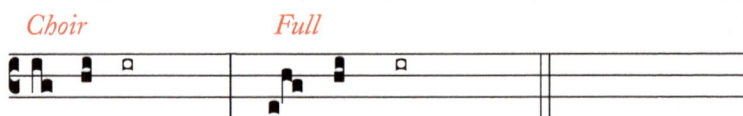

As it was ..., *(etc.)* They cried unto ..., *(etc.)*

Aʟʟᴇʟᴜɪᴀ *Confitebúntur cæli (Common of Martyrs, p. 663)*

Oꜰꜰᴇʀᴛᴏʀʏ *Confitebúntur cæli (Common of Martyrs, p. 664)*

Cᴏᴍᴍᴜɴɪᴏɴ *Tanto témpore (Easter V, p. 331)*

4 May
The English Martyrs
Memorial (OLW Feast)

Iɴᴛʀᴏɪᴛ *Ecce óculi Dómini (St. Joseph the Worker, p. 543)*

Aʟʟᴇʟᴜɪᴀ *Sancti tui*   *Ps. 116:13b*

Cantor / *All*

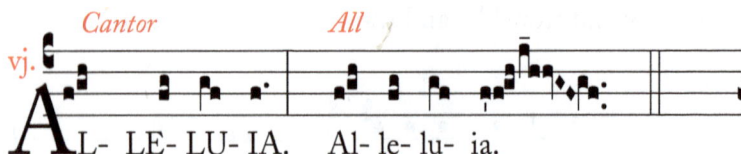

vj. Aʟ- ʟᴇ- ʟᴜ- ɪᴀ.   Al- le- lu- ia.

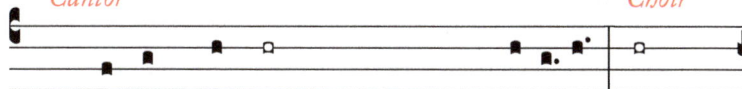

Cantor · *Choir*

℣. Thy Saints, O LORD, shall grow as the li-ly: and as the

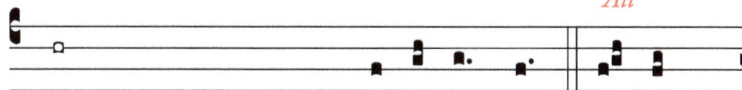

All

odour of balsam shall they be be-fore thee.   Al - le-

Cantors

lu- ia.   ℣. Right dear in the sight of the

Choir · *All*

LORD is the death of his Saints. Al - le- lu- ia.

OFFERTORY *Confitebúntur cæli* *(Common of Martyrs, p.664)*

COMMUNION *Gaudete, iusti*   *Ps. 33:1*

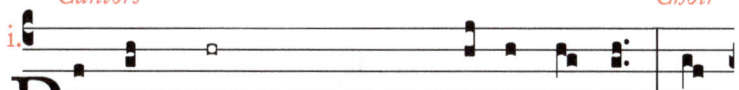

Cantors · *Choir*

i.

RE-JOICE in the LORD, alleluia, O ye right-eous: for

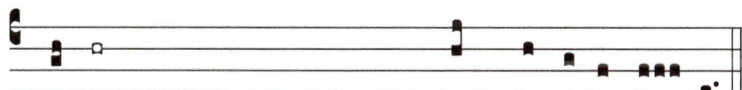

it becometh well the just to be thank-ful. Al-le- lu- ia.

Verses from Psalm 33:2-4,12-15,18-22 *may be sung.*

5 May, Saint Asaph, Bishop *(OLW, Wales only)*
From the Common of Confessors: For a Bishop (pp. 678–684).

6 May
Saint John the Apostle in Eastertide
(OLW, CSP, Canada only)

INTROIT *Protexísti (Common of Martyrs, p. 662)*

ALLELUIA *Iustus ut palma (Common of An Abbot, p. 709)*

OFFERTORY *Confitebúntur cæli (Common of Martyrs, p. 664)*

COMMUNION *Lætábitur iustus (Common of Martyrs, p. 665)*

10 May, Saint Damien de Veuster, Priest *(CSP)*
From the Common of Confessors: For a Missionary (pp. 688–692).

12 May, Saints Nereus and Achilleus, Martyrs
From the Common of Martyrs: For Several Martyrs (pp. 666–670 or, during Eastertide, p. 670).
Saint Pancras, Martyr
From the Common of Martyrs: For One Martyr (pp. 659–662 or, during Eastertide, pp. 662–665).

13 May, Our Lady of Fatima
From the Common of the Blessed Virgin Mary (pp. 647–651).

14 May
Saint Matthias, Apostle
Feast

INTROIT *Vocem iucunditátis (Easter VI, p. 333)*

or, outside of Eastertide **Mihi autem nimis** *(St. Barnabas, Apostle, p. 559)*

GRADUAL *Nimis honoráti sunt*   Ps. 139:17,18

Cantors   *Choir*

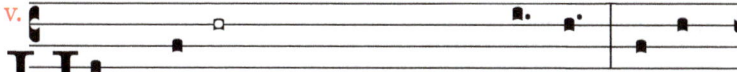

HOW dear are thy friends unto me, O God: O how

Cantor   *Choir*

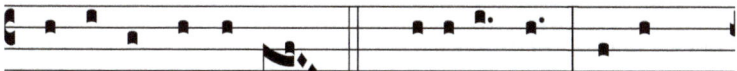

great is the sum of them. ℣. If I tell them: they are

more in num-ber than the sand.

ALLELUIA *Ego vos elégi*   Jn. 15:16) 116:13b

Cantors   *All*

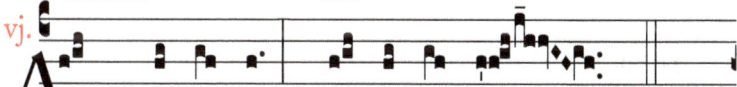

AL- LE- LU- IA. Al- le- lu- ia.

Cantor   *Choir*

℣. I have chosen you out of the world: that ye should go

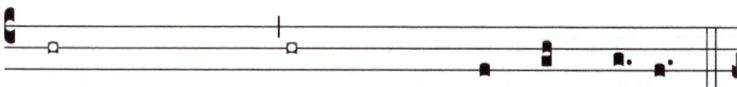

and bring forth fruit, and that your fruit should re-main.

All

Al - le- lu- ia.

or in Eastertide, AL. *Confitebúntur cæli (Common of Martyrs, p 663)*

OFFERTORY *Repléti sumus*   *Ps. 90:14*

Cantor   *Choir*

O SA-TISFY us with thy mer-cy and that soon: so shall we

rejoice and be glad all the days of our life. Al- le- lu- ia.

COMMUNION *Ego vos elégi (Easter VI, p. 337)*

15 May, Saint Isidore *(CSP)*
From the Common of Holy Men and Women: For Any Holy Man (p.702).

18 May, Saint John I, Pope and Martyr
From the Common of Martyrs: For a Martyr Pope or Bishop (pp. 652-655); or from the Common of Confessors: For a Holy Pope (pp. 675-678).

19 May, Saint Dunstan, Bishop *(OLSC, OLW)*
Saint Dunstan, Ethelwold and Oswald, Bishops *(CSP)*
From the Common of Confessors: For a Bishop (pp. 678-684).

20 May, Saint Bernardine of Siena, Priest

From the Common of Confessors: For a Missionary (pp. 688-692);
or from the Common of Holy Men and Women: For Religious (pp. 705-708)

21 May, Saint Christopher Magallanes, Priest, and Companions, Martyrs

From the Common of Martyrs: For Several Martyrs (pp. 666-670 or,
during Eastertide, p. 670).

Saint Godric of Finchale, Religious *(OLW)*

From the Common of Holy Men and Women: For Religious (pp. 705-708).

Saint Helena *(OLW)*

From the Common of Holy Men and Women: For Any Matron or
Holy Woman (pp. 702-705).

22 May, Saint Rita of Cascia, Religious

From the Common of Holy Men and Women: For Religious (pp. 705-708).

23 May, Saint Petroc, Abbot *(OLW)*

From the Common of Holy Men and Women: For an Abbot or Abbess
(pp. 708-711).

24 May
Our Lady, Help of Christians
Patron of Australia

Solemnity

INTROIT *Salve, sancta Parens (January 1, p. 68)*

ALLELUIA *Virga Iesse (Common of The BVM, p. 650)*

OFFERTORY *Felix namque es (January 1, p. 70)*

COMMUNION *Beáta víscera (Common of The BVM, p. 651)*

Saint Aldhelm, Bishop *(OLW)*

From the Common of Confessors: For a Bishop (pp. 678-684).

25 May, Saint Bede the Venerable,
Priest and Doctor of the Church *(OLW Memorial)*
From the Common of Doctors of the Church (pp. 693-695); or from
the Common of Holy Men and Women: For Religious (pp. 705-708).
Saint Gregory VII, Pope
From the Common of Confessors: For a Holy Pope (pp. 675-678).
Saint Mary Magdalene de' Pazzi, Virgin
From the Common of Virgins (pp. 696-701); or from the Common of
Holy Men and Women: For Religious (pp. 705-708).

26 May
Saint Philip Neri, Priest
Feast

INTROIT *Cáritas Dei (Vigil of Pentecost, p. 361)*

GRADUAL *Veníte, fílii (Trinity VII, p. 406)*

ALLELUIA *O quam Bonus (Ember Friday in Whitsun Week, p.*
377, without second versicle)

OFFERTORY *Bénedic, ánima mea (Christmas II, p. 74)*

COMMUNION *Magna est glória eius (21 September, St. Matthew,*
p.605)

27 May
Saint Augustine of Canterbury, Bishop
Patron of the Ordinariate of Our Lady of the Southern
Cross
(OLSC, OLW: Feast)

INTROIT *Sacerdótes tui (Common of Confessors, p. 681)*

GRADUAL *Sacerdótes eius (Common of Confessors, p. 682)*

ALLELUIA *Iuravit Dóminus (Common of Confessors, p. 682)*

OFFERTORY *Véritas mei (Common of Confessors, p. 683)*

COMMUNION *Beátus servus (Common of Confessors, p. 684)*

28 May, Saint Gregory VII, Pope *(OLW, Vide supra, 25 May)*
Saint Mary Magdalene de' Pazzi, Virgin *(OLSC, Vide supra, 25 May)*

31 May
Visitation of the Blessed Virgin Mary
Feast

INTROIT *Gaudeamus... Mariae (Common of the BVM, p. 647)*
or IN. *Salve sancta Parens (January 1, p. 68)*

GRADUAL *Benedícta et venerábilis (Common of the BVM, p. 648)*

ALLELUIA *Felix es, sacra Virgo*

Cantor   *All*

vj.

AL- LE- LU- IA.   Al- le- lu- ia.

Cantors

℣. Hap-py art thou, O sacred Virgin Mary, and most

Choir

worthy of all praise: for out of thee hath arisen the Sun of

All

righteousness, Christ our Lord Al - le- lu- ia.

In Eastertide: AL. *Virga Iesse (Common of the BVM, p.650)*

OFFERTORY *Beáta es, Virgo María (Masses of St. Mary, p. 756)*

COMMUNION *Beatam me dicent (August 15, p. 593)*

Saturday after the Second Sunday after Pentecost
**The Immaculate Heart of the Blessed Virgin Mary
Memorial**

INTROIT *Meditátio cordis mei*   *Ps. 19:14,1*

Cantors

vij.

LET the meditation of my heart be alway ac-cep-ta-ble

Choir   *FINE*

in thy sight: O LORD, my strength and my re-dee-mer.

Cantors   *Choir*

Ps. The hea-vens declare the glo-ry of God: and the

Cantor

firmament show-eth his han-dy-work. Glo-ry be ..., *(etc.)*

Choir   *Full*

As it was ..., *(etc.)* Let the meditation ..., *(etc.)*

GRADUAL *Exsultábit cor meum*   *Ps. 13:5b,6; 45:17*

Cantors   *Choir*

MY heart is joyful in thy sal-va-tion: I will sing

of the LORD because he hath dealt so lovingly with me;

yea, I will praise the Name of the LORD Most High-est.
Cantors

℣. They shall remember thy Name from one generation to
Choir

an-o-ther: there-fore shall the people give thanks unto

thee, world with-out end.

ALLELUIA *Parátum cor meum* *(Trinity XX, p. 457)*

OFFERTORY *Meditabor* *(Lent II, p. 151)*

COMMUNION *Narrabo omnia* *(Trinity I, p. 386)*

INTROIT *Loquébar de testimóniis tuis* *(Common of Virgins, p. 670)*

GRADUAL *Os iusti meditábitur*   *Ps. 37:31,32*

Cantor

v.

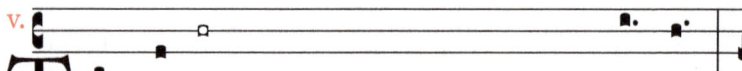

THE mouth of the righteous is exercised in wis-dom:

Choir   *Cantor*

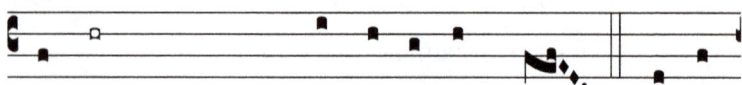

and his tongue will be talk-ing of judge-ment. ℣. The law

Choir

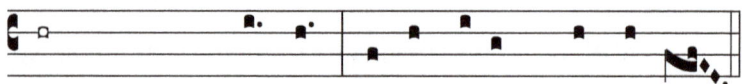

of his God is in his heart: and his go-ings shall not slide.

ALLELUIA *Qui séquitur me*   *Jn. 8:12*

Cantors   *All*

vj.

AL- LE- LU- IA.   Al- le- lu- ia.

Cantor

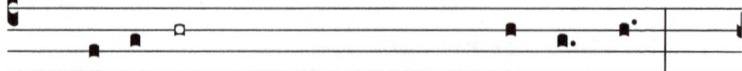

℣. He that followeth me shall not walk in dark-ness:

Choir

but shall have the light of e-ter-nal life.

All

Al - le- lu- ia.

OFFERTORY *Levábo óculos meos (Lent I Mon., p.138)*
or in Eastertide, OF. *Confitebúntur cæli (Common of Martyrs,*
p.664)

COMMUNION *Quod dico vobis in ténebris*   *Mt. 10:27*

Cantors

i.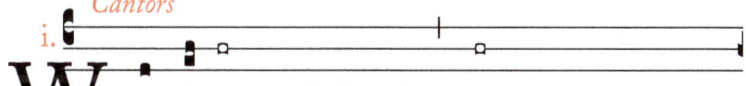

WHAT I tell you in darkness, that speak ye in the

Choir

light, saith the Lord: and what ye hear in the ear, that

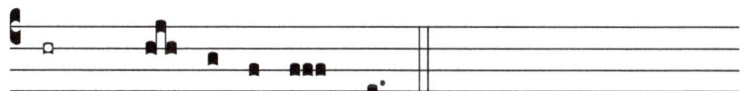

preach ye up-on the house-tops.

Psalm 126 *may be sung.*

or in Eastertide, CO. *Laetábitur iustus (Common of Martyrs,*
p. 665)

2 June, Saints Marcellinus and Peter, Martyrs
From the Common of Martyrs: For Several Martyrs (pp. 666–670 or, during Eastertide, pp. 670).

3 June, Saint Charles Lwanga and Companions, Martyrs
From the Common of Martyrs: For Several Martyrs (pp. 666–670 or, during Eastertide, pp. 670).

5 June
Saint Boniface, Bishop and Martyr
Memorial

INTROIT *Loquébar de testimóniis tuis (Common of Martyrs, p. 670)*

GRADUAL *Veníte, fílii (Trinity VII, p. 406)*

ALLELUIA *Invéni David (Baptism of the Lord, p. 82)*

OFFERTORY *Benedícam Dóminum (Trinity V, p. 399)*

COMMUNION *Signa eos (Ascension, p. 345)*
or in Eastertide Co. *Lætábitur iustus (Common of Martyrs, p. 665)*

6 June, Saint Norbert, Bishop
From the Common of Confessors: For a Bishop (pp. 668–684); or from the Common of Holy Men and Women: For Religious (pp. 705–708).

9 June, Saint Ephrem, Deacon and Doctor of the Church
From the Common of Doctors of the Church (pp. 643–646).
Saint Columba, Abbot
From the Common of Holy Men and Women: For an Abbot or Abbess (pp. 708–710).

JUNE
11 June
Saint Barnabas, Apostle
Memorial

INTROIT *Mihi autem nimis*   Ps. 139:17,1)

Cantor

vij.

RIGHT dear, O God, are thy friends unto me, and

Choir

held in high-est hon-our: their rule and governance

FINE   *Cantor*

is ex-cee-ding stead-fast. *Ps.* O LORD, thou hast searched

Choir

me out, and known me: thou knowest my down-sitting,

Cantor

and mine up-ris-ing..   Glo-ry be ..., *(etc.)*

Choir   *Full*

As it was ..., *(etc.)* Right dear, O God, ..., *(etc.)*
or in Eastertide IN. *Vocem iucundidátus (Easter VI, p. 333)*

559

GRADUAL *In omnem terram*   *Ps. 19:4,1*

Cantor   *Choir*

THEIR sound is gone out into all lands: and their

Cantors

words unto the ends of the world.   ℣. The hea-vens

Choir

declare the glory of God: and the firmament

show-eth his han-dy-work.

ALLELUIA *Ego vos elégi (14 May, Saint Matthias, p. 549)*

OFFERTORY *Constítues eos príncipes*   *Ps. 45:16,17*

Cantors   *Choir*

THOU shalt make them prin-ces in all lands: they shall

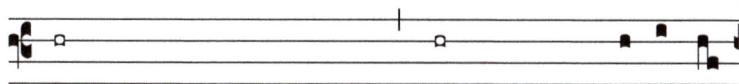

remember thy Name, O LORD, from one gen-er-a-tion to

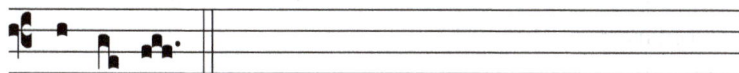

an- o- ther.
or in Eastertide OF. *Repléti sumus (14 May, St. Matthias, p. 550)*

COMMUNION *Vos, qui secúti*   *Mt. 19:28*

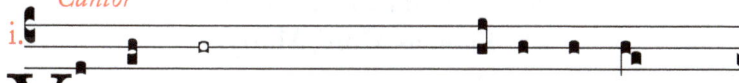

Cantor

E which have followed me shall sit up-on twelve

Choir

thrones: judg-ing the twelve tribes of Is- ra- el.
Verses from Psalm 19:1-6 *may be sung.*

or in Eastertide CO. *Ego vos elégi (Easter VI, p. 337)*

13 June, Saint Anthony of Padua, Priest and Doctor of the Church *(Memorial)*
From the Common of Confessors: For a Priest (pp. 685-687); or from the Common of Doctors of the Church (pp. 693-695); or from the Common of Holy Men and Women: For Religious (pp. 705-708).

16 June, Saint Richard of Chichester, Bishop
From the Common of Confessors: For a Bishop (pp. 678-684).

19 June, Saint Romuald, Abbot

From the Common of Holy Men and Women: For an Abbot or Abbess (pp. 708-710).

20 June, Saint Alban, Martyr

From the Common of Martyrs: For One Martyr (pp. 659-662).
OLW (Wales only): Saints Alban, Julius and Aaron, Protomartyrs of Britain
From the Common of Martyrs: For Several Martyrs (pp. 666-670).

21 June, Saint Aloysius Gonzaga, Religious

From the Common of Confessors: For a Priest (pp. 688-692); or from the Common of Holy Men and Women: For Religious (pp. 705-708).

22 June
**Saints John Fisher, Bishop,
and Thomas More, Martyrs**
Memorial (OLW Feast)

INTROIT *Multae tribulatiónes*   *Ps. 34:19,20,1*

Cantor

vij.

GREAT are the troubles of the righteous, but the

Choir

LORD delivereth him out of all: the LORD keepeth all his

FINE   *Cantor*

bones, so that not one of them is bro-ken. *Ps.* I will

Choir

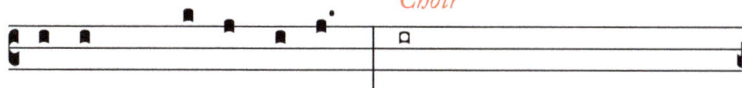

give thanks un-to the LORD: his praise shall ever,

Cantor *Choir*

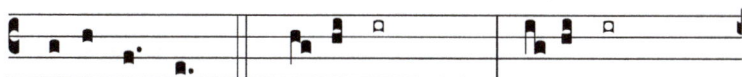

be in my mouth. Glo-ry be ..., *(etc.)* As it was ..., *(etc.)*

Full

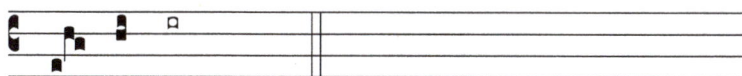

Great are the, ..., *(etc.)*

GRADUAL *Accedite ad eum* *Ps. 34:5,15*

Cantors *Choir*

v.

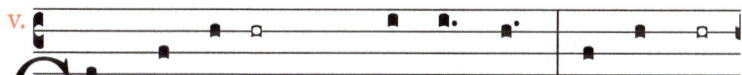

COME un-to him and be en-light-ened: and your faces

Cantors

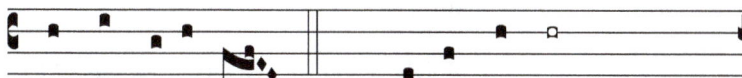

shall not be a-shamed. ℣. The eyes of the LORD are over

Choir

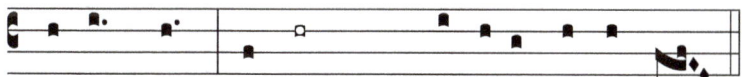

the right-eous: and his ears are op-en un-to their prayers.

ALLELUIA *Sancti tui, Dómine*   *Ps. 145:10b,11*

Cantors   *All*

AL- LE- LU- IA.   Al- le- lu- ia.

Cantors   *Choir*

℣. Thy Saints give thanks unto thee, O LORD: and tell

All

the glory of thy king-dom.   Al - le- lu- ia.

OFFERTORY *Mirábilis Deus* *(Common of Martyrs, p. 669)*

COMMUNION *Iustórum ánimæ* *(All Saints, p. 621)*

23 June, Saint Paulinus of Nola, Bishop
From the Common of Confessors: For a Bishop (pp. 678-684).
Saint Etheldreda (Audrey), Virgin *(OLSC, OLW)*
From the Common of Virgins (pp. 696-701).
Saints Hilda, Etheldreda, Mildred and All Holy Nuns *(CSP)*
From the Common of Holy Men and Women: For Religious (pp. 705-708).

THE NATIVITY OF SAINT JOHN THE BAPTIST
Solemnity
At the Vigil Mass

INTROIT *Ne tímeas (Sapientiatide, p. 41)*

GRADUAL *Fuit homo*   *Jn. 1:6*

Cantors   *Choir*

THERE was a man sent from God: whose name was

Cantors

John. ℣. The same came for witness, to bear witness to

Choir

the light: to make ready a people pre-par-ed for the Lord.

ALLELUIA *Beatus vir qui timet (Common of Saints, p. 706)*
OFFERTORY *Glória et honóre (Common of Martyrs, p. 661)*
COMMUNION *Magna est glória eius (21 Sep., St. Matthew, p. 605)*

At the Mass during the Day

INTROIT *De ventre*   *Is. 49:1,2; Ps. 92*

Cantors

vij.

FROM the womb of my mother the LORD hath called

me by my name;   and hath made my mouth as it were

Choir

a sharp sword: be-neath the shadow of his hand hath

FINE

he hidden me, and hath made me like a pol-ished ar-row.

Cantors   *Choir*

Ps. It is a good thing to give thanks un-to the LORD: and to

sing praises unto thy Name, O Most High-est.

Cantors

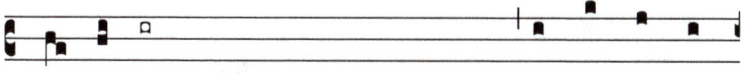

Glo- ry be to the Father, and to the Son, and to the Ho-

Choir

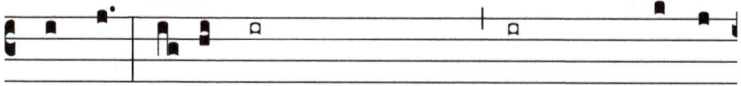

ly Ghost: As it was in the beginning, is now, and ev- er

Full

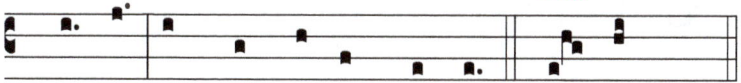

shall be: world with- out end. A- men. From the..., *(etc.)*

GRADUAL *Priúsquam*   *Jer. 1:5* ℣. *9*

Cantors

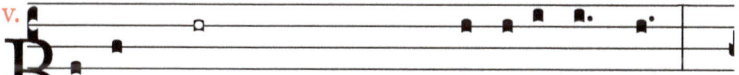

℣. BE-FORE I formed thee in the bel-ly I knew thee:

Choir

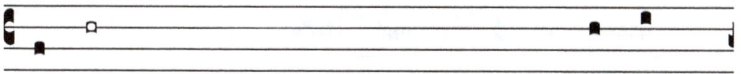

and before thou camest forth out of the womb I sanc-

Cantors

ti-fi-ed thee.   ℣. The LORD put forth his hand and

567

Choir

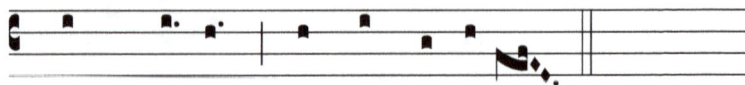

touched my mouth: and spake un-to me.

ALLELUIA *Tu puer*   *Lk.* 1:76

vj.

Cantors   *All*

AL- LE- LU- IA.   Al- le- lu- ia.

Cantors

℣. Thou, child, shalt be called the Prophet of the High-est:

Choir

for thou shalt go before the face of the Lord to pre-pare

All

his ways.   Al - le- lu- ia.

OFFERTORY *Iustus ut palma florébit,* *Ps. 92:11*

Cantors

ij.

THE righ-teous shall flou-rish like a palm-tree:

Choir

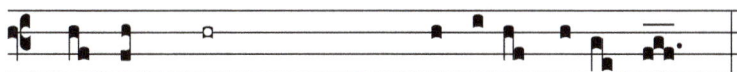

and shall spread abroad like a ce-dar in Le-ba-non.

COMMUNION *Tu, puer* *Luke 1:76*

Cantors

i.

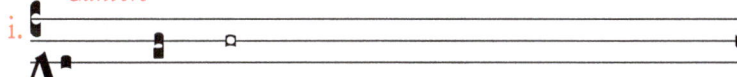

AND thou, child, shalt be called the Prophet

Choir

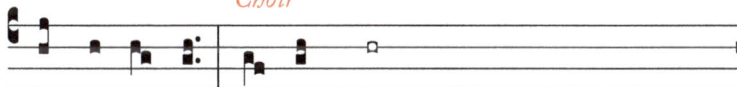

of the high-est: for thou shalt go before the face of the

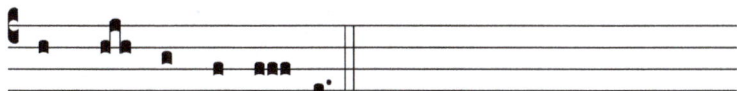

Lord to pre-pare his ways.

The Benedictus *may be sung.*

27 June, Saint Cyril of Alexandria, Bishop and Doctor of the Church

From the Common of Confessors: For a Bishop (pp. 678-681); or from the Common of Doctors of the Church (pp. 693-695).

28 June
Saint Irenaeus, Bishop and Martyr
Memorial

From the Common of Martyrs: For a Martyr Pope or Bishop (pp. 652–655),
or For a Martyr Bishop (pp. 655–659); or from the Common of Confessors:
For a Bishop (pp. 678–684).

INTROIT *Loquétur Dóminus pacem*   *Ps 85:8,1*

Cantors   *Choir*

THE LORD shall speak peace un-to his peo-ple: and to

FINE   *Cantors*

his Saints, that they turn not a- gain. *Ps.* LORD, thou

Choir

art become gracious un-to thy land: thou hast turned

Cantors

away the cap-ti-vi-ty of Ja-cob.   Glo-ry be ..., *(etc.)*

Choir   *Full*

As it was ..., *(etc.)* The Lord shall ..., *(etc.)*

SAINTS PETER AND PAUL, APOSTLES
Solemnity
At the Vigil Mass

INTROIT *Dicit Dóminus Petro*   *Jn. 21:18,19; Ps. 19:1*

Cantors

vij.

THE Lord saith unto Peter, When thou wast young,

thou girdedst thyself, and walkedst whi-ther thou would-est:

Choir

but when thou shalt be old, thou shalt stretch forth thy

hands, and another shall gird thee, and carry thee

whither thou wouldest not; this spake he, signifying by

FINE *Cantors*

what death he should glo- ri- fy God. *Ps.* The hea-vens

Choir

declare the glo-ry of God: and the firmament show-eth

Cantors *Choir*

his han-dy-work. Glo-ry be ..., *(etc.)* As it was ..., *(etc.)*

Full

The Lord saith ..., *(etc.)*

GRADUAL *In omnem terram (June 11, St. Barnabas, p. 560)*

ALLELUIA *Constítues eos príncipes* *Ps. 45:16,17*

Cantors *All*

vj. AL- LE- LU- IA. Al- le- lu- ia.

Cantors *Choir*

℣. Thou shalt make them princes in all lands: they shall

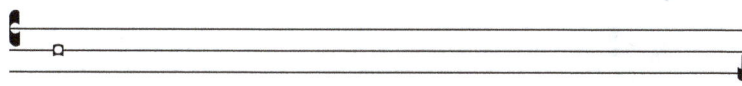

remember thy Name, O LORD, from one generation

All

to an- o- ther..   Al - le- lu- ia.

OFFERTORY *Mihi autem nimis* *(Jan. 25, p. 503)*
COMMUNION *Simon Ioannis (Easter III, p. 323)*

At the Mass during the Day

INTROIT *Nunc scio vere*   *Acts 12:11; Ps. 139:1*

Cantors

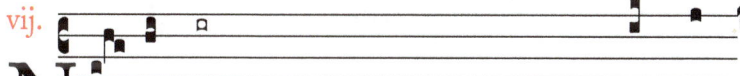

vij.

N OW I know of a surety that the LORD hath sent his

Choir

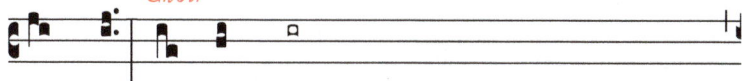

An - gel: and hath delivered me from the hand of Herod,

FINE

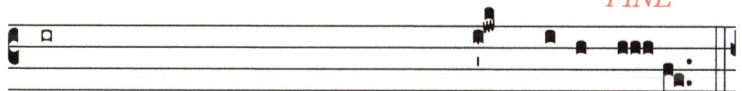

and from all the expectation of the peo - ple of the Jews.

Cantors

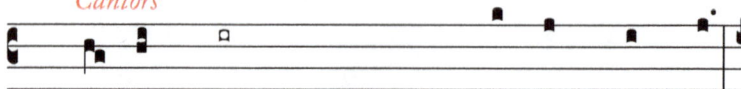

Ps. O LORD, thou hast searched me out, and known me:

Choir

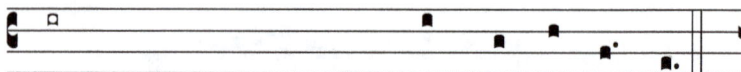

thou knowest my down-sitting and mine up - ris - ing.

Cantors   *Choir*   *Full*

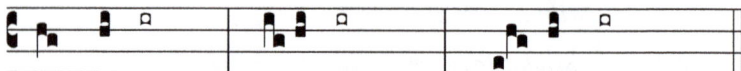

Glo-ry be..., *(etc.)* As it was..., *(etc.)* Now I know..., *(etc.)*

GRADUAL *In omnem terram (June 11, St. Barnabas, p. 560)*

ALLELUIA *Tu es Petrus (Common of Confessorss, p. 676)*

OFFERTORY *Constítues eos príncipes (June 11, St. Barnabas, p. 560)*

COMMUNION *Tu es Petrus (Chair of St. Peter, p. 530)*

30 June, The First Martyrs of the Holy Roman Church
From the Common of Martyrs: For Several Martyrs (pp. 666-670).

1 July, St. Oliver Plunkett, Bishop and Martyr *(OLSC, OLW)*

From the Common of Martyrs: For a Martyr Pope or Bishop (pp. 652-655), or For a Martyr Bishop (pp. 655-659); or from the Common of Confessors: For a Bishop (pp. 678-684).

CSP(US only): Saint Junipero Serra, Priest
From the Common of Confessors: For a Missionary (pp. 688-692), or For a Priest (pp. 685-687).

3 July
SAINT THOMAS, APOSTLE
Feast

INTROIT *Mihi autem nimis (June 11, St. Barnabas, p. 559)*

GRADUAL *Nimis honoráti sunt (May 14, St. Matthias, p. 549)*

ALLELUIA *Gaudéte iusti (Holy Family, p. 64)*

OFFERTORY *In omnem terram (Feb. 22, Chair of St. Peter, p. 529)*

COMMUNION *Mitte manum tuam (Easter II, p. 318)*

4 July, Saint Elizabeth of Portugal

From the Common of Holy Men and Women: For Any Matron or Holy Woman (pp. 702-705).

5 July, Saint Saint Anthony Zaccaria, Priest

From the Common of Confessors: For a Priest (pp. 685-687); or from the Common of Holy Men and Women: For Religious (pp. 705-708), or For an Educator (p. 711).

Saint Elizabeth of Portugal *(CSP US only)*
Vide supra, 4 July

6 July, Saint Maria Goretti, Virgin and Martyr

From the Common of Martyrs: For a Virgin Martyr (pp. 670-674).

7 July, Blessed Peter To Rot, Martyr *(OLSC)*

From the Common of Martyrs: For One Martyr (pp. 659-662); or from the Common of Holy Men and Women: For an Educator (p. 711).

9 July, Saint Augustine Zhao Rong, Priest, and Companions, Martyrs

From the Common of Martyrs: For Several Martyrs (pp. 666–670).

Our Lady of the Atonement
(CSP)

From the Common of the Blessed Virgin Mary (pp. 647–651).

INTROIT *Stabant iuxta crucem (St. Mary in Passiontide, p. 201)*

ALLELUIA *Stabat Sancta María (Our Lady of Sorrows, p. 602)*

11 July
Saint Benedict, Abbot
Patron of Europe
Memorial (OLW: Feast)

INTROIT *Os iusti meditábitur (Common of Confessors, p. 685)*

GRADUAL *Dómine, prævenísti eum (Common of Holy Men and Women, for an Abbot or abbess, p. 708)*

ALLELUIA *Iustus ut palma (Common of Holy Men and Women, p. 709)*

OFFERTORY *Desidérium ánimæ (Common of Holy Men and Women, p. 710)*

COMMUNION *Fidelis servus et prudens (Common of Confessors, p. 680)*

12 July, Saint John Jones, Priest and Martyr *(OLW Wales only)*
From the Common of Martyrs: For One Martyr (pp. 919–920).

13 July, Saint Henry
From the Common of Holy Men and Women: For Any Holy Man (p. 702).

14 July, Saint Camillus de Lellis, Priest *(except US)*
From the Common of Confessors: For a Priest (pp. 685-687).
Saint Kateri Tekakwitha, Virgin *Memorial (CSP US only)*
From the Common of Virgins (pp. 696-701).

15 July, St. Bonaventure, Bishop and Doctor of the Church
(CSP Memorial)
From the Common of Confessors: For a Bishop (pp. 678-684); or from the Common of Doctors of the Church (pp. 693-695).
Saint Swithun, Bishop *(OLSC, OLW)*
From the Common of Confessors: For a Bishop (pp. 678-684).

16 July, Our Lady of Mount Carmel
From the Common of the Blessed Virgin Mary (pp. 647-651).
Saint Osmund, Bishop *(OLW)*
From the Common of Confessors: For a Bishop (pp. 678-684).

14 July, Saint Camillus de Lellis, Priest *(CSP. US only)*
Vide supra 14 July

20 July, Saint Apollinaris, Bishop and Martyr
From the Common of Martyrs: For a Martyr Pope or Bishop (pp. 652-655), or For a Martyr Bishop (pp. 635-659).
Saint Margaret of Antioch, Martyr *(OLW)*
From the Common of Martyrs: For a Virgin Martyr (pp. 670-674).

21 July, Saint Lawrence of Brindisi,
Priest and Doctor of the Church
From the Common of Confessors: For a Priest (pp. 685-687); or from the Common of Doctors of the Church (pp. 693-695); or from the Common of Holy Men and Women: For Religious (pp. 705-708).

PROPER of SAINTS and HOLY DAYS
22 July
Saint Mary Magdalene
Memorial

INTROIT *Tibi dixit cor meum* *(Lent II, p. 150)*

GRADUAL *Audi, filia* *(Aug.15, Annunciation, p. 592)*

ALLELUIA *Surréxit Dóminus de sepulchro* *(Easter Tues., p. 303)*

OFFERTORY *Deus, Deus meus* *(Easter IV, p. 327)*

COMMUNION *Notas mihi fecisti* *(Lent III Weds., p. 172)*

23 July
Saint Bridget of Sweden, Religious
Patron of Europe
(OLW Feast)

INTROIT *Cognóvi* *(Common for any matron or holy woman, p. 702)*

GRADUAL *Diffusa est gratia* *(St. Mary Mother of God, p. 69)*

ALLELUIA *Specie tua* *(Common of Holy Men and Women, p. 703)*

OFFERTORY *Diffúsa est grátia* *(Candlemas, p. 518)*

COMMUNION *Dilexísti* *(Common of Holy Men and Women, p. 704)*

24 July, Saint Sharbel Makhlūf, Priest
From the Common of Confessors: For a Priest (pp. 685–687); or from the Common of Holy Men and Women: For Religious (pp. 705–708).

25 July
SAINT JAMES, APOSTLE
Feast

INTROIT *Mihi autem nimis (June 11, St. Barnabas, p. 559)*

GRADUAL *Constítues eos príncipes* Ps. 45:16,17

Cantor *Choir*

THOU shalt make them princes in all lands: they shall

Cantor

re-mem-ber thy Name, O LORD. ℣. In-stead of thy

Choir

fathers thou shalt have chil-dren: there-fore shall the

peo-ple give thanks un-to thee.

ALLELUIA *Ego vos elégi (13 May, St. Matthias, p. 549)*
OFFERTORY *In omnem terram (Feb. 22, Chair of St. Peter, p. 529)*
COMMUNION *Ego vos elégi (Easter VI, p. 337)*

PROPER of SAINTS and HOLY DAYS
26 July
Saints Joachim and Anne,
Parents of the Blessed Virgin Mary
Memorial (CSP [Canada only]: Feast)

INTROIT *Sapiéntiam sanctórum*   *Sir. 44:15,14; Ps. 33:1*

Cantor

vij.

LET the people tell of the wisdom of the Saints, and let

Choir

the Church show forth their praise: their names shall live

FINE   *Cantor*

for e-ver-more. *Ps.* Re-joice in the LORD, O ye right-eous:

Choir

for   it becometh well the just to be thank-ful.

Cantor   *Choir*   *Full*

Glo-ry be ..., *(etc.)* As it was ..., *(etc.)* Let the, ..., *(etc.)*

GRADUAL *Exultábunt sancti*   *Ps. 149:5,1*

Cantor   *Choir*

LET the Saints be joyful with glo-ry: let them

Cantor

re-joice in their beds. ℣. O sing unto the LORD a new

Choir

song: let the congregation of Saints praise him.

ALLELUIA *O Joachim*

Cantor   *All*

AL- LE- LU- IA. Al- le- lu- ia.

Cantors

℣. O ho-ly Joachim, spouse of Saint Anne, of the gracious

Choir

Virgin the fa-ther: here to the need of thy ser-vants

581

All

bring aid.　　Al - le- lu- ia.

OFFERTORY *Lætámini in Domino*　　　　　　*Ps. 32:12*

Cantor　　　　　　　　　　　　　　　　　*Choir*

ij. BE glad, O ye righteous, and re-joice in the LORD: and be

joyful, all ye that are true of heart.

COMMUNION *Ierúsalem, surge (Advent II, p. 24)*

29 July, Saint Martha *Memorial*
From the Common of Virgins (pp. 696-701).

30 July, St. Peter Chrysologus, Bishop and Doctor of the Church
From the Common of Confessors: For a Bishop (pp. 678-684); or from the Common of Doctors of the Church (pp. 693-695).

31 July
Saint Ignatius of Loyola, Priest
Memorial

INTROIT *In Nómine Iesu* *(Weds. in Holy Week, p. 238)*

GRADUAL *Iustus ut palma* *(Common of Confessors, p. 686)*

ALLELUIA *Beatus vir qui suffert* *(Common of Confessors, p. 686)*

OFFERTORY *Véritas mea* *(Common of Confessors, p. 283)*

COMMUNION *Qui meditábitur* *(Ash Weds., p. 128)*

1 August, Saint Alphonsus Liguori, Bishop and Doctor of the Church *Memorial*
From the Common of Confessors: For a Bishop (pp. 678-681); or fromthe Common of Doctors of the Church (pp. 693-695).

2 August, Saint Eusebius of Vercelli, Bishop
From the Common of Confessors: For a Bishop (pp. 678-681).

Saint Peter Julian Eymard, Priest
Common of Holy Men and Women: For Religious (pp. 705-708); or from the Common of Confessors: For a Priest (pp. 678-681).

3 August, Saint Germanus of Auxerre, Bishop *(Wales only)*
From the Common of Confessors: For a Bishop (pp. 678-68).

4 August, Saint John Mary Vianney, Priest *Memorial*
From the Common of Confessors: For a Priest (pp. 685-687).

5 August, The Dedication of the Basilica of Saint Mary Major
From the Common of the Blessed Virgin Mary (pp. 647-651.

Saint Oswald, Martyr
From the Common of Martyrs: For One Martyr (pp. 659-662).

6 August
THE TRANSFIGURATION OF THE LORD
Feast

INTROIT *Tibi dixit cor meum (Lent II, p. 150)*

Or: INTROIT *Illuxérunt coruscátiones*   *Ps. 77:18; 84:1,2*

THE light-nings shone up-on the ground: the earth

FINE *Cantor*

was moved and shook with-al. *Ps.* O how amiable are

Choir

thy dwellings, thou LORD of hosts: my soul hath a desire

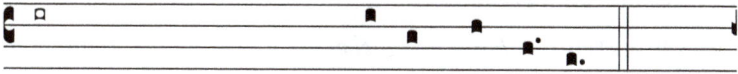

and longing to enter into the courts of the Lord

Cantor *Choir* *Full*

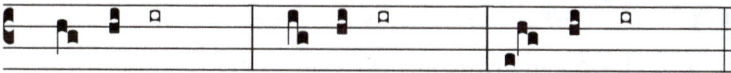

Glo-ry be ..., *(etc.)* As it was ..., *(etc.)* The light-..., *(etc.)*

GRADUAL *Speciósus forma (Christmas II, p. 73)*

ALLELUIA *Candor est* *Wis. 7:26*

Cantor *All*

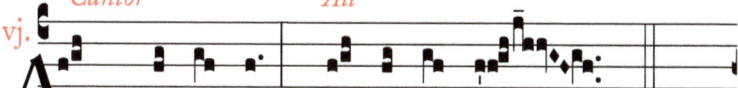

vj. AL- LE- LU- IA. Al- le- lu- ia.

Cantor *Choir*

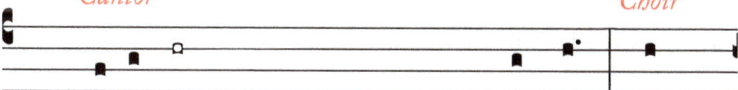

℣. He is the brightness of the everlast-ing light: the

unspotted mirror, and the image of his good-ness.

All

Al - le- lu- ia.

OFFERTORY *Glória et honóre (Common of Martyrs, p. 661)*

Or: OFFERTORY *Glória et divítiæ*   *Ps. 112:3*

Cantor

ij. RICH-ES and plenteousness shall be in his house:

Choir

and his righteousness endureth for ev-er.   Al- le- lu- ia.

COMMUNION *Visiónem (Lent II, p. 151)*

7 August, Saint Sixtus II, Pope, and Companions, Martyrs
From the Common of Martyrs: For Several Martyrs (pp. 666-670).
Saint Cajetan, Priest
*From the Common of Confessors: For a Priest (pp. 685-687); or from
the Common of Holy Men and Women: For Religious (pp. 705-708).*
Saint Saint Dominic, Priest *(OLSC)*
Vide infra, 8 August

8 August
Saint Dominic, Priest
Memorial (CSP, OLW)

Introit *Sapiéntiam sanctórum (Sts. Joachim and Anne, p. 580)*

Gradual *Iustus ut palma (Common of Confessors, p. 686)*

Al. *Iustus germinabit (29 Aug. Passion of St. John the Baptist, p. 597)*

Offertory *Veritas mea (Common of Confessors, p. 683)*

Co. *Fidelis servus et prudens (Common of Confessors, p 680)*

SAINT MARY OF THE CROSS, VIRGIN *(OLSC)*

Solemnity

Introit *Veníte, benedícti (Weds. in the Octave of Easter, p. 305)*

Gradual *Dilexisti (Common of Virgin Martyrs, p. 671)*

Alleluia *Adducentur (St. Catherine of Siena, p. 541)*

Offertory *Fíliæ regum (Common of Virgins p. 700)*

Communion *In hoc cognóscent* Jn. 13:35

Cantor

By this shall all men know that ye are my dis-ci-ples:

Choir

if ye have love one to an-o-ther.

The Magnificat *or* Psalm 45:1,10-15 *may be sung.*

PROPER of SAINTS and HOLY DAYS
9 August
Saint Teresa Benedicta of the Cross, Virgin and Martyr, Patron of Europe
(OLW: Feast)

INTROIT *Dilexísti (Common of Virgins, p. 696)*

GRADUAL *Dilexísti (Common of Virgin Martyrs, p. 671)*

ALLELUIA *Hæc est virgo sápiens*

Cantor / *All*

AL- LE- LU- IA.   Al- le- lu- ia.

Cantor / *Choir*

℣. This is a wise vir-gin: and one of the number

All

of the pru-dent.   Al - le- lu- ia.

OFFERTORY *Filiae regum (Common of Virgins, p. 700)*

COMMUNION *Quinque prudéntes vírgines (Common of Virgins, p. 700)*

AUGUST
10 August
SAINT LAWRENCE, DEACON AND MARTYR
(Feast)

INTROIT *Conféssio (Thursday, Lent I, p. 144)*

GRADUAL *Probásti, Dómine*   *Ps. 17:3*

Cantor   *Choir*

THOU hast proved and visited mine heart in the

Cantors   *Choir*

night sea-son. ℣. Thou hast tried me with fire: and hast

found no wick-ed-ness in me.

ALLELUIA *Levíta Lauréntius*

Cantor   *All*   *Cantor*

AL- LE- LU- IA. Al- le- lu- ia.   ℣. The Le-

Choir

vite Lawrence wrought a good work: who by the sign of

All

the Cross gave light to the blind Al - le- lu- ia.

OFFERTORY *Conféssio*   *Ps. 96:6*

Cantor   *Choir*

GLO-RY and wor-ship are be-fore him: pow-er and

honour are in his sanc-tu- a- ry.

COMMUNION *Qui mihi minístrat (Lent V, p. 193)*

11 August, Saint Clare, Virgin *(Memorial)*
From the Common of Virgins (pp. 696-701); or from the Common of Holy Men and Women: For Religious (pp. 705-708).

12 August, Saint Jane Frances de Chantal, Religious
From the Common of Holy Men and Women: For Religious (pp. 705-708).

13 August, Saints Pontian, Pope, and Hippolytus, Priest, Martyrs
From the Common of Martyrs: For Several Martyrs (pp. 666-670).

14 August, Saint Maximillian Mary Kolbe, Priest and Martyr *(Memorial)*
From the Common of Martyrs: For One Martyr (pp. 659-662).

AUGUST
15 August
THE ASSUMPTION
OF THE BLESSED VIRGIN MARY
Solemnity
At the Vigil Mass

INTROIT *Vultum tuum deprecabúntur (Masses of St. Mary, p. 753)*

GRADUAL *Benedícta et venerábilis (Common of the BVM, p. 648)*

ALLELUIA *Felix es, sacra Virgo (Visitation of the BVM, p. 553)*

OFFERTORY *Beáta es, Virgo María (Masses of St. Mary, p. 756)*

COMMUNION *Beáta víscera (Common of the BVM. p. 651)*

At the Mass during the Day

INTROIT *Signum magnum*   *Rev. 12:1, Ps. 98:1*

Cantor

THERE ap- peared a great wonder in heaven:

Choir

A woman cloth-ed with the sun, and the moon under

FINE

her feet; and upon her head a crown of twelve stars.

Cantor   *Choir*

Ps. O sing unto the LORD a new song: for he hath done

591

Cantor　　　　*Choir*

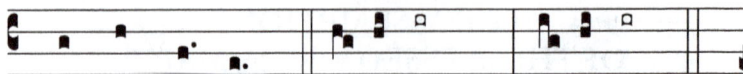

mar- vel- lous things. Glo- ry be...*(etc.)* As it was..., *(etc.)*

Full

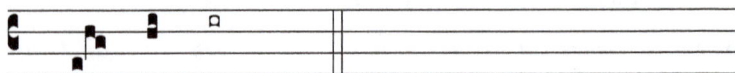

There ap-peared..., *(etc.)*

or In. *Gaudeámus... Maríæ (Common of the BVM, p. 647)*

Gradual *Audi, fília*　　　　　　　　　　　　　　*Ps. 45*

Cantor

v.

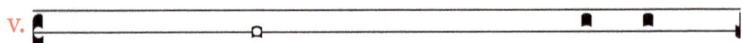

Hear- ken, O daughter, and consider, in- cline

Choir

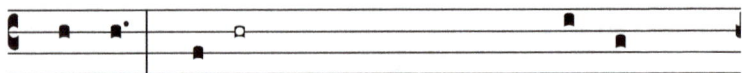

thine ear:　for the King delighteth greatly in thy

Cantor

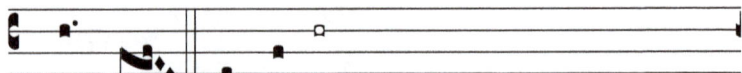

beau- ty.　℣. All glor-ious the King's daughter

Choir

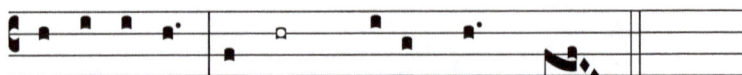

en-ter-eth in: her clothing is of wrought gold.

592

ALLELUIA *Assúmpta est*

Cantor   *All*

AL- LE- LU- IA.   Al- le- lu- ia.

Cantor   *Choir*

℣. Ma- ry is taken up into hea- ven: the hosts of

All

An- gels re-joice.   Al - le- lu- ia.

OFFERTORY *Assúmpta est*

Cantor   *Choir*

MA- RY is taken up in- to hea- ven: The An- gels

rejoice and glorify the LORD. Al- le- lu- ia.

COMMUNION *Beátam me dicent*   *Luke 1:48. 49*

Cantor   *Choir*

ALL ge- nerations shall call me bless-ed: for he that

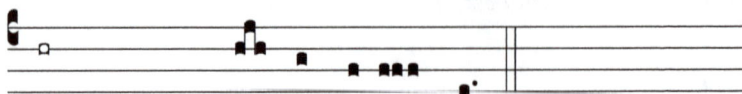

is mighty hath done to me great things.

Verses from The Magnificat may be sung.

16 Saint Stephen of Hungary
From the Common of Holy Men and Women: For Any Holy Man (p. 702).

19 August, Saint John Eudes, Priest
From the Common of Confessors: For a Priest (pp. 685-687); or from the Common of Holy Men and Women: For Religious (pp. 705-708).

20 August, Saint Bernard, Abbot and Doctor of the Church *(Memorial)*
From the Common of Doctors of the Church (pp. 603-695); or from the Common of Holy Men and Women: For an Abbot or Abbess (pp. 708-710).

21 August, Saint Pius X, Pope *(Memorial)*
From the Common of Confessors: For a Holy Pope (pp. 675-678).

22 August
The Queenship of the Blessed Virgin Mary
Memorial

INTROIT *Salve, sancta Parens (St. Mary, Jan. 1, p. 68)*

GRADUAL *Posuísti, Dómine*   *Ps. 21:4,3b,2*

HOU hast set, O LORD, a crown of pure gold up-on

her head. ℣. Thou hast given her, her heart's de-sire:

Choir

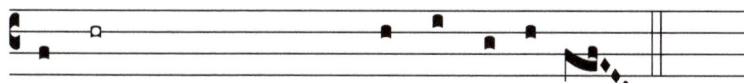

and hast not denied her the re-quest of her lips.

ALLELUIA *Posuísti, Dómine (Common of Martyrs, p. 661)*

OFFERTORY *Recordáre, Virgo Mater (Passion Week, p. 210)*

COMMUNION *Diffúsa est grátia*　　　　　　　　*Ps. 45:2b*

Cantor　　　　　　　　　　　　*Choir*

i.

FULL of grace are thy lips: be-cause God hath blessed

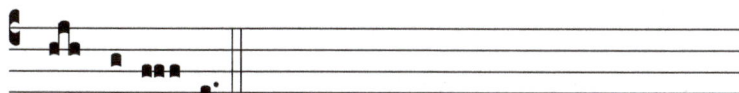

thee for   e- ver.

Verses from **Psalm 45:1, 10-15** *may be sung.*

23 August, Saint Rose of Lima, Virgin
From the Common of Virgins (pp. 696–701).

24 August

SAINT BARTHOLOMEW, APOSTLE
Feast

INTROIT *Mihi autem nimis (June 11, St. Barnabas, p. 559)*

GRADUAL *Constítues eos príncipes (July 25, St. James, p. 579)*

ALLELUIA *Te gloriósus*

Cantor　　　　　　　　　*All*

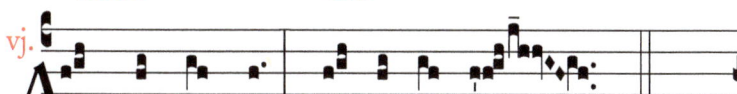

vj.

AL- LE- LU- IA.   Al- le- lu- ia.

Cantor

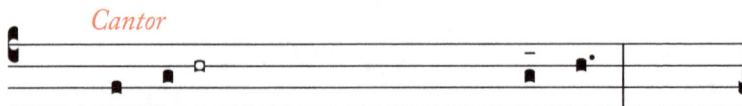

℣. The glo-ri-ous company of the Ap-os-tles:

Choir   *All*

praise thee, O God.   Al - le- lu- ia.

OFFERTORY *Mihi autem nimis (Jan. 25, p. 503)*

COMMUNION *Vos, qui secúti (June 11, St. Barnabas, p. 561)*

25 August, Saint Saint Louis
From the Common of Holy Men and Women: For Any Holy Man (p. 702).

Saint Joseph Calasanz, Priest
From the Common of Holy Men and Women: For an Educator (p. 711); or from the Common of Confessors: For a Priest (pp. 685-687).

26 August, Bl. Dominic of the Mother of God, Priest *(OLW)*
From the Common of Confessors: For a Priest (pp. 685-687); or from the Common of Holy Men and Women: For Religious (pp. 705-708).

Saint David Lewis, Martyr *(OLW, Wales only)*
From the Common of Martyrs: For One Martyr (pp. 659-662); or from the Common of Confessors: For a Priest (pp. 685-687).

27 August, Saint Monica *(Memorial)*
From the Common of Holy Men and Women: For Any Matron or Holy Woman (pp. 702-705).

28 August, Saint Augustine of Hippo, Bishop and Doctor of the Church *(Memorial)*
From the Common of Confessors: For a Bishop (pp. 678-684); or from the Common of Doctors of the Church (pp. 693-695).

29 August
The Passion of Saint John the Baptist
Memorial (CSP, Canada only: Feast)

INTROIT *Loquebar de testimoniis tuis* *(Common of Martyrs, p. 670)*

GRADUAL *Iustus ut palma* *(Common of Confessors, p. 686)*

ALLELUIA *Iustus germinábit* Hos. 14:6

Cantor *All*

vj. AL- LE- LU- IA. Al- le- lu- ia.

Cantor *Choir*

℣. The right-eous shall grow as the li-ly: and flourish

All

for ev-er be-fore the LORD. Al - le- lu- ia.

OF. *In virtúte tua* *(Common of Holy Men and Women, p. 707)*

CO. *Posuísti, Dómine* *(Common for a Martyr Bishop, p. 659)*

30 August, Saints Margaret Clitherow, Anne Line, and Margaret Ward, Martyrs
From the Common of Martyrs: For Several Martyrs (pp. 666-670); or from the Common of Holy Men and Women: For Any Matron or Holy Woman (pp. 702-684).

31 August, St. Aidan, Bishop, and the Saints of Lindisfarne
From the Common of Confessors: For a Bishop (pp. 678-684).

PROPER of SAINTS and HOLY DAYS
1 September
OUR LADY OF THE SOUTHERN CROSS
OLSC: Solemnity

INTROIT *Gaudeámus... Maríæ (Common of the BVM, p. 647)*

GR. *Benedícta et venerábilis (Common of the BVM, p. 648)*

ALLELUIA *Post partum (Jan. 1, St. Mary, p. 69)*

OFFERTORY *Ave, María (Common of the BVM, p. 651)*

COMMUNION *Beáta víscera (Common of the BVM, p. 651)*

3 September
Saint Gregory the Great
Pope and Doctor of the Church
Memorial (OLW: Feast)

INTROIT *Sacerdótes Dei (Common of a Martyr Bishop, p. 655)*

GRADUAL *Iurávit Dóminus*   *Ps. 110:4,1*

Cantor | *Choir*

THE LORD hath sworn and will not re-pent: Thou art

Cantor

a priest for ever, after the order of Mel-chi-se-dech. ℣. The

Choir

LORD said unto my Lord: Sit thou on my right hand.

ALLELUIA *Spíritus sanctus docébit vos* *(Tuesday in Whitsun Week, p. 373)*

OFFERTORY *Véritas mea* *(Common of Confessors, p. 683)*

COMMUNION *Fidélis servus et prudens* *(Common of Confessors, p. 680)*

4 September, Saint Cuthbert, Bishop

From the Common of Confessors: For a Bishop (pp. 678-684).

8 September
THE NATIVITY OF THE BLESSED VIRGIN MARY
Feast

INTROIT *Salve, sancta Parens* *(St. Mary, Jan. 1, p. 68)*

GRADUAL *Benedícta et venerábilis* *(Common of the BVM, p. 648)*

ALLELUIA *Solémnitas*

Cantor *All*

vj. AL- LE- LU- IA. Al- le- lu- ia.

Cantor *Choir*

℣. This is the festival of the glorious Virgin Ma-ry: of the

seed of Abraham, sprung from the tribe of Ju-dah, of the

599

All

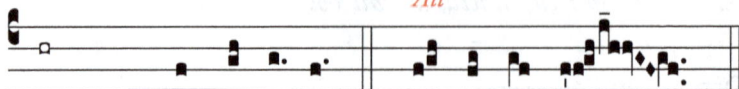

the noble stem of Da-vid.   Al - le- lu-   ia.

OFFERTORY *Beáta es, Virgo María (Masses of S. Mary, p. 755)*

COMMUNION *Beátam me dicent (Assumption, p. 593)*

9 September, Saint Peter Claver, Priest *(CSP: Memorial)*
From the Common of Confessors: For a Priest (pp. 685-687).

12 September, The Most Holy Name of Mary
From the Common of the Blessed Virgin Mary (pp. 647-651).

13 September, Saint John Chrysostom,
Bishop and Doctor of the Church *(Memorial)*
From the Common of Confessors: For a Bishop (pp. 678-684); or from
the Common of Doctors of the Church (pp. 693-695).

14 September
THE EXALTATION OF THE HOLY CROSS
(HOLY CROSS DAY)
Feast

INTROIT *Nos autem gloriári (Maundy Thursday, p. 243)*

GRADUAL *Christus factus est (Good Friday, p. 256)*

ALLELUIA *Dulce lignum*

AL- LE- LU- IA.   Al- le- lu- ia.

Cantor

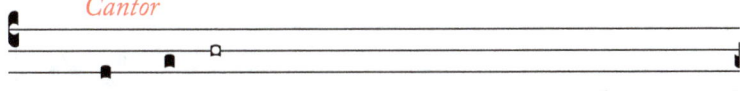

℣. Sweet-est wood, sweetest iron, that bare so sweet a

Choir

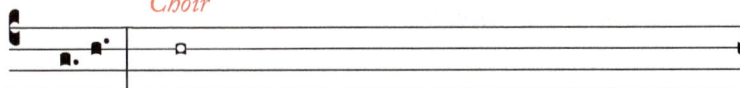

Bur-den: which only was counted worthy to sustain the

All

King of hea-ven and its Lord.   Al - le- lu- ia.

OFFERTORY   *Prótege, Dómine*

Cantor

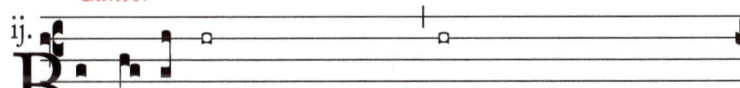

ij. BY the sign of the holy Cross, defend, O LORD, thy

Choir

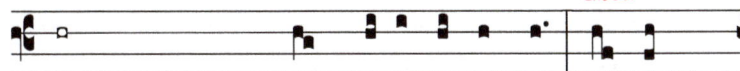

people from all the snares of our e-ne-mies: that the

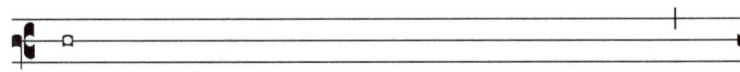

service which we render may be pleasing unto thee,

[musical notation]

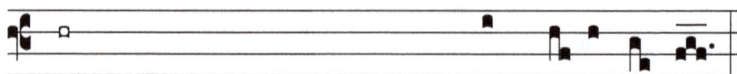

and our sacrifice acceptable in thy sight, al- le- lu- ia.

COMMUNION *Per signum crucis*

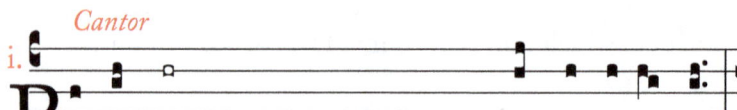

Cantor

[musical notation]

i.

BY the sign of the Cross, deliver us from our e-ne-mies:

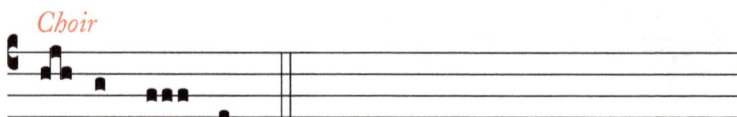

Choir

[musical notation]

O LORD our God.

Psalm 18:1-3,18,38,39,41,48-50 *may be sung.*

15 September
Our Lady of Sorrows
(Saint Mary at the Cross)
Memorial

INTROIT *Stabant iuxta crucem (St. Mary in Passiontide, p. 201)*

GRADUAL *Deus vitam meam (Lent III, Monday, p. 166)*

ALLELUIA *Stabat sancta María*

Cantor   *All*

[musical notation]

vj.

AL- LE- LU- IA.   Al- le- lu- ia.

Cantor

℣. There stood mournful by the Cross of our Lord

Choir

Je-sus Christ: holy Mary, Queen of Heaven, and La-dy

All

of the world.   Al - le- lu- ia.

SEQUENCE *Stabat Mater dolorósa (St. Mary in Passiontide, p. 204)*

OFFERTORY *Recordáre, Virgo Mater (Passion Week, p. 210)*

COMMUNION *Redíme me (Passion Week, p. 198)*

16 September, Saints Cornelius, Pope,
and Cyprian, Bishop, Martyrs *(Memorial)*
From the Common of Martyrs: For Several Martyrs (pp. 666-670).

17 September, Saint Robert Bellarmine,
Bishop and Doctor of the Church
*From the Common of Confessors: For a Bishop (pp. 678-684); or from
the Common of Doctors of the Church (pp. 693-695).*
Saint Ninian, Bishop *(OLW)*
From the Common of Confessors: For a Bishop (pp. 678-684).
Saint Edith of Wilton, Religious *(OLW)*
*From the Common of Virgins (pp. 696-701); or from the Common of
Holy Men and Women: For Religious (pp. 705-708).*

19 September, Saint Januarius, Bishop and Martyr

From the Common of Martyrs: For a Martyr Pope or Bishop (pp. 652-655), or For a Martyr Bishop (pp. 655-659).

Saint Theodore of Canterbury, Bishop

From the Common of Confessors: For a Bishop (pp. 678-684).

Saint Adrian, Abbot *(CSP)*

From the Common of Holy Men and Women: For an Abbot or Abbess (pp. 708-710).

20 September, Saint Andrew Kim Tae-go˘n, Priest, Paul Cho˘ng Ha-sang and Companions, Martyrs *(Memorial)*

From the Common of Martyrs: For Several Martyrs (pp. 666-670).

21 Setember
SAINT MATTHEW, APOSTLE AND EVANGELIST
(Feast)

INTROIT *Os iusti meditábitur (Common of Confessors, p. 685)*

GRADUAL *Beátus vir qui timet (Common of Martyrs, p. 660)*

ALLELUIA *Te gloriósus (St. Bartholomew, August 24, p. 595)*

OFFERTORY *Posuísti, Dómine*   *Ps. 21:3b,4*

Cantor

THOU hast set, O LORD, a crown of pure gold up-on his

Choir

head: he asked life of thee, and thou gavest him a long life.

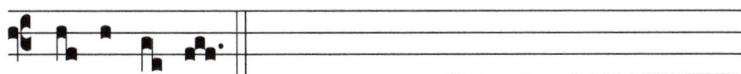

Al- le- lu- ia.

COMMUNION *Magna est glória eius* *Ps. 21:5*

Cantor   *Choir*

HIS hon-our is great in thy sal-va-tion: glo-ry and

great worship shalt thou lay up-on him, O LORD.

Psalm 21:1-4,6,13 *may be sung.*

23 September, Saint Pius of Petrelcina, Priest *(Memorial)*
*From the Common of Confessors: For a Priest (pp. 685-687); or from
Common of Holy Men and Women: For Religious (pp. 705-708).*

24 September
OUR LADY OF WALSINGHAM
Feast (OLW: Solemnity)

INTROIT *Terríbilis est (Common of the Dedication of a Church, p. 643)*
or IN. *Roráte cæli (Advent IV, p. 35)*

GRADUAL *Unam pétii (Holy Family, p. 64)*
or GR. *Tóllite portas (Masses of St. Mary, p. 752)*

ALLELUIA *Diffúsa est grátia (Common of a Virgin Martyr, p. 672)*
or AL. *Et ingressus Angelus (March 25, Annunciation, p. 536)*

OFFERTORY *Adorábo ad templum*   *Ps. 138:2*

Cantor

ij.

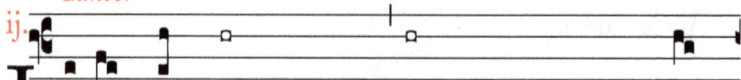

I WILL come into thy house, I will worship toward thy

Choir

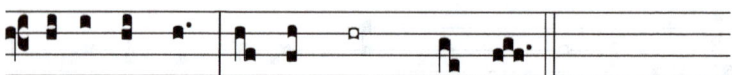

ho-ly tem-ple: and give praise to thy Name.

or OF. *Ave, María (Common of the Blessed Virgin Mary, p. 651)*

COMMUNION *Beátus homo*   *Prov. 8:34,35*

Cantor

i.

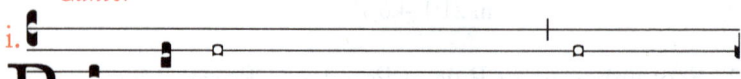

BLES-SED is the man that heareth me, waiting at the

Choir

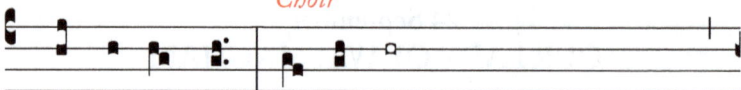

posts of my doors: for who-so findeth me, findeth life,

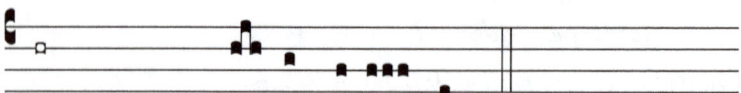

and shall obtain fa-vour of the LORD.

Psalm 122 may be sung.

or CO. *Ecce virgo concípit (Advent IV, p. 38)*

25 September, Saints Cosmas and Damian, Martyrs
(CSP Canada Only) vide infra, 26 September

26 September, Saints Cosmas and Damian, Martyrs
From the Common of Martyrs: For Several Martyrs (pp. 666-670).
Saints Jean Brébeuf and Isaac Jogues, Priests,
and Companions , Martyrs *(CSP, Canada only) Feast*
Vide infra, 19 October.

27 September, Saint Vincent de Paul, Priest *(Memorial)*
From the Common of Confessors: For a Priest (pp. 685-687).

28 September, Saint Wenceslaus, Martyr
From the Common of Martyrs: For One Martyr (pp. 659-662).
Saint Lawrence Ruiz and Companions, Martyrs
From the Common of Martyrs: For Several Martyrs (pp. 666-670).

29 Septembert
SAINTS MICHAEL, GABRIEL,
AND RAPHAEL, ARCHANGELS
(MICHAELMAS)
(Feast)

IN. *Benedícite Dóminum (Votive Mass for Holy Angels, p. 740)*

GRADUAL *Benedícite Dóminum*   *Ps. 103:20,1*

Cantor

O PRAISE the LORD, all ye Angels of his, ye that

Choir

ex-cel in strength: ye that fulfil his commandment, and

Cantor

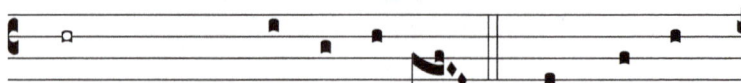

hearken unto the voice of his words. ℣. Praise the LORD,

Choir

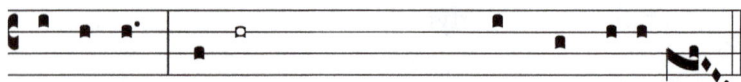

O my soul: and all that is within me praise his ho-ly Name.

ALLELUIA *Sancte Míchael*

Cantor   *All*

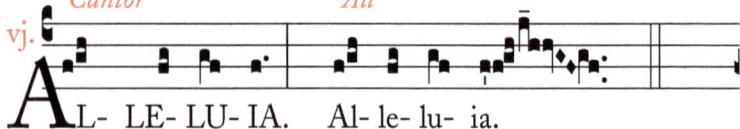

vj. AL- LE- LU- IA.   Al- le- lu- ia.

Cantor

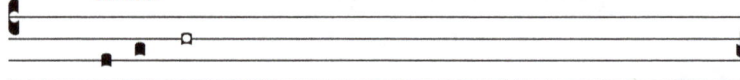

℣. Ho-ly Michael Archangel, defend us in the day of

Choir

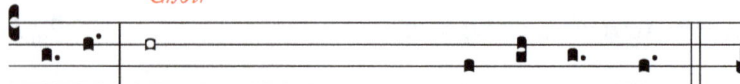

ba-tle: that we perish not in the dread-ful judge-ment.

All

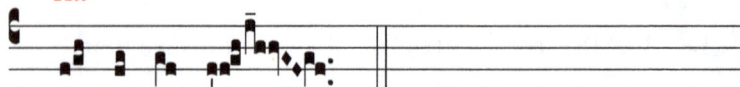

Al - le- lu-   ia.

OFFERTORY *Stétit ángelus (Votive Mass for Holy Angels, p. 744)*

608

COMMUNION *Benedícite omnes ángeli*   *Dan. 3:58*

Cantor   *Choir*

i.

O YE Angels of the Lord, bless ye the Lord: sing ye

praises, and magnify him a-bove all for e-   ver

Verses from the Benedicite *may be sung.*

30 September, Saint Jerome, Priest and Doctor of the Church *(Memorial)*

From the Common of Confessors: For a Priest (pp. 685-687); or from the Common of Doctors of the Church (pp. 693-695).

PROPER of SAINTS and HOLY DAYS
1 October
Saint Thérèse of the Child Jesus, Virgin and Doctor of the Church
Memorial

From Common of Virgins (pp. 696–701); or from the Common of Doctors of the Church (pp. 693–695).

INTROIT *Ego autem in Dómino (Lent III, Weds., p. 170)*

2 October
Holy Guardian Angels
Memorial

IN. *Benedícite Dóminum (Votive Mass for Holy Angels, p. 740)*

GRADUAL *Angelis suis (Lent I, p. 133)*

ALLELUIA *Benedícite Dómino*   *Ps. 103:21*

Cantor   *All*

A̶L- LE- LU- IA.   Al- le- lu- ia.

Cantor   *Choir*

℣. O praise the LORD, all ye his hosts: ye servants of his

All

that do his plea-sure.   Al - le- lu- ia.

OFFERTORY *Immíttet ángelus (Trinity XIV, p. 432)*

COMMUNION *Benedícite, omnes ángeli (Michaelmas, p. 609)*

3 October, St .Thomas of Hereford, Bishop *(OLSC, OLW)*
From the Common of Confessors: For a Bishop (pp. 678-684.

4 October
Saint Francis of Assisi
Memorial
From the Common of Holy Men and Women: For Religious (pp. 705-708).

INTROIT *Nos autem gloriári (Maundy Thursday, p. 243)*
with the following Psalm verse:

Cantor   *Choir*

Ps.   I cried unto the LORD with my voice: yea, even unto

the Lord did I make my sup-pli-ca-tion. Glo-ry be ..., *(etc.)*

6 October, Saint Bruno, Priest
From the Common of Holy Men and Women: For Religious (pp. 705-708);
or from the Common of Confessors: For a Priest (pp. 685-687).
Blessed Marie Rose Durocher, Virgin *(CSP)*
From the Common of Virgins (pp. 696-701).

7 October
Our Lady of the Rosary
Memorial

INTROIT *Vultum tuum deprecabúntur (Masses of St. Mary, p. 753)*

GRADUAL *Propter veritatem*   *Ps. 45:4b,10,11*

Cantor

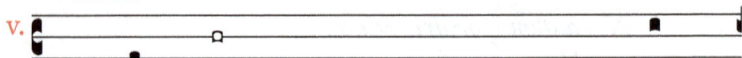

℣.

Be-CAUSE of the word of truth, of meekness, and

Choir

righ-teous-ness: and thy right hand shall teach thee

Cantor

ter-ri-ble things. ℣. Hear-ken, O daughter, and consider,

Choir

incline thine ear: so shall the King have pleasure

in thy beau-ty.

ALLELUIA *Felix es, sacra Virgo (May 31, Visitation of the BVM, p. 553)*

OFFERTORY *Ave, María (Common of the BVM, p. 651)*

612

COMMUNION *Floréte flores*   *Sir. 39:19*

Cantor

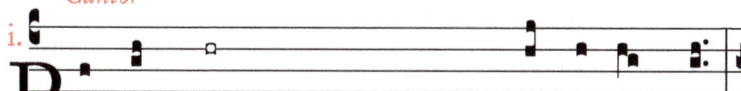

PUT forth flowers as a lily, spread a-broad a sweet smell:

Choir

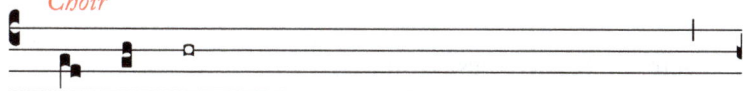

and bring forth leaves in grace, sing a song of praise,

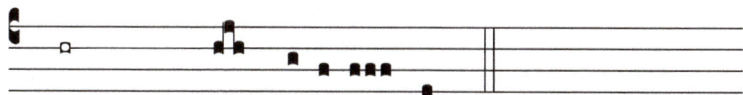

and bless the LORD in all his works.
Psalm 45:1,9b-15 *may be sung.*

8 October, Saint Denis, Bishop and Companions, Martyrs
From the Common of Martyrs: For Several Martyrs (pp. 666-670).
Saint John Leonardi, Priest
From the Common of Confessors: For a Missionary (pp. 688-692).

9 October, Blessed John Henry Newman, Priest
Patron of the Ordinariate of Our Lady of Walsingham
(OLW: Feast; OLSC: Memorial)
From the Common of Confessors: For a Priest (pp. 685-687).

10 October, Saint Paulinus of York, Bishop
(OLSC, OLW)
From the Common of Confessors: For a Bishop (pp. 678-684).

11 October, Saint John XXIII, Pope
From the Common of Confessors: For a Holy Pope (pp. 675-678).
Saint Ethelburga, Abbess *(OLW)*
From the Common of Holy Men and Women: For an Abbot or Abbess
(pp. 708-710).

12 October, Saint Wilfrid, Bishop
From the Common of Confessors: For a Bishop (pp. 678-684).

13 October, Saint Edward the Confessor
From the Common of Holy Men and Women: For Any Holy Man (p. 702).

14 October, Saint Callistus I, Pope and Martyr
From the Common of Martyrs: For a Martyr Pope or Bishop (pp. 652-655); or from the Common of Confessors: For a Holy Pope (pp. 675-678).

15 October, Saint Teresa of Jesus, Virgin and Doctor of the Church
From the Common of Virgins (pp. 696-701); or from the Common of Doctors of the Church (pp. 693-695).

16 October, Saint Hedwig, Religious
From the Common of Holy Men and Women: For Religious (pp. 705-708), or For Any Matron or Holy Woman (pp. 702-705).

Saint Margaret Mary Alacoque, Virgin
From the Common of Virgins (pp. 696-701).

Saint Richard Gwyn, Martyr *(OLW, Wales only)*
From the Common of Martyrs: For One Martyr (pp. 659-662).

17 October
Saint Ignatius of Antioch, Bishop and Martyr
Memorial

INTROIT *Nos autem gloriári (Maundy Thursday, p. 243) with the folloing Psalm verse:*

Cantor   *Choir*

Ps. LORD, re-mem-ber Da-vid: and all his trou-ble.

GRADUAL *Ecce sacérdos magnus (Common of Confessors, p. 679)*

ALLELUIA *Qui séquitur me (Justin, Martyr, 1 June, p. 556)*

OFFERTORY *Glória et honóre (Common of Martyrs, p. 661)*

COMMUNION *Fruméntum Christi*

Cantor   *Choir*

I AM the wheat of Christ: let me be ground by the

teeth of beasts, that I may be found pure bread.

Psalm 34:1,5,15,17-20,22 *may be sung.*

18 October
SAINT LUKE, EVANGELIST
Feast

INTROIT *Mihi autem nimis (June 11, St. Barnabas, p. 559)*

GRADUAL *In omnem terram (June 11, St. Barnabas, p. 560)*

ALLELUIA *Ego vos elegi (May 13, St. Matthias, p. 549)*

OFFERTORY *Mihi autem nimis (January 25, p. 503)*

COMMUNION *Vos, qui secúti (June 11 St. Barnabas, p. 561)*

19 October

Saints Jean de Brébeuf and Isaac Jogues, Priests,
and Companions, Martyrs *(CSP, USA only, Memorial)*

INTROIT *Clamavérunt iusti*   *Ps. 34:17,1*

Cantor

vij.

THE right-eous cry, and the LORD hear-eth them:

Choir   *Cantor*

and de-livereth them out of all their trou-bles. *Ps.* I will

Choir

always give thanks un-to the LORD: his praise shall ever

Cantor   *Choir*

be in my mouth.   Glo-ry be ..., *(etc.)*   As it was ..., *(etc.)*

All

The right-eous ..., *(etc.)*

GRADUAL *Anima nostra sicut passer* *(March 7, Perpetua and Felicitas, p. 531)*

ALLELUIA *Confitémini Dómino* *(Rogation, p. 340)*

OFFERTORY *Lætámini in Dómino* *(July 26, Joachim & Anne, p. 582)*

COMMUNION *Iustórum ánimæ* *(Votive Mass of All Saints, p. 747)*

St. Paul of the Cross, Priest *(OLSC, OLW, CSP: Canada only)*
From the Common of Confessors: For a Priest (pp. 685-687).
Saint Frideswide, Abbess *(OLSC, OLW)*
From the Common of Holy Men and Women: For an Abbot or Abbess
(pp. 708-710).

20 October, St, Paul of the Cross, Priest *(CSP USA only)*
Vide supra, 19 October

22 October, Saint John Paul II, Pope
From the Common of Confessors: For a Holy Pope (pp. 675-678).

23 October, Saint John of Capistrano, Priest
From the Common of Confessors: For a Missionary (pp. 688-692; or from
the Common of Holy Men and Women: For Religious (pp. 705-708).

24 October, Saint Anthony Mary Claret, Bishop
From the Common of Confessors: For a Missionary (pp. 688-692), or
For a Bishop (pp. 678-684).

25 October
SIX WELSH MARTYRS & THEIR COMPANIONS
(OLW Wales only, Feast)
From the Common of Martyrs: For Several Martyrs (pp. 662-665).

26 October, Saints Chad and Cedd, Bishops *(OLSC, OLW)*
From the Common of Confessors: For a Bishop (pp. 678-684).

28 October
SAINTS SIMON AND JUDE, APOSTLES
Feast

INTROIT *Iudicant sancti (Votive Mass of All Saints, p. 746)*

GRADUAL *Constítues eos príncipes (July 25, St. James, p. 579)*

ALLELUIA *Nimis honoráti sunt*   *Ps. 139:17*

Cantor   *All*

AL- LE- LU- IA.   Al- le- lu- ia.

Cantor

℣. How dear are thy friends unto me, O God, and held

Choir

in highest hon-our: their rule and governance is

All

ex-ceed-ing stead-fast.   Al - le- lu- ia.

OFFERTORY *In omnem terram (Feb. 22, Chair of St. Peter, p. 529)*

COMMUNION *Ego vos elégi (Easter VI, p. 337)*

1 November
ALL SAINTS DAY
Solemnity

INTROIT *Gaudeámus ... Sanctórum ómnium*   *Ps. 33:1*

Cantor

vij.

RE-JOICE we all, and praise the LORD, celebrating a

Choir

holy-day in ho-nour of all the Saints: in whose solemnity

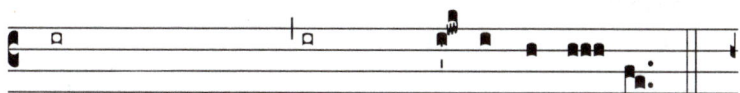

the Angels are joyful, and glo-ri-fy the Son of God.

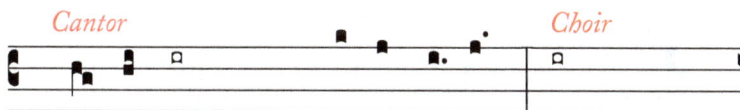

Cantor   *Choir*

Ps. Re-joice in the Lord, O ye righ-teous: for it

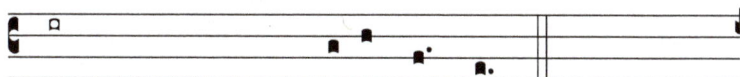

becometh well the just to be thank-ful.

Cantor   *Choir*   *Full*

Glo-ry be ..., *(etc.)* As it was ..., *(etc.)* Re-joice we ..., *(etc)*

GRADUAL *Timéte Dóminum*   *Ps. 34:9,10b*

Cantor   *Choir*

℣. O FEAR the LORD, all ye Saints of his: for they that

Cantor

fear him lack no-thing. ℣. But they that seek the LORD:

Choir

shall want no manner of thing that is good.

ALLELUIA *Veníte ad me*   *Mt. 11:28*

Cantor   *All*

℣j. AL- LE- LU- IA.   Al- le- lu- ia.

Cantor

℣. Come un-to me, all ye that labour and are heavy la-den:

Choir   *All*

and I will give you rest.   Al - le- lu- ia.

OFFERTORY *Iustórum ánimæ* *Wis. 3:1,2,3*

Cantor

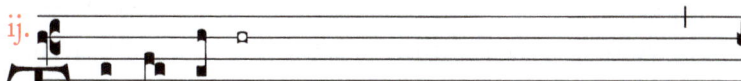

HE souls of the righteous are in the hand of God,

Choir

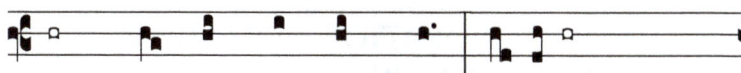

and no tor-ment shall touch them: in the eyes of the

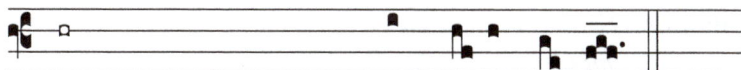

foolish they seemed to die, but they are in peace.

COMMUNION *Beáti mundo corde* *Mt.5:8,9,10*

Cantor

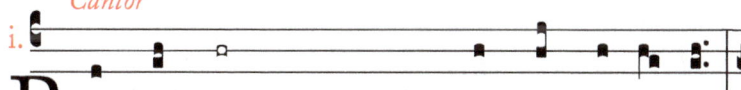

LESS-ED are the pure in heart, for they shall see God:

Choir

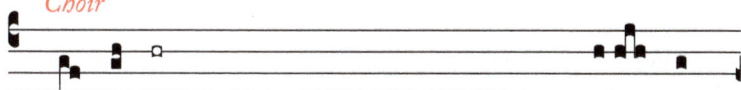

bless-ed are the peacemakers, for they shall be call-ed

Cantor

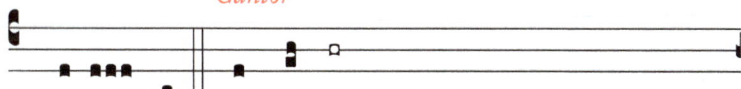

sons of God. Bless-ed are they that are persecuted for

Choir

righ-teous-ness' sake: for theirs is the king-dom of heaven.

Psalm 126 *may be sung.*

2 November
COMMEMORATION OF ALL THE
FAITHFUL DEPARTED (All Souls)

INTROIT *Requiem ætérnam (Masses for the Dead, p. 770)*

GRADUAL *Requiem aeternum (Masses for the Dead, p. 771)*
or GR. *Si ambulem (Saturday, Lent III, p. 175)*

for the TRACT *Sicut cervus (Holy Saturday, p. 275, vv. 1,2,3)*
or TR. *De profúndis (Masses for the Dead, p. 773)*

SEQUENCE *Dies Iræ (Masses for the Dead, p. 775)*

OF. *Dómine Iesu Christe (Masses for the Dead, p. 780)*
or OF. *O pie Deus (Masses for the Dead, p. 784)*

CO. *Pro quorum memória (Masses for the Dead, p. 782)*
or CO. *Lux ætérna (Masses for the Dead, p. 783)*

3 November, Saint Martin de Porres, Religious
From the Common of Holy Men and Women: For Religious (pp. 705-708).
Saint Winefride, Virgin *(OLW)*
From the Common of Virgins (pp. 696-701).

4 November, Saint Charles Borromeo, Bishop *(Memorial)*
From the Common of Confessors: For a Bishop (pp. 678-684).

6 November, Saint Illtud, Abbot *(OLW: Wales only)*
From the Common of Holy Men and Women: For an Abbot or Abbess
(pp. 708-710).

7 November, Saint Willibrord, Bishop *(OLSC, OLW)*
From the Common of Confessors: For a Bishop (pp. 678-684).

Blessed Marie Rose Durocher, Virgin *(CSP)*
From the Common of Virgins (pp. 696-701).

8 November
ALL SAINTS OF ENGLAND *or* WALES *(OLW)*
Feast

INTROIT *Iudicant sancti* *(Votive Mass of All Saints, p. 746)*

GRADUAL *Exultábunt sancti* *(July 26, Joachim & Anne, p. 581)*

ALLELUIA *Veníte ad me* *(Nov. 1, All Saints, p. 620)*

OFFERTORY *Exultábunt sancti*   *Ps. 149:5,6*

Cantor

LET the Saints be joyful with glory,   let them re-joice

Choir

in their beds: let the praises of God be in their mouths.

COMMUNION *Iustórum ánimæ* *(Votive Mass of All Saints, p. 747)*

9 November
THE DEDICATION OF THE LATERAN BASILICA
Feast

INTROIT *Deus in loco sancto (Trinity XI, p. 419)*

GRADUAL *Lætátus sum (Trinity XVIII, p. 448)*

ALLELUIA *Bene fundata est domus (Common of the Dedication of a Church, p. 644)*

OFFERTORY *Dómine Deus (Common of the Dedication of a Church, p. 645)*

COMMUNION *Ierusalem quæ ædificátur (Lent IV, p. 180)*

10 November, Saint Leo the Great, Pope and Doctor of the Church *(Memorial)*
From the Common of Confessors: For a Holy Pope (pp. 675-678); or from the Common of Doctors of the Church (pp. 693-695).

11 November, Saint Martin of Tours, Bishop *(Memorial)*
From the Common of Confessors: For a Bishop (pp. 678-684).

12 November, St. Josaphat, Bishop and Martyr *(Memorial)*
From the Common of Martyrs: For a Martyr Pope or Bishop (pp. 652-655), or For a Martyr Bishop (pp. 655-659); or from the Common of Confessors: For a Bishop (pp. 678-684).

13 November, Saint Frances Xavier Cabrini, Virgin *(Memorial CSP: USA only)*
From the Common of Virgins (pp. 696-701).

15 November, Saint Albert the Great, Bishop and Doctor of the Church
From the Common of Confessors: For a Bishop (pp. 678-684); or from the Common of Doctors of the Church (pp. 693-695)

16 November, Saint Margaret of Scotland
From the Common of Holy Men and Women: For Any Matron or Holy Woman (pp. 702-705).

Saint Gertrude, Virgin
From the Common of Virgins (pp. 696-701); or from the Common of Holy Men and Women: For Religious (pp. 705-708).

Saint Edmund of Abingdon, Bishop *(OLW)*
From the Common of Confessors: For a Bishop (pp. 678-684).

17 November, Saint Elizabeth of Hungary, Religious *(CSP Memorial)*
From the Common of Holy Men and Women: For Any Matron or Holy Woman (pp. 705-708).

Saint Hilda, Abbess *(OLSC, OLW)*
From the Common of Holy Men and Women: For an Abbot or Abbess (pp. 708-710).

Saint Hugh of Lincoln, Bishop *(OLSC, OLW)*
From the Common of Confessors: For a Bishop (pp. 678-684).

18 November, Dedication of the Basilicas of Saints Peter and Paul, Apostles
From the Common of the Dedication of a Church (pp. 643-646).

Saint Rose Philippine Duchesne, Virgin *(CSP: USA only)*
From the Common of Virgins (pp. 696-701).

20 November, Saint Edmund, Martyr
From the Common of Martyrs: For One Martyr (pp. 659-662).

21 November
The Presentation of the Blessed Virgin Mary
Memorial

From the Common of the Blessed Virgin Mary (pp. 647-651).

IN. *Vultum tuum deprecabúntur* *(Masses of St. Mary, p. 653)*

22 November, Saint Cecilia, Virgin and Martyr *(Memorial)*
From the Common of Martyrs: For a Virgin Martyr (pp. 670-674); or from the Common of Virgins (pp. 696-701).

23 November, Saint Clement I, Pope and Martyr

From the Common of Martyrs: For a Martyr Pope or Bishop (pp. 652-655); or from the Common of Confessors: For a Holy Pope (pp. 675-678).

Saint Columban, Abbot

From the Common of Confessors: For a Missionary (pp. 688-692); or from the Common of Holy Men and Women: For an Abbot or Abbess (pp. 708-710).

Blessed Miguel Agustín Pro, Priest and Martyr *(CSP)*

From the Common of Martyrs: For One Martyr (pp. 659-662); or from the Common of Confessors: For a Priest (pp. 685-681).

24 November, Saint Andrew Dũng-Lạc, Priest, and Companions, Martyrs *(Memorial)*

From the Common of Martyrs: For Several Martyrs (pp. 666-670).

25 November, St. Catherine of Alexandria, Virgin and Martyr

From the Common of Martyrs: For a Virgin Martyr (pp. 670-674); or from the Common of Virgins (pp. 696-701).

30 November
SAINT ANDREW, APOSTLE
Feast

INTROIT *Dóminus secus mare (Epiphany III, p. 90)*

GRADUAL *In omnem terram (June 11, St. Barnabas, p. 560)*

ALLELUIA *Diléxit Andréam*

AL- LE- LU- IA.   Al- le- lu- ia.

℣. The Lord loved An-drew: as a sweet-smell-ing sa-vour.

Al - le- lu- ia.

OFFERTORY *Mihi autem nimis (January 25, p. 503)*

COMMUNION *Veníte post me (Epiphany III, p. 94)*

or CO. *Dicit Andréas Simóni*   *Jn. 1:41,42*

AN-DREW saith unto his bro-ther Si-mon: We have

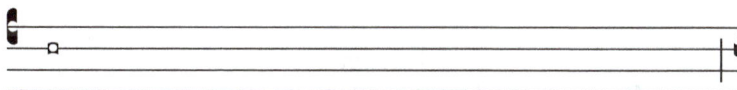

found the Messiah, which is being interpreted, the Christ:

and he brought him to Je- sus.

Psalm 34:1,5,6,14-20 *may be sung.*

PROPER of SAINTS and HOLY DAYS

1 December, Saint Edmund Campion, Priest and Martyr
(OLSC, OLW: Memorial)
From the Common of Martyrs: For One Martyr (pp. 659-662); or from the Common of Confessors: For a Priest (pp. 685-687).

3 December, Saint Francis Xavier, Priest *(Memorial)*
From the Common of Confessors: For a Missionary (pp. 688-692), or For a Priest (pp. 685-687).

4 Dec. St. John Damascene, Priest and Doctor of the Church
From the Common of Confessors: For a Priest (pp. 685-687); or from the Common of Doctors of the Church (pp. 693-695).

6 December, Saint Nicholas, Bishop
From the Common of Confessors: For a Bishop (pp. 678-684).

7 December, Saint Ambrose, Bishop and Doctor of the Church *(Memorial)*
From the Common of Confessors: For a Bishop (pp. 678-684); or from the Common of Doctors of the Church (pp. 693-695).

8 December
THE IMMACULATE CONCEPTION OF THE BLESSED VIRGIN MARY
Patronal Feastday of the United States of America
Solemnity

INTROIT *Gaudens gaudébo*　　　　Is. 61:10; Ps. 30:1

Cantor

I WILL greatly rejoice in the LORD my God; yea my

soul shall be joyful and glad in him; for he hath clothed

628

Choir

me with the garments of sal-va-tion: he hath covered

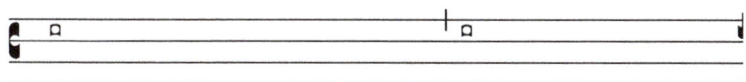

me with the robe of righteousness, as a bride adorneth

FINE   *Cantor*

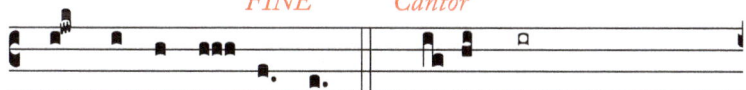

her-self with her jew- els. *Ps.* I will magnify thee, O

Choir

LORD, for thou hast set me up: and not made my foes to

Cantor   *Choir*

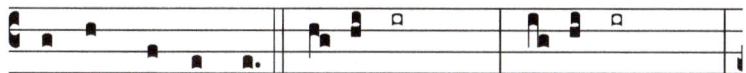

tri-umph o- ver me. Glo- ry be..., *(etc.)* As it was..., *(etc.)*

Full

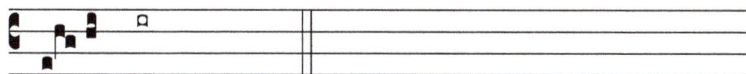

I will greatly..., *(etc.)*

GRADUAL *Benedícta es tu* *(Feb. 11, Our Lady of Lourdes, p. 525)*

629

ALLELUIA *Tota pulchra es*   *Song of Songs 4:7*

Cantor   *All*

vj.

AL- LE- LU- IA.   Al- le- lu- ia.

Cantor   *Choir*

℣. All fair art thou, O Ma- ry : nor is original sin found

All

in thee   Al - le- lu- ia.

OF. *Ave, María* *(Common of the Blessed Virgin Mary, p. 651)*

COMMUNION *Gloriósa dicta*   *Ps. 87:2; Lk. 1:49*

Cantor

i.

GLOR-IOUS things are spoken of thee, O Ma- ry:

Choir

for he that is mighty hath done great things to thee.

Verses from The Magnificat *may be sung.*

630

9 December, Saint Juan Diego Cuauhtlatoatzin
From the Common of Holy Men and Women: For Any Holy Man (p. 702).

10 December, Saint John Roberts, Priest and Martyr *(OLW, Wales only)*
From the Common of Martyrs: For One Martyr (pp. 659-662); or from the Common of Confessors: For a Priest (pp. 685-687).

11 December. Saint Damasus I, Pope
From the Common of Confessors: For a Holy Pope (pp. 675-678).

12 December
Our Lady of Guadalupe
CSP: Feast

INTROIT *Salve, sancta Parens (St. Mary, Jan 1, p. 68)*

GRADUAL *Quæ est ista* Song 6:10; Sir. 50:8

Cantor

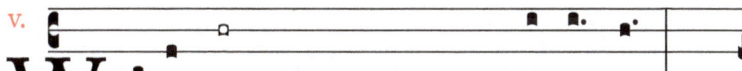

WHO is she that looketh forth as the mor-ning:

Choir *Cantor*

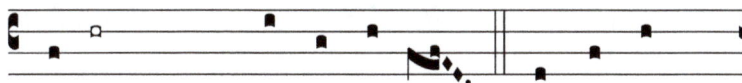

fair as the moon, clear as the sun? ℣. And as the

Choir

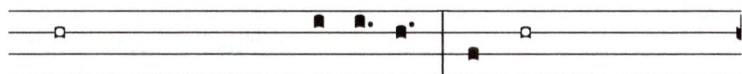

giving light in clouds of glo-ry: and as the flower of

roses in the days of spring.

ALLELUIA *Flores apparuerunt* *Song 2:12*

Cantor *All*

vj.

AL- LE- LU- IA. Al- le- lu- ia.

Cantor *Choir*

℣. The flow-ers appear on the earth: the time of prun-ing

All

is come Al - le- lu- ia.

OFFERTORY *Elegi et sanctificavi* *2 Chron. 7:16*

Cantor

ij.

NOW have I chosen and hallowed this house, that my

Choir

Name may be there for ev-er: and mine eyes and my

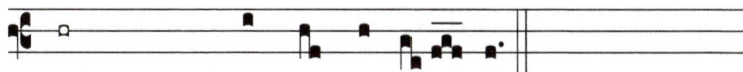

heart shall be there per- pe- tu- al- ly.

COMMUNION *Non fecit*   *Ps. 147:20*

HE hath not dealt so with a-ny na-tion: nei-ther

have the heathen know-ledge of his laws.

Verses from **Psalm 147** *may be sung.*

13 December, Saint Lucy, Virgin and Martyr (Memoria)
From the Common of Martyrs: For a Virgin Martyr (pp. 670-674); or from the Common of Virgins (pp. 696-701).

14 December, Saint John of the Cross, Priest and Doctor of the Church *(Memorial)*
From the Common of Confessors: For a Priest (pp. 685-687); or from the Common of Doctors of the Church (pp. 693-695).

21 Dec., St. Peter Canisius, Priest and Doctor of the Church
From the Common of Confessors: For a Priest (pp. 685-687); or from the Common of Doctors of the Church (pp. 693-695).

23 December, Saint John of Kanty, Priest
From the Common of Confessors: For a Priest (pp. 685-687).

26 December
SAINT STEPHEN, THE FIRST MARTYR
Feast

INTROIT *Et enim sedérunt príncipes*　　　*Ps. 119:23,86,1*

Cantor

vij.

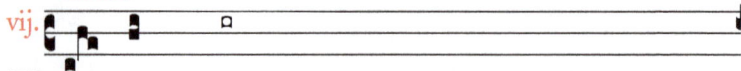

PRIN-CES moreover did sit, and did witness falsely

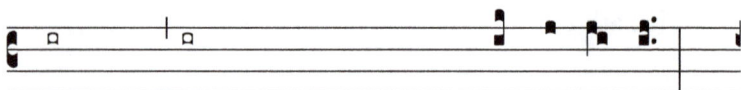

against me, and the ungodly pressed sore up-on me:

Choir

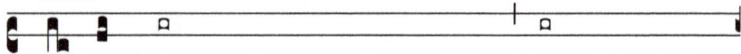

O LORD my God, stand up to help me; for thy servant

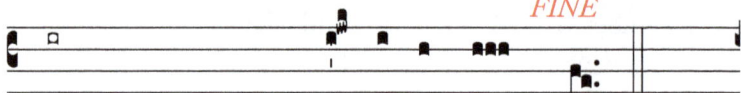

FINE

is occupied continually in thy com-mand-ments.

Cantor

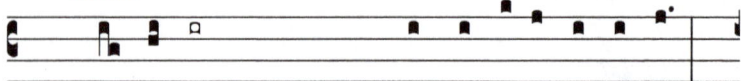

Ps. Bles-sed are those that are un-de-fil-ed in the way:

Choir　　　　　　　　　*Cantor*

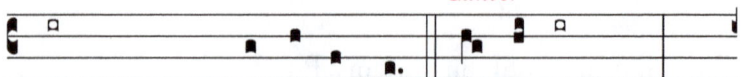

and walk in the law of the LORD. Glo- ry be..., *(etc.)*

Choir   *Full*

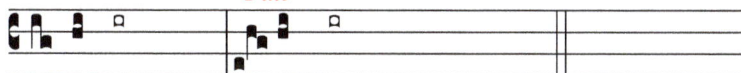

As it was..., *(etc.)* Prin-ces moreover..., *(etc.)*

GRADUAL *Sedérunt príncipes*   *Ps. 119:23,86; 108:25*

Cantor   *Choir*

v.

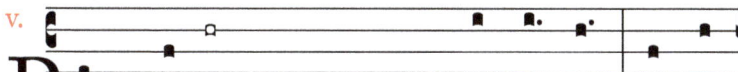

PRIN-CES also did sit and speak a-gainst me: wick-ed

Cantor

men have per-se-cut-ed me. ℣. Help me, O LORD

Choir

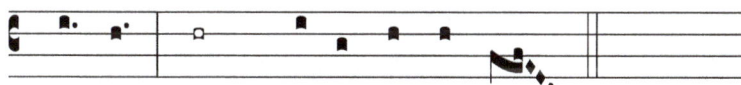

my God: save me for thy mer-cies' sake.

ALLELUIA *Video cælos*   *Acts 7:56*

Cantor   *All*

vj.

AL- LE- LU- IA. Al- le- lu- ia.

635

Cantor   *Choir*

℣. I see the heavens o-pen-ed: and Jesus standing on the

All

right hand of God   Al - le- lu- ia.

OFFERTORY *Elegérunt Apóstoli Stéphanum*   *Acts 6:5; 7:59*

Cantor

ij. THE A-pos-tles chose Stephen the Levite, a man full

Choir

of faith and of the Ho-ly Ghost: whom the Jews stoned

as he prayed, saying, Lord Je-sus, re-ceive my spi- rit.

COMMUNION *Video cælos*   *Acts 7:56,59,60*

Cantor

i. LO, I see the heavens opened, and Jesus standing on the

636

Choir

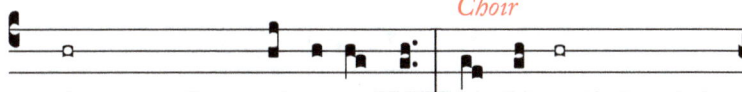

right hand of the pow-er of God: O Lord Jesus receive

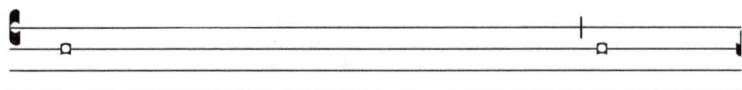

my spirit, and lay not this sin to their charge for they

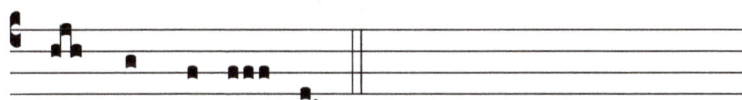

know not what they do..

Psalm 119:1,78,86,95,150,153,157,161,173 *may be sung.*

27 December
SAINT JOHN, APOSTLE AND EVANGELIST
Feast

INTROIT *In médio ecclésiæ (Common of Doctors of the Church, p. 693)*

GRADUAL *Exiit sermo inter fratres*   *Jn. 21:23*

Cantor

v.

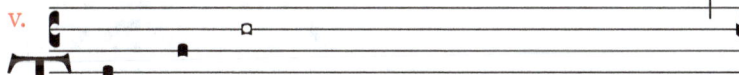

THEN went this saying abroad among the brethren,

Choir

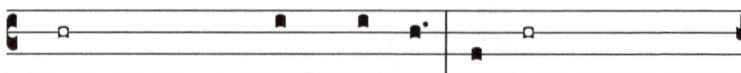

that that disciple should not die: yet Jesus said not unto

Cantor

him, He shall not die.   ℣. But, If I will that he tarry till

Choir

I come: fol-low thou me.

ALLELUIA *Hic est discípulus ille*   Jn. 21:24

Cantor   *All*   *Cantor*

vj. AL- LE- LU- IA.   Al- le- lu- ia.   ℣. This is

Choir

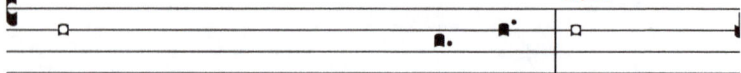

the disciple which testifieth of these things: and we know

All

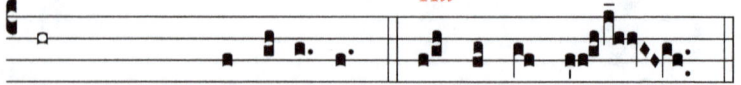

that his tes-ti-mo-ny is true   Al - le- lu- ia.

OF. *Iustus ut palma* *(Common of Doctors of the Church, p. 695)*

Communion *Exiit sermo inter fratres*   *Jn. 21:23*

Cantor

i.

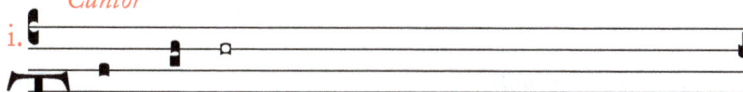

T HEN went abroad this saying among the brethren,

Choir

that that dis-ci-ple should not die: yet Je-sus said not

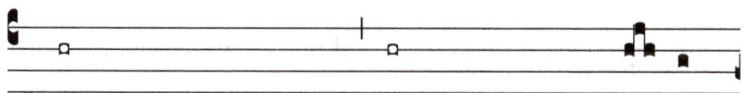

unto him, He shall not die; but, If I will that he tar-ry

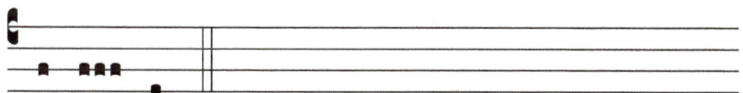

till I come.

Psalm 89:1,3-5,8,20-22,25 *may be sung.*

28 December
THE HOLY INNOCENTS, MARTYRS
Feast

INTROIT *Ex ore infántium*   *Ps. 8:2,1*

Cantor

vij.

OUT of the mouth of very babes, O God, and of

Choir

sucklings, hast thou per-fect-ed praise: be-cause of thine

FINE   *Cantor*   *Choir*

ad- ver- sa- ries. *Ps.* O LORD our Go-ver-nor: how

Cantor

excellent is thy Name in all the world. Glo- ry be..., *(etc.)*

Choir   *Full*

As it was..., *(etc.)* Out of the mouth..., *(etc.)*

GRADUAL *Anima nostra sicut passer (March 7, Perpetua & Felicitas, p. 531)*

ALLELUIA *Laudáte púeri* *(Masses for the Dead, p. 788)*

OFFERTORY *Anima nostra sicut passer* *(6 Feb., Paul Miki, p. 524)*

COMMUNION *Vox in Rama audíta est*   *Mt. 2:18*

Cantor

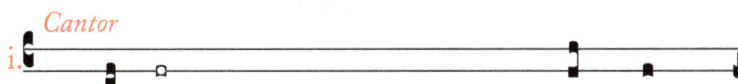

IN Ra-mah a voice was heard, lamentation and great

Choir

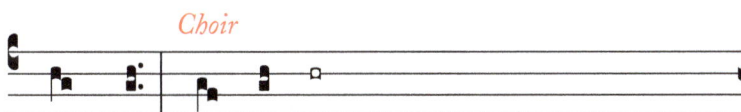

mourn-ing: Ra-chel weeping for her children, and would

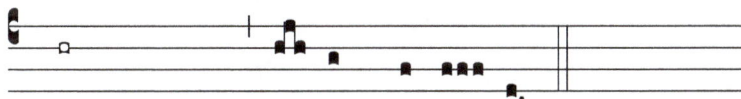

not be comforted, be-cause they are not.

Psalm 79:1-5,14ab,14c *may be sung.*

29 December
Saint Thomas Becket, Bishop and Martyr
Patron of Pastoral Clergy in England and Wales
(OLW: Feast)

IN. *Loquébar de testimóniis tuis* *(Common of Martyrs, p. 670)*

GRADUAL *Ecce sacérdos magnus (Common of Confessors, p. 679)*

ALLELUIA *Ego sum pastor bonus*   *Jn. 10:14*

Cantor   All

vj.

AL- LE- LU- IA.   Al- le- lu- ia.

Cantor   Choir

℣. I am the good Shep-herd: and know my sheep,

All

and am known of mine.   Al - le- lu- ia.

OFFERTORY *Posuísti, Dómine (21 Sept., St. Matthew, p. 604)*

COMMUNION *Servíte Dómino (Sat.after Ash Weds., p. 130)*

31 December, Saint Sylvester I, Pope
From the Common of Confessors: For a Holy Pope, (pp. 675-678).

COMMONS

Common of the Dedication of a Church

INTROIT *Terríbilis est*   *Gen. 28:17,22; Ps. 84:1*

Cantor

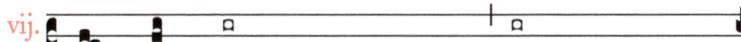

O HOW awesome is this place: this is the house of

Choir

God, and gate of hea-ven: and men shall call it

FINE

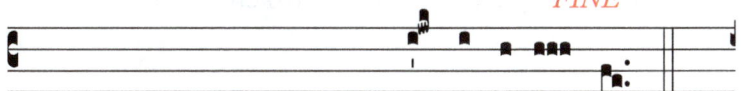

the pa-lace of God.

or (the pa-lace of God. Al-le-lu-ia. Al- le- lu- ia.)

Cantor

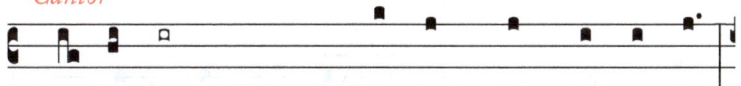

Ps. O how amiable are thy dwell-ings, thou LORD of hosts:

Choir

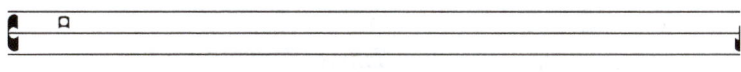

my soul hath a desire and longing to enter into the

Cantor   *Choir*

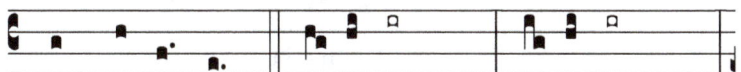

courts of the LORD. Glo- ry be..., *(etc.)* As it was..., *(etc.)*

Full

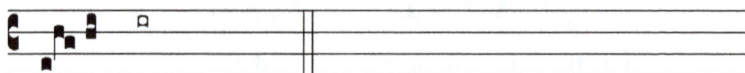

O how awesome.., *(etc.)*

GRADUAL *Locus iste*

Cantor   *Choir*

℣.

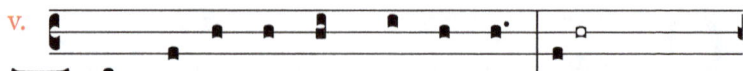

THIS dwell-ing is God's han-dy-work: it is a mystery

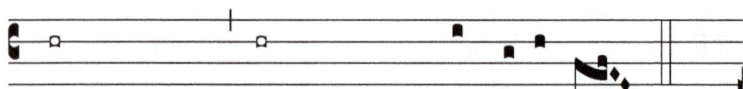

beyond all price, that cannot be spo-ken a-gainst.

Cantor

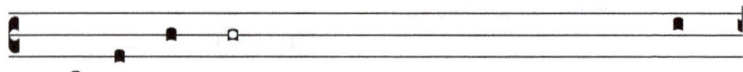

℣. O God, in whose presence the choirs of Angels are

Choir

stand-ing: gra-cious-ly hear the prayers of thy ser-vants.

ALLELUIA *Adorábo (Epiphany IV, p. 97)*
or ALLELUIA *Bene fundata est domus*

Cantor   *All*

vj.

AL- LE- LU- IA. Al- le- lu- ia.

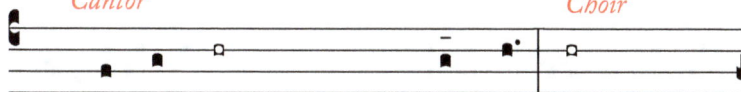

Cantor · *Choir*

℣. The house of God is surely found-ed: stablished

All

up-on the rock. Al - le- lu- ia.

TRACT *Qui confídunt (Lent IV, p. 178)*
In Eastertide AL. *Adorábo (p. 97) and* ℣. *Bene fundata, (above)*

OFFERTORY *Dómine Deus*   1 *Chron. 29:17,18*

Cantor

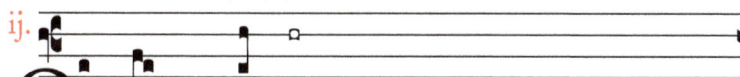

ij.

O LORD God, in the uprightness of my heart I have

Choir

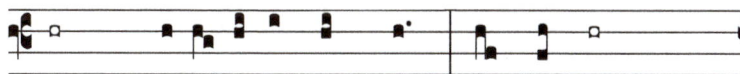

willingly of-fer-ed all these things; and now I have seen

Cantor

with joy thy people, which are pre-sent here: O LORD God

Choir

of Israel, keep for ever this i-ma-gi-na-tion, of the heart

(musical notation)

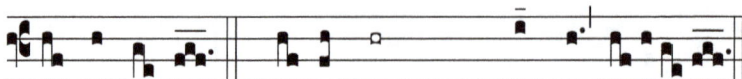

of thy peo-ple. *or* of the heart of thy peo-ple. Al-le-lu-ia.

COMMUNION *Domus mea*   *Mt. 21:13*

Cantor

i.

(musical notation)

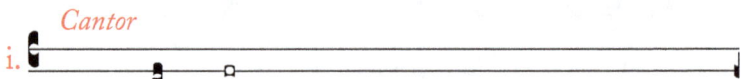

MY house shall be called of all nations the house of

Choir

(musical notation)

prayer, saith the LORD: in it everyone that asketh

Cantor

(musical notation)

receiveth, and he that seek-eth find-eth; and to him that

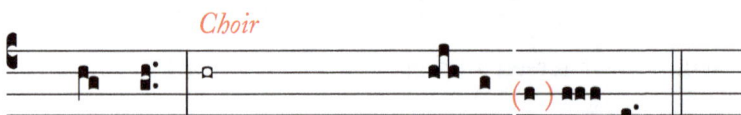

Choir

(musical notation)

knock-eth,   it shall be o- pen-ed.
or knock-eth, it shall be opened. Al- le-   lu- ia.

Psalm 84:1-4,8-11 *may be sung.*

COMMON OF THE BLESSED VIRGIN MARY

INTROIT *Salve sancta Parens* *(January 1, p. 68)*
or for feasts: IN. *Gaudeámus... Maríæ* Ps. 45:1

Cantor

vij.

RE-JOICE we all in the LORD, keeping holy-day in

Choir

honour of the Blessed Vir-gin Ma-ry: in whose feast* the

FINE *Cantor*

Angels rejoice and glori-fy the Son of God. *Ps.* My heart

Choir

is inditing of a good mat-ter: I speak of the things which

Cantor

I have made un-to the King. Glo- ry be..., *(etc.)*

Choir *Full*

As it was..., *(etc.)* Re-joice we all..., *(etc.)* *(or* solemnity)
647

GRADUAL *Benedícta et venerábilis*

Cantor

℣.

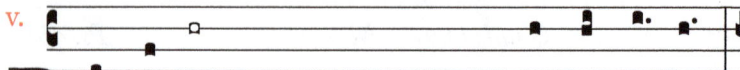

BLES-ED and venerable art thou, O Vir-gin Ma-ry:

Choir

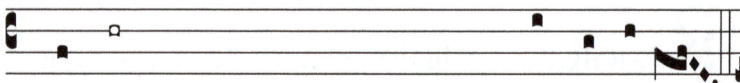

who without spot wast found the Mother of the Sav-iour.

Cantor

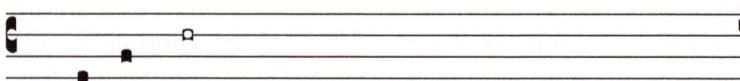

℣. Vir-gin Mother of God, he whom the world con-

Choir

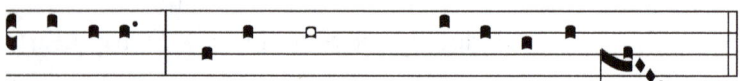

tain-eth not: be-ing made man, lay hid in thy womb.

ALLELUIA *Post partum (January 1, p. 69)*
in Advent AL. *Ave, María*   Lk. 1:28,42

Cantor   *All*

vij.

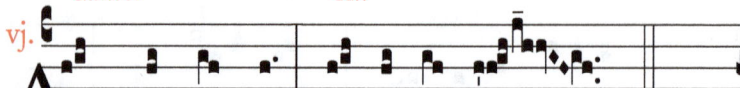

AL- LE- LU- IA.   Al- le- lu- ia.

Cantor

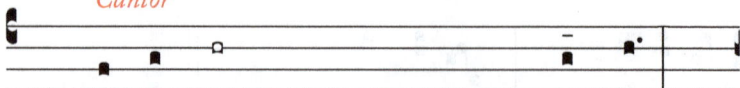

℣. Hail, Ma-ry, full of grace; the LORD is with thee:

Choir

blessed art thou among women, and blessed is the

All

fruit of thy womb.   Al - le- lu- ia.

During Pre-Lent and Lent, the following is said in place of the Alleluia:
TRACT *Gaude, María*

Cantor

viij.

RE-JOICE, O Virgin Ma-ry: thou alone all he-re- sy

Choir

didst slay. ℣. Thou the Archangel Gabriel's mes-sage:

Cantor

didst be-lieve. ℣. While yet a Virgin, bearing God and

Man: thou after childbirth, Virgin, inviolate didst re-main.

Choir

℣. Mother of God: in-ter-cede for us.,

in Eastertide A<small>L</small>. *Virga Iesse*   *Num. 17:8b; Lk. 1:28,42*

Cantor   *All*

A<small>L</small>- LE- LU- IA.   Al- le- lu- ia.

Cantor

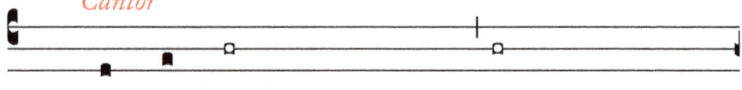

℣. Now hath blossomed Jesse's rod; a Virgin bears both

Choir

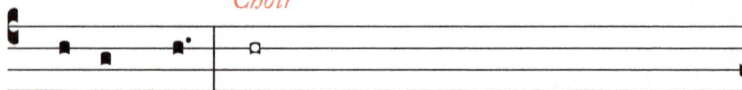

Man and God: God restoreth peace to men, high and low

All

are one a-gain.   Al - le- lu- ia.

Cantor   *Choir*

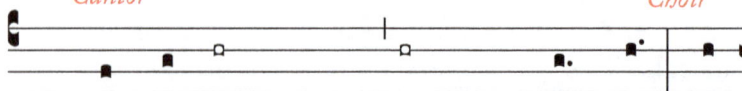

℣. Hail, Ma-ry, full of grace; the Lord is with thee: Bles-

All

sed art thou a-mong wo-men.   Al - le- lu- ia.

OFFERTORY *Ave, María*   *Lk. 1:28,42*

Cantor

AIL Ma-ry, full of grace; the LORD is with thee:

Choir

bles-sed art thou among women, and blessed

is   the   fruit of thy womb.
or is the fruit of thy womb. Al- le- lu- ia.

COMMUNION *Beáta víscera*   *Lk. 11:27*

Cantor   *Choir*

LES-SED is the womb of the Vir-gin Ma-ry: that

bore the Son of the   e-ver-last-ing Fa-ther.
or bore the Son of the everlasting Father. Al- le-   lu- ia.

Psalm 45:1,9-15 *or* The Magnificat *may be sung,*

COMMONS
COMMON OF MARTYRS
1. For a Martyr Pope or Bishop

INTROIT *Státuit ei*   *Sir. 45:24; Ps. 132:1*

Cantor

vij.

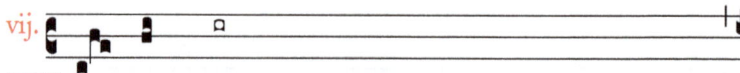

THE LORD hath established a covenant of peace with him,

Choir

and made him a chief of his peo-ple: that he should have

FINE

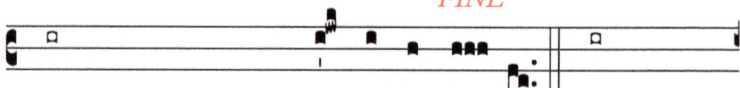

the priestly dignity for ev- er and ev- er. (*or* the priestly

FINE

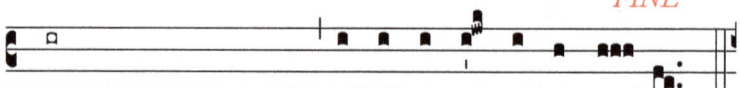

dignity for ever and ever. Al-le-lu- ia. Al- le- lu- ia.)

Cantor   *Choir*

Ps. LORD, re-mem-ber Da-vid: and all his trou-ble.

Cantor   *Choir*   *Full*

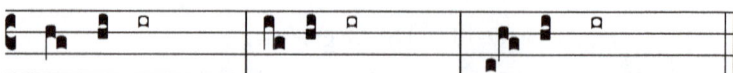

Glo- ry be..., *(etc.)* As it was..., *(etc.)* The Lord hath..., *(etc.)*

GRADUAL *Invéni David*   *Ps. 89:21,22,23*

Cantor

v.

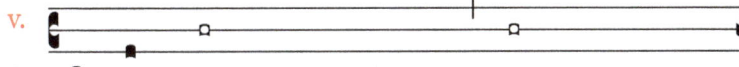

I HAVE found David my servant; with my holy oil

Choir

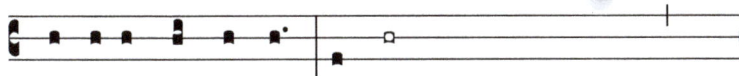

have I a-noint-ed him: my hand shall hold him fast,

Cantor

and my arm shall strength-en him. ℣. The e-ne-my shall

Choir

not be able to do him vio-lence: the son of wickedness

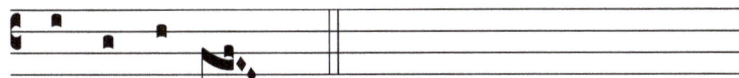

shall not hurt him.

ALLELUIA *Tu es sacérdos*   *Ps. 110:4b*

Cantor   *All*

vj.

AL- LE- LU- IA.   Al- le- lu- ia.

653

Cantor   *Choir*

℣. Thou art a priest for ev-er: after the order of

All

Mel-chi-se-dech. Al - le- lu- ia.

During Pre-Lent and Lent, the following is said in place of the Alleluia:
Tʀᴀᴄᴛ *Desidérium ánimæ eius*   Ps. 21:2,3

Cantor

viij.

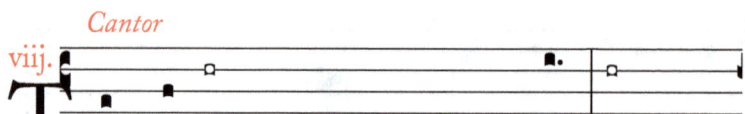

THOU hast given him his heart's de-sire: and hast

Choir

not denied him the request of his lips. ℣. For thou

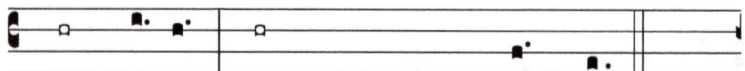

shalt meet him: with the blessings of good-ness.

Cantor   *Full*

℣. Thou shalt set a crown: of pure gold up-on his head.

Oꜰꜰᴇʀᴛᴏʀʏ *Véritas mea (Common of Confessors, p. 683)*

COMMUNION *Semel iurávi* *Ps. 89:34b,35,36*

Cantor

i.

I HAVE sworn once by my holiness, his seed shall en-

dure for ever, and his throne is like as the sun be-fore me:

Choir

he shall stand fast for evermore as the moon, and as the

faithful   wit-ness in hea-ven.
or faithful witness in heaven. Al- le-   lu- ia.

Psalm 89:1,5-7,21,25,29,34 *may be sung.*

2. For a Martyr Bishop

INTROIT *Sacerdótes Dei* *Dan. 3:84,87,57*

Cantor   *Choir*

vij.

O YE priests of the Lord, bless ye the Lord: O ye holy

FINE

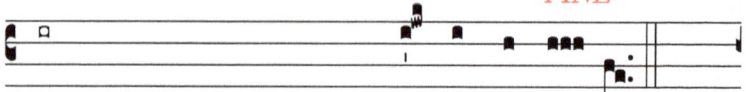

and humble men of heart, ex-alt him for ev- er.
or exalt him for ever. Allelu- ia. Al- le- lu- ia.

Cantor

Choir

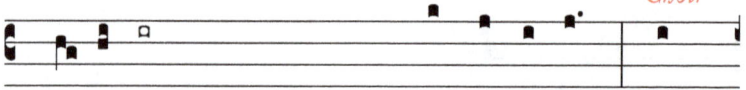

Ps. O all ye works of the Lord, bless ye the Lord: praise

Cantor

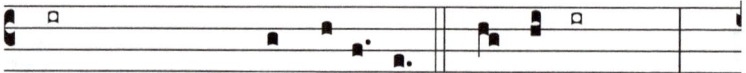

him and magnify him for ev-er.　Glo- ry be..., *(etc.)*

Choir

Full

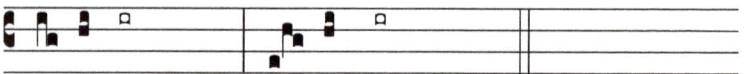

As it was..., *(etc.)* The Lord hath..., *(etc.)*

GRADUAL *Glória et honóre*　　　　　　　　　　Ps. 8:5,6

Cantor

Choir

v.

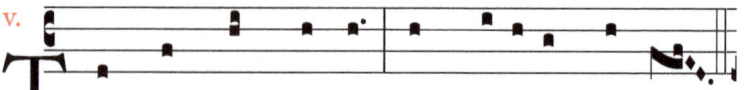

THOU hast crown-ed him with glo-ry and wor-ship.

Cantor

Choir

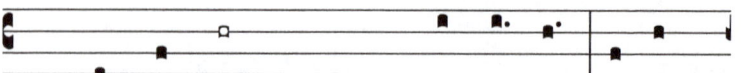

℣. Thou hast made him to have do-min-ion　　of the

works of thy hands, O LORD..

ALLELUIA *Hic est sacerdos*

Cantor   *All*

vj.

AL- LE- LU- IA.   Al- le- lu- ia.

Cantor   *Choir*

℣. This is the priest: whom the Lord hath cho-sen.

All

Al - le- lu- ia.

During Pre-Lent and Lent, the following is said in place of the Alleluia:
TRACT *Beátus vir qui timet*   *Ps. 112:1,2,3*

Cantor

viij.

BLES-SED is the man that feareth the LORD: he hath

Choir

great delight in his com-mand-ments. ℣. His seed shall

(musical notation)

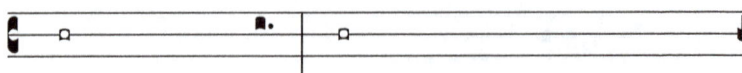

be mighty upon earth: the generation of the faithful

Cantor

(musical notation)

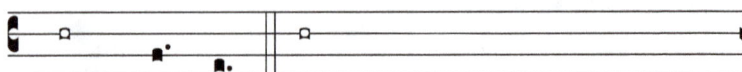

shall be bless-ed. ℣. Riches and plenteousness shall be

Full

(musical notation)

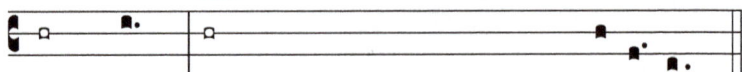

in his house: and his righteousness endureth for ev-er.

OFFERTORY *Inveni David*   *Ps. 89:21,22*

Cantor

ij. *(musical notation)*

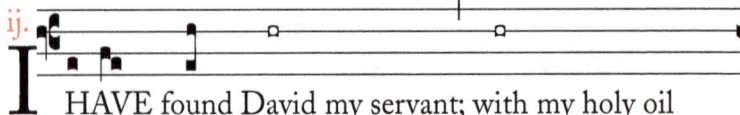

I HAVE found David my servant; with my holy oil

Choir

(musical notation)

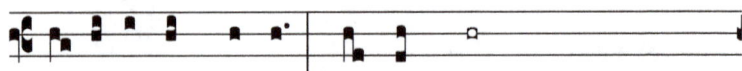

have I a-noint-ed him: my hand shall hold him fast, and

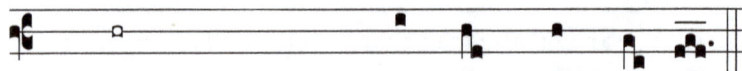

(musical notation)

my   arm shall strength-en him.
or my arm shall strengthen him. Al- le- lu- ia.

COMMUNION *Posuísti, Dómine* *Ps. 21:3b*

i.

T HOU hast set a crown of pure gold up-on his head,

O LORD. *or* upon his head, O LORD. Al- le- lu- ia.

Psalm 21:1,2,4-7,13 *may be sung.*

3. For One Martyr
I. Out of Eastertide

INTROIT *In virtúte tua* *Ps. 21:1,2,3*

Cantor

vij.

T HE right-eous shall rejoice in thy strength, O LORD:

Choir

ex-ceed-ing glad shall he be in thy salvation; thou hast

FINE *Cantor*

giv-en him his heart's de-sire. *Ps.* For thou hast preceded

Choir

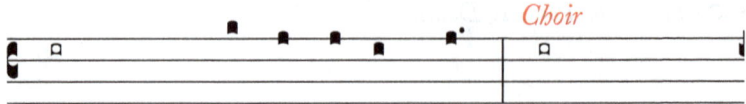

him with the bless-ings of good-ness: and hast set

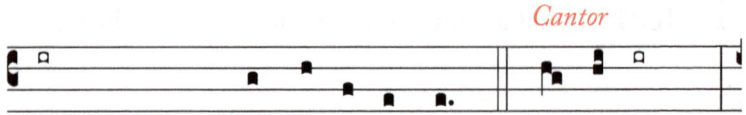

Cantor

a crown of pure gold up-on his head. Glo- ry be..., *(etc.)*

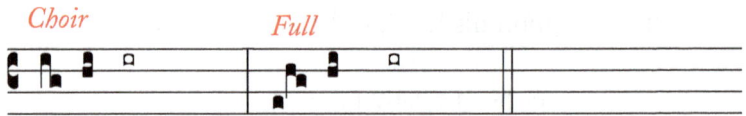

Choir　　　　*Full*

As it was..., *(etc.)* The right-eous..., *(etc.)*

GRADUAL *Beátus vir qui timet*　　　　*Ps. 112:1,2*

Cantor　　　　　　　　　　　　　　　　*Choir*

℣.

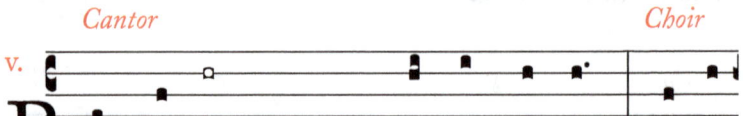

BLESS-ED is the man that fear-eth the LORD: he hath

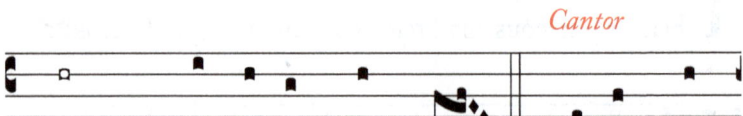

Cantor

great delight in his com-mand-ments. ℣. His seed shall

Choir

be mighty up-on earth: the generation of the faithful

shall be bless-ed .

ALLELUIA *Posuísti, Dómine*   *Ps. 21:3b*

Cantor   *All*

AL- LE- LU- IA. Al- le- lu- ia.

Cantor   *Choir*

℣. Thou hast set a crown of pure gold up-on his head,

All

O LORD. Al - le- lu- ia.

During Pre-Lent and Lent, the following is said in place of the Alleluia:
TRACT *Desidérium ánimæ eius (supra, p. 654)*

OFFERTORY *Glória et honóre*   *Ps. 8:5,6*

Cantor

THOU hast crowned him with glo-ry and wor-ship:

Choir

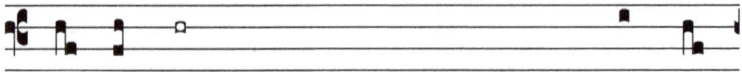

and hast made him to have dominion of the works of

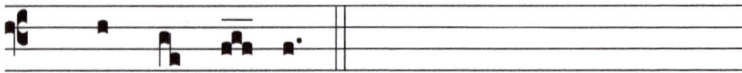

thy hands, O LORD.

COMMUNION *Qui vult venire*   *Mt. 16:24*

Cantor   *Choir*

IF an-y man will come af-ter me: let him deny himself

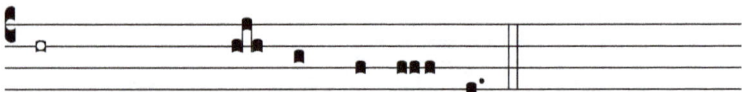

and take up his cross, and fol-low me.

Psalm 34:1,5,6,14-20 *may be sung.*

II. In Eastertide

INTROIT *Protexísti*

Cantor

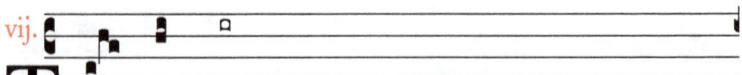

THOU hast hidden me, O God, from the gathering

662

Choir

together of the froward, al-le-lu-ia: from the insurrection

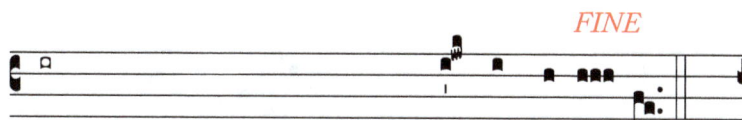

FINE

of the workers of iniquity. Allelu-ia. Al- le- lu- ia.

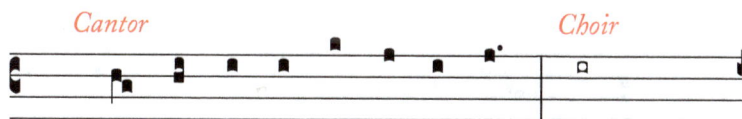

Cantor　　　　　　　　　　　　　　　*Choir*

Ps. Hear my voice, O God, in my prayer: preserve my

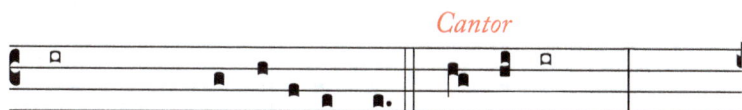

Cantor

life from fear of the e-ne-my　Glo- ry be..., *(etc.)*

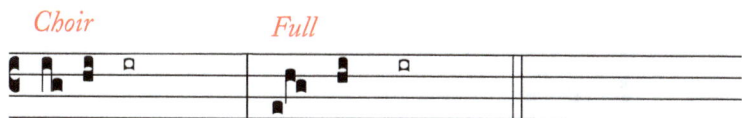

Choir　　　　　　　*Full*

As it was..., *(etc.)* Thou hast hidden..., *(etc.)*

ALLELUIA *Confitebúntur cæli*　　　　　　*Ps. 89:5; 21:3b*

Cantor　　　　　　　*All*

vj.

AL- LE- LU- IA.　Al- le- lu- ia.

Cantor

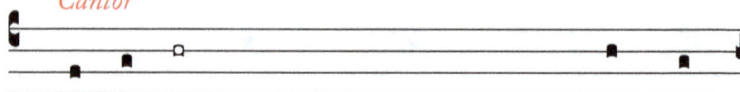

℣. O LORD, the very heavens shall praise thy won-drous

Choir

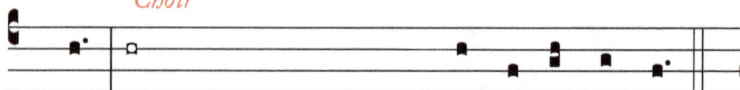

works: and thy truth in the congrega-tion of the Saints.

All *Cantor*

Al - le- lu-˜ ia.   ℣. Thou hast set, O LORD:

Choir

a crown of pure gold up-on his head.

All

Al - le- lu- ia.

OFFERTORY *Confitebúntur cæli*   Ps. 89:5

Cantor

ij.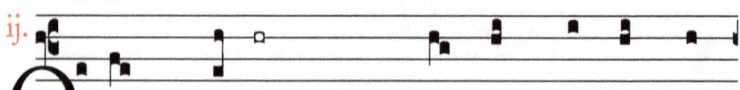

O LORD, the very heavens shall praise thy won-drous

Choir

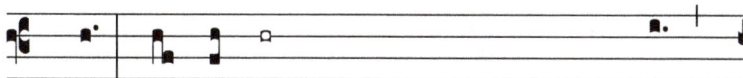

works: and thy truth in the congregation of the Saints.

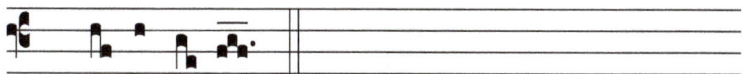

A- le- lu- ia.

COMMUNION *Lætábitur iustus*   *Ps. 64:10*

Cantor

i.

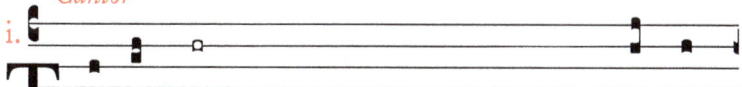

THE right-eous shall rejoice in the Lord, and put his

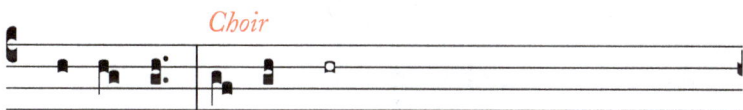

Choir

trust in him: and all they that are true of heart shall be

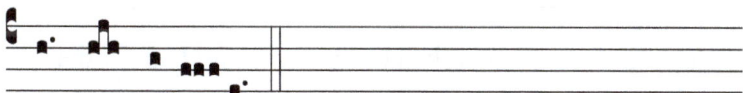

glad. Al- le- lu- ia.

Psalm 34:1,5,6,14-20 *may be sung.*

COMMONS
4. For Several Martyrs
I. Out of Eastertide

INTROIT *Intret in conspéctu*　　　　　*Ps. 79:12,13,1*

Cantor

vij.

O LET the sorrowful sighing of the prisoners come

before thee, O LORD: reward thou our neighbours

Choir

sevenfold in-to their bos-om: let the vengeance of thy

servants' blood that is shed be openly showed up-on the

FINE　　*Cantor*

hea-then. *Ps.* O God, the heathen are come into thine

Choir

inheritance, thy holy temple have they de-fil-ed:　and

Cantor

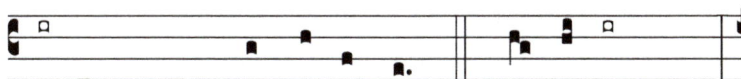

made Jerusalem an heap of stones.   Glo- ry be..., *(etc.)*

Choir   *Full*

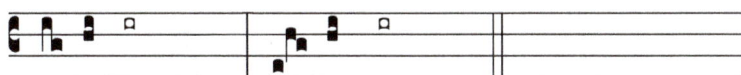

As it was..., *(etc.)*   O   let the..., *(etc.)*

GRADUAL   *Gloriósus Deus*   *Ex. 15:11,6*

Cantor   *Choir*

℣.

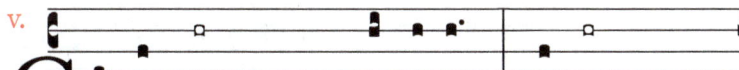

GOD is glorious in his ho-ly ones: mar-vellous in

Cantor

majesty, do-ing won-ders. ℣. Thy right hand, O LORD,

Choir

is become glorious in pow-er: thy right hand hath

dashed in pie-ces the e-ne-my.

667

ALLELUIA *Córpora sanctórum* *Sir. 44:14*

vj.

Cantor *All*

A̱L- LE- LU- IA. Al- le- lu- ia.

Cantor *Choir*

℣. The bo-dies of the Saints are buried in peace: but

All

their name liv-eth for ev-er-more Al le- lu- ia.

During Pre-Lent and Lent, the following is said in place of the Alleluia:

TRACT *Qui séminant in lácrimis* *Ps. 126:6,7*

viij.

Cantor *Choir*

ṮHEY that sow in tears: shall reap in joy. ℣. He that

now goeth on his way weep-ing: and beareth forth

Cantor

good seed. ℣. He shall doubtless come again with joy:

Full

and bring his sheaves with him.

OFFERTORY *Mirábilis Deus*   *Ps. 68:35*

Cantor   *Choir*

GOD is won-der-ful in his Saints: ev-en the God of

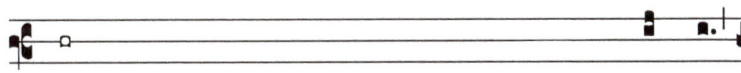

Israel, he will give strength and power unto his peo-ple;

bles-sed be God.

COMMUNION *Et si coram homínibus*   *Wis. 3:4,6*

Cantor

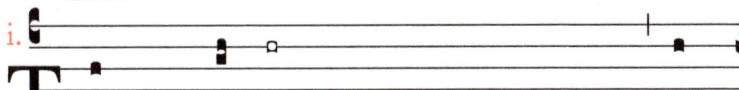

THOUGH they be punished in the sight of men, yet

Choir

hath God proved them: as gold in the furnace hath he

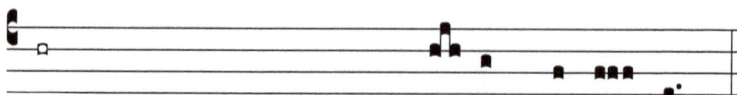

tried them, and received them as a burnt- of- fer- ing.

Canticle, Wis. 3:1-3,5,9ab,9c *may be sung.*

II. In Eastertide

INTROIT *Protexísti (supra, p. 662)*

ALLELUIA *Confitebúntur cæli (supra, p. 663)*

OFFERTORY *Confitebúntur cæli (supra, p. 664)*

COMMUNION *Lætábitur iustus (supra, p. 665)*

5. For A Virgin Martyr

INTROIT *Loquébar de testimóniis tuis*   *Ps. 119:46,47,1*

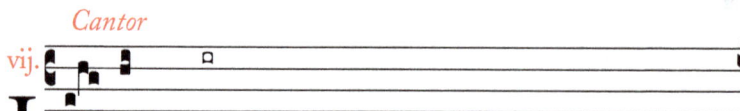

HAVE spoken of thy testimonies, even before kings,

and was not a-sham-ed: and my delight hath been in thy

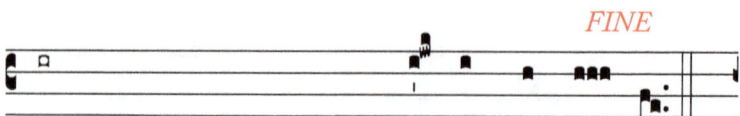

commandments, which I have loved ex- ceed- ing- ly.

FINE

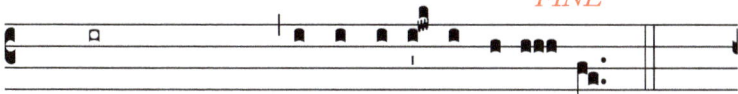

(*or* loved exceedingly. Al-le- lu-ia. Al- le- lu- ia.)

Cantor

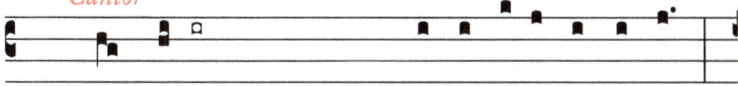

Ps. Bless-ed are those that are un-de-fi-led in the way:

Choir　　　　　　　　　　　　　*Cantor*

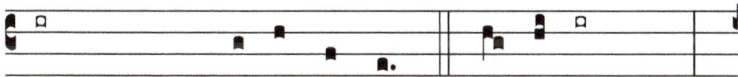

and walk in he law of the LORD.. Glo- ry be..., *(etc.)*

Choir　　　　　　*Full*

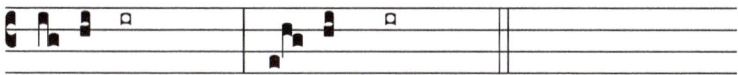

As it was..., *(etc.)*　I　have spoken..., *(etc.)*

GRADUAL *Dilexísti*　　　　　　　　　　　　Ps. 45:7

Cantor　　　　　　　　　　　*Choir*

v.

THOU hast loved right-eous-ness: and ha-ted

Cantor

i- ni- qui- ty.　℣. Where-fore God, even thy God:

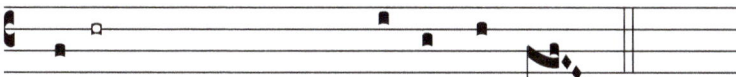

hath anointed thee with the oil of glad-ness.

671

ALLELUIA *Diffúsa est grátia*   *Ps. 45:2b*

Cantor   *All*

vj.

AL- LE- LU- IA.   Al- le- lu- ia.

Cantor   *Choir*

℣. Full of grace are thy lips: because God hath blessed

All

thee for ev-er.   Al le- lu- ia.

In Eastertide the Gradual is omitted and the following versicle is addded:

Cantor   *Choir*

℣. In thy comeliness and in thy beau-ty: go forth, ride

All

prosperous-ly, and reign.   Al le- lu- ia.

During Pre-Lent and Lent, the following is said in place of the Alleluia:

TRACT *Veni, sponsa Christi*   *Cf. Ps. 45:7,4*

Cantor

viij.

COME thou bride of Christ, receive the crown, which

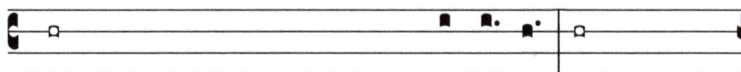

the LORD hath prepared for thee for ev-er: for whose

Choir

love thou didst shed thy blood. ℣. Thou hast

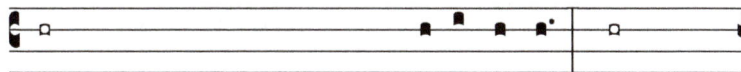

loved righteousness, and hated i-ni-qui-ty: therefore

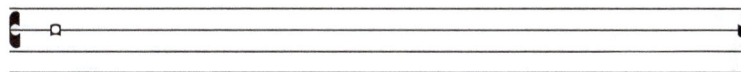

God, even thy God, hath anointed thee with the oil of

Cantor

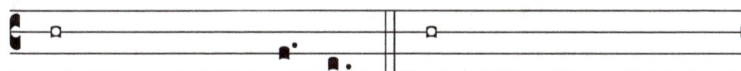

gladness above thy fel-lows ℣. In thy comeliness and in

Full

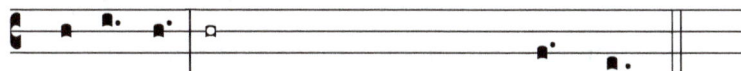

thy beau-ty: go forth, ride prosperously, and reign.

COMMONS

OFFERTORY *Afferéntur*   *Ps. 45:14b*

Cantor

ij.

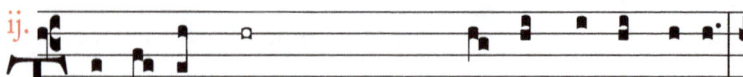

T HE vir-gins that be her fellows shall bear her com-pa-ny:

Choir

they shall be   brought un-to thee.
or they shall be brought un-to thee. Al- le- lu- ia.

COMMUNION *Confundántur supérbi*   *Ps. 119:78,80*

Cantor

i.

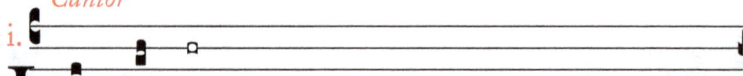

L ET the proud be confounded, for they go wickedly

Choir

about to des-troy me: but I will be occupied in thy

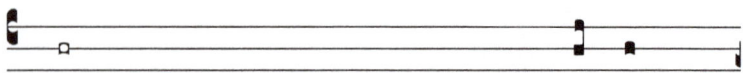

commandments, and in thy statutes, that I be not

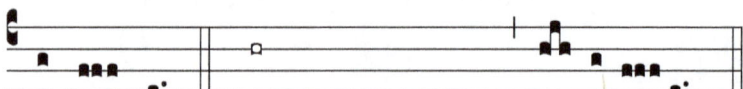

a-sham-ed.   *or* that I be not ashamed. Al- le- lu- ia.

Psalm 118:1,41,85,113,123,157,161,174 *may be sung.*

COMMON OF CONFESSORS
1. For a Holy Pope

INTROIT *Si díligis me*   *Jn. 21:17; Ps. 30:1*

Cantor   *Choir*

IF thou lovest me, Sim-on Pe-ter: feed my lambs, feed

FINE

my sheep. *(or* feed my lambs, feed my sheep. Al-le-lu- ia.

FINE   *Cantor*   *Choir*

Al- le- lu- ia.) *Ps.* I will magni-fy thee, O LORD: for thou

hast set me up and not made my foes to tri-umph ov-er me.

Cantor   *Choir*   *Full*

Glo- ry be..., *(etc.)* As it was..., *(etc.)* If thou lovest..., *(etc.)*

GRADUAL *Exáltent eum* *(Feb. 22, Chair of St. Peter, p.528)*

675

ALLELUIA *Tu es Petros* *Mt. 16:18; Ps. 45:16b,17*

Cantor *All*

vj.

AL- LE- LU- IA. Al- le- lu- ia.

Cantor *Choir*

℣. Thou art Peter, and upon this rock: I will build my

All

Church. Al - le- lu- ia.

During Eastertide the Gradual is ommitted and the following is added:

Cantor *Choir*

℣. Thou shalt make them princes in all lands: they shall

All

remem-ber thy Name, O LORD. Al - le- lu- ia.

During Pre-Lent and Lent, the following is said in place of the Alleluia:

TRACT *Annuntiávi iustítiam túam*   Ps. 40:11,12,13

Cantor

viij.

I HAVE declared thy righteousness in the great

Choir

con-gre-ga-tion: lo, I will not refrain my lips, O LORD,

Cantor

and that thou know-est. ℣. I have not hid thy righteous-

Choir

ness within my heart: my talk hath been of thy truth and

Cantor

of thy sal-va-tion ℣. I have not kept back thy loving

Choir

mercy and truth: from the great congre-ga-tion.

677

OFFERTORY *Ecce dédi vérba méa*   *Jer. 1:9,10*

Cantor   *Choir*

ij.

B E-HOLD, I have put my words in thy mouth: see, I

have set thee over the nations and over the kingdoms, to

pull down and to des-troy, to build and to plant.

(or destroy, to build and to plant. Al- le- lu- ia.*)*

COMMUNION *Tu es Pétrus (Feb. 22, Chair of St. Peter, p.529)*

2. For a Bishop
I

INTROIT *Státuit ei*   *(Common of Martyrs, p. 651)*

GRADUAL *Ecce sacérdos magnus*   *Sir. 44:16,20*

Cantor   *Choir*

Bᴇ-HOLD, a might-y prel-ate: who in his lifetime

Cantor

was pleas-ing un-to God.   ℣. There was none found like

Choir

un-to him: that observed the law of the Most High.

ALLELUIA *Tu es sacérdos*   *Ps. 110:4b*

Cantor   *All*

Aʟ- LE- LU- IA.   Al- le- lu- ia.

Cantor   *Choir*

℣. Thou art a priest for ev-er: after the order of

All

Mel-chi-se-dech.   Al - le- lu- ia.

In Eastertide the Gradual is ommitted and the following is added:

COMMONS

Cantor *Choir*

℣. This is a priest: whom the LORD hath crowned.

All

Al - le- lu- ia.

During Pre–Lent and Lent, the following is said in place of the Alleluia:
TRACT *Beátus vir qui timet*   *(Common of Martyrs, p. 657)*

OFFERTORY *Inveni David*   *(Common of Martyrs, p. 657)*

COMMUNION *Fidélis servus et prudens*   *Lk. 12:42*

Cantor

i. A FAITH-FUL and wise steward, whom the LORD

Choir

hath made ruler ov-er his house-hold: to give them their

portion of meat in due sea-son.
(*or* portion of meat in due sea-son. Al- le-   lu- ia.)
Psalm 112:1-9 *may be sung.*

680

Common of Confessors
II

INTROIT *Sacerdótes tui*   *Ps. 132:9,10,1*

Cantor

LET thy priests, O LORD, be clothed with righteousness,

Choir

and let thy Saints sing with joy-ful-ness: for thy servant

FINE

David's sake, turn not away the face of thine An-oint-ed.
(*or* of thine Anointed. Alle-lu- ia. Al- le- lu- ia.)

Cantor   *Choir*

Ps. LORD, re-mem-ber Da-vid: and all his trou-ble.

Cantor   *Choir*   *Full*

Glo- ry be..., *(etc.)* As it was..., *(etc.)* Let thy priests..., *(etc.)*

GRADUAL *Sacerdótes eius*   *Ps 132:17,18*

Cantor   *Choir*

I WILL deck her priests with health: and her Saints

shall re-joice and sing. ℣. There shall I make the horn of

Choir

David to flou-rish: I have ordained a lantern for

mine An-oint-ed.

ALLELUIA *Iuravit Dóminus*   *Ps 110:4*

Cantor   *All*

AL- LE- LU- IA.   Al- le- lu- ia.

Cantor   *Choir*

℣. The LORD hath sworn and will not re-pent: Thou art

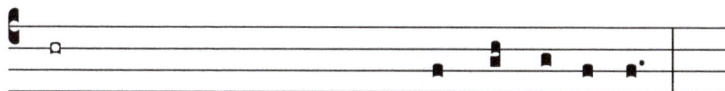

a priest for ever, after the order of Mel-chi-se-dech.

All

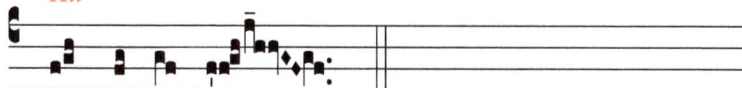

Al - le- lu- ia.

In Eastertide the Gradual is ommitted and the following is added:

Cantor   *Choir*

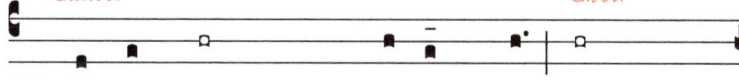

℣. The LORD loved him and ad-orned him: he clothed

All

him with a robe of glo-ry   Al - le- lu- ia.

During Pre-Lent and Lent, the following is said in place of the Alleluia:
TRACT *Beátus vir qui timet*   (*Common of Martyrs, p. 657*)

OFFERTORY *Véritas mea*   *Ps. 89:25*

Cantor

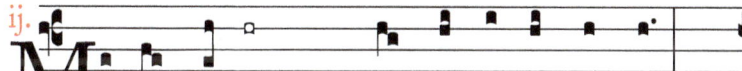

ij.

MY truth al-so and my mer-cy shall be with him:

Choir

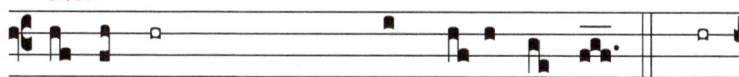

and in my Name shall his horn be ex- al- ted. (*or* horn

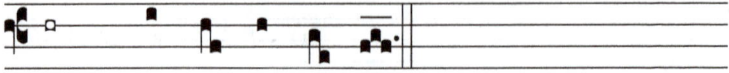

be ex-al-ted. Al- le- lu- ia.)

COMMUNION *Beátus servus*   *Mt. 24:46,47*

Cantor

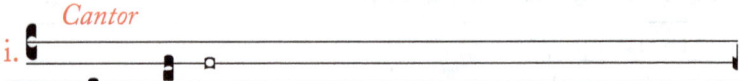

BLES-SED is the servant whom the LORD when he

Choir

cometh shall find watch-ing: ve-ri-ly I say unto you, he

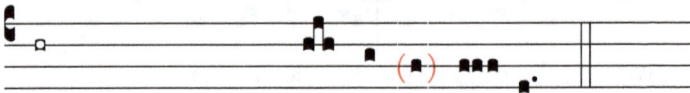

shall make him a ruler o- ver all his goods.
(*or* over all his goods. Al- le-   lu- ia.)

Psalm 33:1-5,12-14,17-21
or **Psalm 72:1,2,4,10-13**
or **Psalm 121** *may be sung.*

3. For a Priest

INTROIT *Os iusti meditábitur*   *Ps. 37:31,32,1*

Cantor

vij.

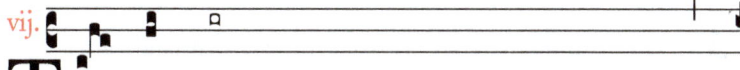

THE mouth of the righteous is exercised in wisdom,

Choir

and his tongue will be talk-ing of judge-ment: the law of

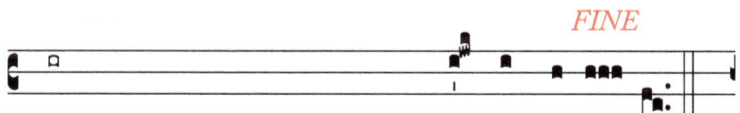

FINE

his   God is in his heart.
(or his God is in his heart. Allelu-ia. Al- le- lu- ia. *)*

Cantor   *Choir*

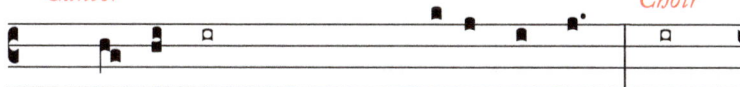

Ps. Fret not thyself because of the un-god-ly: neither

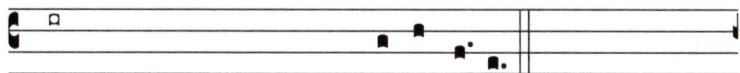

be thou envious against the e- vil do-ers.

Cantor   *Choir*   *Full*

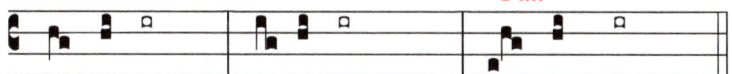

Glo- ry be..., *(etc.)* As it was..., *(etc.)* The mouth of..., *(etc.)*

GRADUAL *Iustus ut palma*   *Ps. 92:11,12,2*

Cantor   *Choir*

v.

THE right-eous shall flourish like a palm tree: and

shall spread abroad like a cedar in Lebanon in the house

Cantor

of the LORD. ℣. To tell of thy loving-kindness early in

Choir

the morn-ing: and of thy truth in the night sea-son.

ALLELUIA *Beátus vir qui suffert*   *Jas. 1:12; Sir, 45:9*

Cantor   *All*

vj.

AL- LE- LU- IA.   Al- le- lu- ia.

Cantor

℣. Bles-sed is the man that endureth temp-ta-tion:

Choir

for when he is tried he shall re-ceive the crown of life.

All

Al - le- lu- ia.

In Eastertide the Gradual is ommitted and the following is added:

Cantor   *Choir*

℣. The Lᴏʀᴅ loved him and a-dorned him: he clothed

All

him with a robe of glo-ry.   Al - le- lu- ia.

During Pre-Lent and Lent, the following is said in place of the Alleluia:
Tʀᴀᴄᴛ *Beátus vir qui timet*   *(Common of Martyrs, p. 657)*

Oꜰꜰᴇʀᴛᴏʀʏ *Véritas mea*   *(supra, p. 683)*

Cᴏᴍᴍᴜɴɪᴏɴ *Beátus servus*   *(supra, p. 684)*

687

COMMONS
4. For a Missionary

Cantor

vij.

G OD be merciful unto us, and bless us, and show us the

light of his countenance, and be mer-ci-ful un-to us:

Choir

that thy way may be known upon earth, thy saving health

FINE

a-   mong all   na-tions.
(*or* among all nations. Allelu-ia. Al- le- lu- ia.)

Cantor   *Choir*

Ps. Let the peoples praise thee, O God: yea, let all the

Cantor

peo-ples praise thee..   Glo- ry be..., *(etc.)*

688

Choir   *Full*

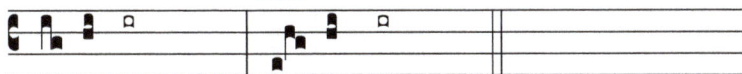

As it was..., *(etc.)*   God be merciful..., *(etc.)*

GRADUAL   *Confiteántur tibi*   *Ps 67:5,7*

Cantor   *Choir*

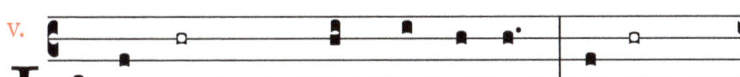

LET all the peoples praise thee, O God: yea, let all the

Cantor   *Choir*

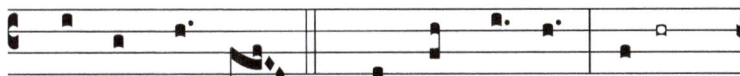

peo-ples praise thee. ℣. God shall bless us: and all the

ends of the world shall fear him.

ALLELUIA   *Iubiláte Deo*   *Ps. 100:1,2*

Cantor

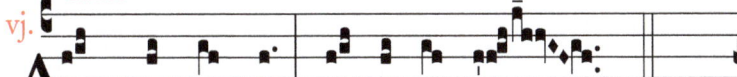

AL- LE- LU- IA.   Al- le- lu- ia.

Cantor   *Choir*

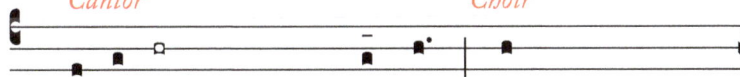

℣. O be joyful in God, all ye lands: serve the LORD with

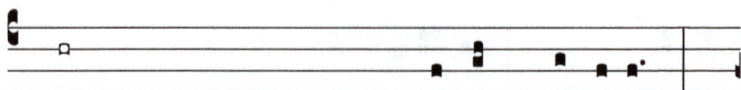

gladness, and come before his pres-ence with a song.

Al le- lu- ia.

In Eastertide the Gradual is ommitted and the following is added:

Cantor   *Choir*

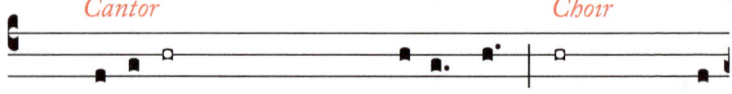

℣. Be ye sure that the Lᴏʀᴅ he is God: and it is he that

All

hath made us   Al - le- lu- ia.

During Pre-Lent and Lent, the following is said in place of the Alleluia:

Tʀᴀᴄᴛ *Annuntiáte inter gentes*   *Ps. 96:3,4,5*

Cantor

viij.

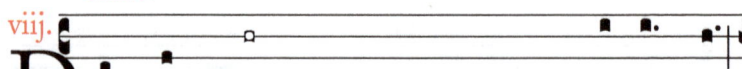

D E-CLARE the honour of the Lᴏʀᴅ unto the hea-then:

Choir   *Cantor*

and his wonders un-to all peo-ples. ℣. For the Lᴏʀᴅ

Choir

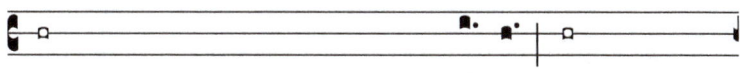

is great, and cannot worthily be prais-ed: he is more

Cantor

more to be feared than all gods. ℣. As for the gods of the

Choir

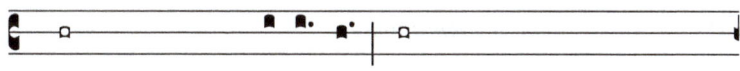

heathen, they are but i-dols: but it is the LORD that made

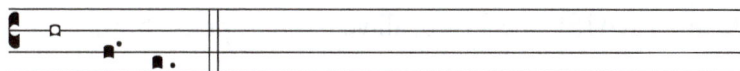

the hea-vens.

OFFERTORY *Afférte Dómino*   *Ps. 96:7,8,9*

Cantor

ij.

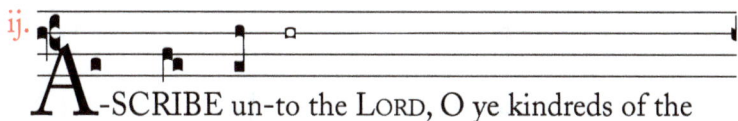

A-SCRIBE un-to the LORD, O ye kindreds of the

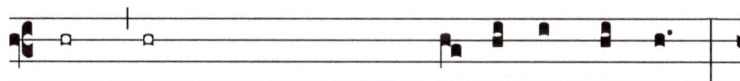

peoples; ascribe unto the LORD wor-ship and pow-er:

Choir

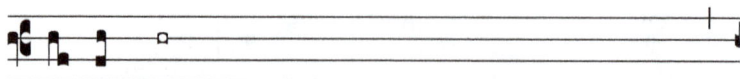

a-scribe unto the LORD the honour due unto his Name;

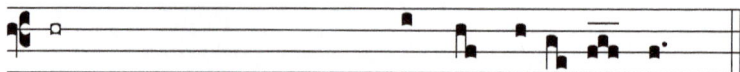

O worship the LORD in the beau-ty of ho- li- ness.
(*or* in the beauty of ho-li- ness. Al- le- lu- ia.)

COMMUNION *Laudáte Dóminum*   *Ps. 117:1,2*

Cantor

i.

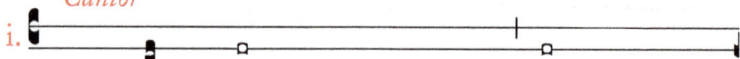

O PRAISE the LORD, all ye nations; praise him,

Choir

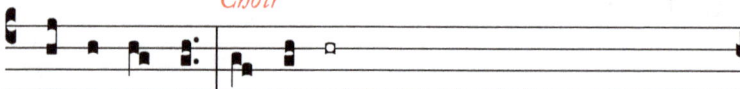

all ye peo-ples: for his merciful kindness is ever more and

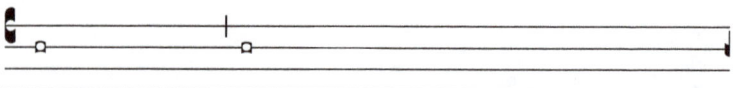

more toward us; and the truth of the LORD

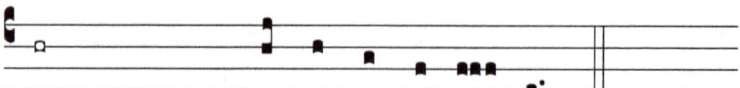

en-dur-eth for e- ver.
(*or* en-dur-eth for e- ver. Al- le- lu- ia.)

Psalm 96:1-2,10,13 *may be sung.*

COMMON OF DOCTORS OF THE CHURCH

INTROIT *In médio ecclésiæ*   *Sir. 15:5; Ps 92:1*

Cantor

vij.

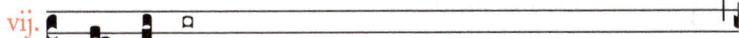

IN the midst of the congregation he opened his mouth;

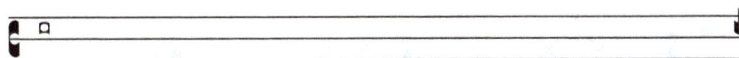

and the LORD filled him with the spirit of wisdom and

Choir   *FINE*

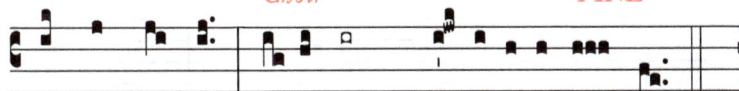

un-der-stand-ing: in a robe of glo-ry he ar-rayed him.

Choir   *FINE*

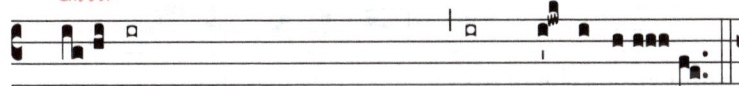

(*or* in a robe of glory he arrayed him. Allelu-ia. Al-le-lu-ia.)

Cantor

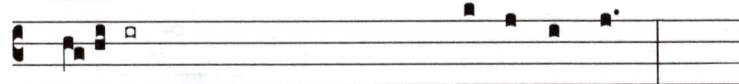

Ps. It is a good thing to give thanks un-to the LORD:

Choir

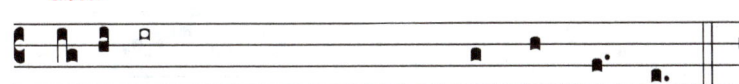

and to sing praises unto thy Name, O Most High-est.

693

Cantor *Choir* *Full*

Glo- ry be..., *(etc.)* As it was..., *(etc.)* In the midst..., *(etc.)*

GRADUAL *Os iusti meditábitur* *(June 1, St. Justin, p.556)*

ALLELUIA *Amávit eum Dóminus*   *Sir. 45:9; Hos. 14:6*

Cantor   *All*

vj.

AL- LE- LU- IA.   Al- le- lu- ia.

Cantor   *Choir*

℣. The LORD loved him, and a-dorned him: he clothed

All

him with a robe of glo-ry   Al - le- lu- ia.
During Eastertide the Gradual is ommitted and the following is added:

Cantor   *Choir*

℣. The right-eous shall grow as the li-ly: and flourish

All

for ever be-fore the LORD. Al - le- lu- ia.

Common of Doctors of the Church

During Pre-Lent and Lent, the following is said in place of the Alleluia:
TRACT *Beátus vir qui timet*   *(Common of Martyrs, p. 657)*

OFFERTORY *Iustus ut palma florébit*   *Ps. 92:11*

Cantor   *Choir*

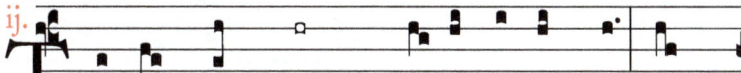

THE, right-eous shall flour-ish like a palm tree: and

shall spread abroad like a ce- dar in Le-ba-non.

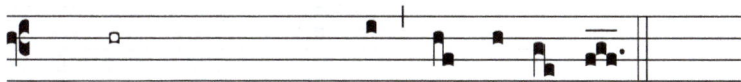

(or like a cedar in Leba-non. Al- le- lu- ia.*)*

COMMUNION *Fidélis servus (Common of Confessors p. 680)*

695

COMMON OF VIRGINS

INTROIT *Dilexísti*   *Ps .45:7,1*

Cantor

vij.

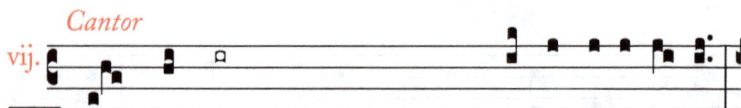

THOU hast loved righteousness, and hat-ed in-i-qui-ty:

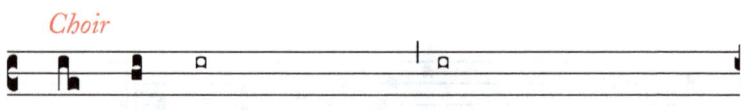

Choir

where-fore God, even thy God, hath anointed thee with

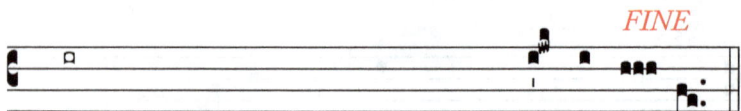

FINE

the oil of gladness   ab-ove thy fel-lows.
(*or* the oil of gladness above thy fellows. Al- le- lu- ia.)

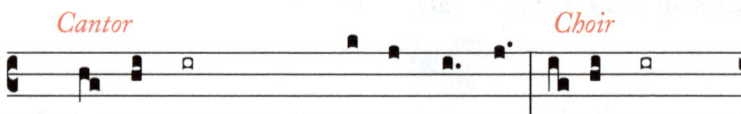

Cantor   *Choir*

Ps. My heart is inditing of a good mat-ter: I speak of the

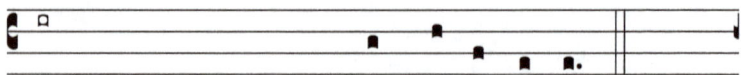

of the things which I have made un-to the King.

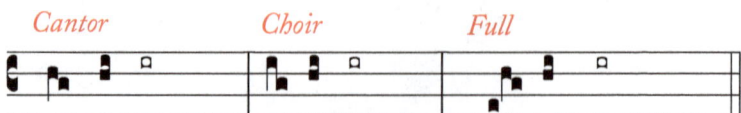

Cantor   *Choir*   *Full*

Glo- ry be..., *(etc.)* As it was..., *(etc.)* Thou hast loved..., *(etc.)*

696

GRADUAL *Specie tua* *Cf. Ps. 45:4b*

Cantor   *Choir*

v.

IN thy comeliness and in thy beau-ty: go forth,

Cantor

ride pros-per-ous-ly, and reign. ℣. Be-cause of the

Choir

word of truth, of meekness, and right-eous-ness: and thy

right hand shall teach thee ter-ri-ble things.

ALLELUIA *Afferentur* *Ps. 45:14b,11*

Cantor   *All*

vj.

AL- LE- LU- IA. Al- le- lu- ia.

Cantor

℣. The vir-gins that be her fellows shall bear her com-pa-ny:

697

Choir

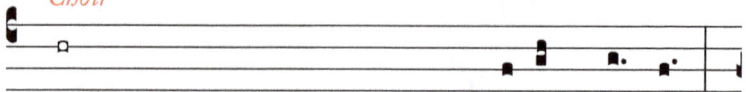

they shall be brought unto thee with joy and glad-ness.

All

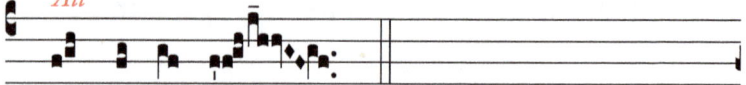

Al - le- lu- ia.

During Eastertide the Gradual is ommitted and the following is added:

Cantor   *Choir*

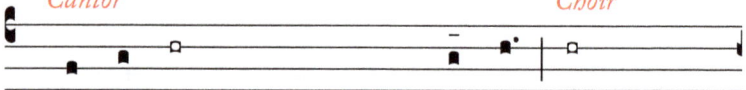

℣. In thy comeliness and in thy beau-ty: go forth, ride

All

prosper-ous-ly, and reign. Al - le- lu- ia.

During Pre-Lent and Lent, the following is said in place of the Alleluia:

TRACT *Audi, filia*   *Cf. Ps 45:9-15*

Cantor

viij.

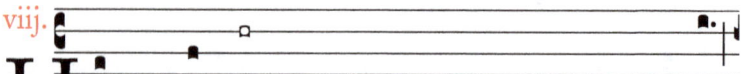

HEAR-KEN, O daughter, and consider, incline thine ear:

Choir   *Cantor*

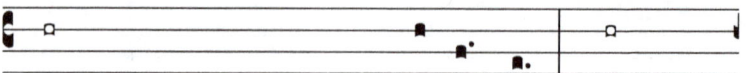

for the King hath pleasure in thy beau-ty. ℣. The rich also

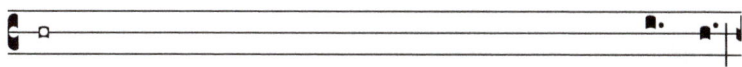

among the people shall make their supplication be-fore thee:

Choir

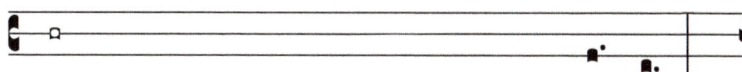

kings' daughters are among thy honourable wo-men.

Cantor

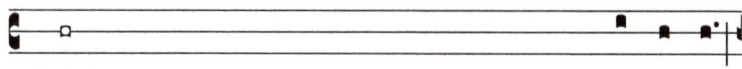

℣. She shall be brought unto the King in raiment of need-le-work

Choir

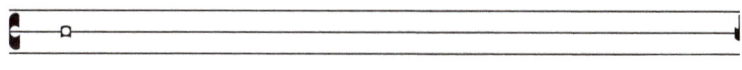

the virgins that be her fellows shall bear her company, and

Cantor

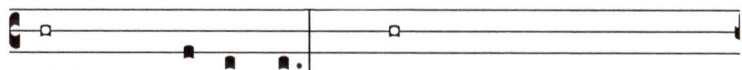

be brought un-to thee. ℣. With joy and gladness shall

Choir

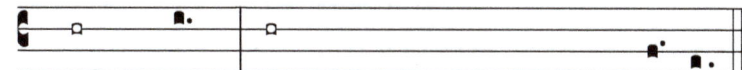

they be brought: and shall enter into the King's pal-ace.

OFFERTORY *Filiae regum* *Ps. 45:9*

Cantor

KINGS' daugh-ters are among thine ho-nour-ab-le

Choir

wo-men: up-on thy right hand doth stand the queen in

a vesture of gold, wrought about with di-vers co-lours.

(*or* wrought about with divers co-lours. Al- le- lu- ia.)

COMMUNION *Quinque prudéntes vírgines* *Mt. 25:4,6*

Cantor

THE five wise virgins took oil in their vessels with

Choir

their lamps: and at midnight there was a cry made,

Behold the Bridegroom cometh;

go ye out to meet Christ the LORD.
(*or* go ye out to meet Christ the LORD. Al- le- lu- ia.)

Psalm 45:1,9-15 *may be sung.*

COMMON OF HOLY MEN AND WOMEN

1. For Any Holy Man

INTROIT *Os iusti meditábitur* *(Common of Confessors, p. 685)*

GRADUAL *Iustus ut palma* *(Common of Confessors, p. 686)*

ALLELUIA *Beátus vir qui suffert* *(Common of Confessors, p. 686)*

TRACT *Beátus vir qui timet* *(Common of Martyrs, p. 657)*

OFFERTORY *Véritas mea* *(Common of Confessors, p. 683)*

COMMUNION *Beátus servus* *(Common of Confessors, p. 684)*

2. For Any Matron or Holy Woman

INTROIT *Cognóvi*   *Ps. 119:75,120,1*

Cantor

vij.

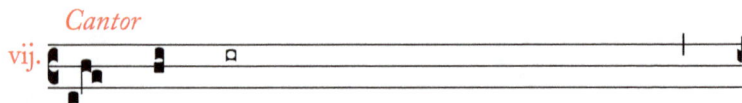

I KNOW, O LORD, that thy judgements are right,

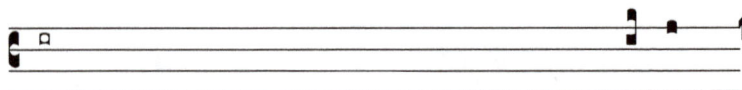

and that thou of very faithfulness hast caused me to be

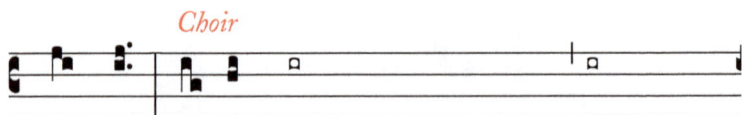

Choir

trou-bled: my flesh trembleth for fear of thee, and I am

702

FINE

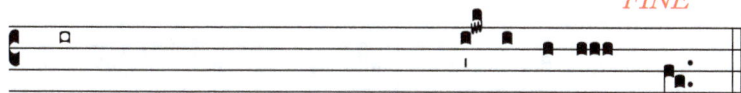

a-　　　　　　　　　fraid of thy judge-ments.
(or a-fraid of thy judgements. Allelu-ia. Al- le- lu-　ia.*)*

Cantor

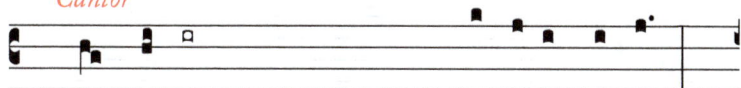

Ps. Bles-sed are those that are unde-fi-led in the way:

Choir　　　　　　　　　*Cantor*

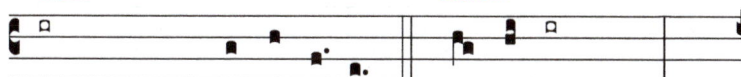

and walk in he law of the LORD. Glo- ry　be..., *(etc.)*

Choir　　　　　*Full*

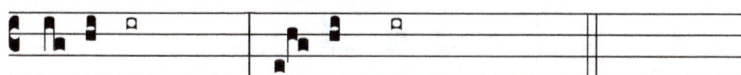

As it was..., *(etc.)*　I　know, O LORD..., *(etc.)*

GRADUAL *Diffúsa est grátia (St. Mary, Mother of God, p. 69)*

ALLELUIA *Specie tua*　　　　　　　　　*Cf. Ps. 45:4*

Cantor　　　　　*All*

vj. AL- LE- LU- IA.　Al- le- lu- ia.

Cantor　　　　　　　　　*Choir*

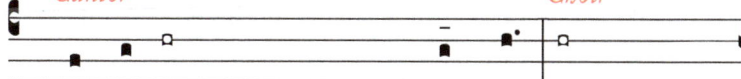

℣. In thy comeliness and in thy beau-ty:　go forth, ride

All

pros-per-ous-ly, and reign. Al - le- lu- ia.

During Eastertide the Gradual is omitted and the following is added:

Cantor

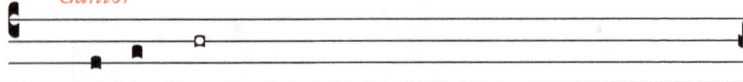

℣. Be-cause of the word of truth, of meekness, and

Choir

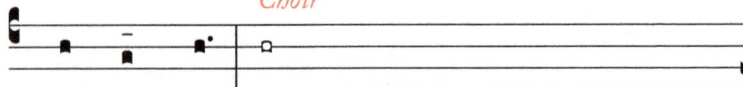

right-eous-ness: and thy right hand shall teach thee

All

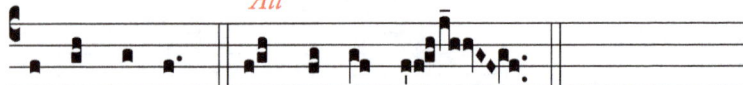

ter-ri-ble things. Al - le- lu- ia.

During Pre-Lent and Lent, the following is said in place of the Alleluia:

Tract *Veni sponsa Christi (Common of Martyrs, p. 672)*

Offertory *Diffúsa est grátia (Candlemas, p. 518)*

Communion *Dilexísti iustítiam*   Ps. 45:7

Cantor

i.

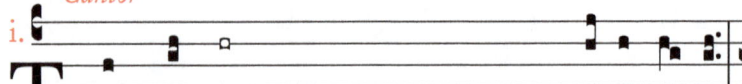

THOU hast loved righteousness, and hated i-ni-qui-ty:

Choir

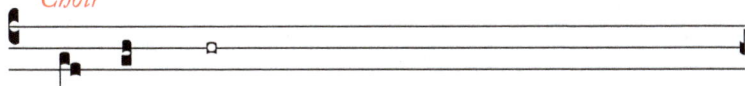

where-fore God, even thy God, hath anointed thee with

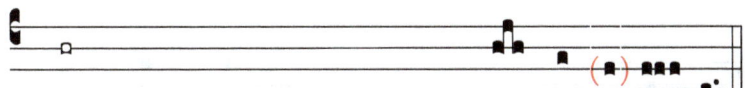

the oil of gladness   a-bove thy fel-lows.
(*or* the oil of gladness above thy fellows. Al- le-   lu- ia.)

Psalm 45:1,9-15 *may be sung.*

3. For Religious

INTROIT *Iustus ut palma*   *Ps. 92:11,12,1*

Cantor

vij.

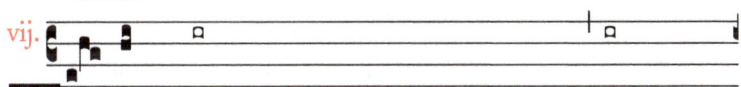

THE right-eous shall flourish like a palm tree, and shall

Choir

spread abroad like a ce-dar in Le-ba-non: such as are

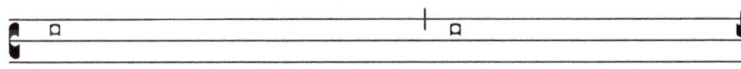

planted in the house of the LORD shall flourish in the court

FINE

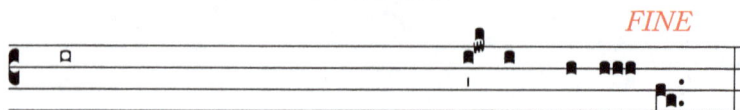

of   the house of our God.
(*or* of the house of our God. Allelu- ia. Al- le- lu- ia.)

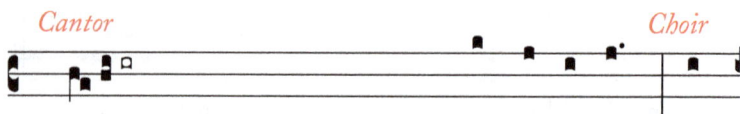

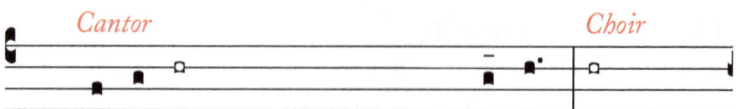

Cantor   *Choir*

Ps. It is a good thing to give thanks un-to the LORD: and

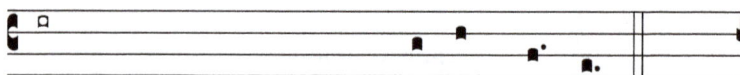

to sing praises unto thy Name, O Most High-est.

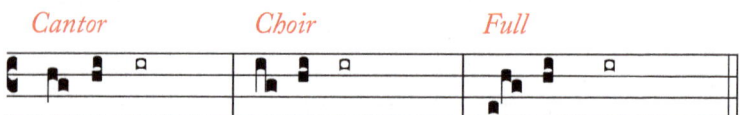

Cantor   *Choir*   *Full*

Glo- ry   be..., *(etc.)* As it was..., *(etc.)*   The righ-teous..., *(etc.)*

GRADUAL   *Os iusti meditábitur (June 1, St. Justin, p. 556)*

ALLELUIA *Beátus vir qui timet*   *Ps. 112:1; Hos. 14:6*

Cantor   *All*

vj. AL- LE- LU- IA.   Al- le- lu- ia.

Cantor   *Choir*

℣. Bles-sed is the man that feareth the LORD: he hath great

706

All

delight in his com-mand-ments. Al - le- lu- ia.

During Eastertide the Gradual is omitted and the following is added:

Cantor　　　　　　　　　　　　　　　　　*Choir*

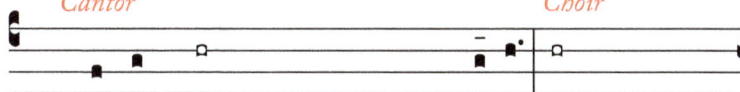

℣. The right-eous shall grow as the li-ly: and flourish for

All

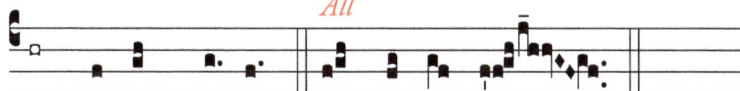

ever be-fore the Lord. Al - le- lu- ia.

Tract *Beatus vir qui timet (Common of Martyrs, p. 657)*

Offertory *In virtúte tua*　　　　　　　　　　*Ps. 21:1,2*

Cantor

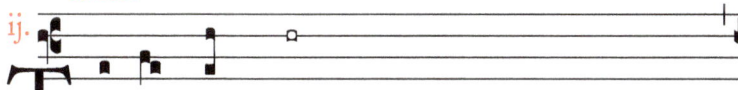

ij. THE right-eous shall re-joice in thy strength, O Lord;

Choir

exceeding glad shall he be of thy sal-va-tion: thou hast

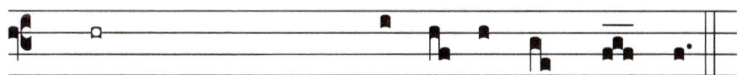

giv-en him his heart's de- sire.
(*or* given him his heart's des-ire. Al- le- lu- ia.)

COMMUNION *Amen dico vobis: quod vos*   *Mt. 19:28,29*

i.

VE-RI-LY I say un-to you: that ye who have forsaken

all, and followed me, shall receive an hundredfold, and

shall inherit   ev- er-last- ing life.
(*or* shall inherit everlasting life. Al- le-   lu- ia.)

Psalm 21:1-6,13 *may be sung.*

4. For An Abbot or Abbess

INTROIT *Os iusti meditábitur (Common of Confessosrs, p. 685)*

GRADUAL *Dómine, prævenísti eum*   *Ps. 21:3,4*

v.

THOU hast prevented him with the blessings of good-ness:

and hast set a crown of pure gold up-on his head.

708

Cantor

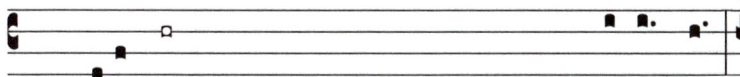

℣. He ask-ed life of thee, and thou gavest him a long life:

Choir

yea, even for ev-er and ev-er.

ALLELUIA *Iustus ut palma*   *Ps 92:11; Ho.s 14:6*

Cantor   *All*

vj.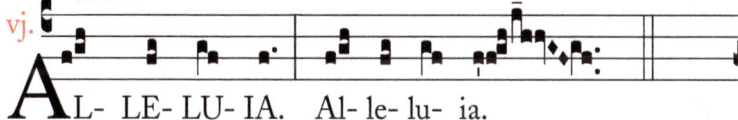

AL- LE- LU- IA.   Al- le- lu- ia.

Cantor   *Choir*

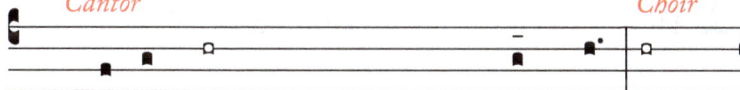

℣. The right-eous shall flourish like a palm tree: and shall

All

spread abroad like a ce-dar in Le-ba-non.   Al - le - lu-

In Eastertide the Gradual is omitted and the following is added:
Cantor

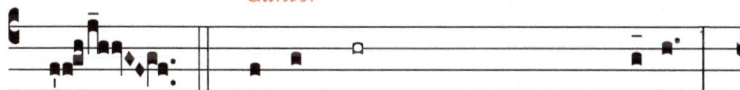

ia.   ℣. The right-eous shall grow as the li-ly:

(musical notation)

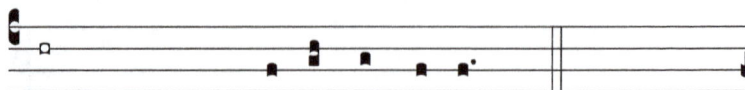

and flourish for ev-er be-fore the LORD.

All

(musical notation)

Al - le- lu- ia.

TRACT *Beátus vir qui timet (Common of Martyrs, p. 657)*

OFFERTORY *Desidérium ánimæ*   *Ps. 21:2,3b*

Cantor

ij. *(musical notation)*

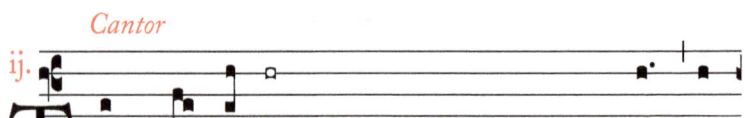

THOU hast giv-en him his heart's desire, O LORD, and

Choir

(musical notation)

hast not denied him the re-quest of his lips: thou hast set

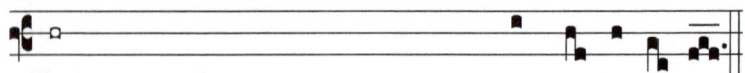

(musical notation)

set a crown of pure   gold up-on his head.
(*or* set a crown of pure gold upon his head. Al- le- lu- ia.)

COMMUNION *Fidélis servus et prudens*
                    (Common of Confessors, p. 680)

5. For An Educator

INTROIT *Iustus ut palma (supra, p. 705)*

GRADUAL *Os iusti meditábitur (June 1, St. Justin, p. 556)*

ALLELUIA *Beátus vir qui timet (supra, p. 706)*

TRACT *Beátus vir qui timet (Common of Martyrs, p. 657)*

OFFERTORY *In virtúte tua (supra, p. 707)*

COMMUNION *Amen dico vobis: quod vos (supra, p. 708)*

RITUAL MASSES

For the Administration of Baptism

INTROIT *Sitiéntes*   *Ps. 119:75,120,1*

Cantor

vij.

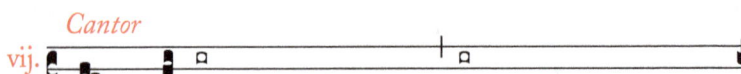

COME, ev-eryone that thirsteth, come ye to the waters,

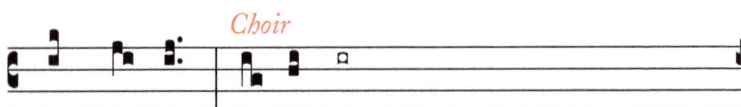

Choir

saith the LORD: and ye that have no money, come and

FINE   *Cantor*

drink with glad-ness. *Ps.* Hear my law, O my peo-ple:

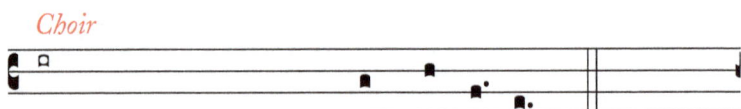

Choir

incline your ears unto the words of my mouth.

Cantor   *Choir*   *Full*

Glo- ry be..., *(etc.)* As it was..., *(etc.)* Come, ev-er..., *(etc.)*

Eastertide: IN. *Edúxit Dóminus (Saturday in the Easter 8ᵛᵉ, p. 314)*

GRADUAL *Beáta gens (Trinity XVII, p 441)*

ALLELUIA *Confitémini Dómino (Rogationtide, p 340)*
or AL. *Verba mea (Trinity I, p 385)*
for the TRACT *Sicut cervus (Holy Saturday, p. 275, verses 1–3)*

OFFERTORY *Factus est Dóminus*   *Ps. 18:1b,2*

Cantor   *Choir*

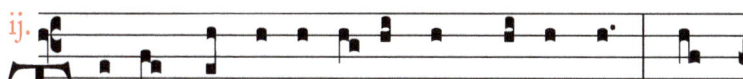

HE LORD is my sto-ny rock, and my de-fence: my

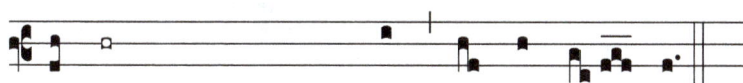

Sa-viour, my God, and my might, in whom I will trust.

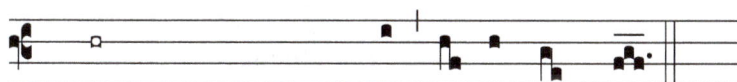

(*or* ...might, in whom I will trust. Al- le- lu-   ia.)

COMMUNION *Omnes qui in Christo baptizáti estis*
                                    (Baptism of the Lord, p. 83)

For the Conferral of Confirmation

INTROIT *Dum Sanctificátus*   *(Vigil of Pentecost, p. 362)*
or IN. *Caritas Dei*   *(Vigil of Pentecost, p. 361)*

GRADUAL *Beáta gens (Trinity XVII, p 441)*

ALLELUIA *Emítte Spíritum (Vigil of Pentecost, p 363)*
or AL. *Veni, Sancte Spíritus (Votive Mass of the Holy Spirit, p. 739)*

OFFERTORY *Confírma hoc (Whitsunday, p. 370)*

COMMUNION *Beáti mundo corde (Nov 1, All Saints, p. 621)*
or P.T. CO. *Non vos relínquam (Easter VI, p. 336)*

RITUAL MASSES
HOLY MATRIMONY

1.

INTROIT *Deus in loco sancto* *(Holy Family, p. 63)*

GRADUAL *Timéte Dóminum (Nov. 1, All Saints, p. 620)*

ALLELUIA *Mittat vobis* *Ps. 20:2; 134:4*

vj. **Cantor** **All**

AL- LE- LU- IA. Al- le- lu- ia.

Cantor **Choir**

℣. The LORD send you help from the sanc-tu-a-ry: and

All

strengthen you out of Si-on. Al le- lu- ia.

In Eastertide the Gradual is omitted and the following is added:

Cantor **Choir**

℣. The LORD that made heaven and earth: give you

All

blessing out of Si-on. Al - le- lu- ia.

714

Holy Matrimony

During Pre-Lent and Lent, the following is said in place of the Alleluia:

TRACT *Ecce sic benedicétur*   *Ps. 128:5,6,7*

Cantor

LO thus shall the man be bles-sed: that feareth the LORD.

Choir

℣. The LORD from out of Sion shall so bless thee: that

thou shalt see Jerusalem in prosperity all thy life long.

Cantor   *Full*

℣. Yea, thou shalt see thy children's child-ren: and peace

upon Is-ra-el.

OFFERTORY *In te sperávi*   *(Holy Family, p. 65)*

COMMUNION *Beáti mundo corde*   *(Nov 1, All Saints, p. 621)*

INTROIT *Deus Israel*   *Tob. 7:8; Ps. 128:1*

Cantor

vij.

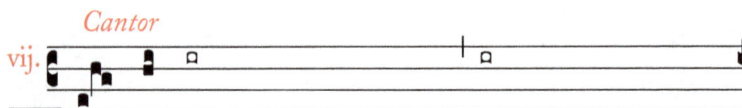

THE God of Israel make you one, and may he be with you

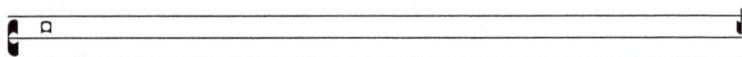

even as he had mercy of two that were the only begotten of

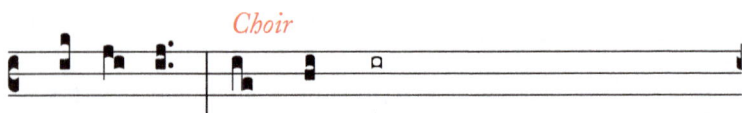

Choir

their fa-thers: grant them mercy, O LORD, and finish their

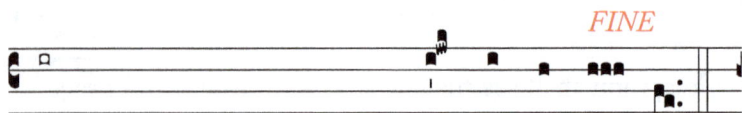

FINE

life   in health with joy.
(*or* life in health with joy. Allelu-ia.   Al- le- lu-   ia.)

Cantor   *Choir*

Ps. Bles-sed are all they that fear the LORD: and walk in

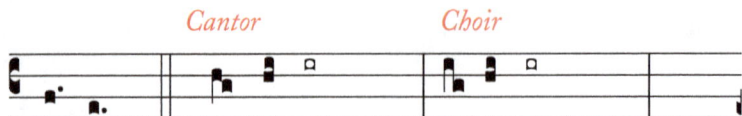

Cantor   *Choir*

his ways.   Glo- ry   be..., *(etc.)* As it was..., *(etc.)*

Full

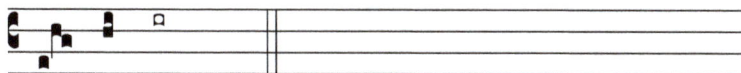

The God of..., *(etc.)*

GRADUAL *Uxor tua*   *Ps. 128:3,4*

Cantor   *Choir*

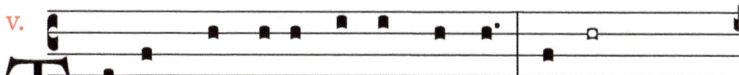

THY wife shall be as the fruit-ful vine: up-on the

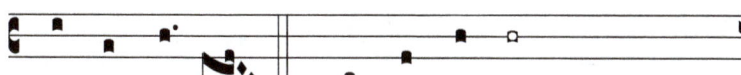

walls of thy house. ℣. Thy child-ren like the olive-

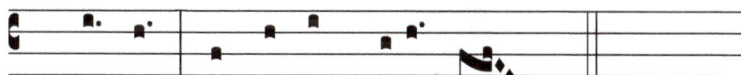

branch-es: round a-bout thy ta- ble.

ALLELUIA *Mittat vobis (supra, p. 714)*

TRACT *Ecce sic benedicétur (supra, p. 715)*

OFFERTORY *In te sperávi (Holy Family, p. 65)*

COMMUNION *Ecce sic benedicétur* Ps. 128:5,7

Cantor

i.

LO, thus shall the man be blessed that fear-eth the LORD:

Choir

yea, thou shalt see thy children's children,

and peace up-on Is- ra- el.
(*or* and peace upon Is-ra- el. Al- le- lu- ia.)

Psalm 128:1-4,6, *may be sung.*

VOTIVE MASSES

Votive Mass of the Most Holy Trinity

Introit *Benedícta sit* *(Trinity Sunday, p. 379)*

Gradual *Benedíctus es* *(Trinity Sunday, p. 380)*

Alleluia *Benedíctus es* *(Trinity Sunday, p. 380)*

During Pre-Lent and Lent, the following is said in place of the Alleluia:

Tract *Te Deum Patrem*

Cantor

viij.

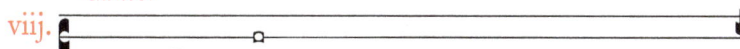

WITH our whole heart we confess thee, we praise and

Choir

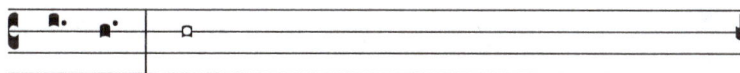

bless thee: O God the Father unbegotten, O Only

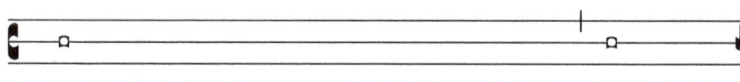

Begotten Son, O Holy Ghost the Comforter, holy

Cantor

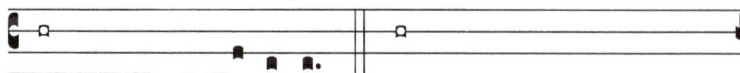

and undivided Tri-ni-ty. ℣. For thou art great, and dost

Choir *Cantor*

wondrous things: thou art God a-lone. ℣. Thine be the

Full

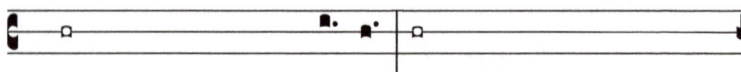

praise, and thine the glo-ry: and thine the thanksgiving,

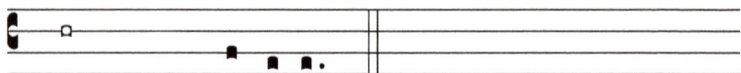

O everlasting Tri-ni-ty.

or in Eastertide ALLELUIA *Benedíctus es, Dómine* *Dn. 3:52*

Cantor *All*

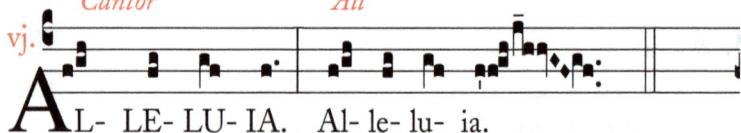

vj. AL- LE- LU- IA. Al- le- lu- ia.

Cantor

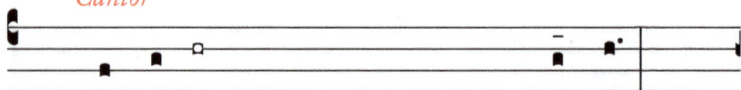

℣. Bless-ed art thou, O Lord God of our fa-thers:

Choir *All*

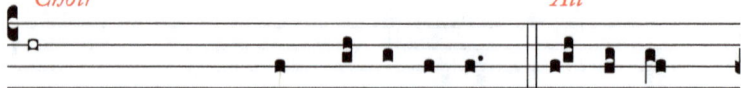

and worthy to be praised for ev-er-more. Al - le- lu-

Cantor

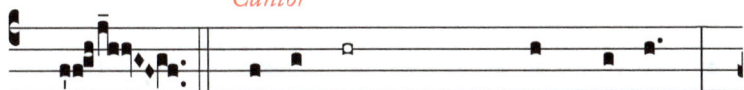

ia. ℣. Let us bless the Father, and the Son,

Choir   *All*

with the Ho-ly Ghost.   Al- le- lu- ia.

OFFERTORY *Benedíctus sit* *(Trinity Sunday, p. 381)*
COMMUNION *Benedícimus Deum* *(Trinity Sunday, p. 382)*

Votive Mass of the Most Holy Eucharist

INTROIT *Cibavit eos* *(Corpus Christi, p. 477)*

GRADUAL *Oculi ómnium* *(Corpus Christi, p. 478)*

ALLELUIA *Caro mea vere* *(Corpus Christi, p. 478)*

TRACT *Ab ortu solis* *(Maundy Thursday, p. 244)*
or in Eastertide
ALLELUIA *Cognovérunt discípuli*   Lk. 24:35; Jn. 6:56,57

Cantor   *All*

vj.

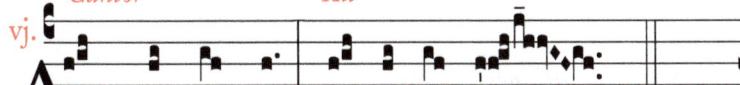

AL- LE- LU- IA.   Al- le- lu- ia.

Cantor   *Choir*

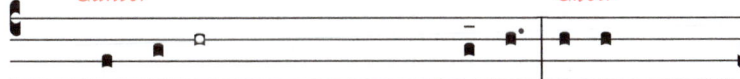

℣. The dis-ci-ples knew the Lord Je-sus: in the

All

break-ing of the bread. Al - le- lu-

Cantor

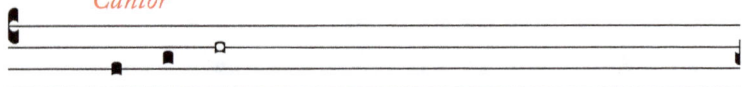

℣. My Flesh is meat indeed, and my Blood is drink

Choir

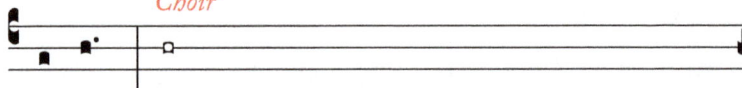

in-deed: he that eateth my Flesh and drinketh my Blood,

All

dwelleth in me, and I in him.   Al- le- lu- ia.

OFFERTORY *Portas cæli (Corpus Christi, p. 487)*

COMMUNION *Qui manducat (Corpus Christi, p. 488)*

Votive Mass of the Most Sacred Heart

INTROIT *Cogitationes (Sacred Heart, p. 489)*

GRADUAL *Dulcis et rectus (Sacred Heart, p. 490)*

ALLELUIA *Tollite iugum (Sacred Heart, p. 490)*

VOTIVE MASSES

During Pre-Lent and Lent, the following is said in place of the Alleluia:
TRACT *Miséricors*   Ps. *103:8,9,10*

Cantor

viij.

THE LORD is full of compassion and mer-cy: long-

Choir

suffering and of great good-ness. ℣. He will not always be

Cantor

chid-ing: neither keepeth he anger for ev-er.   ℣. He hath

Full

not dealt with us after our sins: nor regarded us according

to our wick-ed-nes-ses.

or in Eastertide

ALLELUIA *Tollite iugum*   Mt. *11:29,28*

Cantor   *All*

vj.

AL- LE- LU- IA.   Al- le- lu- ia.

723

Cantor

℣. Take my yoke upon you and learn of me, for I am

Choir

meek and lowly of heart: and ye shall find rest un-to your

All　　　　　　　　　　*Cantor*

souls. Al - le- lu- ia.　　℣. Come un-to me all ye

Choir

that labour and are heavy la-den: and I will give you rest.

All

Al- le- lu- ia.

OFFERTORY *Impropérium (Palm Sunday, p. 232)*

or P.T. OF. *Holocáustum*　　　　　　　　Ps. 40:9,10

Cantor

ij.

BURNT-of-fer-ings and sacrifice for sin hast thou not

Choir

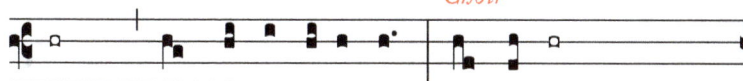

required: then said I, Lo, I come;   in the volume of the

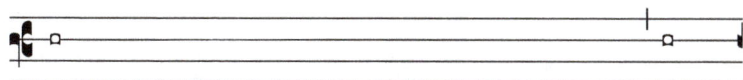

book it is written of me that I should fulfil thy will; O my

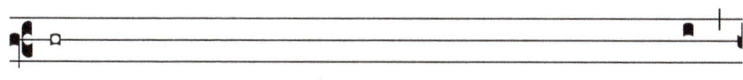

God, I am content to do it, yea thy law is within my heart.

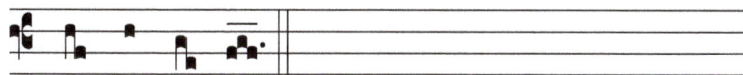

Al- le- lu- ia.

COMMUNION *Unus mílitum* *(Sacred Heart, p. 491)*

Votive Mass of our Lord Jesus Christ
Supreme and Eternal High Priest

INTROIT *Iurávit Dóminus*   *Ps. 110:4,1*

Cantor   *Choir*

vij.

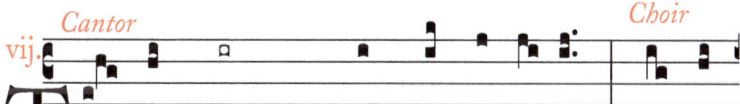

HE LORD hath sworn, and will not re-pent: Thou art

FINE

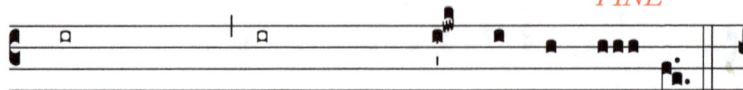

a Priest for ever, after the order of Mel-chi- se- dech.
(or Melchisedech. al- le- lu- ia, al - le- lu- ia.)

Cantor *Choir*

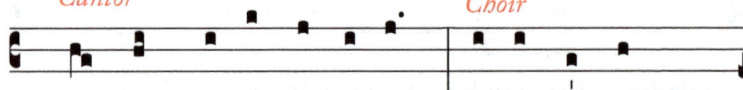

Ps. The LORD said un-to my Lord: Sit thou on my

Cantor *Choir*

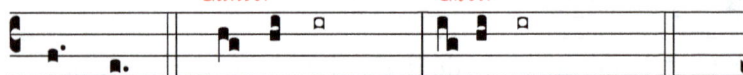

right hand. Glo- ry be *(etc.)* As it was...., *(etc.)*

Full

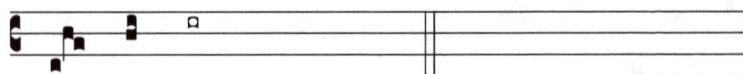

The LORD hath sworn,..., *(etc.)*

GRADUAL *Spíritus Dómini*   *Lk. 4:18*

Cantor

v.

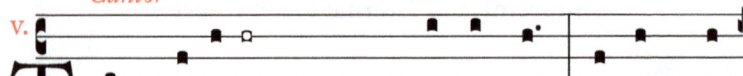

THE Spir-it of the LORD is up-on me: be-cause he

Choir

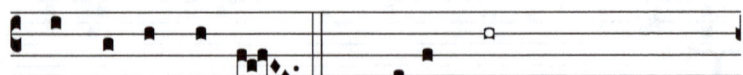

hath an-oint-ed me. ℣. He hath sent me to preach

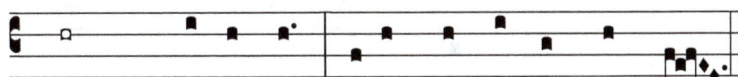

the Gospel to the poor: to heal the bro-ken-heart-ed.

ALLELUIA *Iesus autem eo*   *Heb. 7:24; Lk. 4:18*

vj.

Cantor   *All*

AL- LE- LU- IA.   Al- le- lu- ia.

Cantor   *Choir*

℣. But Je-sus, because he continueth ev-er: hath an un-

All

change-a-ble priest-hood. Al - le- lu- ia.

During Eastertide the Gradual is omitted and the following is added:

Cantor

℣. The Spi-rit of the LORD is upon me, because he hath

Choir

anointed me to preach the Gospel to the poor: he hath

727

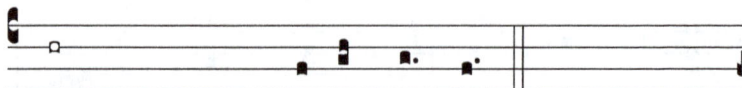

sent me to heal the bro-ken-heart-ed.

All

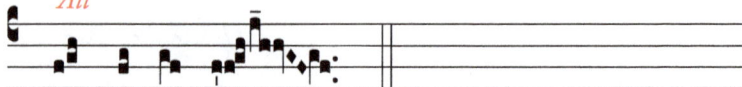

Al - le- lu- ia.

During Pre-Lent and Lent, the following is said in place of the Alleluia:
TRACT *Exsúrge, Dómine Deus* Ps. 10:13,15,16

Cantor

viij.
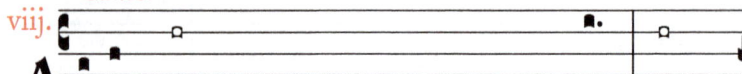

A-RISE, O LORD God, and lift up thine hand: forget

Choir

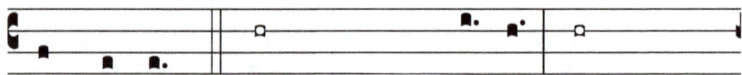

not the poor.. ℣. Surely thou hast seen it: for thou be-

Cantor

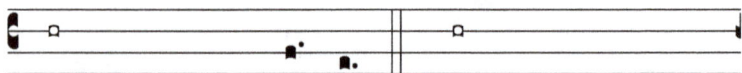

holdest trouble and sor-row. ℣. The poor committeth him-

Full

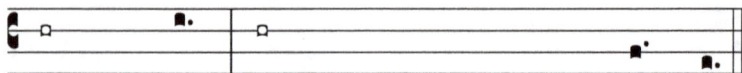

self unto thee: for thou art the helper of the friend-less.

728

OFFERTORY *Christus unam*   *Heb. 10:12,14*

Cantor

ij.

CHRIST, aft-er he had offered one sacrifice for sins

Choir

for ever, sat down on the right hand of God: for by one of-

fering he hath perfected for ever them that are sanc-ti-fi-ed.

(*or* that are sancti-fied. Al- le- lu- ia.)

COMMUNION. *Hoc corpus*   *I Cor. 11:24, 25*

Cantor

i.

THIS is my Body, which is broken for you; this cup is

Choir

the new co-ve-nant in my Blood: this do ye, as oft

as ye drink it, in re-   mem- brance of me.
(*or* in remembrance of me. Al-   le- lu- ia.

Verses from Psalm 23 *or* 116:10-16 *may be sung.*

Votive Mass of the Holy Cross

INTROIT *Nos autem gloriári (Maundy Thursday, p. 243)*

GRADUAL *Christus factus est (Good Friday, p. 256)*

ALLELUIA *Dulce lignum (Holy Cross, p. 600)*

During Pre-Lent and Lent, the following is said in place of the Alleluia:
TRACT *Adorámus te, Christe*

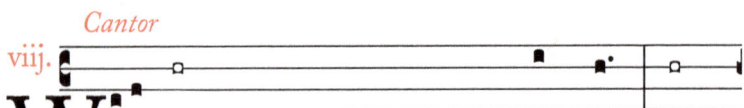

Cantor

viij.

WE a-dore thee, O Christ, and we bless thee: because

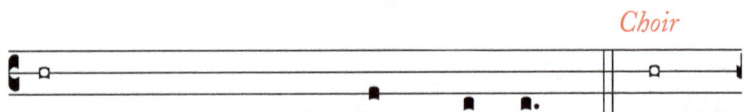

Choir

by thy Cross thou hast re-deemed the world. ℣. We adore

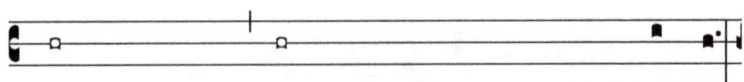

thy Cross, O Lord, we commemorate thy glorious Pas-sion:

730

(musical notation)

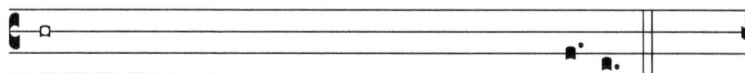

have mercy upon us, thou who didst suffer for us.

Cantor

(musical notation)

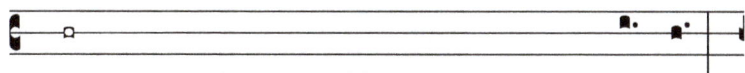

℣. O blessed Cross, which alone wast counted wor-thy:

Full

(musical notation)

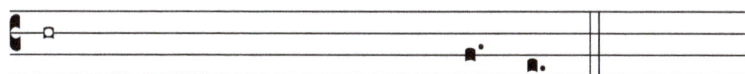

to sustain the King of Heaven and its Lord.

or in Eastertide:

Alleluia *Dícite in géntibus*   *Cf. Ps. 96:10*

(musical notation)

vj.

A̱L- LE- LU- IA.   Al- le- lu- ia.

Cantor   *Choir*

(musical notation)

℣. Tell it out among the hea-then: that the Lord hath

All

(musical notation)

reign-ed from the Tree.   Al - le- lu- ia.

Cantor

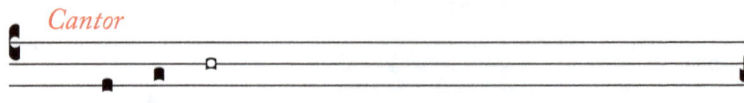

℣. Sweet-est wood, sweetest iron, that bare so sweet a

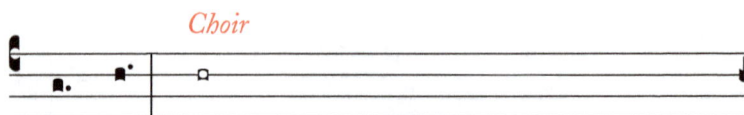

Choir

Bur-den: which only was counted worthy to sustain the

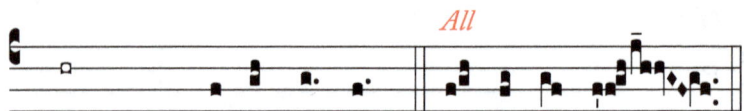

All

King of hea-ven and its LORD.   Al- le- lu- ia.

OFFERTORY *Prótege, Dómine* *(Holy Cross, p. 601)*

COMMUNION *Per signum crucis*

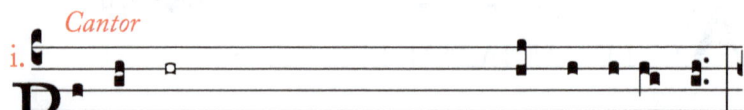

Cantor

i.

BY the sign of the Cross, deliver us from our e-ne-mies:

Choir

O LORD our God.   *or* O LORD our God. Al- le- lu- ia.

Psalm 18:1-3,18,38,39,41,48-50 *may be sung.*

Votive Mass of the Five Wounds

INTROIT *Humiliávit*   *Phil. 2:5,6, Ps. 89:1*

Cantor

vij.

THE LORD Jesus Christ humbled himself unto death,

Choir

even the death of the Cross: where-fore God also hath

highly exalted him, and given him a Name which is

FINE

above   e-   ver-   y   name.
(*or* above every name. allelu-ia,   al - le-   lu- ia.)

Cantor

Ps. My song shall be alway of the loving-kind-ness of the LORD:

Choir   *Cantor*

from one generation to an-o-ther.   Glo- ry be *(etc.)*

733

Choir   *Full*

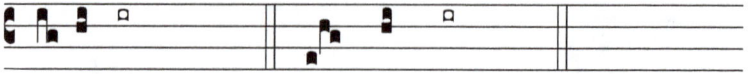

As it was...., *(etc.)*   The LORD Jesus..., *(etc.)*

GRADUAL *Impropérium*   *Ps.69:21,22*

Cantor

℣.

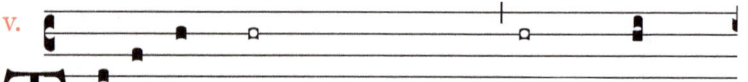

THY re-buke hath broken my heart; I am full of

Choir

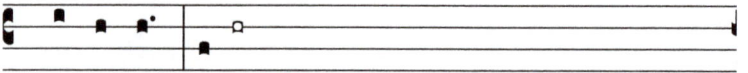

hea-vi-ness: I looked for some to have pity on me, but

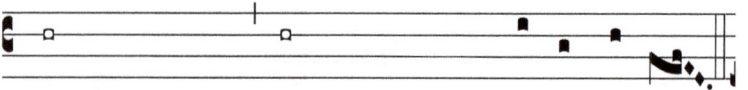

there was no man, neither found I any to com-fort me.

Cantor   *Choir*

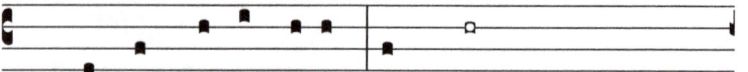

℣. They gave me gall to eat: and when I was thirsty,

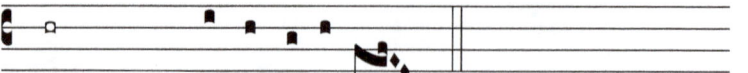

they gave me vin-e-gar to drink.

ALLELUIA *Ave, Rex noster*

Cantor *All*

vj.

AL- LE- LU- IA. Al- le- lu- ia.

Cantor

℣. Hail, our King, Jesus Christ, who alone didst pity our

Choir

sins and trans-gres-sions: in obedience to the Father,

thou wast led to the Cross, even as a meek lamb to the

All

slaugh-ter. Al - le- lu- ia.

During Eastertide the Gradual is omitted and the following is added:

Cantor *Choir*

℣. To thee be glory, ho-san-na: to thee the crown of

All

highest praise and hon-our.   Al - le- lu- ia.

During Pre-Lent and Lent, the following is said in place of the Alleluia:

TRACT *Iudica me*   *Ps. 43:1,2; 35:11; 129:3; 22:17b,18*

Cantor

viij.

GIVE sen-tence with me, O God,   and defend my

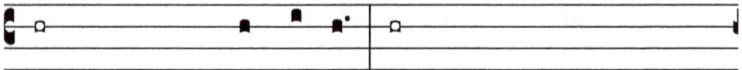

cause against the un-god-ly: O deliver me from the

Choir

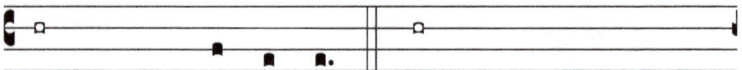

deceitful and wick-ed man. ℣. For thou art the God of

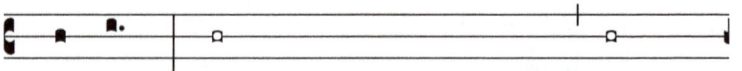

my strength: why hast thou put me from thee? and why go

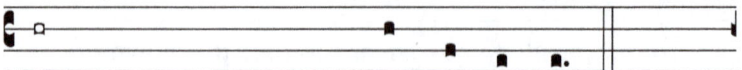

I so heavily, while the enemy op-pres-seth me?

Cantor

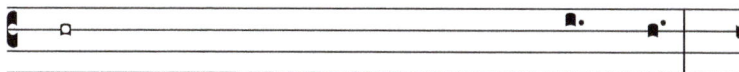

℣. For there are false witnesses risen up a-gainst me:

Choir

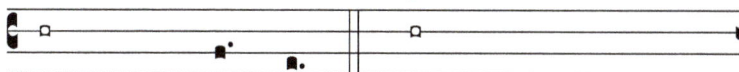

and such as speak wrong. ℣. The ploughers ploughed

Choir

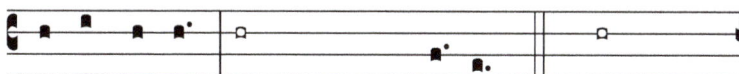

up-on my back: and made long fu-rows ℣. They stand

Full

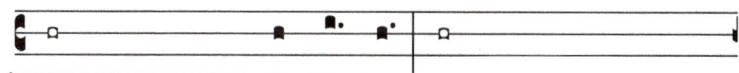

staring and looking up-on me: they part my garments

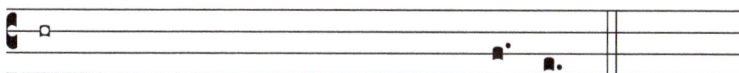

among them; and cast lots upon my ves-ture.

OFFERTORY *Surgentes testes iniqui*　　*Cf. Ps. 35:11; 22:17*

Cantor

ij.

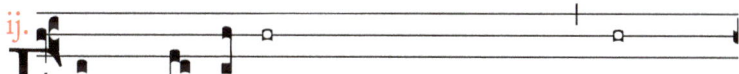

FALSE wit-nes-ses did rise up against me;　without

Choir

mercy they have sought to slay me: and they spared not

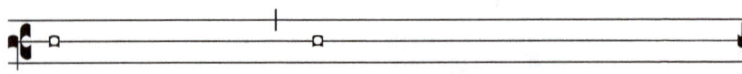

to spit upon my face; with their lances they wounded me,

and all my bones have been out of joint.

(or out of joint. Al- le- lu- ia.)

COMMUNION *Fodérunt manus meas*

Cantor   *Choir*

i.

THEY pierc-ed my hands and my feet: I may tell all

my bones.   *or* I may tell all my bones. Al- le- lu- ia.

Psalm 22:12-16,18 *may be sung.*

Votive Mass of the Holy Spirit

INTROIT *Spíritus Dóminii (Whitsunday, p. 366)*

GRADUAL *Beáta gens (Trinity XVII, p. 441)*

ALLELUIA *Veni Sancte Spíritus*

AL- LE- LU- IA.   Al- le- lu- ia.

℣. Come, Ho-ly Ghost, and fill the hearts of thy faithful

peo-ple: and kindle in them the fire of thy love.

Al - le- lu- ia.

During Pre-Lent and Lent, the following is said in place of the Alleluia:

TRACT *Emítte Spíritum*   *Ps. 104:30; Ws. 12:1*

O SEND forth thy Spirit, and they shall be made:

Choir

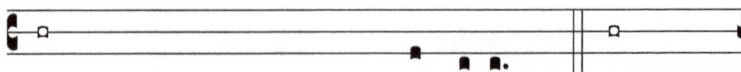

and thou shalt renew the face of the earth. ℣. O how

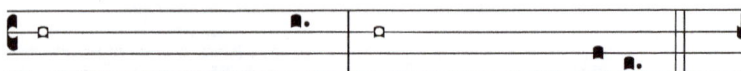

good and sweet, O Lord: is thy Spirit with-in us.

Cantor

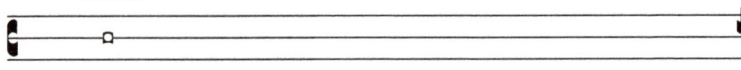

℣. Come, Holy Ghost, and fill the hearts of thy faithful

Full

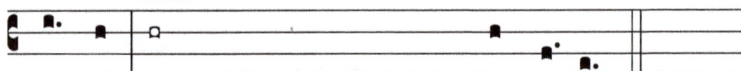

peo-ple: and kindle in them the fire of thy love.

or in Eastertide: AL. *Emítte Spiritum (Whitsunday, p. 367)*

OFFERTORY *Confírma hoc (Whitsunday, p. 370)*

COMMUNION *Factus est repénte (Whitsunday, p. 371)*

Votive Mass of the Holy Angels

INTROIT *Benedícite Dóminum*   *Ps. 103:20,1*

Cantor

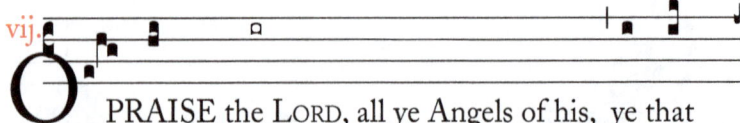

vij.

O PRAISE the Lord, all ye Angels of his, ye that

Choir

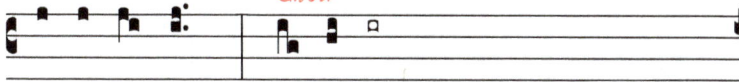

ex-cel in strength: ye that fulfil his commandment,

and hearken unto the   voice   of   his words.
(*or* voice of his words. allelu-ia,   al - le-   lu- ia.)

Cantor   *Choir*

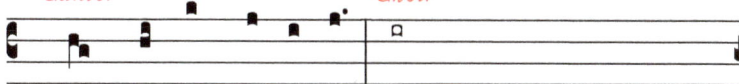

Ps. Praise the LORD, O my soul: and all that is within me

Cantor   *Choir*

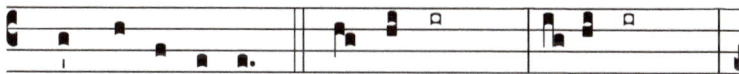

praise his ho-ly Name. Glo- ry be *(etc.)* As it was...., *(etc.)*

Full

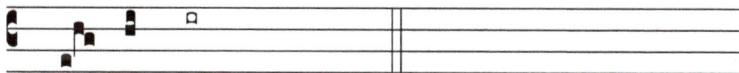

O praise the LORD ..., *(etc.)*

GRADUAL *Laudáte Dóminum*   *Ps. 148:1,2*

Cantor   *Choir*

v.

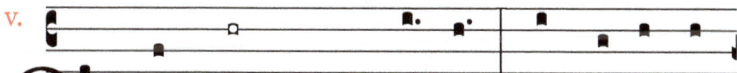

O PRAISE the LORD of hea-ven: praise him in the

Cantor   *Choir*

height. ℣. Praise him all ye Angels of his: praise him all

his host.

ALLELUIA *In conspéctu angelórum*   Ps. 138:1b,2; Mt. 28:2

Cantor   *All*

vj. AL- LE- LU- IA.   Al- le- lu- ia.

Cantor

℣. In the presence of the Angels will I praise thee,

Choir

O LORD my God: I will worship toward thy holy temple,

All

and praise thy Name. Al - le- lu- ia.
During Eastertide the Gradual is ommitted and the following is added:

742

Cantor

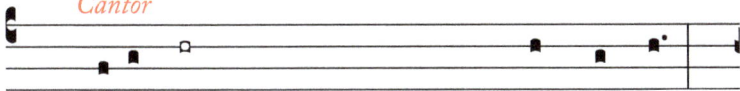

℣. The An-gel of the LORD descended from hea-ven:

Choir

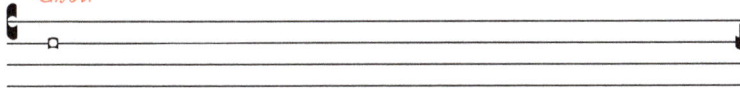

and came and rolled back the stone from the door,

All

and sat up-on it.   Al - le- lu- ia.

During Pre-Lent and Lent, the following is said in place of the Alleluia:
TRACT *Benedícite Dóminum*   *Ps. 103:20,21,22*

Cantor

viij.

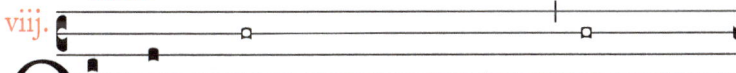

O PRAISE the LORD, ye Angels of his, ye that excel

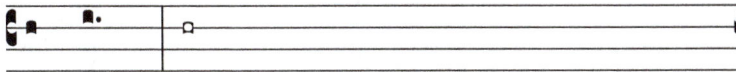

in strength: ye that fulfil his commandment, and hearken

Choir

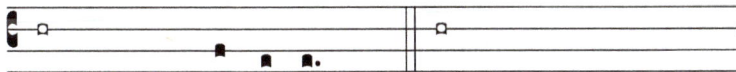

unto the voice of his words.   ℣. O praise the LORD, all ye

743

(musical notation)

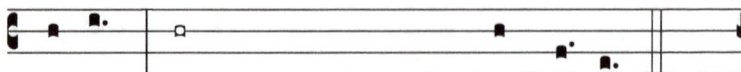

his hosts: ye servants of his, that do his plea-sure.

Cantor   *Full*

(musical notation)

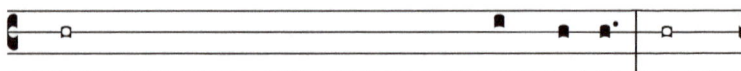

℣. O speak good of the Lord, all ye works of his: in all

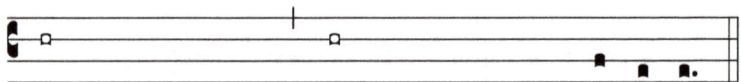

(musical notation)

places of his dominion, praise thou the Lord, O my soul.

Offertory *Stétit ángelus*   *Rev. 8:3,4*

Cantor

ij. *(musical notation)*

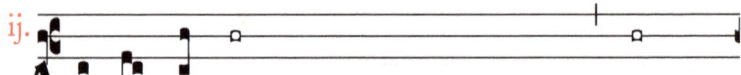

AN An-gel stood by the altar of the temple, having a

Choir

(musical notation)

golden cen-ser in his hand: and there was given unto him

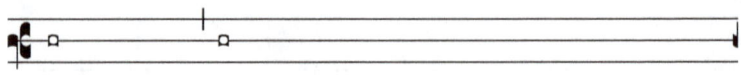

(musical notation)

much incense, and the smoke of

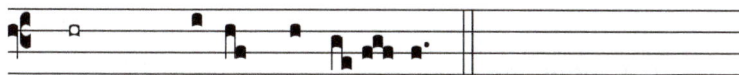

the incense as-cen-ded up to God.

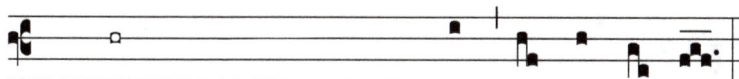

(*or* the incense ascended up to God. Al- le- lu- ia.)

COMMUNION *Angeli, archángeli*

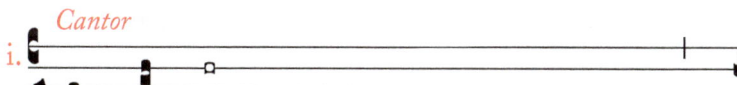

Cantor

i.

AN-GELS, Archangels, Thrones and Dominations,

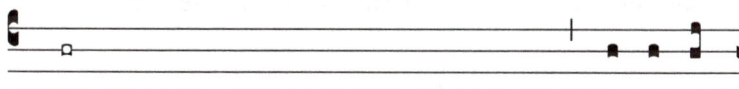

Principalities and Powers, heavenly Virtues, Che-ru-bim

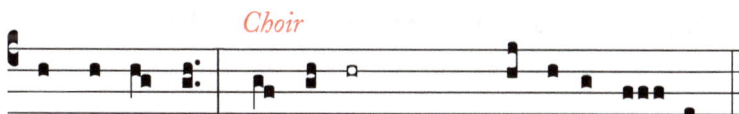

Choir

and Se-ra-phim: bless ye the LORD for ev-er and ev- er.

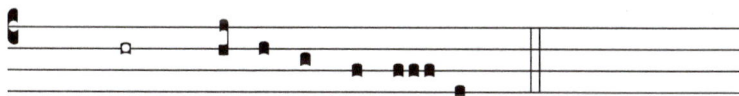

or for ever and ev-er. Al- le- lu- ia.

Verses from the Bendicite *may be sung.*

745

Votive Mass of All Saints

INTROIT *Iudicant sancti*   *Wis. 3:8; Ps. 33:1*

Cantor

vij.

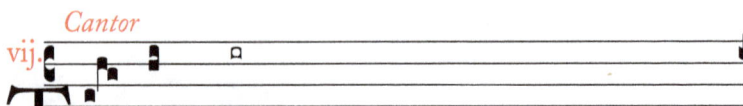

THE Saints shall judge the nations, and have dominion

Choir

ov-er the peo-ple: and the LORD their God shall reign

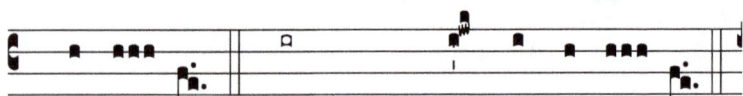

for ev- er. (*or* for ever allelu-ia, al - le - lu- ia.)

Cantor   *Choir*

Ps. Rejoice in the LORD, O ye right-eous: for it becometh well

Cantor   *Choir*

the just to be thank-ful. Glo- ry be *(etc.)* As it was...., *(etc.)*

Full

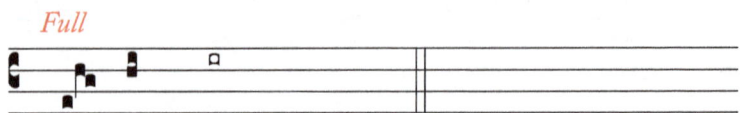

The Saints shall ..., *(etc.)*

VOTIVE MASSES

GRADUAL *Timéte Dóminum (Nov. 1, All Saints, p. 620)*

ALLELUIA *Veníte ad me (Nov. 1, All Saints, p. 620)*

During Pre-Lent and Lent, the following is said in place of the Alleluia:

TRACT *Qui séminant in lácrimas*   *Ps. 126:6,7*

Cantor   *Choir*

viij.

THEY that sow in tears: shall reap in joy. ℣. He that

now goeth on his way weep-ing: and beareth forth

Cantor

good seed. ℣. He shall doubtless come again with joy:

Full

and bring his sheaves with him.

OFFERTORY *Iustórum ánimæ (Nov. 1, All Saints, p. 621)*

COMMUNION *Iustórum ánimæ*   *Wis. 3:1,2,3*

Cantor

i.

THE souls of the righteous are in the hand of God, and

Choir

no tor-ment shall touch them: in the eyes of the foolish

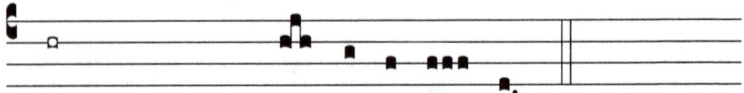

they seemed to die, but they are in   peace.

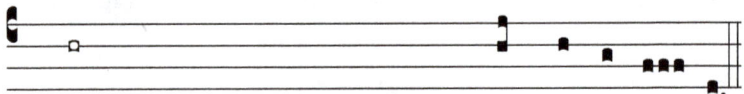

or they seemed to die, but they are in peace. Al- le- lu-   ia.

Canticle Wisd. 3:4-9 *may be sung.*

or Co. *Beáti mundo corde (Nov. 1, All Saints, p. 621)*

Votive Mass of Saint Joseph

INTROIT *Iustus ut palma (Common for Religious, p. 705)*

GRADUAL *Dómine, prævenísti eum (C. for an Abbot, p. 708)*

ALLELUIA *Amávit eum Dóminus (C. Doctors, p. 694)*

TRACT *Beátus vir qui timet (Common of Martyrs p. 657)*

OFFERTORY *Véritas mea (Common of Confessors p. 683)*

COMMUNION *Ioseph fili David*   *Mt. 1:20*

Cantor

i.

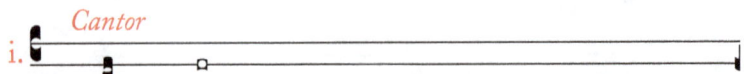

JO-SEPH, thou son of David, fear not to take unto

Choir

thee Ma-ry thy wife: for that which is conceived in her

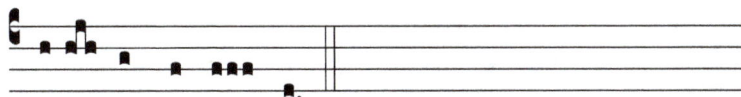

is of the Ho- ly Ghost.

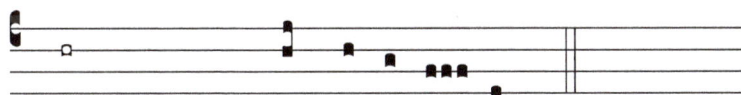

or is of the Holy Ghost. Al- le- lu- ia.

Verses from Psalm 112:1-9 *may be sung.*

Votive Mass of Saint Peter and Saint Paul

INTROIT *Mihi autem nimis (June 11, St. Barnabas, p. 559)*

GRADUAL *Constítues eos príncipes (July 25, St. James, p. 579)*

ALLELUIA *Mihi autem nimis* *Ps. 139:17*

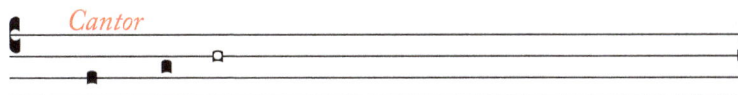

Cantor   *All*

j.

AL- LE- LU- IA. Al- le- lu- ia.

Cantor

℣. Right dear are thy friends unto me, O God, and held

Choir

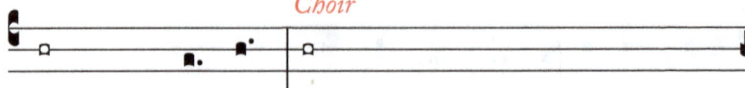

in highest hon-our: their rule and governance is

All

ex-ceed-ing stead-fast. Al - le- lu- ia.

During Pre-Lent and Lent, the following is said in place of the Alleluia:

TRACT *Qui séminant in lácrimas (supra, p. 747)*

OFFERTORY *In omnem terram (Feb. 22, Chair of St. Peter, p. 529)*

COMMUNION *Vos, qui secúti*   *Mt. 19:28*

Cantor

i.

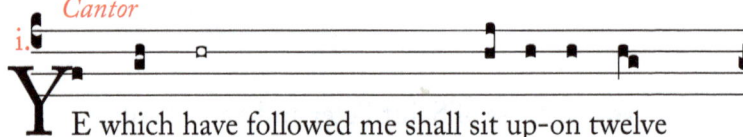

Y E which have followed me shall sit up-on twelve

Choir

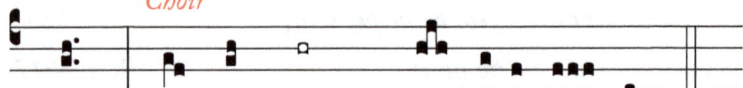

thrones: judg-ing the twelve tribes of Is- ra- el

or the twelve tribes of Isra-el. Al- le- lu- ia.

Verses from Psalm 19:1-6 *may be sung.*

MASSES OF ST. MARY
1. From Advent to Christmas

INTROIT *Roráte, cæli*   *Is. 45:8; Ps. 85:1*

Cantor

vij.

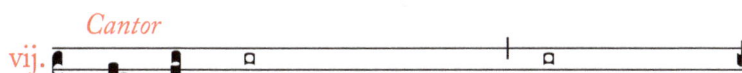

DROP down, ye heavens, from above, and let the skies

Choir

pour down righ - teous - ness: let the earth open,

FINE   *Cantor*

and bring forth a Sa - viour. *Ps.* LORD, thou art become

Choir

gracious un-to thy land: thou hast turned away the cap-

Cantor

ti- vi- ty of Ja- cob.   Glo-ry be *(etc.)*

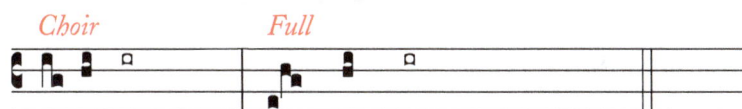

Choir   *Full*

As it was...., *(etc.)* Drop down,ye haevens,..., *(etc.)*

751

GRADUAL *Tóllite portas*   *Ps. 24:7,3,4*

Cantor

℣. LIFT up your heads, O ye gates; and be ye lift up,

Choir

ye e-ver-last-ing doors: and the King of glo-ry shall

Cantor

come in.   ℣. Who shall ascend into the hill of the LORD,

Choir

or who shall stand in his ho- ly place? E-ven he that

hath clean hands, and a pure heart.

or GR. *Benedícta et venerábilis (Common of the BVM, p. 648)*

ALLELUIA *Ave, María (Common of the BVM, p. 648)*

OFFERTORY *Ave María (Common of the BVM, p. 651)*

COMMUNION. *Ecce virgo (Advent IV, p. 38)*

2. From Christmas to Candlemas

Introit *Vultum tuum deprecabúntur*   *Ps. 45:12b,14b,15,1*

Cantor

vij.

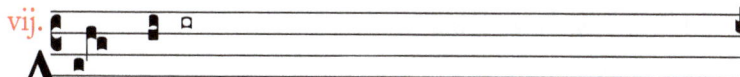

ALL the rich among the people shall make their

Choir

sup-pli-ca-tion be-fore thee: the vir-gins that be her

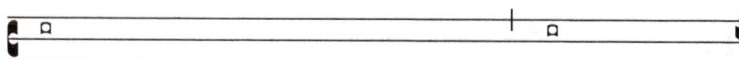

fellows shall be brought unto the King; they that bear

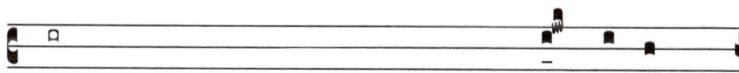

her company shall be brought unto thee with joy and

Cantor

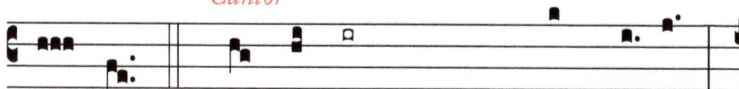

glad-ness. *Ps.* My heart is inditing of a good mat-ter:

Choir

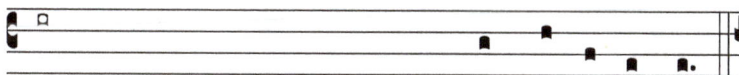

I speak of the things which I have made un-to the King.

Cantor   *Choir*   *Full*

Glo- ry be *(etc.)* As it was...., *(etc.)* All the rich..., *(etc.)*

GRADUAL *Spaciósus forma (Christmas II, p. 73)*

ALLELUIA *Post partum (January 1, p. 69)*

During Pre-Lent and Lent, the following is said in place of the Alleluia:
TRACT *Gaude María (Common of the BVM, p. 649)*

OFFERTORY *Benedícta et venerábilis*   *Cf. Ps. 35:11; 22:17*

Cantor

ij.

BLES-SED art thou, O holy Virgin Mary, and most

Choir

wor-thy of all praise: that bore the Son of the

ev-er-last-ing Fa-ther.

COMMUNION *Beáta víscera (Common of the BVM, p. 651)*

3. From Candlemas to Passiontide

INTROIT *Salve sancta Parens* *(January 1, p. 68)*

GRADUAL *Benedícta et venerábilis* *(Common of the BVM, p. 648)*

ALLELUIA *Virga Iesse* *Num. 17:8b*

Cantor *All*

AL- LE- LU- IA.   Al- le- lu- ia.

℣. Now hath blossomed Jesse's rod; a Virgin bears both

Choir

Man and God: God restoreth peace to men, high and low

All

are one a-gain.   Al- le- lu- ia.

After Septuagesima, the following is said in place of the Alleluia:

TRACT *Gaude María* *(Common of the BVM, p. 649)*

OFFERTORY *Benedícta et venerábilis* *(supra, p. 754)*

COMMUNION *Beáta víscera* *(Common of the BVM, p. 651)*

4. From Easter to Pentecost

INTROIT *Salve sancta Parens* *(January 1, p. 68)*

ALLELUIA *Virga Iesse* *(Common of the BVM, p. 650)*

OFFERTORY *Beáta es, virgo María*

Cantor

ij.

BLES-SED art thou, O Virgin Mary, who didst bear

Choir

the Cre-a-tor of all things: thou brought-est forth him who

made thee, and for ever remainest a Vir-gin. Al-le-lu-ia.

COMMUNION *Beáta víscera* *(Common of the BVM, p. 651)*

5. From Pentecost to Advent

INTROIT *Salve sancta Parens* *(January 1, p. 68)*

GRADUAL *Benedícta et venerábilis* *(Common of the BVM, p. 648)*

ALLELUIA *Post partum* *(January 1, p. 69)*

OFFERTORY *Ave María* *(Common of the BVM, p. 651)*

COMMUNION *Beáta víscera* *(Common of the BVM, p. 651)*

VARIOUS OCCASIONS

In Any Necessity

INTROIT *Salus pópuli* *(Trinity XIX, p. 451)*
or IN. *Exsúrge, quare abdórmis* *(Sexagesima, p. 114)*
GRADUAL *Liberásti nos* *(Trin. XXIII-XXVI, p. 469)*
or GR. *Salvum fac servum tuum* *(Ember Friday in Lent, p. 146)*

ALLELUIA *Propítius esto, Dómine* *Ps. 79:9b,10*

Cantor *All*

AL- LE- LU- IA. Al- le- lu- ia.

Cantor

℣. Be mer-ci-ful unto our sins, O LORD; wherefore do

Choir

the hea-then say: Where is now their God?

All

Al- le- lu- ia.

or AL. *Veníte ad me* *(Nov. 1 All Saints, p. 620)*
or AL. *Dómine, exáudi* *(Trinity XVII, p. 442)*

During Pre–Lent and Lent, the following is said in place of the Alleluia:

TRACT *Miserére mihi*   *Ps. 31:10,11,12*

Have mer-cy upon me, O Lord, for I am in trou-ble:

and mine eye is consumed for very heaviness, yea, my soul

Choir

and my bo-dy. ℣. For my life is waxen old with hea-vi-ness:

Cantor

and my years with mourn-ing. ℣. My strength faileth me

Full

because of mine in- i- qui- ty: and my bones are

con-sum-ed.

or, in Eastertide: AL. *Propítius esto, Dómine Ps. 79:9b,10; 31:8*

Cantor　　　　　　　*All*

AL- LE- LU- IA.　Al- le- lu- ia.

Cantor

℣. Be mer-ci-ful unto our sins, O LORD; wherefore do

Choir　　　　　　　*All*

the hea-then say: Where is now their God?　Al- le- lu-

Cantor

ia.　　　　℣. I will be glad and rejoice in thy mer-cy:

Choir

for thou hast considered my trouble, and hast known my

All

soul in ad-ver-si-ties.　Al- le- lu- ia.

OFFERTORY *Exáudi Deus* *(Monday in Lent III, p. 166)*
or OF. *Si ambulávero* *(Trinity XIX, p. 453)*
or OF. *Dómine Deus salútis* *(Ember Sat. in Lent, p. 149)*

759

COMMUNION *Meménto verbi tui* *(Trinity XX, p. 458)*
or CO. *Petite et accipiétis* *(Rogationtide, p. 341)*

For the Pope or Bishop

Minor Propers may be taken from the Mass In Any Necessity, supra, p.757.

INTROIT *Sacerdótes tui* *(Common of Confessors II, p. 681)*
GRADUAL *Sacerdótes eius* *(Common of Confessors II, p. 682)*

For the Election of the Pope

Minor Propers may be taken from the Votive Mass of the Holy Spirit, p. 739.

For the Priest Himself

Minor Propers may be taken from the Mass In Any Necessity, supra, p.757.

INTROIT *Spíritus Dómini* *(Whitsunday, p. 366)*

For the Propagation of the Faith

Minor Propers may be taken from the Mass In Any Necessity, supra, p.757.

For Christian Unity

INTROIT *Salvos nos fac*   *Ps. 106:45,1*

Cantor

vij.

DE-LI-VER us, O LORD our God, and gather us from

Choir

a-mong the na-tions: that we may give thanks unto thy

holy Name, and make our boast of thy praise. (*or* make

our boast of thy praise, allelu-ia,   al - le- lu-   ia.)

Cantor   *Choir*

Ps. O give thanks un-to the LORD, for he is gra-cious: and

Cantor

his mercy en-dur-eth for e-ver.   Glo- ry be *(etc.)*

761

Choir   *Full*

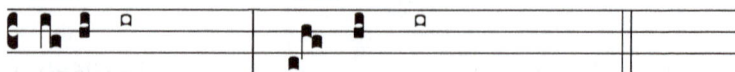

As it was...., *(etc.)*   De- li- ver us,..., *(etc.)*

GRADUAL *Rogáte pacem*   *Ps. 122:6,7*

Cantor   *Choir*

℣.

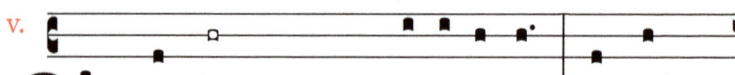

O PRAY for the peace of Je-ru-sa-lem: they shall

Cantor

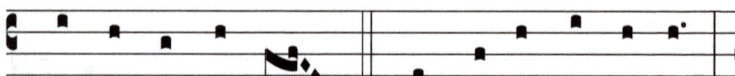

pros-per that love thee.   ℣. Peace be with-in thy walls:

Choir

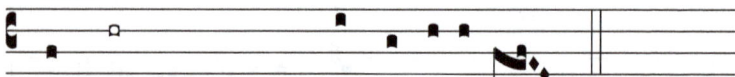

and plenteousness with-in thy pa-la-ces.

ALLELUIA *Lauda, Ierusalem*   *Ps. 147:12*

Cantor   *All*

vj

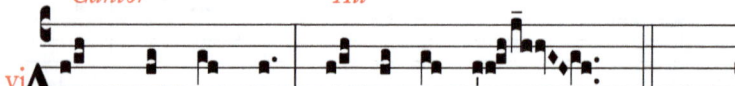

AL- LE- LU- IA.   Al- le- lu- ia.

Cantor   *Choir*

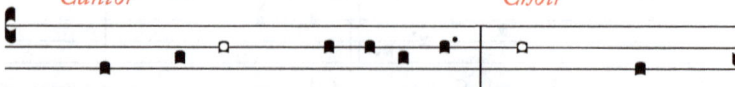

℣. Praise the LORD, O Je-ru-sa-lem: praise thy God,

O Si- on.   Al- le- lu- ia.

During Pre-Lent and Lent, the following is said in place of the Alleluia:

TRACT *Notus in Iudaéa*   *Ps. 76:1,2*

Cantor

viij.

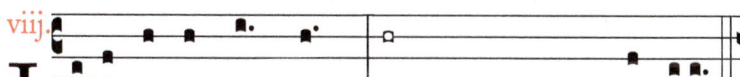

IN Ju-dah is God known: his Name is great in Is-ra-el.

Choir

℣. At Salem is his ta-ber-na-cle: and his dwelling in Si-on.

Cantor   *Full*

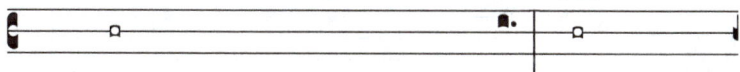

℣. There brake he the arrows of the bow: the shield, the

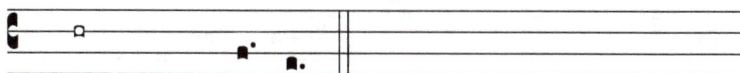

sword, and the bat-tle.

OFFERTORY *Det vobis*   *Rom. 15:5,6*

Cantor

ij.

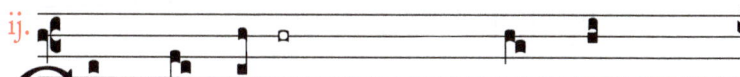

GOD grant you to be like-minded one towards

763

Choir

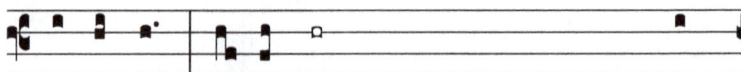

an-o-ther: that ye may with one mind and one mouth

glo- ri- fy God. (*or* that ye may with one mind and one

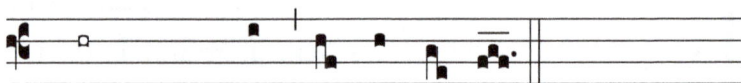

mouth glorify God. Al- le- lu- ia.)

COMMUNION *Unus panis*   *1 Cor 10:17*

Cantor

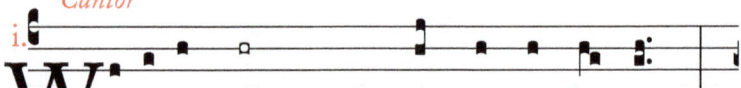

i.

WE be-ing many are one bread, and one bo-dy:

Choir

for we are all partakers of one bread and one cup.

(*or* of one bread and one cup. Al- le- lu- ia.)

Verses from Psalm 23 *may be sung.*

VARIOUS OCCASIONS
For the Sick

Minor Propers may be taken from the Mass In Any Necessity, supra, p.757.

For the Pilgrims or Travellers

Minor Propers may be taken from the Mass In Any Necessity, supra, p.757.

In Thanksgiving for the Gift of Human Life

Minor Propers may be taken from the Mass In Any Necessity, supra, p.757.

For the Blessing of Human Labour
(also for Labour Day)

Minor Propers may be taken from the Mass In Any Necessity, supra, p.757.

INTROIT *Sapiéntia reddídit*　　　　　　　*Wis. 10:17; Ps. 127:1*

Cantor

WIS-DOM rendered to the just the wages of their

labours and conducted them in a won-der-ful way:

Choir

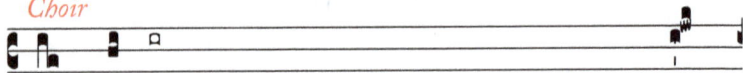

and she was to them for a covert by day and for the light

FINE   *Cantor*

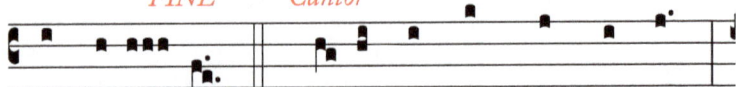

of stars by night. *Ps.* Ex-cept the LORD build the house:

Choir   *Cantor*

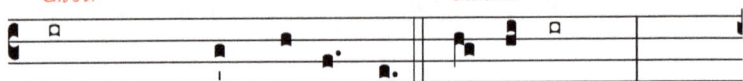

they labour in vain that build it.   Glo- ry be *(etc.)*

Choir   *Full*

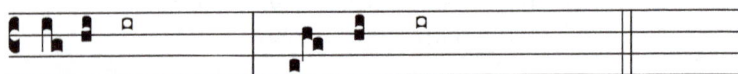

As it was...., *(etc.)*   Wis-dom rendered..., *(etc.)*

GRADUAL *Beátus quicumque*   *Ps. 128:1,2*

Cantor   *Choir*

v.

BLES-SED are all they that fear the LORD: that walk

Cantor

in his ways.   ℣. Thou shalt eat the labours of thy hands:

Choir

it shall be well with thee.

In Thanksgiving for the Blessings of Harvest

Minor Propers may be taken from the Mass In Any Necessity, supra, p.757.

INTROIT *Cibavit eos (Corpus Christi, p. 477)*

In The Nation
(For Civic Observances)

Minor Propers may be taken from the Mass In Any Necessity, supra, p.757.

In Time of War or Civil Disturbance

Minor Propers may be taken from the Mass In Any Necessity, supra, p.757.

INTROIT *Reminíscere (Ember Weds, in Lent, p. 141)*
ALLELUIA *Qui pósuit*   *Ps. 148:3*

AL- LE- LU- IA. Al- le- lu- ia.

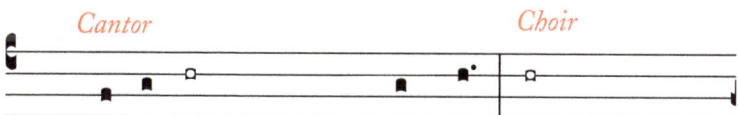

℣. He ma-keth peace in thy bor-ders: and filleth thee

767

All

with the flour of wheat.   Al- le- lu- ia.

OLSC

26 January Australia Day

INTROIT *Confitébor tibi*   *Ps. 57:10,11*

Cantor

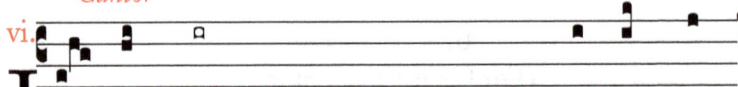

vi.

I WILL give thanks unto thee, O LORD, a-mong the

Choir   *FINE*

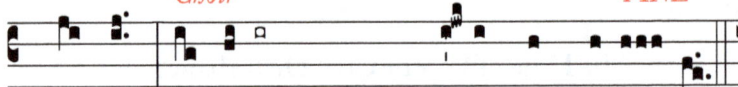

peo-ples: and I will sing unto thee a-mong the na-tions.

Cantor

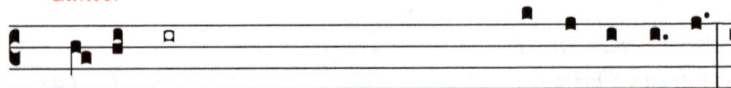

Ps. For the greatness of thy mercy reacheth un-to the hea-vens:

Choir   *Cantor*

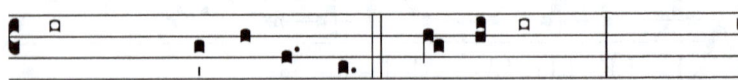

and thy truth un-to the clouds. Glo- ry be *(etc.)*

Choir   *Full*

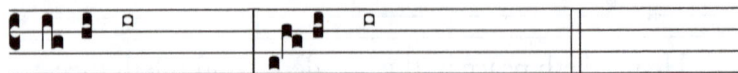

As it was...., *(etc.)*   I will give thanks..., *(etc.)*

VARIOUS OCCASIONS

GRADUAL *Benedícam Dóminum* (*Trinity XII, p. 424*)

ALLELUIA *Exsultábo et lætábor* Ps. 31:8

Cantor *All*

AL- LE- LU- IA. Al- le- lu- ia.

Cantor *Choir*

℣. I will be glad and rejoice in thy mer-cy: for thou

hast considered my trouble, and hast known my soul in

All

ad-ver-si-ties. Al- le- lu- ia.

OFFERTORY *Bénedic, ánima mea* (*Christmas II, p. 74*)

COMMUNION *Tóllite hóstias* (*Trinity XVIII, p. 450*)

CSP
Thanksgiving Day

Minor Propers may be taken from the Mass In Any Necessity, supra, p.757.

GRADUAL *Oculi ómnium* (*Corpus Christi, p. 478*)

Remembrance Day, Memorial Day, Anzac Day

Minor Propers may be taken from Masses for the Dead, below

FOR THE DEPARTED
1. For The Funeral

INTROIT *Requiem ætérnam*   *IV Esd. 2:34–35; Ps.65:1,2*

Cantors

vij.

REST e - ter - nal grant un - to them, O LORD:

Choir   *FINE*

and let light per - pe - tu - al shine up - on   them.

Cantors   *Choir*

Ps. Thou, O God, art praised in Si - on,   and unto thee

shall the vow be performed in Je - ru - sa - lem:

Cantors   *Choir*

Thou that hear - est the prayer, un - to thee shall all flesh

Full

come.   Rest e - ter - nal ..., *(etc.)*

770

MASSES FOR THE DEAD

GRADUAL *Requiem ætérnam*   *IV Esd. 2:34–35; Ps.112:6,7*

Cantors   *Choir*

REST e - ternal grant to them, O Lord: and let light

Cantors

perpetual shine up - on them. ℣. The righ - teous shall be

Choir

had in everlasting re - mem - brance: he will not be

afraid of any e- vil tid - ings.

or GR. *Si ambulem (Saturday, Lent III, p. 175)*

771

MASSES FOR THE DEAD

If desired an optional **Alleluia** *may be used except during the season of Lent:*

ALLELUIA *De profúndis (Trinity XXIII–XXVI, p. 470)*

or AL. *In éxitu (Trinity XXI, p. 461)*

or AL. *Lætatus sum (Advent II, p. 23)*

or AL. *Requiem ætérnam*   *IV Esd. 2:34-35*

Cantors / All

AL- LE- LU- IA.   Al- le- lu- ia.

Cantors / Choir

℣. Rest e-ter-nal grant to them, O LORD: and let light

perpetual shine up-on them.   Al- le- lu- ia.

or for priests and religious: AL. *Ego vos elegi (May 13, St. Matthew, p. 549)*

MASSES FOR THE DEAD

TRACT *Absólve Dómine*

Cantors

viij

AB - SOLVE, O Lord, the souls of all the faithful de-

Choir

par - ted: from every bond of sin. ℣. And by the succour

of thy grace: may they be found worthy to escape the

Cantors

avenging judge-ment. ℣. And enjoy the bliss:

Full

of ever- last - ing light.

or TR. *De profúndis*   *Ps 130:1-5*

Cantors

viij.

OUT of the deep have I called unto thee, O LORD:

773

MASSES FOR THE DEAD

Choir

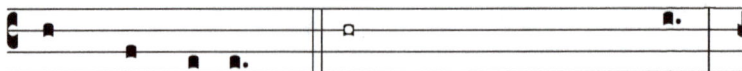

Lord, hear my voice. ℣. O let thine ears consider well:

Cantors

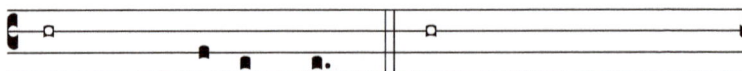

the voice of my com-plaint. ℣. If thou, LORD, wilt be

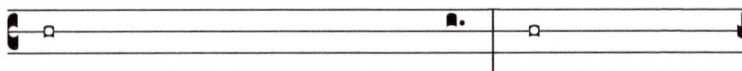

extreme to mark what is done a-miss: O Lord, who may

Choir

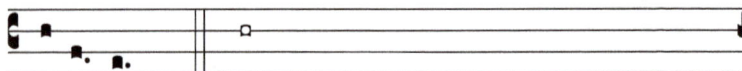

a-bide it? ℣. For to thee belongeth mercy and

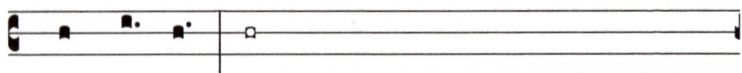

com-pas-sion: and for thy Name's sake have I waited

for thee, O God.

MASSES FOR THE DEAD

i.

1. Day   of wrath and doom im- pend-ing
7. What   shall I, frail man, be plead- ing?
13. Through the   sin-ful   wo- man shriv- en,

Da-   vid's word with Si- byl's blend-ing!
Who   for   me   be in- ter- ced- ing,
Through the   dy- ing thief for- giv- en,

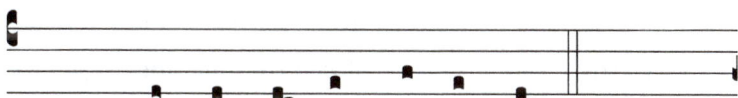

Heaven and earth in ash- es end-ing!
When the   just are mer- cy need-ing?
Thou   in me   a   hope hast giv- en.

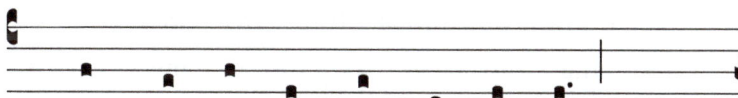

2.   O, what fear man's bo- som ren- deth,
8. King   of ma- jes- ty   tre- men-dous,
14. Worth- less are my prayers and sigh- ing,

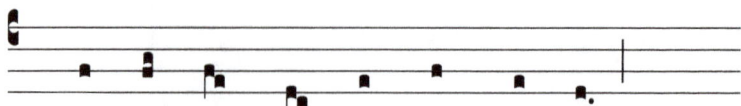

When from heav'n the Judge de- scend-eth,
Who dost free sal- va- tion send us
Yet good Lord, in grace com-ply- ing,

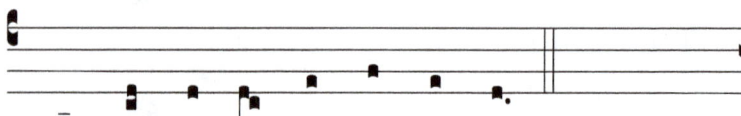

On Whose sen-tence all de- pend- eth!
Fount of pi- ty, then be- friend us!
Res- cue me from fires un-dy- ing.

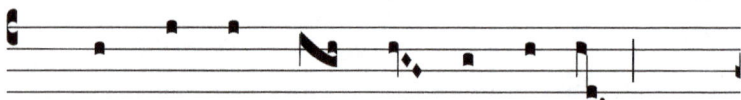

3. Won-drous sound the trum-pet fling-eth,
9. Think, kind Je- su! — my sal- va- tion
15. With thy sheep a place pro- vide me,

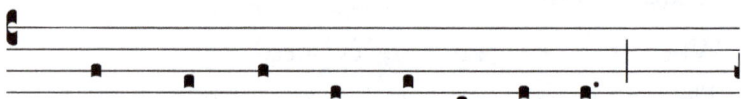

Through earth's se- pul-chres it ring- eth,
Caused thy won-drous In-car- na- tion;
From the goats a- far di- vide me,

MASSES FOR THE DEAD

All be-fore the throne it bring- eth.

Leave me not to re-pro- ba- tion.

To thy right hand do thou guide me.

4. Death is struck, and na- ture quak- ing,

10. Faint and wea- ry thou hast sought me,

16. When the wick- ed are con- found- ed,

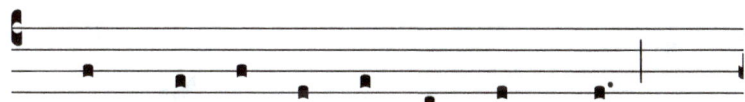

All cre- a- tion is a- wak- ing,

On the Cross of suff-'ring bought me;

Doom'd to shame and woe un- bound- ed,

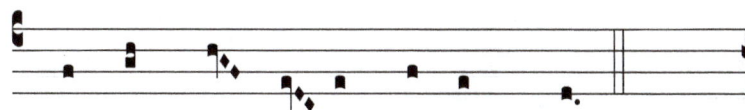

To its Judge an an-swer mak- ing.

Shall such grace be vain- ly brought me?

Call me, with thy Saints sur-round- ed.

5. Lo! the book ex- act- ly word-ed,
11. Right-eous Judge! for sin's pol- lu- tion
17. Low I kneel, with heart sub-mis- sion

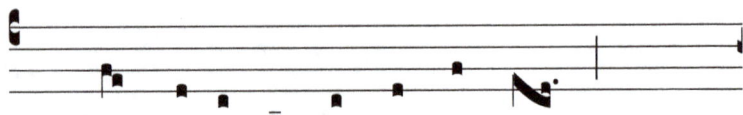

Where- in all hath been re- cord-ed;
Grant thy gift of ab- so- lu- tion,
See, like ash-es my con-tri- tion!

Thence shall judge- ment be a- ward-ed.
Ere that day of re- tri- bu- tion.
Help me in my last con-di- tion!

(to v. 18 below).

6. When the Judge his seat at-tain- eth,
12. Guil- ty, now I pour my moan- ing,

And each hid- den deed ar- raign-eth,
All my shame with an-guish own-ing;

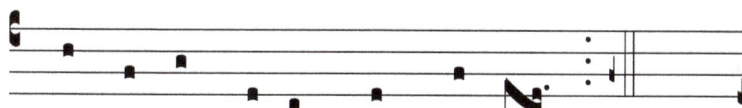

Noth- ing un- a-veng'd re- main-eth.
Spare, O God, thy sup- pliant groan-ing!

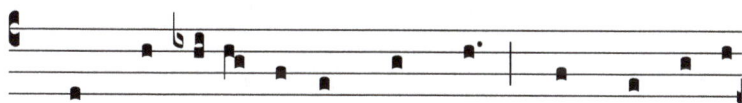

18. Ah! that day of tears and mourn-ing! From the dust of

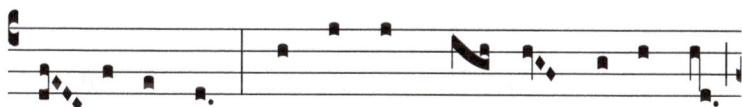

earth re-turn-ing, Man for judge-ment must pre-pare him:

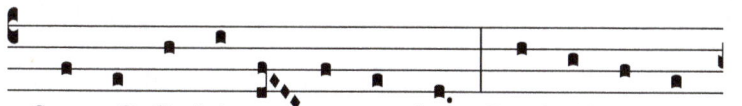

Spare, O God, in mer-cy spare him! Lord, all-pity-ing

Je- su blest, Grant them thine e- ter-nal rest. A- men.

OFFERTORY *Dómine Iesu Christe*

Cantors

ij.

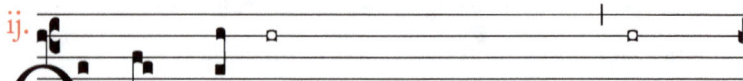

O LORD Je - sus Christ, King of Majesty, deliver

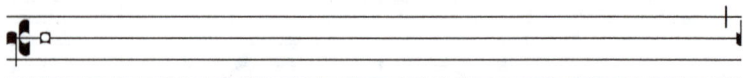

the souls of all the faithful departed from the hand of hell,

Choir

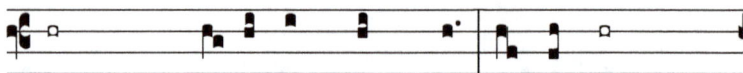

and from the pit of de - struc - tion: de - li - ver them

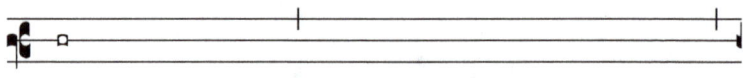

from the lion's mouth; that the grave devour them not;

that they go not down to the realms of dark - ness.

Cantors

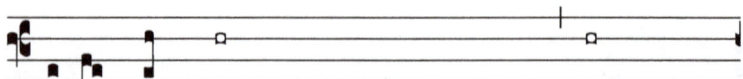

But let Mich - ael, the holy standard-bearer, make speed to

Choir

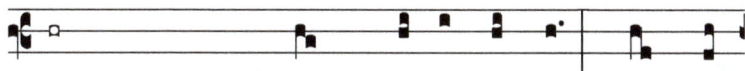

restore them to the bright - ness of glo - ry: which thou

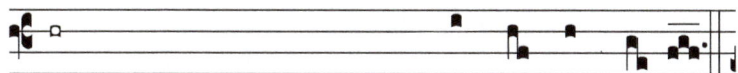

didst promise in ages past to A - bra - ham and his seed.

Cantors

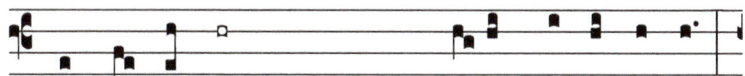

℣. Sac - ri - fice and prayer do we of - fer un - to thee, O Lord:

Choir

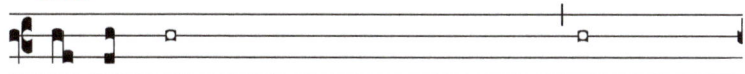

do thou accept them for the souls departed, in whose

Cantors

memory we make this o - bla - tion: And grant them, O

Choir

Lord, to pass from death un- to life: which thou didst

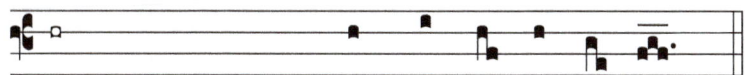

promise in ages past unto A - bra - ham and his seed.

781

MASSES FOR THE DEAD

COMMUNION *Pro quorum memória*

i.

T O them in whose memory the Body of Christ is

re-ceived: grant, O LORD, rest ev-er-last- ing. ℣. And let

light perpetual shine up-on them. To them in whose

whose memory the Blood of Christ is re-ceived: grant, O

LORD, rest ev-er-last-ing

Verses from Psalm 130:1-8 *may be sung.*

or Co. *Lux ætérna*   *IV Esd. 2:35*

Cantors

i.

LET light eternal shine, O LORD, up - on them:

Choir

for end - less ages with thy blessed ones, for thou art

Cantors

gra - cious. ℣. Rest e-ter-nal grant unto them, O LORD:

Choir

and let light perpetual shine up-on them. For end-less

ages with thy blessed ones: for thou art gra-cious.

Verses from Psalm 130:1-8 *may be sung.*

2. For all the Faithful Departed

INTROIT *Requiem ætérnam (supra, p. 770)*

GRADUAL *Requiem ætérnam (supra, p. 771)*

ALLELUIA *optional (supra, p. 772)*

MASSES FOR THE DEAD

TRACT *Absólve Dómine* *(supra, p. 773)*

The Sequence Dies irae *may be sung or said, (supra, p. 775)*

OFFERTORY *Dómine Iesu Christe* *(supra, p. 780)*

or OF. *O pie Deus*

Cantors

ij.

O KIND Cre- ator, who hast recalled the first man to

eternal glory: O good Shepherd, who on thy loving

shoulder hast brought again the lost sheep to the sheep-

fold: O just Judge, when thou shalt come for judge-ment:

Choir

de-li-ver from death the souls of them whom thou hast

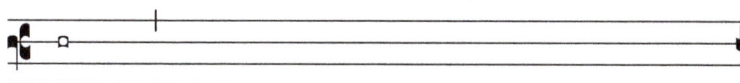

redeemed. Nor give to the beasts the souls of them that

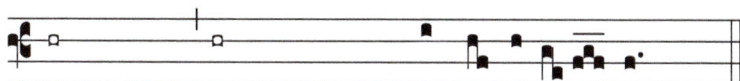

confess thee: nor forsake them ut-ter-ly for e- ver.

COMMUNION *Pro quorum memória (supra, p. 782)*
or CO. *Lux ætérna (supra, p. 783)*

3. On the Anniversary of Death

INTROIT *Requiem ætérnam (supra, p. 770)*

GRADUAL *Requiem ætérnam (supra, p. 771)*
or GR. *Si ambulem (Saturday, Lent III, p. 175)*

ALLELUIA *optional (supra, p. 772)*

TRACT *Absólve Dómine (supra, p. 773)*

or TR. *De profúndis (supra, p. 773)*

The Sequence Dies irae *may be sung or said, (supra, p. 775)*

OFFERTORY *Dómine Iesu Christe (supra, p. 780)*
or OF. *O pie Deus (supra, p. 784)*

COMMUNION *Pro quorum memória (supra, p. 782)*
or CO. *Lux ætérna (supra, p. 783)*

MASSES FOR THE DEAD
4. For an Infant or Child

INTROIT *Abstérget Deus*   *Rev. 21:4, cf. Ps. 17:16*

Cantors

GOD shall wipe away all tears from their eyes; and

there shall be no more death, neither sor-row, nor cry-ing:

Choir

nei-ther shall there be any more pain, for the former

FINE   *Cantors*

things are passed a- way. *Ps.* They will behold thy

Choir

pre-sence in right-eous-ness: and they will be satisfied

Cantors

when thy glory is man-i-fest-ed.   Glo-ry be,...*(etc.)*

Choir   *Full*

as it was..., *(etc.)*   God shall...*(etc.)*

or in Eastertide:

In. *Veníte, benedícti*   Mt. 25:34; Ps. 96:1

Cantors

vij.

COME, ye blessed of my Father, inherit the kingdom,

Choir

al- le- lu- ia: which hath been prepared for you from the

FINE

foundation of the world. Allelu-ia. Al- le- lu- ia.

Cantors   *Choir*

Ps. O sing unto the Lord a new song: sing unto the

Cantors

Lord, all the whole earth. Glo-ry be,...*(etc.)*

Choir　　　　　　*Full*

as it was..., *(etc.)*　Come, ye blessed...*(etc.)*

GRADUAL *Beáta gens (Trinity XVII, p. 441)*

ALLELUIA *Laudáte, púeri*　　　　　　　　　　　　*Ps. 113:1*

Cantors　　　　　　*All*

vj.

AL- LE- LU- IA.　Al- le- lu- ia.

Cantors　　　　　　　　　　　　　*Choir*

℣. Praise the LORD, ye chil-dren: O praise the Name

All

of the LORD..　Al- le- lu- ia.

OFFERTORY *Inténde voci (Trinity I, p. 385)*

COMMUNION *Dóminus regit me (Saturday, Lent IV, p. 188)*
or in Eastertide: CO. *Omnes qui in Christo baptizáti estis*
　　　　　　　　　(The Baptism of the Lord , p. 83)

ORDINARY COMMON TONES

On Sundays at the Aspersion of Holy Water

Out of Eastertide

ANTIPHON *Asperges me*　　　　　　　　　　　　*Ps. 51:9, 3*

Priest or cantor　　　　　*Choir*

vij.

THOU shalt purge me * with hys- sop, O LORD, and I

shall be clean: thou shalt wash me,　and　I shall be whi-

FINE　　　　*Cantors*

ter　than snow, *Ps.* Have mer-cy up-on me, O God, *

Choir　　　　　　　　　　*Cantors*

af-ter thy great good - ness.　Glo- ry be to the Father, and

Choir

to the Son, and to the Ho - ly Ghost; * as it was in the

789

(music)

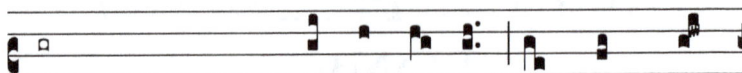

beginning, is now and ev - er shall be, world with - out

Full

(music)

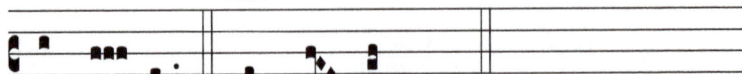

end. A-men. Thou shalt purge..., *(etc.)*
The Gloria Patri *is omitted on Passion Sunday and on Palm Sunday.*

In Eastertide

ANTIPHON *Vidi aquam*   *Ez. 47:1, 9*

Priest or cantor   *Choir*

viij.

(music)

I BE-held wa - ter * is - su - ing out from the tem -

(music)

ple,   on the right-hand side, al - le - lu - ia:

(music)

and all   to whom that wa -ter   came   were   sav-

FINE

(music)

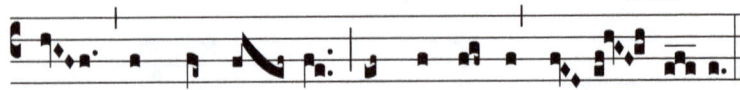

ed,   and they shall say, al - le - lu - ia, al - le - lu - ia.

COMMON TONES

Cantors

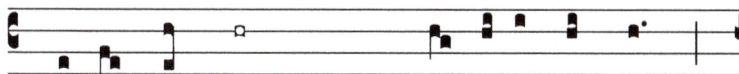

Ps. O give thanks unto the LORD, for he is gra - cious, *

Choir

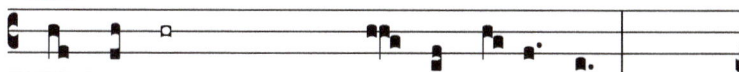

be- cause his mer-cy en - dur - eth for ev - er.

Cantors   *Choir*

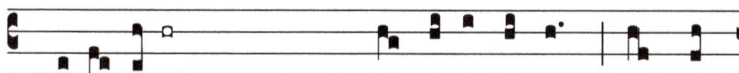

Let Is-ra-el now con-fess that he is gra-cious, and that

Cantors

his mer-cy en - dur - eth for ev - er.   Glo- ry be

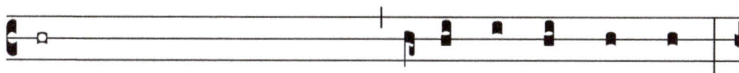

to the Father and to the Son, and to the Ho - ly Ghost; *

Choir

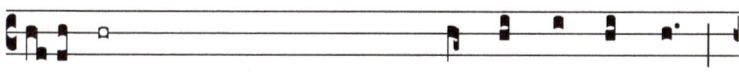

as it was in the beginning, is now and ev - er shall be,

Full

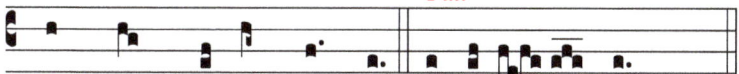

world with - out end. A - men. I be-held wa -ter..., *(etc.)*

791

PRECES

Celebrant

℣. O LORD, show thy mer - cy up - on us. (*P.T.* : up - on

All

us, al - le - lu - ia.) ℟. And grant us thy sal - va - tion

Celebrant

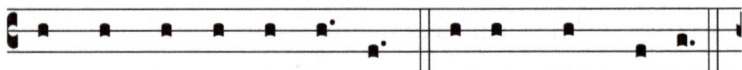

(sal - va - tion, al - le - lu - ia.) ℣. O LORD, hear my prayer,

All   *Celebrant*

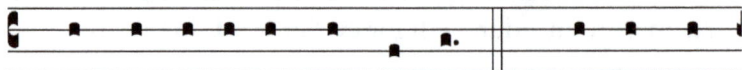

℟. And let my cry come un - to thee. ℣. The LORD be

All

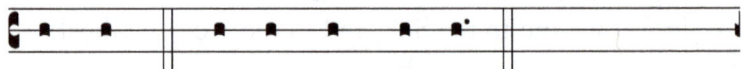

with you. ℟. And with thy spi - rit.

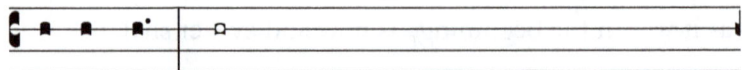

Let us pray.   O Lord, holy Father, Almighty, everlasting
God, we beseech thee to hear us; and vouchsafe to send thy
holy Angel from heaven, to guard and cherish, protect and

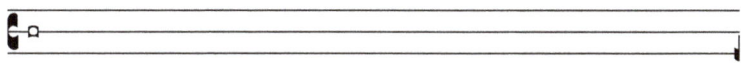

visit, and evermore defend all who are assembled in this

All

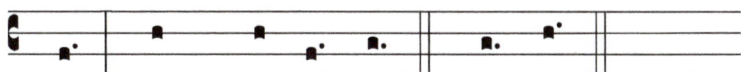

place; through Christ our LORD. ℞. A - men.

After the Consecration

Celebrant

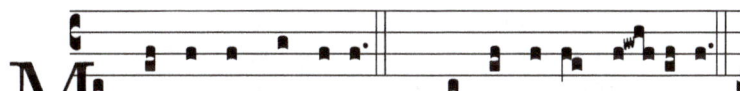

MYs-té- ri- um fí- de- i. *or* Mys-té- ri- um fí- de- i.

All

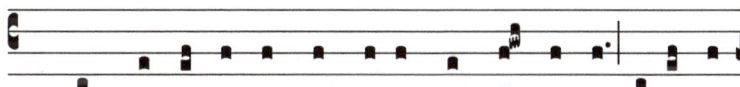

℞. Mor- tem tu- am an-nun-ti-á-mus, Dó-mi-ne, et tu- am

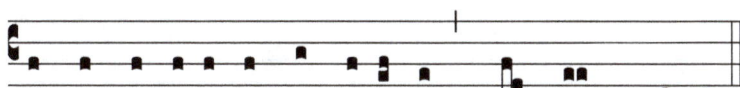

re- sur- rec-ti-ó-nem con-fi-té-mur, do- nec vé- ni- as.

Celebrant

THE my- ste- ry of faith.

or

Celebrant

THE my- ste- ry   of faith.

All

℟. We pro-claim thy Death, O Lord, and pro-fess thy

Re-ur-rec-tion   un-til thou come a-gain.

or

All

℟. We pro-claim thy Death, O Lord, and pro-fess thy

Re-ur-rec-tion   un-til thou come a-gain.

or

All

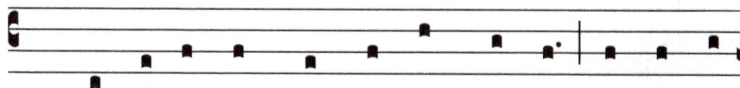

℟. When we eat this bread and drink this cup, we pro-claim

thy Death, O Lord, un-til thou come a-gain.

or

All

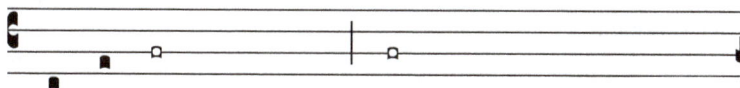

℟. O Sav-iour of the world, who by thy Cross and

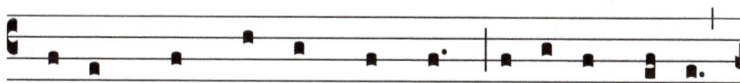

pre-cious Blood hast re-deemed us: save us and help us,

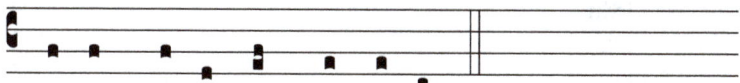

we hum-bly be-seech thee, O Lord.

Index of Chants
Introits

Index of Chants
Introits

Graduals

Index of Chants
Graduals

Index of Chants
Graduals

801

Index of Chants
Graduals

Index of Chants
Alleluia Verses

Index of Chants
Alleluia Verses

Sequences

Tracts

Index of Chants
Tracts

Offertories

Index of Chants
Offertories

Index of Chants
Communions

Index of Chants
Communions

Index of Chants
Communions

Index of Chants
Communions

Index of Chants
Antiphons

Index of Chants
Psalms

Canticles

Index of Chants

Responsories

Varia

INDICES

The following index will assist planning in places where it is desired that the minor propers correspond closely with the Roman Lectionary:

Ordinary Time

Ordinary Time
Week 8

Week 9

Week 10

Week 11

* 9 7 8 0 9 7 9 3 8 0 0 7 5 *